Appraising the Single Family Residence

George F. Bloom, MAI
Henry S. Harrison, MAI

American Institute of Real Estate Appraisers
of the National Association of Realtors
430 N. Michigan Avenue • Chicago, Illinois 60611

Text in Chapter 10 based on *Houses*, first revision, by Henry S. Harrison. Copyright 1976. Used by permission REALTORS National Marketing Institute.®

The authors assume responsibility for the content of this text. Portions of the text were contributed by individual members of the Institute and/or its committees. The opinions and statements set forth herein do not necessarily reflect the viewpoint of the American Institute of Real Estate Appraisers or its individual members, and neither the Institute nor its editors and staff assume responsibility for such expression of opinion or statements.

Library of Congress Catalog Card Number: 77-93119
International Standard Book Number: 0-911780-40-8

First printing: June 1978
Second printing: October 1978
Third printing: April 1980

Foreword

One of the cornerstones of the American Institute of Real Estate Appraisers is to serve as a source of appraisal education and knowledge. With the publication of *Appraising the Single Family Residence,* the Institute takes pride in continuing this tradition.

The book brings together textbook knowledge and information with their actual use and application in preparing an appraisal of a single family residence. A dual purpose work, the book is designed for the novice in real estate appraisal as a primary textbook and for the real estate veteran as a reference source on residential appraising. Highlighting the book are a "math for appraisers" feature, a helpful series of mortgage payment tables and complete model narrative and form appraisal reports.

The Institute is indebted to George F. Bloom and Henry S. Harrison for their cooperative efforts in writing *Appraising the Single Family Residence.* The Institute also wishes to thank its members who provided thoughtful counsel and guidance to the authors in developing this work.

Charles B. Akerson, MAI
1978 President
American Institute of Real
Estate Appraisers

Introduction

A comprehensive textbook on the subject of appraising the single family residence has never been available to the real estate industry. It is the desire of the authors of this text, *Appraising the Single Family Residence*, to meet that need; it is their hope that it will be used widely throughout the real estate and allied industries by everyone involved with single family residences.

Certainly this book will be useful to the professional real estate appraiser in valuing single family residences. REALTORS®, brokers and sales associates, all of whom deal with the value of houses daily, should also find it invaluable. Representatives of financial institutions involved in making home loans, housing contractors and builders and government and quasi-government officials have in this book a handy reference source. Lay persons and trade persons may use it to help them make decisions to buy, sell, build, renovate, lease or rent. Individuals dealing with the valuation of residential real estate for courts and ad valorem taxation proceedings will find this book a source of standard acceptable practices.

This book has been written to complement *The Appraisal of Real Estate*, the first major and most widely distributed textbook of the American Institute of Real Estate Appraisers.

Although the American Institute of Real Estate Appraisers is the publisher of *Appraising the Single Family Residence*, the book is the product of the authors, who bear complete responsibility for its content. Any questions of fact, interpretation of principles, discussion of theory and illustration of the application of methods and techniques is wholly the work of the authors who stand strongly behind their beliefs. Anyone involved in real estate knows that markets are erratic and that the application of theories and techniques may vary depending on social, government, economic and environmental pressures. This book emphasizes the importance of principles and theories because they are the foundation on which application and technique rest.

The authors intend that this book do many things and serve many functions. First and foremost the book follows the premise that fundamental concepts of appraisal theory and principles are basic and critical to the professional application of the appraisal process. All of the basic ideas come "from the field" via the many devoted members of the appraisal profession, whose experiences have been converted over the last five decades into orderly and categorized rules, guidelines, steps, techniques and methods. From this experience, principles and theory have been developed, which are the basis of this book; they have withstood the test of time and the authors present them for acceptance and use by the appraisal student as "wholly dependable."

This book stands as a comprehensive self-contained document on the valuation of single family residences. The practical aspects of the subject have not been discarded, however, for all methods, techniques, steps and applications are explained and illustrated.

Another philosophy of the authors is that all sides of every issue should be presented. Dogmatism has been virtually eliminated in favor of reporting all practical methods and techniques. Such an approach may frustrate some who prefer one answer or method to be dictatorially given. In a field so comprehensive as real estate valuation, however, the authors feel strongly that every professional must be open-minded, objective and unbiased.

If this text helps students to become professional appraisers and aids others who use it to be more professional, the primary goal of the authors is accomplished.

G.F.B. and H.S.H.

Acknowledgments

There is no way for the authors to express adequately their thanks and appreciation to the many designated and staff members of the American Institute of Real Estate Appraisers for their contributions to *Appraising the Single Family Residence*. Although the relations between the authors and the Institute were based on a formal, written contract, much was done by many well beyond that required in the contract. The mutuality of interest and the sincere desire to assist in the development of the best possible book permeated all contacts and discussions throughout the time the manuscript was in process.

Among those to whom the authors are indebted in a variety of ways are:

Jack K. Mann, MAI, Jackson, MS, 1974 president of AIREA.

Robert W. Ford, MAI, Modesto, CA, 1975 president of AIREA.

Walter Winius Jr., MAI, Phoenix, AZ, 1976 president of AIREA.

William T. Van Court, MAI, Denver, CO, 1977 president of AIREA.

Charles B. Akerson, MAI, Boston, MA, 1978 president of AIREA.

E. T. Compere, Jr., MAI, Abilene, TX, 1977 AIREA National Education Committee Chairman.

J. B. Featherston, MAI, Wichita Falls, TX, 1978 AIREA National Education Committee Chairman, who reviewed material on the Institute's Code of Ethics and made many helpful suggestions.

John G. Hoppe, Jr., MAI, Oak Park, IL, 1977 AIREA Division of Courses Chairman, who in both an official capacity and as a close personal friend was persistent throughout that this book be one of high quality and a contribution to appraisal literature.

Stephen R. Wheelock, MAI, Burlington, VT, 1977 AIREA Course VIII Subcommittee Chairman; and Donald Dean Potter, MAI, Vancouver, WA, of the Course VIII Subcommittee, who contributed many ideas and suggestions for the practical application of the book

John D. Dorchester, Jr., MAI, Tulsa, OK, 1976-1977 AIREA Division of Publications Chairman, who in addition to providing much guidance and solving many issues also prepared the mortgage tables and wrote portions of the market data approach chapter and the material on linear and multiple regression analysis.

Peter D. Bowes, MAI, Denver, CO, 1978 AIREA Division of Publications Chairman.

William S. Stripling III, MAI, Atlanta, GA; Stephen T. Crosson, MAI, Dallas, TX; and Ronald P. Nelson, MAI, Santa Monica, CA, Division of Publications Review Subcommittee.

Everett W. Fenton, MAI, Seattle, WA, 1977 RM Required Examinations Subcommittee Chairman; and Frank E. Bredice, MAI, Montpelier, VT, and Don C. Peete, MAI, Prairie Village, KS, of the RM Examinations Subcommittee, who reviewed the model appraisal and made constructive criticism.

Richard L. Lodge, MAI, St. Louis, MO, 1977 Chairman of the Textbook Revision Subcommittee, who offered suggestions for coordinating this text with *The Appraisal of Real Estate*.

Raymond E. Froula, MAI, Chicago, whose appraisal report for the 1976 Pan American Real Estate Appraisal Congress served as the basis for the model narrative appraisal in this text; and Walter R. Kuehnle, MAI, Chicago, who assisted in making the report available to the authors.

Robert P. LaPorte, Jr., and Thomas B. Martin, whose demonstration appraisal reports were used as guidelines in the model narrative appraisal report and also in portions of the text.

Alvin L. Wagner, Jr., RM, Flossmoor, IL, who provided material for the model appraisal.

Carlton W. Cole, MAI, Coral Gables, FL, who drafted the drawing for the model appraisal.

Many other members of the Institute, including David S. Mason, MAI, and Harvey P. Jeffers, MAI, who made suggestions, offered encouragement, sent critiques and generally urged the authors to produce a professional product.

The staff of the Appraisal Institute: William A. Collis, Executive Vice President; Stephen C. Cummins, Director of Education; and Janet Seefeldt, Director of Publications.

REALTORS® National Marketing Institute, who granted permission for the use of material from *Houses: The Illustrated Guide to Construction, Design & Systems* in Chapter 10 of this text (including all of the illustrations in that chapter).

Dr. Joseph Lambert, who supplied material on statistics.

Emily Emerson, New Haven, CT, and Charlotte Pitcher, Mary Holmes and Lou Ann Moulden, Bloomington, IN, who helped the authors in manuscript preparation.

Julie and Eve Harrison, who besides giving up many hours that rightfully were theirs, cut and pasted uncounted numbers of galley proofs.

Ruth Lambert Harrison, New Haven, CT, who did much of the initial editing, typing, rewriting and proofing, must be recognized for her consistent interest, encouragement and contribution.

To all others not specifically mentioned who contributed to this text the authors are indebted.

The close relationship that this project necessitated between the authors has produced an even closer friendship. Many hours spent together have produced not only a tangible product but a distinct camaraderie, compassion and total respect for each other. May it last forever.

In writing a book of this type, many ethical and moral issues needed to be resolved and the use of langauge carefully scrutinized for meaning. The authors were always concerned with commission as well as omission. In a document of this type, a consistent issue is "short-run vs. long-run" implications. Throughout its writing, however, the long-run consequences have been preserved as was the mutual understanding between the authors.

George F. Bloom, MAI, SRPA
Bloomington, Indiana
Henry S. Harrison, MAI, SRPA
New Haven, Connecticut

The Authors

George F. Bloom, MAI, SRPA, is Professor of Real Estate Administration and Chairperson of Real Estate Area, School of Business and Real Estate Director, Indiana University, Bloomington, Indiana. Dr. Bloom has been active in the appraisal of all property types since 1947. He received the MBA and DBA in real estate from Indiana University following 4½ years in the U.S. Marine Corps during World War II. He received the MAI designation in 1954. He also holds the SRPA designation of the Society of Real Estate Appraisers.

In addition to teaching both graduate and undergraduate real estate courses at Indiana University, Dr. Bloom has been active in organizations of the real estate industry. He serves as director of the Indiana REALTORS® Institute and developed the approved real estate salesmen's course for the Indiana Real Estate Commission. As a REALTOR®, he has served as board president, state education chairman and national director. He was founding president of the American Real Estate and Urban Economics Association in 1965 and 1966.

Dr. Bloom served the Appraisal Institute as National Education Committee Chairman and as a member of the National Executive Committee in 1974 and 1975. He also served as a member of the Sixth Edition Textbook Revision Subcommittee. He has taught the Appraisal Institute's Courses I, I-A, I-B, II and VIII and the Society's Course 101.

Dr. Bloom is co-author of *Real Estate* with Dr. Arthur M. Weimer and Dr. Homer Hoyt, a principles book in its seventh edition. He is a member of the real estate fraternities Lambda Alpha and Rho Epsilon.

Henry S. Harrison, MAI, SRPA, is president of Harrison Appraisal Company, New Haven, Connecticut, affiliated with Real Property Analysts, Inc. He has been a practicing real estate appraiser since 1956. He has a BS in economics from the Wharton School of Finance and Commerce, University of Pennsylvania, and a master's degree in adult education (real estate and appraising) from Goddard College, Vermont. He is a retired major in the U.S. Air Force.

Mr. Harrison has been active locally and nationally in real estate organizations. He served as 1977 Connecticut Chapter president and National Public Relations Committee Chairman of the American Institute of Real Estate Appraisers. In 1975 he received the Institute's Professional Recognition Award. He has also been president of the Connecticut Chapter and vice governor of the Society of Real Estate Appraisers. He is 1978 vice president and director of the Greater New Haven Board of REALTORS® and in 1976 was named its REALTOR of the Year.

Mr. Harrison has taught the Appraisal Institute's Course I-A (serving as chairman of the Course I-A Subcommittee in 1975) and Course VIII and the Society's courses 101 and 201. Together with John G. Hoppe, Jr., MAI, he developed and presented around the country a seminar entitled "Houses, Houses, Houses."

A nationally recognized author and lecturer, Mr. Harrison's previous publications include numerous articles and the books, *Houses: The Illustrated Guide to Construction, Design & Systems* and *Houses: Student Workbook,* both published by the REALTORS National Marketing Institute®, and *Harrison's Illustrated Guide How to Fill Out a Residential Appraisal Report (FHLMC Form 70-FNMA Form 1004).* His column, "The Residential Appraiser," is a regular feature in the Society of Real Estate Appraisers' journal, *The Real Estate Appraiser.*

Contents

8 Highest and Best Use Analysis 129

Historic Houses
Log Cabins and Other Colonial Reproductions
Solar Houses
Experimental Houses

If a man does not keep pace with his companions, perhaps it is because he hears a different drummer. Let him step to the music which he hears, however measured or far away.

Thoreau: Walden XVIII

The Appraiser and the Appraisal Profession

Thousands of real estate appraisals are made every year, ranging from those of a simple house lot to those of multimillion dollar commercial and industrial complexes. Although the purpose of this text is to concentrate on the appraisal of single family residences, a brief overview of the various needs for real estate appraisals serves as an introduction.

Kinds of Appraisal Assignments

Real estate appraisals are generally made by either staff appraisers of organizations requiring such appraisals or by fee appraisers, who are independent contractors. Almost anyone the appraiser meets can be a potential source of business. The list of those seeking the services of a real estate appraiser includes:

• *Buyers and sellers of homes.* Appraisers assist them in setting listing and offering prices and in making final decisions to complete a sale or purchase.

• *Lending institutions* such as savings and loan associations, savings banks, commercial banks, credit unions, insurance companies, pension funds and investment trusts. Appraisers estimate the market value of property being accepted as loan security. The trust departments of these organizations use appraisers for estate planning and estate disposal. Real estate departments use appraisers to help manage and plan their own activities.

• *Investors.* Appraisers help them acquire and dispose of real estate investments.

• *Architects.* Appraisers help judge the economic feasibility of proposed projects as well as site selection and acquisitions.

• *Builders and developers.* Appraisers help them to make site acquisitions, develop sites to highest and best use, test the feasibility of projects, obtain mortgages and equity financing, attract investors, and assist in the sale of projects.

• *Lawyers.* Appraisers are often hired in behalf of clients. Lawyers also recommend appraisers to help divide property between disputing heirs, partners or clients. They use appraisers for condemnation, tax appeals, estate planning and disposal of estates and a variety of other uses.

• *Tenants.* Appraisers help them estimate fair rental. In condemnation proceedings and business valuations, tenants need appraisers to estimate their leasehold value (leasehold interests are those of the lessee, tenant or renter).

• *Insurers and the insured.* Appraisers estimate the insurable value of property to aid in determining the proper amount of insurance. Appraisers also play an important role in claims adjustments.

• *Accountants.* Appraisers are hired for clients to help estimate the value of assets and to establish rates of depreciation.

• *Business corporations.* Appraisers help acquire and dispose of property, assist in the transfer of employees, evaluate real estate assets, develop real estate programs and plan real estate activities.

• *Nonprofit organizations.* Appraisers help buy and sell real estate and value holdings.

• *Government agencies* at federal, state and local levels. These are all large users of appraisals. Some federal agencies that use appraisals are the Veterans Administration, Federal Housing Administration, Federal Home Loan Mortgage Corporation, General Services Administration, Internal Revenue Service, Post Office Department, Army Corps of Engineers, National Park Service, and Farm Home Administration. State governments use appraisers for highway right-of-way acquisitions, condemnation and purchase of land for schools and other government buildings, parks, open space programs and wetland acquisitions. Local governments depend on appraisers in the process of acquiring property for schools and other government buildings. Redevelopment programs require appraisers for both acquisition and reuse programs. Ad valorem (property) taxes are based on real estate assessments (appraisals).

• *Public utility companies.* Appraisers are needed for the acquisition of rights-of-way for their wires, pipelines and other real estate acquisitions.

The list of users of appraisals is almost endless. It is an expanding function and the need for appraisals appears to be constantly increasing. The field presents good opportunities for those who are willing to acquire the necessary skills to serve the public as professionals.

Objectives of Real Estate Appraisals

The fundamental objective of an appraisal is to estimate value. The need for an appraisal of market value may arise from many situations, including:

1. Transfer of ownership.
2. Financing and credit.
3. Just compensation in condemnation (eminent domain) proceedings.
4. A basis for taxation.
5. To establish rental schedules and lease provisions.
6. Feasibility.

In addition to the need for estimating market value, appraisals are also made to estimate:

1. Insurable value.
2. Going concern value.
3. Liquidation value.
4. Assessed value (may be a percentage of market value).

Although the list does not include all the needs for appraisals, it does indicate the broad scope of the professional appraiser's typical activities.

Definition of an Appraisal

An appraisal is an answer to a question, which may be as limited as: "What is the market value of this house today?" More complicated and sophisticated considerations, such as various interests, equities, historic and future values and other conditions, are often present. An appraisal may answer any question involving the value of an interest in real estate under assumed conditions, provided that both the question and conclusion are fully and clearly stated. The professional appraiser defines an appraisal as "a supported estimate of a defined value."

Contents of the Appraisal Report

Although abbreviated forms of appraisal reports (including verbal) may be acceptable, depending on the requirements of the client, the type of property and the nature of the appraisal assignment, the narrative appraisal report is preferable. It is a formal written document that contains as a minimum:

1. The estimate of value.
2. The effective date of the appraisal.
3. The certification and signature of the appraiser.
4. The objective of the appraisal and definition of value.
5. The qualifying conditions.
6. An adequate description and specific facts about identification and description of the property and its ownership.
7. The factual data.
8. An analysis and interpretation of the data.
9. The processing of the data by one or more of the accepted approaches.
10. Other descriptive supporting material such as maps, charts, and photographs.

The Importance of the Appraiser to the Community

The appraiser is frequently regarded by lenders and the public as the expert in evaluating a neighborhood's strength and weakness. Accordingly, the appraiser must exercise this responsibility with care and be certain that a considered judgment about a community's trend is supportable by objective facts. Emotional arguments or advocacy must never affect the professional appraiser's presentation of demonstrable facts.

Growth of Professionalism in Real Estate Appraising

A profession is a vocation that involves primarily intellectual activities and requires high levels of technical competence, individual responsibility and personal integrity. Historically the first professionals were physicians and surgeons, professors, lawyers, accountants, engineers and the clergy. Today a professional is a member of an organized vital vocation or activity in which the membership is highly competent, thoroughly honest and devoted to the ideal of performing a service to the maximum of their capacity regardless of compensation. A professional has a responsibility to help make the world a better place in which to live.

Appraisers have aspired to professional status in the eyes of the public and the rest of the real estate field for many years. Today appraisals written by appraisers who have achieved some level of professionally recognized expertise usually receive greater acceptance than those prepared by the nonprofessional.

The need for professional real estate appraisers came into focus with the collapse of real estate values during the depression of the 1930s. Prior to that time, real estate appraising as a vocation had been unstructured and little educational material was available, although as early as 1929, the National Association of Real Estate Boards had a publication called *Standards of Appraisal Practice*. To the early appraiser, "market price" meant "market value."

Professional Appraisal Organizations

Since the 1930s a body of knowledge on the theory and practice of real estate appraising has been developed and disseminated. In 1932 the American Institute of Real Estate Appraisers was formed to establish and maintain standards of professional practice in the field of real estate appraising. It is an affiliate organization of what was then known as the National Association of Real Estate Boards, now the National Association of Realtors®. Since its founding, more than 5,000 appraisers have earned its MAI (Member, Appraisal Institute) and RM (Residential Member) designations.

The basic objectives of the American Institute of Real Estate Appraisers are:

1. The establishment of high standards of professional practice and the formulation of minimum standards of professional conduct, which are required of all members and candidates.
2. The establishment of educational standards for the appraisal of real property comprised of all general fields of knowledge with which an appraiser should be acquainted.
3. The encouragement of training of students in educational institutions for careers in real estate appraising.
4. The promotion of research and publication of material considered essential to the realization of the Institute's programs of study with which all professional appraisers should be acquainted.
5. The presentation of seminars, conferences, educational courses and conventions to achieve these ends.

In addition to educational courses and seminars given each year at various times and places around the United States, primarily on college campuses, the Institute makes available a broad range of literature on valuation subjects. (The basic requirements for membership in the American Institute of Real Estate Appraisers and obtaining its designations are presented in Appendix J.)

Other national and regional appraisal organizations, some made up of only real estate appraisers and others who accept affiliated professions and other types of appraisers, include the Society of Real Estate Appraisers, the American Society of Farm Managers and Rural Appraisers, and the Association of Federal Appraisers.

Regardless of how one enters the appraisal profession, the first step is either to take some appraisal courses or obtain on-the-job training. Many appraisers have begun by working for an established appraiser or appraisal firm, either on a full-time or part-time basis. Through such employment, they receive needed education, training and experience. Many colleges and universities now offer programs in real estate appraisal.

Professional Conduct

The essence of our civilization is that people acknowledge the limited right of society to control the activities of individuals for the benefit of the public. In addition, many people conduct their own activities at a higher level than is required by the law or by their fellow humans.

There are several levels of conduct. The first deals with the laws that apply to all the people. In the United States, there are federal, state and local laws. Everyone is required to obey these laws. It makes little difference if one agrees or disagrees with them. If someone does not obey a law, society has the right to punish the law-breaker. (Of course, not all laws are enforced uniformly, and many people break laws and are not caught or punished.)

The second level consists of the laws that apply to certain groups of people. These are laws and rules that regulate special activities such as those of lawyers and doctors. Often one has to obtain a license or permit to participate in such activities. For example, in the real estate field, one must have a license to sell or rent real estate for compensation. Real estate brokers are subject to special laws that control their activities. Other common examples at this level are the laws pertaining to driving automobiles, building houses, practicing medicine, or running a store. Such regulatory laws apply only when one voluntarily engages in a special activity controlled by the legislation or regulation which applies. In some states, real estate appraising falls into this category of control.

The third level consists of various codes of ethics developed by different professional organizations to control the activities of their members. The members of the organization agree to be governed by its code of ethics as one of the conditions of membership. The organization itself develops and enforces the code of ethics. Violators may be disciplined in a variety of ways. The maximum penalty usually is expulsion from the group. The American Medical Association, the American Bar Association, the National Association of Realtors® and the American Institute of Real Estate Appraisers as well as many other organizations have these codes governing the conduct of their members with the public, their clients and among their own members.

The fourth level is commonly referred to as the "golden rule." It encompasses the personal rules people set for themselves to control their own lives according to their personal (and religious) beliefs. Many everyday decisions people make about their professional activities and conduct fall outside the scope of the three preceding levels of conduct. The decision regarding how to act must be made by the individual based on personal standards of conduct. The rewards for functioning at this higher level are personal satisfaction and approval by one's family and peers. The punishment is from one's own conscience and disapproval by others.

Summary

The needs and reasons for real estate appraisals are as varied as the clients who request them. Broadly, a real estate appraisal is "a supported estimate of a defined value." The client's specific needs will give further refinement and shape to the objective of the appraisal report. The validity of the report is strongly based on the competence and integrity of the person performing the appraisal. Over the last 40-plus years, real estate appraising has grown as a profession, based on the development of standards of professional practice and conduct by organizations such as the American Institute of Real Estate Appraisers.

The professional real estate appraiser is charged with a solemn responsibility and obligation to the public and to the profession. In recognition of this professional responsibility, members of the American Institute of Real Estate Appraisers subscribe to a Code of Ethics and Standards of Professional Practice. (The Code of Ethics, known as Regulation No. 10, is described in further detail in Appendix K.)

Review Questions

1. What is an appraisal?
2. What are the minimum contents of an appraisal report?
3. Give a reason why each of the following might require an appraisal of a single family residence:
   a. Buyers
   b. Sellers
   c. Lending institutions
   d. Investors
   e. Architects
   f. Builders
   g. Lawyers
   h. Tenants
   i. Insurers
   j. Accountants
   k. Business corporations
   l. Nonprofit organizations
   m. State government agencies
   n. Federal government agencies
   o. Local government agencies
   p. Public utilities
4. What are the basic ways to enter the real estate appraisal profession?
5. What are the characteristics of a professional?

2

The Nature of Real Property and Value

Real property has economic value and significance only as it satisfies the needs and desires of human beings. The utilization of and the collective desire for real property gives it value. Although land acquires value when it is desired and has a feasible use, the value assigned to a parcel of real estate is not limited to the individual whose desires create it. Reflections of that value have significance for everyone whose welfare might be affected by its utilization. Before value can be discussed, however, the nature of real property must be understood.

Legal Concept of Real Estate

The original legal concept of real estate is more comprehensive than is generally realized. By definition it

> ... includes not only the ground, or soil, but everything that is attached to the earth, whether by course of nature, as trees and herbage, or by .... [society], as houses and other buildings. It includes not only the surface of the earth, but everything under it and over it. Thus, in legal theory, a tract of land consists not only of the portion on the surface of the earth, but is an inverted pyramid having its tip or apex at the center of the earth, extending outward through the surface of the earth at the boundary lines of the tract, and continuing on upward to the heavens.[1]

This, theoretically, is full and complete ownership. However, acts passed by Congress in 1926 and 1938 give the United States complete sovereignty over the air space above the nation. In general, the courts have held that an owner can control only as much air space above the land as can be reasonably utilized, depending upon its location, zoning and other factors governing the use of the property.

---

[1]Robert Kratovil, *Real Estate Law*, 6th ed. (Englewood Cliffs, NJ: Prentice-Hall, Inc., 1974), p. 5.

A variety of terms exists to describe land and the elements thereon, either natural or synthetic.

1. *Real estate.* The physical land and appurtenances, including structures affixed thereon. In some states, by statute, this term is synonymous with real property.
2. *Property.* Synonymous with *rights* as used in the "bundle of rights." It includes the rights to future benefits by ownership or possession of economic goods.
   a. *Real property.* The interests, benefits and rights inherent in the ownership of the physical real estate. It is the bundle of rights with which such ownership is endowed. This term does not include personal property.
   b. *Personal property.* Movable items, those not permanently fixed to and part of real estate. In deciding whether an item is personal property or real estate, four factors must be considered: (1) the manner in which it is annexed, (2) the intention of the party responsible for the annexation (i.e., to leave it permanently or to remove it at some time), (3) the purpose for which the premises are used, and (4) the cost of the item. With some exceptions, items remain personal property *if* they can be removed easily and without damage to the real estate or the item itself.
3. *Chattel.* A legal term referring to any property other than a freehold or fee estate in land. Chattels are treated as personal property but are divided into two subcategories:
   a. *Chattels real.* All interest in real estate that does not constitute a freehold or fee estate in land, including leasehold estates and other interests issuing out of or annexed to real estate.
   b. *Chattels personal.* All movable things.
4. *Fixtures.* Tangible items that previously were personal property and have been attached to or installed in land or a structure in such a way as to become a part of the real estate.

Thus *real estate, real property, personal property, chattels* and *fixtures* are different and precise concepts. The distinctions between them are significant and the appraiser must have a thorough understanding of them.

The chief characteristics of real estate are its immobility and tangibility. Real estate is land and all things of a permanent and substantial nature affixed thereto, whether by nature or people. Real property, however, embraces in its broadest sense the tangible elements of real estate *plus* the intangible attributes that are the rights of ownership. The appraiser is concerned with real property, since the estimate of value made in an appraisal is of the rights and benefits to be derived from the ownership and/or use of real estate.

The major characteristic of personal property is its mobility. Furniture and furnishings, machinery, mortgages and securities of every type comprise personal property.

Chattel is a legal concept referring to nonownership interests in real estate or personal property.

Frequently the distinction between personal property and real estate is so fine that it has required the opinion of the courts to resolve the issue. This has given rise to the law of fixtures. The distinction between personal property and real property is important to the appraiser, since the status of a fixture can determine its contribution to the value of the real property.

Because the distinction between real estate and personal property is not always evident and because it is important in the valuation of real estate, appraisers should be familiar with the law of fixtures as it applies in their area. In case of controversial items, the appraiser may abide by local custom; however, the appraisal report should clearly state the distinction.

Bundle of Rights Theory

The bundle of rights theory holds that the ownership of real property may be compared to a bundle of sticks wherein each stick represents a distinct and separate right or privilege of ownership. These rights, inherent in ownership of real property and guaranteed by law (but subject to certain limitations and restrictions), include the right to occupy and to use real property, to sell it in whole or in part, to bequeath it, and to transfer by contract for specified periods of time the benefits to be derived by occupancy and use of the real estate ("beneficial interests").

Absolute fee simple title to real property is the most complete degree of ownership but some restrictions and reservations are included. It does not guarantee the unrestricted exercise of the entire bundle of rights. These rights and privileges are limited by four powers of government:

1. *Ad valorem taxation.* The right of the state to levy and collect a tax varying with the assessed value of the property. It is a compulsory contribution exacted from all owners of real estate for the general support of the state and for the maintenance of public services. Also included are special assessments that may be levied against certain real estate benefiting from public improvements, usually to offset directly the cost of such improvements.

2. *Eminent domain.* The right reserved by government to take private property by condemnation for public benefit, provided just compensation is paid. As the concept of what constitutes public benefit broadens, there is an apparent trend toward broader interpretation of this right, which has been extended to quasi-government or public bodies such as housing authorities and public utilities.

3. *Police power.* The right to regulate property to promote the safety, health, morals and general welfare of the community via zoning ordinances, building codes, traffic regulations and other restrictions such as fair housing laws.

4. *Escheat.* The reversion to the state of property ownership if the owner dies without a will and with no known legal heirs.

In addition to the controls and restrictions resulting from the four powers of government, appropriate provisions may be inserted into deeds by which properties are transferred that will further restrict property uses. Through private deed restrictions owners can limit property use, establish building restrictions, regulate land coverage, and control property in other ways. Such restrictions may apply to one property or to an entire area. Deed restrictions may be enforced by the original owners, subsequent owners or other affected individuals or organizations. Where restrictions are conditions upon which the deed is given, a reversionary clause may provide that the property will revert to the seller if violations are claimed and can be proved.

Federal, state and local fair housing laws guarantee persons the right to buy, sell, lease, hold and convey property without being subjected to discrimination on the basis of race, color, religion, sex or national origin. These laws have nullified private deed restrictions which limit occupancy on racial, ethnical or religious grounds.

They also prohibit all types of discrimination in housing and rental transactions, so that equal housing opportunity is now often regarded as one of the basic property rights.

Partial Rights or Interests

Partial rights and interests in real estate can be divided into public rights and private rights. Public rights are included in the bundle of rights. Private rights may be classified further as (1) undivided fractional interests or (2) divisions based on physical separation.

Undivided Fractional Interests

Division of earnings or productivity occurs when ownership rests in undivided fractional interests such as either tenancy-in-common or joint tenancy. The value of such fractional interests is usually less than the fraction that ownership bears to the value of the entire property, particularly where the ownership is less than a 50% interest in the property.

• *Land Trusts.* Title is held by a trustee (usually a bank or trust company) for the benefit of the fractional owners.

• *General and Limited Partnerships.* Limited partners share proportionately in the net earnings and other benefits and depreciation but have no voice in the management decisions or responsibility. General partners are usually the persons who develop the partnership, retain special benefits, including the right of management decisions, and are solely liable for all obligations.

• *Cooperative Ownership.* Usually ownership of stock in a corporation owning the entire property. Each stockholder is given a proprietary lease on a unit, subject to certain conditions and obligations as to its use, sub-leasing and sale. Usually the lease or sale is subject to the approval of a board of directors of the cooperative.

• *Corporate Ownership.* Stock ownership in a property that has been incorporated. One of the disadvantages of corporate ownership is that depreciation for income tax purposes cannot be passed through directly to the owner of the fractional interest.

Physical Division

The second category of fractional ownership or interest is a division in the physical use of the property.

FIG. 2-1: Division of Property Rights

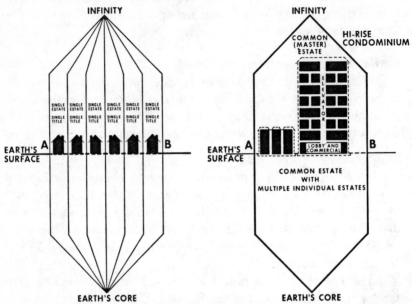

- *Horizontal and Vertical Subdivision.* Horizontal subdivision is the definition of the boundaries of surface areas of a property. Vertical subdivision refers to the division of air rights and subsurface rights. Subsurface rights in the form of oil or mineral rights are commonly leased or sold. Their exclusion may have little effect on surface land values if the terms of conveyance protect the surface use from interference. Subsurface rights may also involve underground pipe and cable lines.

- *Air Rights.* Within the distances normally encompassed above or below land surface, real estate ownership may be considered to be between vertical boundaries above and below the site. Practically, this means that a 100-by-100-foot parcel of land is not a square surface but a cube. Accordingly, this cube may be divided not only vertically, similar to a slice of a layer cake, but also horizontally, as in the individual layers of the cake. The useful height or depth of this cube (number of stories) is limited only by the practicalities of engineering, economics (highest and best use) and zoning.

- *Mineral Rights.* Like air and other rights, mineral rights may be owned, sold, bought and transferred. The estimation of value of each right is becoming a more common appraisal assignment.

• *Easement.* A nonpossessing interest held by one person in land of another person whereby the first person is accorded partial use of such land for a specific purpose. Easements are created to allow access to a property whether it be from public or private land. An easement may be vertical as well as horizontal, such as underground utility lines. Where an easement is granted to allow specific access to or through a property, it may be called a right-of-way.

• *Condominiums.* Ownership of a condominium unit is basically ownership of the cubical area within the confines of its outer walls, floor and ceiling plus common-ownership rights in all public space which, together with all the units, comprise the entire property. The condominium unit is a separate ownership, the title to which is in the name of the owner(s). It may be leased, sold, mortgaged or refinanced separately.

Lease Interests

Lease interests are another type of partial interest in real estate, which can be divided into two types:

• *Leased Fees.* An owner may lease real estate, relinquishing the right of occupancy but retaining the title to the fee, subject to the lease, including the recovery of use at the expiration of the lease, known as the reversionary rights. The value of a leased fee interest is profoundly affected by its length and terms, which may cover a wide range of provisions agreed upon between the parties.

• *Leasehold or Possessory Interest.* The right to the occupancy and use of any benefit in the transferred property granted under any lease, permit, license, concession or other type of contract. It is the opposite of the leased fee. The value of possessory interests usually refers to the value of the interest leased (i.e., the value of the use and occupancy of the property for the lease term, known as a leasehold interest).

Knowing exactly which rights are under consideration is fundamental in appraising. Precise definition customarily is a matter of documentation. In the absence of such definition, it may be necessary to obtain legal opinion. The appraiser, however, should be generally familiar with the broad range of property rights, their more common characteristics, and the usual manner in which they are utilized and transferred.

The Four Great Forces

The value of all real property—including single family residential—is created, maintained, modified or destroyed by the interplay of four great forces that affect human behavior:

1. Social ideals and standards.
2. Economic activities and trends.
3. Government regulations and actions.
4. Physical or environmental forces.

These dynamic forces set the pattern for the variables affecting real estate market values. Combined, they are the essence of cause and effect that influences every parcel of real estate on earth and directly affects both the demand and the supply side of the market.

When these forces are closely examined, it becomes apparent that they are composed of many complex factors that are constantly changing. A partial list of social forces includes:

1. Population growth, decline or stability.
2. Shifts in population density.
3. Changes in family size.
4. Geographical distribution of social groups.
5. Attitudes toward education and social activities.
6. Attitudes toward architectural design and utility.
7. Factors emerging from human social instincts, ideals and moral codes, likes and dislikes.

Economic forces, including the resources and efforts of society to achieve its social goals, are made up of factors such as:

1. Gross national product.
2. Economic trends and activity.
3. Employment trends and wage levels.
4. Availability of money and credit.
5. Price levels, interest rates and tax burdens.
6. All other factors having an effect upon purchasing power.

Forces created by government regulations and activities include:

1. Zoning laws.
2. Building codes.
3. Environmental regulations.

4. Police and fire regulations.
5. Rent controls, national defense measures, special-use permits, and credit controls.
6. Government-sponsored housing and guaranteed mortgage loans.
7. Monetary policies, including all forms of taxation, that affect the free use of real estate.

Physical or environmental forces created by either nature or society encompass:
1. Natural resources.
2. Climate and topography.
3. Characteristics of soil and subsoil to support improvements.
4. Soil fertility.
5. Mineral resources.
6. Flood control and soil conservation.
7. Technological advances affecting land use.

Because all these forces affect cost, price and value, their impact—whether direct or indirect—must be considered in estimating the cost, the probable price or the value of real property. These four forces and the factors comprising them constitute the basic raw material for making an appraisal of value. Any decision on or action about the market value of real estate is based upon an appraisal, whether it is in the form of a formal narrative written report or a verbal estimate of value.

Students of real property valuation are prone to attempt to categorize a factor specifically and concisely under one of the four forces. Often, however, a factor may appear in two or more of the classifications. The reason for itemizing the four major forces is to assist both the beginning and the experienced appraiser in making a comprehensive and thorough analysis of all possible factors and conditions that may affect a real estate decision. To assist in classifying activities and trends in the most appropriate categories, greatest emphasis is given to the force from which the factor tends to stem. For example, the impact of population statistics is typically classified under social forces but the appraiser recognizes that it may be expressed in terms of economic impact as well.

The conclusions drawn from all the forces must be expressed in terms of dollars, but this does not justify the inclusion of all activities under the economic force. Another example of potential conflict in classifying has to do with natural resources. As illustrated so dramatically in the energy crisis, a shortage of fuel is typically expressed economically although the matter is originally and primarily classified as a physical and environmental force.

The Meaning of Value

Because the term *value* has many possible interpretations, its meaning for the valuation of real property must be precise. Value has been defined as *the quantity of one thing that can be obtained in exchange for another or the ratio of exchange of one commodity for another.* Money is the common denominator by which real property value is usually measured.

An appraisal of value is an estimate based on an interpretation by the appraiser of facts and value indications processed and reconciled to produce that estimate as of a specific date. Because the term *appraised value* is too general, the type of value must be precisely defined in the appraisal report. The value most commonly sought in an appraisal is *market value*, although there are other types of value that may be considered depending on the use for which the client requires the appraisal and the nature of the valuation problem being solved. Obviously, the reliability of an appraised value depends on the basic competence and integrity of the appraiser and on the skill with which pertinent data is processed.

The emphasis in appraising is on the *relationship* between a thing desired and the potential purchaser or consumer. The idea that need alone is responsible for the creation of value would imply that value is a characteristic inherent in the object itself. If this concept were true, bread would be intrinsically valuable because it is needed to satisfy hunger. But hunger is limited; therefore, if bread were produced in excess of the need to satisfy all normal hunger, its value would decrease. The value of any object, then, is *not* intrinsic but depends upon the relationship between supply and demand.

An object also cannot have value unless it has utility—that is, unless it is able to satisfy the desire for possession, but utility is also relative to the satisfaction gained from the object. For example, bread has great utility to a hungry person but much less to one who is not hungry.

Although utility is intrinsic to value, utility alone does not establish value. Scarcity also must be present before significant value exists. No object, including a parcel of real estate, can have value unless it possesses in some degree the two factors of utility and scarcity.

Utility and scarcity do not alone create value. The other element necessary if an object is to have value (as defined by the appraiser) is purchasing power—the ability of the individual to participate in the market in order to satisfy the desire to possess. For example, if no one has the purchasing power (money) to buy bread, bread becomes valueless.

The appraiser's interpretation of value can be summarized as follows:

1. Value is not a characteristic inherent in real property itself but depends on the desires of people. It varies from person to person and from time to time, as individual wants vary.
2. An object (real property) cannot have value unless it has utility. Usefulness arouses desire for possession and has the power to give satisfaction.
3. An object (real property) must also be relatively scarce to have value.
4. The desire of a purchaser who has the purchasing power to buy must be aroused for the object to have value.

Unlike rapidly consumed goods, the benefits of real property are realized over a much longer period. Land and its improvements have a useful life usually extending over decades. The value of real property, consequently, is equal to the present value of the future benefits forthcoming from the property. Estimating the market value of the highest and best use is the paramount problem in the valuation of real estate. Any such estimate must take into consideration the social, economic, government and environmental forces that may influence the property's highest and best use. A clear understanding of current and future conditions and the perception to recognize the forces that modify and affect these conditions are essential.

In considering these factors, the professional appraiser should never lose sight of the fact that what must really be interpreted are the reactions of typical users and investors. Appraisers do not make value; they interpret it, chiefly from market evidence. The appraiser must sift through large quantities of data to select those that have the greatest significance relative to market value.

Value-in-Exchange versus Value-in-Use

Market value, or value-in-exchange, is relative. It implies a comparison of available alternative economic goods from which the potential purchaser may make a choice; it also reflects the interactions of buyers, sellers and investors. Value-in-use is the value or importance of an object to a particular owner who may have no intention of exposing it on the open market. Value-in-use has been defined as the value of an economic good to its owner-user based on its productivity (in income, utility or amenity form). Value-in-use does not necessarily represent market value, unless there is a significant number of buyer-users active in the marketplace who are willing and able to pursue the commodity or service.

Most real estate appraisal assignments involve estimates of market value. Numerous definitions of market value have been devised over the years by professional organizations, government bodies and the courts. These definitions are subject to frequent change, and appraisers performing services that may be subject to litigation are cautioned to seek the exact definition of market value that is accepted in the jurisdiction in which the services are performed. A widely accepted definition of market value is:

> The highest price in terms of money which a property should bring in a competitive and open market under all conditions requisite to a fair sale, the buyer and seller each acting prudently, knowledgeably and assuming the price is not affected by undue stimulus. Implicit in this definition is the consummation of a sale as of a specified date and the passing of title from seller to buyer under conditions whereby:
> 1. Buyer and seller are typically motivated.
> 2. Both parties are well informed or well advised and each is acting in self-interest.
> 3. A reasonable time is allowed for exposure in the open market.
> 4. Payment is made in cash or its equivalent.

5. Financing, if any, is on terms generally available in the community at the specified date and typical for the type of property in its locale.
6. The price represents a normal consideration for the property sold unaffected by special financing amounts or terms, services, fees, costs or credits incurred in the transaction.

An expansion of this explanation includes "buyers and sellers" rather than limiting it to a single buyer and seller. This would better represent the actual, open, freely competitive marketplace in which there are (by definition) several or many buyers and sellers of residences. Some prefer to include a further provision for the buyers in that they must be capable of making the purchase (i.e., have purchasing power).

In the process of solving an appraisal problem, one of the earliest decisions that must be made is the kind of value applicable to the situation—value-in-use or value-in-exchange. The decision is based on the problem to be solved. If it is a question of the most probable selling price, then the appraiser is committed to value-in-exchange. If the problem is related to a proposed renovation program, then the most likely kind of value may be its value-in-use to the owner. A financial institution considering a mortgage loan on a residence is primarily concerned about the most likely selling price of the property; therefore, the market value (value-in-exchange) is the appropriate kind of value. Assessed value historically has been based on costs rather than market prices, which tend to relate such values to "use" rather than "market" values. In recent years, however, there has been a trend to relate assessed values to the market rather than solely to costs to reproduce or replace.

Objective versus Subjective Value Concept

Probably the most significant difference between the real estate appraiser's approach to valuation and that of most other professionals in the wide field of valuation is orientation. The real estate appraiser usually estimates market value by studying the type of market of which the property being appraised is a part. The appraiser's interest in the property is not usually in its value to one particular owner or for a single use, but rather for the typical owner and the highest and best use as determined by the market for such property.

At any point in time, the great majority of properties are not available for sale at a price that will attract many buyers. Only after the seller's price is lowered and the buyer's bid is raised is a transaction consummated. The exception to this rule is the subjective value concept, which is related to value-in-use. The subjective value of a commodity is the desirability it is considered to possess in relation to the needs of a single individual. This is also called personal value and is, in fact, a form of anticipation of value-in-use, since it will result in a sale of property at a different price (usually higher) than the market value. The measure of the subjective value of a property is the amount that would be paid by a specific person for possession, which will depend upon the amount of benefits (utility or amenity in nature) that are perceived to exist.

Basic Economic Principles of Real Property Value

The basic principles defined, explained, and illustrated in this section are concerned with their impact upon real property value. The section begins with the broad principle of supply and demand, followed by more specific kinds of real estate principles: anticipation, balance, contribution, increasing and decreasing returns, surplus productivity, change, competition and excess profit, conformity, and substitution.

The last to be discussed, highest and best use, is the most fundamental in understanding real property value. Estimating highest and best use has been described by many appraisers as the most critical step in the total appraisal process. Some steps of the process may be more technical, others may lead more directly to the value conclusion, but none is more basic or fundamental than the concept of highest and best use. It is necessary to use the principles discussed in this chapter in order to reach a sound and defensible highest and best use conclusion. The highest and best use is not a fictitious or artificial determination, and it requires practical and realistic application and conclusions.

Supply and Demand

The principle of supply and demand involves the interrelationship of the desire for a commodity and its scarcity. Demand for a commodity is created by its utility (ability to satisfy a need) and its scarcity and is limited by the financial ability of people to purchase it. The greater the supply of a commodity, the lower its price will tend to be. There is a point, at least theoretically, at which supply and demand are in balance. At this point market value tends to reflect the cost of production or replacement. As the supply increases or demand decreases, the price in the market decreases. Recently this market phenomenon has been called a soft market.

Abstract demand is unlimited — that is, people continually desire more goods. But *effective demand* is limited in the economic sense by the purchasing power of the participants in the market. Because demand is closely related to desire, both advertising and education can greatly influence demand.

Among the factors affecting supply and demand for housing are population changes, purchasing power, and price levels. The supply of housing, for example, is controlled in part by rentals and sales prices and the relationship these bear to the temper of the market. A certain combination of factors must be present in the housing market to stimulate additions to the housing supply. There must be a shortage in the supply of units, a strong demand for housing, and effective purchasing power to satisfy the demand at the rentals and prices offered, which in turn must be high enough to encourage builders to construct new units. If demand is very strong and purchasing power is increasing faster than the ability of the supply to satisfy the increased need, rentals and sale prices for available units rise (inflation results when demand exceeds supply). When increased rentals or sales prices continue to find a ready market, more builders enter the scene, accelerating the pace of additions to the supply. Should this result in an excess of units, prices fall (deflation results when supply exceeds demand).[2]

Other factors influencing the real estate market are the cost of

---

[2]Although all of these relationships and reactions are stated definitely, there may be exceptions (called "phenomena"); furthermore, these are indicated as "tendencies," that is, "the price tends to increase," etc.

labor, taxation of property, the money supply and the cost of financing, rent controls, zoning and other government regulations.

The following principles operate within the structure of the market. Market activity is composed of supply and demand; the interaction of the two is expressed as price. To understand the influence of the market on prices (as well as on values and costs), the appraiser must understand and apply the concept of micro- and macro-economics. *Micro-economics* is the study of the individual property in the market. *Macro-economics* is the study of the industry; in real estate appraising it applies to all the properties of a certain type and their activity in the market.

Obviously a substantial difference exists between the study of an individual residence in its market and the analysis of all such residences as a segment of the market. The basic principles that follow are applicable to both micro and macro situations although the application and interpretation may vary.

Anticipation

Value is created by the expectation of benefits to be derived in the future. The future, not the past, is important in deriving estimates of value. The primary use of past experience is its significance in the forecasting of possible future trends and conditions.

Value may be defined as the present worth of the rights to all prospective future benefits, tangible and intangible, accruing to ownership of real estate. In most cases the quantity, quality and duration of future benefits may be estimated in the light of past experience as disclosed by analysis of the property being appraised and comparable properties.

An illustration of changing attitudes and wants on the part of a segment of the residential market is found in the reactions during the energy crunch in 1974 and 1975. Some consumers in the market altered their desires for housing, changing from larger to smaller units within closer proximity to employment and schools and checked more carefully the costs to heat and cool the structure. Such a significant change in a major part of a market must be considered by the professional appraiser in his or her analysis.

Recent sale prices of comparable houses indicate the attitudes of informed buyers and investors in the market concerning the present value of these anticipated benefits of ownership of a particular property. However, the market value of an individual property is not necessarily established by its past selling price or by the cost to create it.

Balance

Maximum value is achieved when the agents in production[3] are in economic balance. The value of a property depends on the balance of these four:

1. Labor (wages).
2. Capital (the investment in buildings and equipment).
3. Coordination (management or entrepreneurial contribution).
4. Land (rents).

There is a theoretical point of equilibrium in each property that will produce the greatest net return. An imbalance exists when a building represents an underimprovement or overimprovement of its site; one also is present when the cost and amount of special services to the occupants are inadequate or excessive related to the character of the building or neighborhood. These conditions illustrate the principle of balance, affirming that a disadvantage or loss in value attends any excess or deficiency in the contribution of the four agents of production.

The use of goods and services resulting from these agents produces gross income. Gross income is first applied to labor, then to capital, coordination and finally to land.

The principle of balance is applied in the process of estimating highest and best use in appraisal practice. Thus the proper apportionment of the agents in production is essential if maximum net return is to be produced and maximum land value developed. Because land has last claim on the gross income produced by the proper apportionment of the four agents, the land value is residual.

The natural operation of the market is toward balance. This concept applies to individual productive units as well as to all units in a market. It is difficult to alter the relationship of units of production

---

[3]The theories of the classical economists, especially those of David Ricardo, recognized the importance of the agents of production. They are used today to help explain the principle of balance and the residual nature of the value of land.

in an existing building, although it might be accomplished by a renovation program, refinancing or new ownership. New units added to the market use the experience of existing units to maximize their chances of reaching balance.

Three sub-elements of the principle of balance are contribution, increasing and decreasing returns and surplus productivity, each involving the agents in production.

• *Contribution* The principle of contribution (also known as the principle of marginal productivity) is the principle of increasing and decreasing returns applied to a portion or portions of real property. It affirms that the value of any individual agent in production depends on how much it contributes to value by its presence or detracts by its absence. An example of this in the appraisal of residential properties is the valuation of lots of varying depths. The appraiser must estimate the value, if any, that additional depth contributes to a parcel over and above the value of lots of standard depth in the area. If the lot is of less than standard depth, its value would reflect a loss of contribution attributable to the missing piece.

This principle has practical application in estimating the degree of overimprovement, underimprovement, or misplaced improvement in highest and best use analysis.

• *Increasing and Decreasing Returns* Larger amounts of the agents in production produce a greater net income up to a point, at which the maximum value has been developed; any additional expenditures will not produce a return commensurate with such investment. The fertilization of farmland affords a simple example of this principle. Up to a certain point, increasing use of fertilizer results in a greater crop yield; beyond that point, it will not produce an additional return sufficient to warrant the additional cost.

It is frequently necessary to determine the character and size of the structural improvement that will enable the land to produce the greatest net yield. To ascertain this point, hypothetical combinations of probable income and expenses and capital requirements for improvements of various types and sizes should be analyzed. Different combinations may represent higher or lower probable yields.

The process of developing hypothetical improvements to determine that combination of the agents in production providing the greatest yield illustrates the principle of increasing and decreasing returns. It also applies in the estimation of highest and best use—that use indicating the greatest net yield.

• *Surplus Productivity* Surplus productivity is defined as the net income remaining after the four agents in production have been paid. It may be attributed to the land in its present use. Surplus productivity is dependent upon the principles of balance and increasing and decreasing returns and the proper apportionment of the four agents in production.

Change

Change is constantly occurring; in real estate it affects individual properties, neighborhoods and cities. Change can evolve so slowly that its occurrence is almost indiscernible. The appraiser must be sensitive to the subtle as well as the obvious indications of change. The future, not the past, is of primary importance in the valuation of real estate. The appraiser's concern is with the market's view of transition, not permanence. Recognition must be made of the social, economic, governmental and environmental forces at work and their present and future effect on the market value of single family residences.

Individual properties, districts, neighborhoods and entire communities often follow a four-phase lifespan:

1. *Growth.* A period during which there are gains in public favor and acceptance.
2. *Stability.* A period of equilibrium without marked gains or losses.
3. *Decline.* A period of diminishing demand and acceptance.
4. *Renewal.* A period of rejuvenation and rebirth of market demand.

In the market the basis of the value of a property is neither in a price paid for it in the past nor in the cost of its creation, but rather in the prospective amenities and uses that buyers and sellers believe it will provide for them. The actions of the market (sales) reflect informed buyers' opinions of the probable future benefits of ownership. The attitude of the market toward property in a specific neighborhood reflects the probable future trend of that neighborhood. For example, following World War II, more ranch-style houses were built than two-story houses. Buyers in the market developed a preference for one-story houses, reducing the demand for two-story houses.

Competition and Excess Profit

Profit tends to breed competition and excess profit tends to encourage ruinous competition. Profit is defined as that portion of the net income produced by real property over and above the costs of labor, capital, coordination and land (the agents in production).

Profit as applied to real property is not the same as profit obtained from the operation of a business. Normal business profit is the monetary incentive and reward for capital investment. The yield on real property investments also is the monetary incentive for investment in land and buildings. But profit, as it is considered by the appraiser, is the prospective net income remaining after operating costs and adequate returns on land and building(s) have been satisfied. In other words, it is what remains after providing for the agents in production.

Competition is one of the most familiar and easily recognized forces present at all levels of economic activity. Reasonable competition stimulates further creative contribution, but in excess it can destroy profits. A lack of competition, such as created by a monopolistic or oligopolistic situation, must be recognized by the appraiser as being outside the realm of market value definition and considered accordingly in his or her analysis. The appraiser not only recognizes competition in normal situations but also perceives those situations in which it is excessive and, if unchecked, may undermine value. Competition is a product of supply and demand; a proper study of the highest and best use of a property includes current supply and demand factors.

Conformity

Maximum value is realized when a reasonable degree of architectural homogeneity exists and land uses are compatible. Conformity in use is usually a highly desirable feature of real property since it tends to create and maintain value; and maximum value affords the owner a maximum return. Reasonable homogeneity in the principle of conformity implies reasonable similarity; it does not mean monotonous uniformity. Generally, the most satisfactory use of land is realized when it conforms to the standards governing the area in which it is located.

The standards of conformity are subject to the principle of change. For example, racial homogeneity was once considered a sign of social conformity and neighborhood stability. Conversely, racial integration was once considered a sign of social nonconformity and neighborhood decline. Social perceptions and attitudes have changed. The notion that racial or ethnic homogeneity is a requirement for maximum value is without empirical support. Many strong and stable neighborhoods are composed of residents of varied and diverse racial, religious and cultural backgrounds.

Other signs of change may be observed in the fields of architectural design and urban planning. The trend toward multipurpose urban structures and a deliberate mixing of land uses reflects an increasing awareness of the interdependence of land uses.

The elements of conformity are not preconceived standards of development but have evolved as cities have grown and land uses have multiplied. Homeowners have recognized the advantages of living in neighborhoods designed and developed to provide facilities or amenities which add to the benefits of ownership, and they have protected those assets by maintaining conformity through zoning.

Substitution

When several commodities or services with substantially the same utility or benefit are available, the one with the lowest price attracts the greatest demand and widest distribution. The importance and application of this principle can be found in many segments of the economy. In real estate, for example, if two homes offer approximately the same advantages, the prospective buyer will select the one with the lower price.

The principle of substitution is found in each of the three approaches to value:

• *Market Data Approach.* Applicable when there are alternate choices of like or similar residences, market value tends to be set at the price of acquiring an equally desirable substitute property, assuming that no costly delay is encountered in making the substitution.

• *Cost Approach.* No rational person will pay more for a property than that amount by which one can obtain, by purchase of a site and construction of a building without undue delay, a property of equal desirability and utility.

• *Income Approach.* Value tends to be set by the effective investment necessary to acquire, without undue delay, a comparable substitute income property offering an equally desirable net income return.

The principle of substitution is the basis for these premises:

1. The market value of property tends to match the value indicated by the actions of informed buyers in the market for comparable real estate having similar physical and locational characteristics.
2. The cost of producing, through new construction, an equally desirable substitute property *may* set the upper limit of value, if new construction can be completed in a reasonable period of time.
3. The value of a property tends to be related to its competitive position among alternative investment choices producing the same net income.

Highest and Best Use

Fundamental to the concept of value is the theory of highest, best and most profitable use. Highest and best use is the reasonable and probable use that will support the highest present value, as defined, as of the effective date of the appraisal. It is also the use, from among reasonably probable and legal alternative uses, found to be physically possible, appropriately supported and financially feasible and which results in highest land value.

This definition applies specifically to the highest and best use of land. Where a site has existing improvements, the highest and best use of the site *as if vacant* may be different from the existing use. The existing use will continue, however, unless and until land value in its highest and best use exceeds the total value of the property in that use (see Chapter 8).

Implied within these definitions is recognition of the contribution of that specific use to community environment or to community development goals in addition to wealth maximization of individual property owners. Also implied is that the determination of highest and best use results from the appraiser's judgment and analytical skill — that is, that the use determined from analysis represents an opinion, not a fact. In appraisal practice, the concept of highest and best use represents the premise on which value is based. In the context of most probable selling price (market value), another appropriate term to reflect highest and best use would be most probable use.

The most profitable likely use cannot always be interpreted in terms of money. Net return sometimes takes the form of amenities, usually more applicable to houses than other kinds of properties.

Deed restrictions, zoning and government regulations may not conform to current market requirements, and thus the site may remain undeveloped to its highest and best use. If the site has more valuable use potential than allowed by law, and if there is a reasonable probability that a change in use will be permitted, its value will be affected to the extent that a buyer or seller might recognize this potential, after giving due consideration to the expense involved in the change.

The theory of consistent use is an important aspect of the thorough understanding and application of highest and best use. It is discussed in detail in Chapter 8.

Summary

The value of land depends on its usefulness, including all of its improvements and appurtenant rights. Real property is distinct from personal property and chattels. Title is limited by the four great powers of government and frequently by private restrictions and agreements as well. There are many facets to the term *value*, but the real estate appraiser is customarily interested in estimating market value (value-in-exchange). The legal definition of market value becomes most significant when an assignment will involve litigation where precise, legally accepted definitions are required.

Several fundamental economic principles provide the basis for analyzing the action of the real estate market, which are of particular interest to the real estate appraiser:

SUPPLY AND DEMAND
1. Utility and scarcity combined create demand, which is the desire for possession.
2. Demand is effective only when supported by purchasing power.

3. Value is increased if supply is reduced or demand increased.

ANTICIPATION
1. Value is the present worth of the rights to all prospective future benefits accruing to ownership and use of real property.
2. Recent sales prices of comparable properties indicate the market value of such rights and benefits.

BALANCE
1. The value of a property depends on the balance of the four agents in production: labor, capital, coordination and land.

Contribution
1. The principle of contribution deals with increasing and decreasing return applied to a portion or the whole of an improvement.
2. The value of an item in production is measured by its contribution to the net return of the enterprise.
3. Application of this principle is basic to any feasibility study or remodeling or modernization program and in the valuation of lots of varying depths.

Increasing and Decreasing Returns
1. Increased increments of agents in production produce greater net income (increasing returns) up to a point (surplus productivity).
2. The point of maximum contribution of agents in production (point of decreasing returns) attests to the proper combination of agents resulting in highest and best use.
3. Any further increase in the amount of agents in production will decrease the margin between cost of agents and gross income they will produce, resulting in decreased net income returns.
4. The principle of increasing and decreasing returns applied to a proper improvement of the site indicates its highest and best use.

Surplus Productivity
1. Surplus productivity is defined as the net income (often imputable to land) remaining after the costs of labor, capital and coordination have been paid.
2. Land has the last claim on the surplus productivity of the agents in production.

CHANGE
1. Change is constantly occurring.
2. Cities, neighborhoods and individual properties undergo the process of change.

3. The effect of prospective changes is reflected in the market.
4. Change is fundamentally the law of cause and effect.

COMPETITION AND EXCESS PROFITS
1. Competition is a product of the interaction of supply and demand.
2. Profits create competition.
3. Excess profits breed ruinous competition.
4. Profit is the surplus over and above satisfactory return to labor, capital, coordination efforts and land.
5. Competition tends to dissipate the major portion of excess profit, although some part may remain and contribute to increased land value.
6. The value of land is dependent on the use that yields the highest and best return.

CONFORMITY
1. Conformity is the result of a reasonable degree of architectural homogeneity and compatible land uses.
2. The standards of conformity have changed over the years reflecting changes in market attitudes, social trends, economic conditions and public policy.
3. The highest and best land use is generally realized under circumstances of harmony or conformity.
4. The principal purpose of zoning regulation and private restriction is to maintain conformity.

SUBSTITUTION
1. The value of a replaceable property tends to be indicated by the value of an equally desirable substitute property.
2. The value of a property tends to coincide with the value indicated by the actions of informed buyers in the market for comparable properties.
3. Disadvantage attends any excess or deficiency in the supply of the agents in production.
4. Equilibrium (balance) in character, amount and location of essential uses of real estate creates and maintains value.
5. The principle of contribution is related to surplus productivity in that the value of an individual agent in production depends upon how much it adds to or detracts from the income because of its presence.

HIGHEST AND BEST USE
1. Highest and best use is that which, at the time of appraisal, is

the most profitable, likely use of a property. It may also be defined as the available use and program of future utilization that produces the highest present land value.

2. Existing use may not conform to highest and best use.

3. Highest and best use may comprise a combination of a profitable interim (transitional) use and a deferred, more profitable potential use.

4. Highest and best use may be limited by zoning or deed restriction.

5. Improvements must add to the value of the land in order to have value attributed to them.

6. The principle of increasing and decreasing returns affirms the proper apportionment of land and improvement to achieve maximum land value.

7. Balance and consistent use are important collateral considerations in the selection of highest and best use.

Review Questions

1. What is meant by the "legal concept of real estate"?
2. Define and distinguish between "real estate," "real property" and "personal property."
3. What is a "fixture"?
4. What is the "bundle of rights" theory?
5. What are the four great forces affecting real estate value?
6. Define value.
7. Define market value. When might this concept be used in an appraisal?
8. Explain the difference between value-in-use and value-in-exchange. How are these related to subjective and objective value?
9. What characteristics are necessary for an object to have value? How does additional supply or decreased demand affect its value?
10. List the basic economic principles affecting real estate value. Explain and illustrate each.
11. What are the four powers of government affecting real estate?

3

The Appraisal Process

To make a professional appraisal is to solve a problem. The solution requires interpretation, in terms of money, of the combined influence of social, economic, governmental and environmental forces on a specific property. The finished product provides the basis for a decision relating to the property being appraised.

Although the characteristics of different residences can vary greatly, there is little variation in the orderly procedure for solving an appraisal problem. An appraisal problem is defined; the work is planned; and data is acquired, classified, analyzed and reconciled into an estimate of value.

The appraisal process is a series of logical steps which allow the appraiser to make a thorough and accurate appraisal in an efficient manner. The accompanying diagram (Fig. 3-1) is a flow chart illustrating the steps of this procedure.

Definition of the Problem

The first step in an appraisal is problem definition. This eliminates any ambiguity about the objectives of the report and the scope of the analysis or results that follow. There are five major steps in the definition of the appraisal problem:

1. Identification of the real estate to be appraised.
2. Identification of the property rights involved.
3. Determination of the effective date of the value estimate.
4. Statement of the objective of the appraisal.
5. Definition of the value to be estimated in the appraisal.

Identification of Real Estate

A property is first identified physically, by means of a mailing address or other descriptive data. More precise identification is provided by a legal description, available from an existing deed, title

35

FIG. 3-1: The Appraisal Process for the Single Family Residence

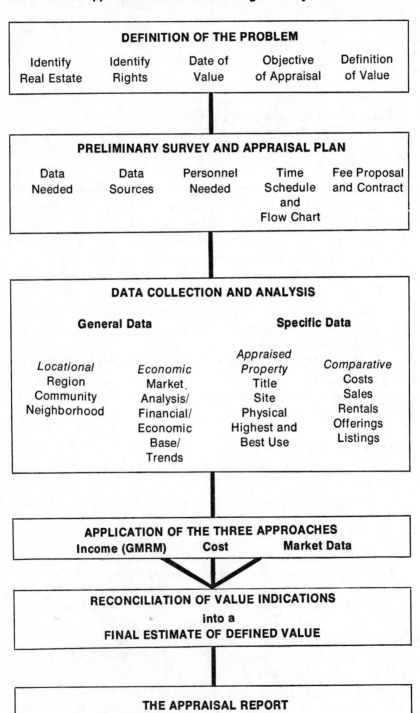

DEFINITION OF THE PROBLEM

| Identify Real Estate | Identify Rights | Date of Value | Objective of Appraisal | Definition of Value |

PRELIMINARY SURVEY AND APPRAISAL PLAN

| Data Needed | Data Sources | Personnel Needed | Time Schedule and Flow Chart | Fee Proposal and Contract |

DATA COLLECTION AND ANALYSIS

General Data   **Specific Data**

Locational
Region
Community
Neighborhood

Economic
Market
Analysis/
Financial/
Economic
Base/
Trends

Appraised Property
Title
Site
Physical
Highest and
Best Use

Comparative
Costs
Sales
Rentals
Offerings
Listings

APPLICATION OF THE THREE APPROACHES
Income (GMRM)   Cost   Market Data

RECONCILIATION OF VALUE INDICATIONS
into a
FINAL ESTIMATE OF DEFINED VALUE

THE APPRAISAL REPORT

policy, mortgage instrument, accredited survey or various public records.

Legal descriptions are derived from land surveys and are incorporated into the public record. Land surveying is a highly technical process, and appraisers should be familiar with the particular land survey system in use in a given area. Current systems of legal description include:

1. *Government survey.* A ground survey system established in 1785 that divides land into townships and sections.
2. *Lot and block.* A reference to a plot of a subdivision recorded in the office of the local recorder.
3. *Metes and bounds.* A system using known referrants, angles east or west of due north or south, and distances given in feet.
4. *Geodetic survey.* A government-designated benchmark system with points located by longitude and latitude.

A legal description, from any source, must be verified to determine that it accurately delineates the appraised property. Whether a complete legal description is to be included in the actual written appraisal is a matter of judgment. In some cases, a lengthy legal description may be incorporated as part of the addendum. Alternatively, reference could be made to its content and location in the public records.

Identification of Property Rights

An appraisal of real property is not directly a valuation of the physical land and improvements; it is a valuation of the rights of ownership. A specific appraisal may require a value estimate of all property rights, while another will analyze only limited rights in property. Ownership of property may be held by an individual, a partnership, a corporation or a group of heirs. When ownership is vested in more than one interest, each may hold an equal or unequal share.

The property rights or interests to be appraised may be fractional interests such as air rights over a specified property, subsurface rights, an easement, a right-of-way or a fee subject to an easement. Because the value of real property is not limited to its physical components, the appraiser cannot define the problem precisely until fully aware of which property rights are involved. Without this knowledge, the appraiser may produce an estimate of value that is irrelevant to the problem. A clear conception of the rights to be appraised will also help the appraiser evaluate the complexity of the problem and the amount of work it will require.

Effective Date of the Value Estimate

Establishing a specific date for the value estimate is an essential step, since the factors that directly affect value are always in the process of change. Thus an estimate of value is only valid for the point in time for which it has been formulated. Generally, appraisal assignments involve a current value estimate. In some cases, however, an appraisal is required as of a date in the past—for example, to determine inheritance taxes or insurance claims or for federal income tax purposes. It frequently has been necessary to appraise property as of March 1, 1913, the date of the inception of the federal income tax law, to establish the capital gains applicable on property owned since that date. In condemnation appraisal work, market value may be as of the date of petition or as of the trial date, depending upon local legal custom.

Objective of the Appraisal

The appraisal answers a question. The question may be as simple as "What is the market value of a property as of a given date?" or "How much insurance will be necessary to protect the owner of a property?" More complex questions may consider the feasibility of a certain project or leasing program or the highest and best use for a parcel of vacant land. These reports go beyond what is included in a traditional appraisal.

The character and direction of the report are directly affected by the nature of the decision a client must make and for which a report is required. The objective or purpose of an assignment will dictate the type and quantity of data to be gathered, the analytical methods to be used and the specific type of report required.

As the use for which an appraisal is needed varies, the arrangement of the report and the emphasis on particular data change to reflect different objectives. A clear statement of the objective of the appraisal avoids misunderstandings and misdirected efforts by the appraiser and prevents dissatisfaction by the client. If the objective of the appraisal is to estimate market value, this value will always be the same no matter what type of a report is required or for whom the report is being made.

Definition of Value

Whereas a property has only one market value as of a given date, there are occasions when other types of value are sought. If, for example, the value estimate is to be based upon a special set of circumstances, these assumptions should be stated within the definition of value. Although market value is sought most frequently in residential appraisals, there may be exceptions. For example, a very large family may buy two adjacent houses and join them with a common passageway. The homes may have been greatly modified to fit a specific purpose, and in this case, an estimate of the value-in-use may be the appropriate value concept.

The fact that others may not understand the exact meaning of terms commonly used by appraisers is another reason for including a written definition of the type of value to be estimated in the appraisal report. An exact definition of value clarifies the appraisal assignment for both the client and the appraiser. A standard definition may be selected from among various texts or one may be written to fit the specific problem being solved. If the appraisal seeks assessed value or insurable value or if the appraisal is to be used in a condemnation proceeding, the appraiser is often required to use a definition of value that is accepted by the assessor, the insurance company, or the courts.

In each case, a clearly written definition of the type of value sought helps the appraiser to choose appropriate data to be considered and the best methods to be used in processing it into a final value conclusion.

Preliminary Survey and Appraisal Plan

A preliminary survey estimating the character, scope and amount of work necessary to solve the problem leads to a definite plan for developing the report.

Data Required

The amount and type of data necessary to solve the problem as stated will depend largely on the characteristics of the property being appraised and on the objective of the appraisal. The appraiser must consider the availability of the needed data. The preliminary survey might include possible sources of specific data to be investigated.

The definition of the problem will also affect the approaches (market data, cost, income) to be used. Because most assignments involve an estimate of market value, the market data approach is basic to such appraisals. Nevertheless, in nearly all appraisals application of all three approaches is fundamental. This means that cost data and income information also should be developed except when the use of one or both of these approaches is not relevant or is impossible or impractical.

The selection of the dominant approach may depend on the question being answered as well as the availability of pertinent data. An estimate of value for insurance purposes might require emphasis on the cost approach. In condemnation cases, the most relevant consideration is establishing market value. The income approach, which uses comparable rental data from the market, is at times useful for supporting values desired in other approaches. A value estimate based solely on the cost approach is seldom acceptable, unless the property appraised is unique and not customarily traded in the market. (Each approach is discussed in further detail later in this chapter and later chapters.)

Personnel and Time Requirements

Orderly planning and scheduling of an appraisal are essential for efficient completion of the assignment. Time and personnel needs to complete an assignment vary with the amount and complexity of the work entailed. In some cases it may involve a matter of days; in more complex situations, it will take longer.

A planned schedule of work to be performed may be helpful, particularly for more complex assignments. Sound working habits for the appraiser and his or her staff begin with a clear understanding of the exact nature of the work to be done by each person, which will expedite efficient completion of an assignment. The appraiser must also recognize those instances when outside assistance is desirable—for example, the need for an engineering opinion concerning soil bearing. The ability to recognize the areas in which to delegate detail assures the appraiser of the most effective use of time.

The appraiser's responsibility is to recognize the nature of the work and to schedule and delegate assignments if additional personnel is available and required. A completion flow chart often helps to systematize the workload.

Fee Proposal and Contract

Many residential appraisals are made for regular clients at a predetermined fee. Other assignments require the appraiser to quote a fee or fee range in advance of a commitment to proceed with the appraisal. The fee may be negotiated on a per-hour or per-diem basis or may be an overall amount (flat fee). The appraiser's experience and familiarity with the cost of operation permits realistic setting of a base figure to cover the actual cost of typical assignments. This requires consideration of the extent of research, personnel and time needed to complete the appraisal. The figure is then adjusted to include an estimate of any additional or unusual expenses specific to a particular assignment. To this subtotal, a remuneration for the appraiser's own contribution is added, and the total is the fee quoted to the client.

The actual amount that may be charged for services performed depends on the appraiser's reputation for experience and sound judgment in the view of the clients. The appraisal report is only paper; with the appraiser's signature, it acquires credibility in proportion to the professional reputation for competence, judgment and integrity of the signator. Competent work is required regardless of fee; thus the fee charged should be adequate for whatever is required by the appraisal assignment.

The appraiser's proposal to a client may be presented verbally or in writing. Regardless of format, it should delineate clearly an understanding of the particular appraisal problem. A typical proposal includes:

1. Identification of the property.
2. A statement of the rights to be appraised.
3. Date of the value estimate and estimated date of delivery of the report.

4. Objective of the appraisal (the question to be answered).
5. Definition of the value to be sought.
6. Form of the report and the number of copies required.
7. Fee quotation, either specifically or within a range.
8. Clarification of responsibility and compensation for any other services, such as court testimony, that may be needed.

Client acknowledgment may take the form of signing a copy of the proposal or by more formal contractual means. Such a commitment is evidence that the client and appraiser agree on the nature of the appraisal problem and on the proposed appraisal plan. This is good professional practice which promotes harmonious relations and avoids misunderstandings.

Data Collection and Analysis

The guiding principle in the collection, analysis and display of data in an appraisal is that it should be relevant to the specific appraisal problem and the value conclusion. Data should not be included unless it applies and is properly analyzed and reconciled.

Data Sources

Appropriate data sources will vary with the nature of the appraisal, although some are useful in nearly every problem. The sources may be divided into two categories, public and private, the latter of which includes the appraiser's own files.

• *Public Records.* Title information is legally on record in the court house or town hall in most communities. These recording systems are usually well classified and maintained so that an accurate title check can be made. City and county offices are the customary sources for information about zoning, traffic regulations, water and sewer lines, public health and other government regulations. In some areas, data about transfers of property, leases and property assessed values is published and sold or distributed by title companies, lending institutions or private publishers.

• *Private Sources.* Data pertinent to the cost analysis of buildings may be found in cost manuals published by several reputable organizations, as part of a continuing service that provides information at regular intervals (see Appendix H). Local cost indices are often published in larger cities. Appraisers may also maintain data on local cost of construction, materials, labor wage scales and contractors' cost breakdowns. Multiple listing systems, real estate brokers' records, classified advertising media, the S.R.E.A. Market Data Center and newspaper items are additional sources of information.

A permanent filing system with an office procedure for its maintenance is a helpful tool for most appraisers in compiling the large volume of general data about the region, community, and neighborhoods in which they operate because it can be used for most assignments. Such data, which is personally collected by the appraiser, gradually accumulates into what is known as an "appraisal plant" or library, which also includes publications devoted to appraising and related business fields as well as cost information, sales data and economic trend analysis.

Data Types

• *General Data.* Background data deals with the locational and economic forces outside the appraised property that influence its value. This includes information about the region, community and neighborhood such as population characteristics, price levels, employment opportunities, economic base analysis, etc. In addition, analysis of current economic conditions such as interest rates, effective purchasing power, construction costs and availability of financing is included here.

• *Specific Data.* Data pertaining to the appraised property includes a description and analysis of the physical characteristics of the property, title and record data, the relation of the site to general land patterns, and highest and best use analysis.

Pertinent title data may include the identity of ownership, type of ownership, existing easements and encroachments, zoning regulations affecting the property, assessed value and taxation and deed or other restrictions.

Descriptive data includes a complete evaluation of the site and the physical improvements and an analysis of condition, layout, style and design. Structural and mechanical quality are also reviewed. Site features such as size, shape, topography, lot and building orientation, utilities and relation to the existing land-use pattern are also analyzed here.

The next step is highest and best use analysis which will provide the base for the rest of the appraisal. The site is analyzed *as if vacant* to estimate the highest and best use. Often it will be the existing use, which reflects the permitted uses of the site under zoning regulations. Frequently, however, the appraiser finds that the existing use does not constitute the highest and best use of the site, that a higher (more intensive) use is permitted within current zoning restrictions, or that a change in permitted use is a reasonable probability that will be recognized by an informed purchaser. Such a determination has great significance in helping the appraiser to arrive at a realistic estimate of value.

• *Comparative Data.* In preparation for the three approaches to value, data is gathered on sales prices, listings, offers, and rentals of properties that are deemed comparable to the property being appraised. Since no two houses are identical, available sale data must be considered the basis of reasonable comparability. Appropriate adjustments reflecting major differences must be made. The subject of comparable sales and the treatment of market data is discussed more fully in Chapter 13.

The total data collection program outlined above is essential for a sound appraisal report. Value conclusions are no better than the reliability of the data considered and the competence of the analysis and reconciliation applied to it.

Good appraisal practice requires that sales, listings and offering data be verified by the buyer, seller or broker. Unverified data may lead to the wrong value estimate.

Application of the Three Approaches to Value

The income, cost, and market data approaches to value are based on three different concepts regarding property, each related to the principle of substitution.

1. Value is related to the economic rental of residential property as indicated by comparable properties.
2. Value is related to the current cost of reproducing or replacing a building less the loss in value from physical deterioration, functional obsolescence and economic obsolescence (accrued depreciation), plus land value.

3. Value is related to the selling prices of recently sold comparable properties when adjustments are considered for time, location, physical characteristics and conditions of sale.

In each assignment, the appraiser considers all three approaches.
For a particular type of property, the value indications obtained in
one or two of the approaches may be most significant; however,
whenever possible, all three approaches are used. There are appraisal problems that do not lend themselves to application of all
three approaches. The income approach, for example, may not be
helpful in the valuation of an owner-occupied home in a market
where houses are rarely rented.

Income Approach

The use of the income approach in valuing residential real estate is
based on the assumption that value is related to the economic rent
(income) that the real estate can be expected to earn. This approach
has its greatest application in areas where there is a substantial
rental market. In neighborhoods that are predominantly owner-
occupied, rental data may be too scarce to permit the use of this
approach.

When sufficient data is available, the appraiser follows these steps
to derive a value indication:

1. Develops an applicable multiplier.
   a. Finds houses that have recently sold in the neighborhood
      that are comparable and were rented at the time of sale.
   b. Divides the sale price of each comparable by the monthly
      rental to derive a monthly rent multiplier, known as a Gross
      Monthly Rent Multiplier (GMRM).
   c. Reconciles the multipliers developed in Step b to obtain a
      single multiplier or range of multipliers applicable to the ap-
      praised property. This is *not* an average; it is a judgment of
      comparability and applicability.
2. Estimates economic rent for the residence being appraised.
   a. Finds comparable rentals in the neighborhood.
   b. Analyzes each comparable rental and compares its features
      with those of the appraised property.
   c. Estimates the adjustments required to obtain an indicated
      rental for the property being appraised.
   d. Considers each comparable carefully, with emphasis on the
      need for adjustments, and formulates an opinion of the
      market (economic) rent of the appraised house based upon
      the actual rents of the comparables.

3. Estimates the value of the residence being appraised.
   a. Multiplies the estimated market rent by the estimated monthly multiplier (or range of multipliers) to obtain an indicated value of the property being appraised via the income approach.

Even if the property being appraised is rented at the time of valuation, it is necessary to consider the market (or economic) rental that would apply if the residence were available for occupancy as of the date of appraisal. The market rent is defined as the rental income a property would command on the open market as indicated by current rentals being paid for comparable space. This may be the same as the contract rent or it may be more or less than the rent specified in an existing lease. As a lease ages, the contract rental usually differs from market rental. In applying the income approach, therefore, the contract rent cannot be used as the market rent *unless* the competitive rents in the market substantiate its applicability.

To develop the GMRM, comparables are chosen that have sold recently in the market and were rented at the time of sale. The selling price of each comparable is divided by its gross monthly rental to obtain this factor. For example, if the appraiser finds single family residences in the subject neighborhood selling for $38,500 and renting for $308 per month, the indicated GMRM will be 125 ($38,500 ÷ $308 = 125).

A value for the appraised property is estimated by multiplying the estimated economic rent by the GMRM. For example, if the economic rental of the property has been estimated to be $315 per month, multiplying the GMRM of 125 by $315 gives an indicated value of $39,375.

The final estimate of value based on the value indication of the income approach will be only as good as the market data used to process it. Therefore data used in this method must be carefully sorted and selected for applicability. Care must be taken to verify the comparability of all sales and rentals selected for processing in this approach, and only properties that are comparable in type, age, size, condition and location should be considered.

In using the GMRM to arrive at an indicated value of the property being appraised, taxes, insurance and other operating expenses of comparable properties used are assumed to be similar to the appraised property. If this is not the case, the appraiser should eliminate such sales from consideration. The appraiser should inspect both the exterior and interior of all comparable properties to adjust properly for differences. Whenever shortcuts are taken that bypass this step, the possibility of error in the final value judgment is substantially increased.

Cost Approach

The appraiser follows five steps to arrive at an indication of value:

1. Estimates the value of the site *as if vacant* and available to be put to its highest and best use.
2. Estimates the current cost of reproducing (or replacing) the existing improvements.
3. Estimates the accrued depreciation from all causes.
4. Deducts the accrued depreciation to arrive at an indicated value of the improvements.
5. Adds the site value developed in Step 1 for a total indicated value for the property.

The site value is estimated on the basis of sales of comparable sites. Depreciation is a combination of the economic penalties that accrue to the property due to disadvantages and deficiencies when it is compared with the "perfect" improvement (see Chapter 8). Depreciation may be classified into three categories:

1. Physical deterioration—wear, tear and disintegration.
2. Functional obsolescence—a lack of desirability in layout, design, material and style, and subsequent loss of utility.
3. Economic obsolescence—the negative effect on value from factors external to the property.

Separate values for the site and proposed improvements are often required to obtain financing for new developments. The cost approach is also useful in estimating the highest and best use based on cost estimates of hypothetical improvements for vacant land.

The reliability of the cost approach depends on obtaining valid figures on which to base the reproduction (or replacement) cost estimate, on proper depreciation analysis and on well-substantiated site values. Relying solely on the cost approach is rarely acceptable professional practice in residential appraising; value indications so obtained should be reconciled with those derived from the market data and income approaches.

Market Data Approach

The appraiser follows these five steps:

1. Finds comparable sales, listings and offerings.[1]
2. Verifies each sale including selling price, terms, motivation, and its bona fide nature.
3. Analyzes each comparable property and compares it to the property being appraised as to time of sale, location, physical characteristics and conditions of sale.
4. Makes the necessary adjustments to compensate for the dissimilarities noted between the comparables and the property being appraised. The adjustments are derived by comparing comparables with each other whenever possible.
5. Derives an indicated value for the house being appraised by comparison with the adjusted selling prices of the comparables.

To estimate the degree of compatibility between two different properties requires considerable judgment and experience. The selling prices of properties deemed most comparable to the property being appraised tend to set the value range. Each comparable used in this approach must be carefully analyzed for similarities and differences relative to the appraised house in each of four elements of comparison, which are:

1. Time of sale, listing or offer.
2. Location in the community and neighborhood.
3. Physical characteristics of the site and improvements.
4. Conditions of sale.

Although the market data approach has wide application, its usefulness is limited in some situations. In an inactive market, the required comparative data to produce a sound value indication may not be obtainable. In the case of wide variations among the physical and locational characteristics of the comparables, adjustments that tend to reduce the reliability of the indicated values must be made. Adjusting for intangibles such as amenities, varying terms and conditions of sale and appropriate treatment of variation in accrued depreciation is particularly difficult.

---

[1] Comparable properties or sites are commonly referred to as "comps."

In spite of these limitations, the market data approach is generally considered the most applicable one in residential appraising, since it reflects most directly the actions of buyers and sellers in the market.

Reconciliation of Value Indications into Final Value Estimate

The next step in the appraisal process is the reconciliation of the value indications obtained in each of the three approaches to derive an estimate of value for the property being appraised.

Under no circumstances are these value indications merely averaged. This would be analogous to asking three people for the right time and then averaging their replies! Rather, the appraiser considers the relative applicability of each of the three approaches to the final estimate of defined value and the reliability of the data used in each approach.

In the reconciliation, the appraiser brings together all of the data and indicated values resulting from the three approaches and evaluates them in a logical cause-and-effect analysis which leads to a supportable value conclusion.

In this process, the appraiser must evaluate the sources and reliability of data, choose the approach or approaches that are most applicable to the specific appraisal problem, and select from among alternative conclusions or indications a value that best represents the defined value of the property being appraised.

For example, in the case of a typical single family residence, where the purpose of the appraisal is to estimate market value for mortgage financing, the market data approach would be greatly emphasized. Alternatively, in a highly active rental market, where most residences are tenant-occupied and are owned as income properties, the income approach would certainly be considered more heavily.

The Appraisal Report

It is generally insufficient to report only the final value estimate to the client. Good appraisal practice requires that it be part of an appraisal report. The report may be a long- or short-form narrative, a form, a letter or certificate or an oral presentation.

Narrative Reports

The appraiser is afforded the best opportunity to support opinions and conclusions and to convince the client of the soundness of the value estimate in a narrative report. Its content and arrangement may vary. A typical report follows the table of contents shown in Fig. 3-2. A complete narrative appraisal report appears as Appendix A to this text. The American Institute of Real Estate Appraisers has guides for the preparation of demonstration appraisals to be used for credit toward Institute designations, which are excellent guides to the preparation of any narrative appraisal (Forms A-20 and A-20A).

Form Reports

Many residential appraisals are made on forms developed by private companies, lending institutions, government agencies and individual appraisers. A popular form is that of the Federal Home Loan Mortgage Corporation and Federal National Mortgage Association (Residential Appraisal Report Form 70/1004). A sample of this form appears as Appendix B.

Forms tend to constrict the appraiser because they do not provide necessary space to display information the appraiser believes is pertinent. Unfortunately, some appraisers merely eliminate this information, which is poor appraisal practice; a solution is to attach additional sheets of paper to the form. Whatever form is used, it should include all the information needed to support the value estimate. AIREA Form A-20B, used in the preparation of demonstration appraisals for credit toward Institute designations, is an excellent guide for any form appraisal.

Letter (Certificate) or Oral Reports

There are situations where a letter or oral report is required because of the circumstances of the assignment. When a letter or oral report is made, the appraiser must preserve the notes and factual records as well as complete memoranda of each analysis, conclusion and opinion contained in the letter or oral report.

FIG. 3-2: Representative Contents of a Narrative Appraisal Report

Part One — Introduction
Title Page
Letter of Transmittal
Table of Contents
Photographs of the Appraised Property
Summary of Salient Facts and Important Conclusions

Part Two — Description, Analysis and Conclusions
Objective of the Appraisal and Definition of Value
Identification of the Property
Property Rights Appraised and Date of Valuation
Regional Data
Community Data
Neighborhood Data
Site Data
Zoning
Highest and Best Use Analysis
Assessment and Taxes
History of the Property
Description of the Improvements
Income Approach — GMRM
Cost Approach
Market Data Approach
Reconciliation and Final Estimate of Value
Underlying Assumptions and Limiting Conditions
Certificate of Appraisal
Qualifications of the Appraiser

Part Three — Addenda
Regional Map
Community Map
Neighborhood Map
Map Showing Comparable Sales and Rentals
Zoning Map
Plot Plan
Floor Plans
Additional Photographs

Summary

The appraisal process is the orderly step-by-step procedure an appraiser follows to produce a valid appraisal. It begins with the definition of the problem to be solved and concludes with a report of the solution in the form of an estimate of the defined value that is sought. The purpose of the appraisal process is to provide the outline for making a thorough, accurate appraisal in an efficient manner.

Most appraisers would agree that making appraisals is an art, not a science. They would further explain that the profession is constantly trying to make appraising more scientific. A big step toward this goal has been the development of the appraisal process. Within this theoretical framework, a concise, logical and clearly supported value conclusion can be presented that will meet the needs of clients as well as the standards of the appraisal profession. New techniques using statistical methods to abstract information from the market, such as multiple regression analysis, are also making the appraisal process more scientific (see Appendix E).

Review Questions

1. What is the purpose of the appraisal process?
2. What are the steps in defining the appraisal problem?
3. List four types of legal description of real estate. Which is used in your area?
4. What rights other than fee simple may be the subject of an appraisal?
5. Why is the date of the value estimate essential in an appraisal?
6. Why must a definition of value appear in the appraisal report?
7. What is the purpose of a fee proposal?
8. What items should a typical proposal contain?
9. What are the three approaches to value?
10. Upon what three concepts regarding real property value are the three approaches based?
11. When might the income approach not be applicable?

4

Metropolitan Area
Economic Analysis

The economic environment of a single family home and the market of which it is a part are of vital concern to the appraiser. A close relationship exists between the economic analysis of the metropolitan area and the analysis of the residential market (see Chapter 5).

The principal characteristic of real estate is fixity of location. Although an oversimplification, it is true that real property is either the benefactor or the victim of its surroundings. Most real estate can be no better than that of which it is a part.

One major limiting factor affecting the market value of real estate is the economic potential of the community in which it is located. Any reasonably qualified analyst recognizes that the marketability of real estate depends heavily upon the economic potential of its community. Just as a close relationship exists between economic development and income-producing properties, such as office buildings or retail stores, there also is a high correlation between the economic potential of the community and the marketability of a single family residence. This chapter deals with the steps in analyzing the economic base and relating its impact to the market value of a single family residence.

Definition of Metropolitan Area Economic Analysis

Metropolitan area economic analysis has many other names. It frequently is referred to as economic base analysis, regional and local economic analysis, and input-output analysis; but the term little economies[1] is a more descriptive name because it refers to the economic health of an area and its ability to bring in income from outside the area. It can be compared to international trade situations,

---

[1]Committee for Economic Development, 1958.

where countries seek to establish favorable balances of trade. For example, if the United States sells more to Japan than Japan sells to the United States, the balance of trade will be in favor of the United States — that is, gold or the equivalent will flow into the United States, thereby enhancing its economic growth.

It is simple to apply this same concept to the economic area of a local community or metropolitan area. Compare and contrast the growth potential of a particular metropolitan area with other metropolitan areas of similar characteristics, size and physical location. Which community is most desirable in which to live? Which community has the greatest growth potential? Which has the greatest protection against unfavorable economic developments? Obviously, the one that rates highest on each of these three questions is the one that has the most favorable future.

Identification of a Metropolitan Area

The boundaries of a metropolitan area must be identified before one can analyze such an area. Most simply, it is the geographic area that is contiguous and operates as one unit. It may cross state boundaries, such as the greater Louisville area or the greater St. Louis area. Quite often it encompasses several counties. It may be the Standard Metropolitan Statistical Area (SMSA) as defined by Bureau of the Census. Recent directives from agencies of the federal government delineate certain economic communities; thus, statistical data is most readily available for these standardized areas. Because quantities of data are necessary to analyze the potential of a specific area, it is well to follow defined areas and regions.

The Growth of Cities

To understand the importance of metropolitan area economic analysis, one must understand why cities exist at all and why they grow in a particular location. Recognition of these elements is essential in understanding the importance of this type of analysis.

Because human beings are social beings, they want to be together. Historically, they came together for defense and self-protection or to facilitate trade among themselves and outsiders or for religious motives. Usually a combination of reasons brought people together into communities. Small village or major metropolitan area of several million people, the reasons for community formation are the same. Problems have developed where many people are clustered together, but these have been offset by the advantages of such an assemblage.

Why did people gather at a particular geographic point to develop a community? One obvious reason was location on established trade routes or other points of transportation access such as rivers. The specific points along such routes may have been established for convenience—for example, a day's travel distance from an established point—or related to access to raw materials and natural resources, such as a waterfall or other source of energy, and to those who were going to be served by the products being developed. Added to these reasons is a catalytic force that has played a greater part in recent community growth—a favorable climate. The greatest growth in the United States in the latter half of this century has been in warmer, more pleasant climates.

Economic Base Analysis

Appraisers are concerned primarily with the economic potential of a community as it affects the market value of the property they are appraising. They must look at the economic potential of a community compared to competitive communities similar to the one in which the property being appraised is located.

Real estate markets depend on growth or the expectation of growth. Although there may be short-run market conditions that are favorable without growth, such circumstances are rare. The market for single family residences depends heavily on families and their economic capacity to purchase homes, which depends on their jobs and the competitive position of such jobs. If the average family income within a specific community is higher than the national or state average, the potential for purchase or construction of homes in that community is greater than in other communities.

It may be helpful to understand the relationship between residential values and the community's economic future by pointing out that certain areas in the United States are recognized for their special economic conditions, both good and bad. Much publicity has been given to Appalachia and its economic problems. The federal government has conducted special programs for this geographic area.

Certain sections of the northeast United States are experiencing marginal economic growth because their major industries have moved to other sections of the country or have become obsolete.

In contrast, some geographic areas are undergoing great physical and economic growth. The "sun belt" has had spectacular growth in the last two decades. Parts of Florida and California, as well as sections in other southwest states, have had spectacular population growth. Along with such growth, however, there must be sound economic development. Population increase alone does not imply substantially sound economic growth; there must be a correspondingly strong economic base to ensure that the community can support itself and be competitive with others.

Basic and Nonbasic Employment

Because the economic potential of a community is dependent on its ability to produce income, metropolitan area economic analysis deals to a great extent with gathering and analyzing employment data. It involves the collection of statistics regarding the total basic employment in the economic community plus similar statistics for nonbasic employment.

Basic employment is the type of employment that attracts dollars from consumers and others *outside* the metropolitan area being analyzed. This kind of employment is, by definition, the basis for the level of the economy in the area. *Nonbasic employment* generates its income from within the community. Lawyers, doctors and service employees, such as the supermarket clerk or city sanitation worker, are included in this category. A community cannot thrive without these people and if they are insufficient in number to satisfy the basic employees, the latter will become dissatisfied and less productive. Ideally, there must be both basic and nonbasic employees in the proper proportion to maximize the whole community's prosperity.

There is no consistent standard ratio of basic to nonbasic employees within an economic community. Such relationships are derived locally and vary in accordance with the income level and nature of the basic employees. If the basic employees are primarily white-collar research and scientific personnel with extremely high levels of income, they will probably require more service; a ratio of two basic to one service employee might be appropriate. In other communities where basic employees have lower income levels, a ratio of three basic to one service employee might be entirely satisfactory. Certain special kinds of communities occasionally have a ratio of one to one. The ratio itself is not important in the analysis of the level and potential of economic activity; however, it does affect the general social and economic climate in terms of the subjective analysis of the community as a good or less satisfactory place to live.

Data on basic employment is collected on an historical as well as a current basis and divided into three major categories: industry; specialty, such as government and recreation; and trade, including retail, wholesale, finance and transportation. These categories are intended to include all types of basic employment and are considered to be the most critical in the estimation of the economic growth of the community being analyzed. They are rated according to predicted employment trends, diversification, and cyclical fluctuation. The importance of diversification in basic employment and the need for types of basic employment that are not subject to cyclical fluctuation have long been recognized.

• *Industry.* This basic employment category, also called manufacturing, includes all components of fabrication, assembly, manufacturing and extractive activities. Industry is the truly essential, critical and fundamental area of employment for most communities, although there are some communities, such as Washington D.C., that have virtually no industry. Most communities, however, look heavily to industrial employment to carry the future of their economy. Accordingly, this analysis is made first and typically is given the greatest weighting in the conclusion.

• *Specialty.* The category includes nonindustrial types of employment, such as government service, education and recreation. For purposes of this analysis, local government employees are not included; only those whose salaries are paid outside local sources, such as a federal court in the community which attracts its income from outside that community, are considered. The fire department is paid from local tax revenue and therefore is not considered base employment. Likewise, education is limited to those institutions that attract most of their operating revenue from outside the economic area, such as a state university or a private college. Local elementary, junior and senior high schools are excluded as basic employment.

Recreation communities, such as Miami Beach; Biloxi, Miss.; or Scottsdale, Ariz., base their employment on providing tourist and retirement services and facilities. Therefore, in such communities the waiter employed in a hotel catering to out-of-town people is a basic employee, but the busboy in a restaurant catering primarily to local citizens is a non-basic employee.

• *Trade.* This category includes positions in retailing, wholesaling, finance and transportation that exist to serve users outside the economic community. A regional shopping center that heavily attracts those outside the community as well as consumers inside the community is partially a basic employer. Major banks serving the entire state or region obviously attract some of their revenue from outside the local economic community. The headquarters of a national bus service or moving company would be primarily a basic employer.

Quality Rating

The procedure for rating the three categories of employment is to look at them individually in light of three quality rating requirements: predicted employment trends, diversification, and cyclical fluctuation.

The grid in Fig. 4-1 illustrates the technique for analyzing the economic base. In the first column are the three major categories of employment; in the second, the components of the quality rating of these three categories. The third column is for the qualitative weighting of the ratings. (This grid is not intended to be used mechanically but to emphasize the most important components to be analyzed, weighed and projected.)

Briefly, the predictable trend for employment opportunities requires the analyst to project the relative position of the types of industry in the local community in competition with other communities and the nation. If the results of the comparison show that this community is in the middle range of all other communities and with national figures, a different kind of future will be forecast than if it is in the top 10% of all communities. In one respect, this technique is similar to the use of GNP for the nation compared to a specific community's gross product.

FIG. 4-1: Analysis Chart for Economic Base

Basic Employees

Category of Employment	Quality Rating	Weighted Rating
Industry	Predicted Employment Trend Diversification Cyclical Fluctuation	
Specialty	Predicted Employment Trend Diversification Cyclical Fluctuation	
Trade	Predicted Employment Trend Diversification Cyclical Fluctuation	
Sum of Weighted Quality Rating		

Estimating the predicted employment trend requires the analyst to project soundly and objectively the growth patterns (decline or increased stability of employment) in each of the factories and other types of industry supporting the local economic base. Such an analysis is not to be a chamber of commerce projection which, by its nature, tends to be optimistic. To be useful for the appraiser, it must be done thoroughly, carefully and with insight.

The second area of quality rating is diversification. Obviously, if one industrial firm hires 50% of all those employed in industry, the risk to the community is greater if a negative trend develops in this organization (or the industry it represents) than if a major employer hires only 15% of all industrial employees. If the latter plant should be moved, shut down or cut employment by half, the community would not suffer so severely.

The third quality rating deals with cyclical fluctuation. Evaluation of this factor is based on how business in the community will fare in the event of recession or depression. Few types of business are recession- or depression-proof. The staple food industry tends to be least affected by recession or depression but high-priced luxury goods tend to drop off in sales the minute the consumer has less money.

This step requires a judgment as to how businesses will rate in the event of adverse conditions. If there is a tendency for overall stability and resistance to such cyclical phenomena, the quality rating would be high. If the majority of the firms can be subject to rapid cutbacks in production or services in the event of unfavorable economic climate, the quality rating would be low.

Industrial, specialty and trade categories of employment are evaluated on the three quality ratings in comparison with the nation and other communities. There may be a tendency for much wider variation in the specialty category, which should be recognized and adjusted for.

The final ratings regarding each of the three categories of employment are totaled to reach a figure applicable to all categories of employment. Such a figure is of value only when it is compared to a rating of similar, competitive communities.

Local Resources

In analyzing the economic potential of a community, consideration is given to its primary physical and human resources. Obviously, a complete and thorough supply of data regarding the people who make up an economic area is essential. Also, inventory must be made regarding its energy sources and physical resources such as mineral and other types of natural resources. Favorable weather and climate conditions may be considered a resource especially in dealing with the recreational potential of a community. Unfavorable factors such as smog, odors, polluted waters or unusual kinds of weather conditions obviously are considered a disadvantage. Capital resources or access to capital is affected by the attitudes of bankers, investors and other financial sources.

Future Economic Activity

The economic base analysis is not merely a collection of data; it is developed so that the analyst can project the economic potential of a defined area. It is useless to collect a mass of data and perform a thorough statistical analysis and then fail to draw clear, concise conclusions regarding the future of the economic entity. This latter step is vital in the analysis of the economic potential of the metropolitan area. Concise and definitive projections regarding the competitive position of the community, compared to other communities and the nation as a whole, are essential. If such projections are not made, there is no validity or justification for the economic base analysis. An example of a typical economic base analysis appears in Figure 4-2.

Economic base analysis is not the only technique used in predicting the economic future of areas. An input/output analysis has been developed by urban economists to rate the economic community on an income and expense basis. It may be further analyzed in terms similar to a profit and loss statement. Urban economists have also developed a regional accounting system that compares one part of a region or area with other parts to see which has competitive advantages. A third type of analysis is referred to as a balance of payments, which is basically a study to reveal historical, current, and future projected capacity for the favorable balance of trade in one economic community compared to the world, the nation, and other economic areas. All economic analysis techniques, however, are projections or estimates of the future. The appraiser must recognize that all prognostications about the future must be used wisely and cautiously.

Sources of Data

Today there is an almost unlimited and unending supply of data covering the items listed above, although data pertaining to local communities quite often is difficult to find. Government agencies at all levels and the Federal Reserve System and its district banks around the country are a primary source of economic data. The Federal Home Loan Bank System, which is closely related to the real estate industry, is also widely known for its economic research with application to local and state areas. Some states have computerized retrieval systems that provide printouts listing historical and current economic, social and governmental data.

Many private organizations also serve as clearing houses for such statistics. Some real estate appraisers and consultants make a practice of collecting pertinent statistical data; such a procedure is costly and justifiable only if kept current. A thorough analysis cannot depend on technique alone; it depends heavily upon sound, resourceful information.

FIG. 4-2: Economic Base Analysis of the City of Utopia

The City of Utopia is the county seat of Love County. It has been designated an SMSA (Standard Metropolitan Statistical Area). The SMSA includes the three counties of Love, Saphire and Pierre, in addition to the City of Utopia. A recent special census of the SMSA revealed a current population of 389,201, ranking it 76th in the United States. The mayor of the greater metropolitan area of Utopia, Pat Turneriski, is proud of the economy of the community and confidently predicts a strong growth pattern for the future. The president of the Greater Utopia Chamber of Commerce proudly talks of the strong industrial base, of the special employment opportunities, and of the manner in which Utopia has grown to serve its entire region.

The data collected by an independent economic analyst reveals other interesting and important facts about the area. There have been heavy commitments made by both state and federal governments. In addition to Utopia being the county seat, the state selected Utopia over a century ago as the site for State University, an internationally recognized institution. As *the* state university, it offers a complete curriculum, including professional schools. The federal government has constructed a complex of office buildings to serve as regional or district offices for the IRS, VA, and several other agencies. Also, one of the federal government's biggest research centers is located in Federal Park.

Utopia's industrial growth has been typical of other major cities, except for its phenomenal growth in the 1960s. Industries grew both in size and number between World Wars I and II. Strong growth followed in the decade after World War II, but spectacular industrial growth came in the 1960s. Due to the special efforts of several community-spirited individuals (known as the Secret Six), 17 new industries were attracted to Utopia through a special program of incentives, tax benefits, and low-cost industrial facilities.

The power structure of the community was altered in the late 1960s when the older community leaders were replaced by a band of "young Turks" who spent much time and money in the campaign to make Utopia versatile and attractive. Almost everyone agrees they have succeeded, but some feel that the growth has been "too much, too fast."

Due to the population increase in the entire region, Utopia has benefited by the addition of many types of activities serving the region, covering approximately 150 miles in all directions. Utopia has become a distribution center of major proportions. It has five super-regional shopping centers to serve the whole region. Five commercial banks have attracted national recognition by their growth and prominence.

The private economic analyst firm developed the following statistics:

Population	389,201
Families	97,521
Gainfully employed	104,000
Per capita personal income	$5,441

Industry	No. of Employees Per Company	Total Number of Employees	Percentage in Largest Employer
1 company	9,000	9,000	21%
1 company	5,000	5,000	
4 companies	3,000	12,000	
5 companies	750-1,000	4,250	
5 companies	500-750	3,250	
15 companies	250-500	5,500	
35 companies	Under 250	4,000	
66		43,000	

Specialty

State university	11,000	39%
Federal government	14,000	
State government	7,000	
City and county government	1,000	
Recreation	3,000	
	36,000	

Trade

Wholesale & distribution	8,000	32%
Retailing	7,000	
Financial	6,000	
Miscellaneous	4,000	
	25,000	

Economic Base Analysis

What does the final rating figure of 16.2% (see breakdown on next page) mean for the Utopia economic area? Is it good, average, high or low?

It can be evaluated only by comparing it to the final rating figure for other economic areas like Utopia. The maximum rating possible in a

ECONOMIC BASE ANALYSIS

FINAL RATING FIGURE 16.2   DATE OF RATING current   NAME OF AREA Utopia
POPULATION (BY CENSUS YEARS) 1940 201,000   1950 222,000   1960 251,000
1970 329,977 Recent Special Census 389,201
SELECTION AND WEIGHING OF CATEGORIES

Categories	Number Employed (Statistical or estimated)		Percent of Total	Category Weights	
	Total	104,000	100%		100%
Industry		43,000	41%	X 2 =	82%
Specialty		36,000	26%	X 2 =	18%
Trade	100% minus sum of other category weights in last column				%

INDUSTRY CATEGORY (Manufacturing, Assembling, Fabricating, and Refining)

	1	2	3	4	5	Rating	Weighted Rating
Predicted Employment Trend	Dec. of 10% and over [14]	Dec. of 1% - 9% [28]	Dec. 0% to inc. of 4% [42]	Inc. of 5% - 9% [56]	Inc. 10% and over [70]	42	
Diversi-fication	50% or over employed in largest industry [3]	30% to 49% employed in largest industry [6]	20% to 29% employed in largest industry [9]	10% to 19% employed in largest industry [12]	Less than 10% employed in largest industry [15]	9	
Cyclical Fluctua-tions	Less than 50% [3]	50% to 59% [6]	60% to 69% [9]	70% to 79% [12]	80% to 100% [15]	6	
					Category Weight 82% x	= 57	47

SPECIALTY CATEGORY (State Type of Activities) University, Governments & Recreation

	1	2	3	4	5	Rating
Predicted Employment Trend	Dec. of 10% and over [14]	Dec. of 1% to 9% [28]	Dec. of 0% to inc. 4% [42]	Inc. of 5% to 9% [56]	Inc. of 10% and over [70]	28
Diversi-fication	50% or over employed in largest industry [3]	30% to 49% employed in largest industry [6]	20% to 29% employed in largest industry [9]	10% to 19% employed in largest industry [12]	Less than 10% employed in largest industry [15]	6
Cyclical Fluctua-tions	Less than 50% [3]	50% to 59% [6]	60% to 69% [9]	70% to 79% [12]	80% to 100% [15]	3
					Category Weight 18% x	= 37	7

TRADE CATEGORY (Trade, Finance, and Transportation)

	1	2	3	4	5	Rating
Predicted Employment Trend	Dec. of 10% and over [14]	Dec. of 1% - 9% [28]	Dec. 0% to inc. 4% [42]	Inc. of 5% - 9% [56]	Inc. of 10% and over [70]	42
Diversi-fication	50% or over employed in largest industry [3]	30% to 49% employed in largest industry [6]	20% to 29% employed in largest industry [9]	10% to 19% employed in largest industry [12]	Less than 10% employed in largest industry [15]	6
Cyclical Fluctua-tions	Less than 50% [3]	50% to 59% [6]	60% to 69% [9]	70% to 79% [12]	80% to 100% [15]	9
					Category Weight 0% x	= 57	0

Sum of Applicable Category Ratings 54

SCOPE OF THE MARKET

	1	2	3	4	5	Rating
Degree of Mktability	Poor [20]	Limited [25]	Moder-ate [30]	Satis-factory [35]	Good [40]	30

ECONOMIC BACKGROUND RATING (Sum of Applicable Category Ratings X
Scope of Market Factor) .... 54 X 30% = 16.2

perfect economic community is 40% (100% as the sum of applicable category ratings times 40, a "good" rating in the degree of marketability). 16.2% looks low in comparison to the perfect rating but, of course, there are no perfect economic communities. A very high range is in the low 20s. Many communities rank in the range of 10. The primary objective of the analysis, however, is to require the analyst to consider thoroughly and objectively all aspects that affect the future economy of a community.

Each of the three categories may be analyzed for its contribution by asking the following pertinent questions:

Industrial Category

What are the types of employees? Are they male, female, skilled, young, old?

What is the nature of the goods being manufactured? Heavy, light, steel, plastic, consumer goods, durable consumer goods, necessities or luxury items?

What is the future of employment? Will the activity increase in the future, remain the same, decline?

How well is industrial employment diversified? Does one company or industry dominate?

Are several small companies with under 250 employees better than or poorer than companies with several thousand employees?

If a refining or extracting industry is involved, when will the resources be depleted? Will they lose their competitive advantage? Will they become monopolistic?

What kind of industry (product) is least cyclical — that is, would decline less in the event of a recession or depression? Luxury goods, staples, steel fabricating for the auto industry, agriculture-related food products?

Special Category (education, government, recreation)

What types of educational institutions are considered basic employers? State universities, private colleges, parochial high schools, middle schools, nursery schools, technical colleges?

What types of government jobs are considered basic employment? City firemen, county sheriff, FBI, U.S. Marshal, IRS employees, Air Force officers, non-coms, and civilians?

Trade Category (trade, finance and transportation)

How can you determine how many retail employees are basic employees? How many are nonbasic?

Are employees of banks and savings and loan associations basic employees or nonbasic employees?

Are employees of wholesale distributors and trucking firms serving the midwest basic or nonbasic?

"Scope of the market" is added to the rating form as a means of testing the competitive position for marketability of the economic area being analyzed in a comparison with other economic areas in terms of how attractive the area is and will be and what demand for services, products and real estate is and will be. This step in the analysis is important because it has such a major impact on the final rating figure. Special care must be used in selecting the appropriate rating. Some of the reasons for the ratings in "scope of the market" may be based on how good the community is as a place to live, which includes other ingredients than pure economic ones. An article in *Business and Economic Review* entitled "What Makes a City a Good Place to Live?" ranks security and protection first, followed by education, government, and public services.[1] Oddly enough, the lowest ranking community attribute was neighborhood, preceded by city planning and city size. Economics was fourth from the bottom. This additional consideration tends to add personality and humanism to the purely economic analysis.

Summary

The whole process of rating the economic base of a community and its future is an attempt to produce an honest and critical analysis of an economic community. In no way can all subjectivity be removed, of course, but at least the analyst would be subject to criticism if too many of the analyst's own likes and dislikes or prejudices are used in developing the ratings. The process is also a way to measure more scientifically the degree of competitiveness among the "little economies" (economic communities). It adds a degree of reliability to the appraiser's conclusions regarding the community in which the house being appraised is located. Communities do vary widely. There are great ones, good ones and some marginal ones. The appraisal process must recognize the impact of the community on the house located in a community. Its marketability will be affected accordingly.

[1]John F. Willenborg and Gerald E. Breger, "What Makes a City a Good Place to Live?," *Business and Economic Review*, Vol. XXIII, No. 6, May 1977.

Summary

A parcel of real estate reflects what surrounds it: the community of which it is a part; the state, district or region; and, of course, its general location within the nation. The economic potential of the community can be analyzed in a logical and orderly manner. This type of rating emphasizes the future economic potential of the community, not its past or present status; the future is paramount in such analyses.

To analyze a metropolitan area, it must be properly identified and its boundaries located. Typically, it is wise to choose an already established type of community for which statistics are already available, such as the SMSA.

Metropolitan area economic analysis requires identification of local resources, the establishment of data sources and the development of clear and careful estimates regarding the future economic potential of the area.

Review Questions

1. How can an analysis of the local economy help a real estate appraiser?
2. Historically why did cities grow? In a particular location?
3. What are some of the economic forces that cause communities to develop?
4. How are income and employment statistics analyzed by the appraiser?
5. What are "basic income sources" in economic base analysis?
6. What are the basic income sources for: a) your community? b) your state capital?
7. What is meant by "non-basic employment"? Can such employment contribute to community growth? Explain.
8. Why is diversification of manufacturing desirable for a community?

5

Analysis of the Single Family Residential Market

The market value of a parcel of real estate cannot be estimated without first understanding its relationship to the real estate market. The appraiser must be familiar with the structure of the market and how it functions, its peculiarities and idiosyncrasies, and its degree of effectiveness. In estimating the market value of a single family residence, the appraiser must have full knowledge of the market in which it is being offered; without this knowledge the estimate may be inaccurate and unreliable.

To obtain this background, the appraiser may use detailed market analyses prepared by experts in that field. The purpose of this chapter is to provide the appraiser with a broad background to facilitate an understanding of market analysis. It is not intended to provide complete instructions on the techniques of making such an analysis. This chapter examines the real estate market, discusses its special economic characteristics and analyzes the relationship of the market and market value estimates.

The Marketplace

All transactions, purchases, sales, leases, exchanges and like activities occur in a market. The marketplace may be a specific location where business is transacted (e.g., the New York Stock Exchange) or it may refer to the *activity* of negotiating toward agreement between parties. The real estate market has no central exchange to facilitate its activities of buying and selling; therefore, when reference is made to the real estate market, it refers to the *activities* of the market.

The major factors in the activity of all markets are demand, supply and price. Demand and supply are causal factors; price is the result or effect of the interaction of the other two, the pressures or lack of activity.

From a brief and general description of the forces operating in the real estate market and the functions they perform, the competitive process may seem to bring about smooth adjustments among supply, demand and prices. This is not necessarily the case. Competition is the main regulative force but the actual operation of the real estate market is far from perfect.

The real estate market is subject to many outside influences such as seasonal activity peaks, general and local economic activity, the availability of financing and government regulations. At any given time these factors can combine to create a buyer's or a seller's market. When supply is greater than demand, prices tend to fall, making it a buyer's market. When demand exceeds supply, prices tend to rise, creating a seller's market.

Any open and free market has a tendency to move toward a point of equilibrium — that is, a point at which supply equals demand. This basic economic principle is clearly understandable because when prices fall, activity on the demand side of the market tends to increase, which results in increased purchases and lowered supply. As demand increases beyond existing supply, prices tend to rise, thereby automatically encouraging suppliers to produce more goods or services for the market. Because of the inefficiencies of most markets, an oversupply can develop, in which case prices drop again and the cycle starts over again.

These statements about the market are generalized and oversimplified. Most markets are more formal and efficient than real estate markets so special effort must be made to understand the real estate market. The reason the real estate market does *not* match other product markets in efficiency is that the real estate market does *not* possess features essential for maximum efficiency, including:

1. Central marketplace.
2. Standardized product, movable and requiring little care or protection.
3. Nonseasonal and noncyclical activity.
4. Simplicity of financing.
5. Minimum legal requirements and restrictions.
6. Free, open market not supervised or regulated by governments.

The real estate market has improved in efficiency over the last two decades because of the contribution of brokers, appraisers, lawyers, title companies, financial institutions, and government agencies; however, it still has not reached the efficiency of most other markets.

Criteria of an Effective Market

Certain restrictions are placed on the real estate market that impair its open and effective functioning. To understand these restrictions, one needs to know the criteria of an effective market. Competition can operate more easily if the goods involved are durable and can bear long carriage and if they can be standardized, graded, and bought and sold from samples. Furthermore, a market requires good organization, preferably with a central exchange that is easily accessible to all and where offers to buy and sell can be cleared with a minimum of difficulty. The more buyers and sellers know about the forces bearing on the market, the more effective market competition becomes. Buyers and sellers must be free from compulsion (for example, where some single group dominates the market) if competition is to be effective. Financing must not be difficult or time consuming; and a minimum of legal requirements and few, if any, government regulations or restrictions can exist.

In a model competitive market, both buyers and sellers are numerous and they are seen as bidding against each other until a price is reached that is agreeable to both parties. The action of any single buyer or seller in this model has only an infinitesimal effect on the market as a whole; but the interactions of all operators taken together create changes in supply, demand, and price. All that any individual buyer can do is buy or not buy, or buy greater or smaller quantities, as prices change. Likewise, an individual seller can choose to sell, not sell, sell more or sell less. If a producer, he or she can produce, not produce, or produce different amounts. The quantities supplied will thus be changed and this will affect price.

The real estate market ranks comparatively low in effectiveness among various types of markets, and it differs in several ways from the model of a competitive market outlined above. In general, real estate cannot be standardized, graded, or bought and sold from samples. Also, real estate transactions involve a variety of legal rights that may differ from property to property, and every transfer of real property involves many legal formalities and much documentation.

Financing may be a severe restriction on the free action of the market.

In some real estate markets a single buyer may have a significant effect due to the relative "thinness" of the market, such as that for unimproved land. This is similar to the over-the-counter securities market where stocks are traded in limited volume.

Economic Characteristics of the
Single Family Residence

To understand the operation of the single family residential market, the appraiser must first appreciate the special economic characteristics of the single family residence. Real estate is different from most economic goods, in terms of its size, the manner in which it is used and the way in which it is marketed. Four special economic characteristics of single family residences make them distinct and separate from most other economic goods: fixity of location, long life, large economic units, and the interdependence of public and private property. These four characteristics affect the reaction of buyers and sellers in the marketplace.

Fixity of Location

Land stays where it is; it is location in itself. Added to this is the lack of mobility of the dwellings that are built upon the sites. Even today's "mobile home" is not truly mobile. Because of fixity of location, each residential property is unique; no two properties can possibly be identical because the site for each is different. Two models of a manufactured home may be built by the same builder with exactly the same interiors and exteriors, but both houses cannot sit on the same lot. The total package may differ in that one may be located on an inside lot and the other on a corner lot. The market will recognize this difference.

The second factor of fixity of location is that the surroundings of each residence have a direct impact on the marketability and livability of such a residence. This is referred to as "neighborhood impact." A single family residence located in a neighborhood in which all the other houses are much older and in poorer condition will be looked upon by buyers in a different light from the same residence in a neighborhood of its approximate age and in good condition. Other factors on neighborhood are discussed in the next chapter.

The third feature of fixity of location is that by its very nature the markets are more limited. Buyers or users must come to the product; the product cannot be moved to the buyers. Therefore, existing inventories of houses must depend on the market that is active in the community or can be attracted to it. To fully appreciate the operation of the residential market, this pertinent point must be remembered.

The fourth special feature of fixity of location deals with the legal distinctions applicable to real property. Real property has more special legal complications, limitations and provisions than virtually all other types of economic goods. An automobile, for instance, is conveyed from one owner to another by the simple registration certificate. A real estate transaction may involve many title complications and resultant recording requirements. While these may be looked upon as a handicap, the intention is protection for the owners rather than a limitation. The additional complications of legal arrangements obviously affect the marketability or the operation of exchanges in the market.

Long Life

Although land itself, the surface of the earth, is endurable, the buildings built upon it will not last forever. However, in terms of other economic goods, a house has a long life. Most houses are useful for 30 to 50 years; some are still being lived in after 200 years. Most types of houses have an economic life of many decades and even the most poorly built building can probably be used for at least 10 to 20 years.

Long duration and physical existence mean that once constructed, the product will remain in inventory (on the market) for a long time. It is not quickly consumed like other products. Once the product is added to inventory, it will be a factor in a specific locational market for a long time. Furthermore, it takes a reasonably long period to add new units to a specific market. Six months is probably a minimum period for the most efficient homebuilder; two years or longer may be required under certain circumstances.

Large Economic Units

The median sale price of a residential unit in the United States now has exceeded the $50,000 range. Not many people make such a purchase frequently; rather, it may be once in a lifetime. In most cases special financing arrangements are necessary so that the buyer can afford the purchase. This requirement complicates the marketing of the product. While much progress has been made in streamlining the financing process, it still is a time-consuming factor and, in some cases, prevents a buyer in the market from becoming an effective bargainer. Obviously, such a matter is heavily weighed in analyzing the demand aspects of the residential market.

Interdependence of Private and Public Property

The fourth economic characteristic of single family residences is the interdependence of private and public property. No matter how well built or architecturally attractive it may be, a house's usability depends upon its accessibility. Because of fixity of location, the residence must be reached by public access. It must have street and sidewalk access. Many other types of dependence on the public sector are needed to make a house livable. Most houses depend heavily on public utilities — sanitary sewer, water, gas, electricity, and telephone. Public transportation is an important factor in many kinds of living units. The close relationship of schools, public recreation areas and other public facilities either enhances or detracts from the marketability of a home.

The four special characteristics outlined above must be related to the economic characteristics of the real estate market. The housing unit is a product in the market; the market is made up of buyers interested in such a product and sellers desirous of selling their commodities. The interreaction of the market is directly affected by the special characteristics of the product. The following section analyzes the special economic characteristics of the residential real estate market.

Economic Characteristics of the Market

The following is a partial list of factors that influence the operation of the residential real estate market:

1. The uniqueness of each parcel of real estate.
2. Local restrictive factors, such as taxes, zoning regulations, rent controls, availability of services, environmental controls.
3. The general economic climate and outlook.
4. The lack of machinery for selling short.
5. The variability of improvements. Lack of standardization may create desirable features or hidden defects.
6. Long lease periods, causing some properties to be removed from the market for a length of time.
7. Uninformed buyers and sellers.
8. Buyers limited to those who are able to take advantage of bargains or the necessities of the seller.
9. Financing terms, which influence prices.
10. Possibility of legal complications in the exchange. Agreements must be in writing to be legally enforceable.
11. Title, which must be clear and saleable.
12. Sentimental attachment on the part of seller, creating an unwillingness to sell for the market value.

Market Variations

Real estate markets can be classified according to types of properties, scope, and whether transfers are permanent (sales) or temporary (rentals, leases). The rental and sale markets are not mutually exclusive because they form parts of a larger whole, but the rental market is not characterized by the wide variations that occur in the permanent transfer of properties. The rental market is similar in nature to a consumer goods market and the sale market to a producer goods market. Usually variations in market activities in consumer goods are not so marked as those in producer goods.

The rental market does, however, influence selling prices and the rate of construction. In a seller's market, prices may move high enough to stimulate new construction. If more new buildings are constructed than can be absorbed at prices characteristic of a seller's market, a long period of time may be required for absorption to take place.

Demand Pressures

An increase in rents and selling prices is normally the result of an increase in the demand for space, although a cost-push inflationary trend may result in across-the-board higher prices. In short-run periods, demand conditions are of greater importance than those of supply. The basic element in demand is purchasing power, which includes income and the terms and availability of financing. When an increase in demand occurs, an expansion of activity usually follows. Expansion of economic opportunities usually is necessary to attract people or to increase their incomes. Similarly, a loss of such opportunities tends to depress the real estate market.

An increase in population growth does not cause real estate activity to increase substantially unless there is a simultaneous increase in purchasing power on the part of the newcomers. Likewise, the lack of population growth does not necessarily prevent an expansion from occurring if incomes advance and financing terms are liberal.

Inflexible Supply

Wide variations in real estate activity can be explained largely in terms of the relative inflexibility of the supply of space. People may be willing or need to live in more crowded conditions for a variety of reasons, although they are usually unwilling to live under these conditions when incomes increase. Under depressed economic conditions new construction tends to decrease because it will not pay to build at the existing low sales prices. But as the population expands in number and in purchasing power, the large supply of vacant units typical of depressed periods tends to be rapidly absorbed. When the percentage of vacant units reaches a low figure, prices begin to rise. Hence, the rate of profit is increased, and it becomes profitable for builders to construct new units again.

Market Expansion

In the early stages of economic expansion, construction of single family houses tends to dominate because many are constructed for consumers with incomes sufficient to make downpayments, even if the houses would not command rents sufficient to yield a normal monetary return on their costs. Similarly, business firms may expand plants or stores. As expansion progresses, however, it becomes profitable to construct apartment buildings, business blocks, industrial structures, shopping centers and office buildings that are financed primarily for pecuniary return.

The period of construction usually begins with a period of easy credit. During such a period it may be quite easy to finance projects of various types. As new buildings absorb vacant land and subdividing activity gathers momentum, a land boom may result if the pressure to build continues to increase. Large areas may be added to the supply of land available to a community. As outward movement from the city center occurs, the available area increases in a manner comparable to the square of the radius of a circle.

Expenditures for public improvements tend to increase at the same time that the volume of building and subdividing gains momentum. The nature of this type of expansion does not allow it to be done piece by piece or in small quantities. A sewer trunkline, for example, may open many thousands of acres to development.

Market Contraction

Inasmuch as the market does not operate "in balance," there tends to be a "teeter-totter" action—too much on one side or the other, rarely balanced. Eventually, supply will begin to exceed demand. It becomes difficult to transfer properties and the sources of credit begin to tighten, which results in delinquencies. This decline in demand and increase in foreclosures signals a period of economic decline. Many sectors of the real estate market may still maintain a peak level of activity because a marked decline in rents has not yet been experienced. Operating expenses may increase, however, and further foreclosures are likely to take place. The fact that real estate is financed more on a debt than an equity basis probably helps to intensify the variations that occur. Thus those who finance real estate may unsuspectingly make or break the market.

If foreclosures continue to increase as credit tightens, the entire market is affected. Prices fall and land values decline. Just as net rentals rise more rapidly than gross rentals in the early period of expansion, they fall more rapidly because of the fixed charges involved. Hence profits are wiped out and market activity falls to low levels.

A recession in the real estate market is intensified during a simultaneous general recession. If incomes drop, vacancies increase and rents decline. Foreclosures increase rapidly, first on leased properties (apartment and office buildings), as rents decline faster than operating expenses. If a long recession ensues, foreclosures extend to single family residences and owner-occupied business properties. As a result, real estate prices are forced down.

A large volume of foreclosures is characteristic of a depressed real estate market. Following the foreclosure process, properties are refinanced. The financial wreckage is cleared away to make way for a new period of expansion, which usually results from some special impetus to increase demand for real estate supply.

Analysis of the Real Estate Market

Purpose of Market Analysis

The objective of the analysis governs the pattern it takes, the information employed and the degree of detail used. Because each market analysis is individual and unique, the priority and emphasis assigned to the topics of consideration may vary.

The first step is to state the objective: What is the purpose of the analysis? An analysis may be used for many reasons, such as to learn what has happened in a specific market in the past, to conclude what market conditions prevail currently or to project market activity in the future. It may seek to answer whether a builder should start a new project or a lender should risk financing single family residences.

The problems involved in making a market analysis generally fall into two major categories: (1) those pertaining to short-run objectives and (2) those pertaining to long-run objectives. For example, a builder may be concerned with the immediate marketability of his houses; a lender may be concerned with property stability over the next 30 years.

Defining the purpose of the analysis helps to determine which of these two considerations should be given the most weight, the sector of the market that should be emphasized, and the appropriate intensity with which the market should be studied. In defining the purpose of the market analysis, the particular market segment under discussion must be isolated and identified. The whole market, or general climate, affects the segmented markets within it. These segments may be defined by geographical location, type, age, or value range of the property.

Major Topics of Analysis

The main topics in the analysis of single family residential markets are supply factors, demand factors or a combination of both.

• *Supply Factors.* The first item under this heading is an inventory of the existing stock of all housing units in the defined market area. The Census Bureau's statistics on housing is the primary source of this data, which is updated at regular intervals.

Next under supply factors are new construction volume and costs, including:

1. Recent building rate—new housing starts.
2. Conditions in the building industry as they relate to construction costs—availability and price of agents of production.
3. Actual and potential changes in building technology and how they might affect construction costs.
4. Relationship of construction costs to sale prices.
5. Cost of improving raw land and supply available.

Among sources of information will be the Bureau of the Census, Bureau of Labor Statistics, city and county building departments and planning commissions, real estate boards and builders' groups.

The third supply factor is the vacancy rate, one of the important indicators of real estate market conditions and trends. A high vacancy rate results in lowered prices and rents, even when demand is high. Normal vacancy for single family homes is usually less than 5% and for apartments, slightly over 5%. Business units may run somewhat higher. These are general guidelines that may vary from place to place. If the supply of vacant units exceeds a normal percentage, the market is oversupplied and/or short in demand. Competition may force prices and rents downward, followed by a decrease of new construction. When the vacancy rate declines, rents and prices increase, and optimistic entrepreneurs begin the process of adding more units to the market.

Vacancy information may be obtained from local real estate boards, the post office, local public utility companies and property managers. Vacancy ratios for different market segments should be computed separately because one part of the market may have a shortage of space while another has a surplus.

• *Demand Factors.* First under this heading is general population change (past, present and predictable future trends), including:

1. Changes in population numbers — current population.
2. Changes in population distributions.
3. Ratios in different population segments — for example, ratio between elementary school enrollment and population, net migration figures, marriage and divorce rates.

Again, sources of information include the Census Bureau, utility companies (the current population can be estimated by multiplying the present number of electric or water meters by the ratio of population to number of meters at the time of the last census), local chamber of commerce, county offices, school districts and visitors bureau.

Changes in preferences and taste are an important demand factor. Within any real estate market, the shifts that occur in the preference and tastes of the consumers may be difficult to identify or evaluate. Many real estate professionals rely on their own experience and observation to guide them, almost intuitively, with respect to such changes. Surveys may not reveal basic shifts in preference, especially for goods that are unfamiliar to consumers, even though once available consumers may flock to buy. Preference and taste are highly subjective and therefore very difficult to quantify and predict.

Any change in market prices or rents that persists for a year or more is a strong market trend indicator. Of special importance is the range between the listing and actual sales price, compared property by property. Similarly, the difference between the rental rate asked and finally paid is a reflection of the strength of the market. The length of time to dispose of properties on the market also indicates its strength. When long periods are required to dispose of property, the market is weakening, assuming, of course, that prices have been set at a reasonable competitive level.

Variations in market activity are reflected in the number of real estate transfers. The county recorder's office can supply figures on the number of deeds, mortgages and foreclosures recorded. Studies of this data covering fairly long periods of time are desirable. This data may be related to population trends, vacancy ratios, prices, rents, cost indices and the volume of construction. Such relationships provide a good indication of the present position of the market with regard to past periods. This overall perspective should allow an accurate prediction for future market activity.

• *Combined Supply and Demand Factors.* Business conditions, employment and income and financing conditions all fall within this category.

Estimates of general business trends usually precede the analysis of a specific real estate market. Local markets follow national economic trends to the degree they represent a typical cross-section of the economy. The appraiser must note whether local conditions follow closely or deviate significantly from general trends.

The most important factors to consider when studying local business conditions are employment and incomes. Sources for this type of information include local chambers of commerce, state employment services, local employers and monthly business reviews published by certain universities and financial institutions. These reports give information on local business activities, including retail sales activity, real estate transfers, new housing starts, and electricity production.

Recent changes in employment or incomes have a vital influence on all phases of local real estate market activity. Of special significance are potential developments likely to strengthen or diminish the demand for specific types of properties. Such developments must be related directly to the specific market problem under discussion. If local incomes are good and income prospects favorable, the real estate market is likely to be active (unless there has already been a great surge of building and a large unused inventory). Even though no new residents are attracted to the city, higher incomes mean an increase in the demand for housing. Heavier spending leads to greater demand for commercial property. Thus, demand for real estate can rise in a locality even though there has been no major increase in population. Similarly, demand falls with a decline in incomes, even if there has been no loss of population.

It is important in analyzing real estate markets to know what sections of the city are occupied by high-, middle- or low-income families. For cities of 50,000 population or more, data is available on a census tract basis including the average monthly rent and average value of owner-occupied houses, which give indications of income ranges in an area.

The terms and availability of financing are also primary factors in determining the strength or weakness of demand for real estate. When financing is readily available at attractive interest rates, the demand for property is strengthened. A tight money market tends to limit demand for real estate. Financing conditions vary not only from region to region but also from one real estate market to another. The availability of funds for the real estate market is dependent on the yield an investor can anticipate from his investment. For instance, if the bond market is offering a higher return on invested funds than the mortgage market, funds are diverted away from the real estate market. Information regarding the real estate finance market can be obtained from many different sources including publications of the Federal Reserve System, Federal Home Loan Banks, or from financial newspapers, lending institutions, magazines and journals.

Relative Prices and Relationships

Of major importance in market analysis are *relative prices*. For example, construction costs may be rising, but if rents, selling prices and incomes are rising proportionately, further construction is likely to continue. An upward or downward trend in prices and rents may cause buyers, investors and property users to expect still further changes in the same direction and accentuate the trend that has been developing.

An increase in funds available for real estate investment, resulting in more favorable financing terms, may stimulate market activity even though no other basic changes have occurred. The effect of rising incomes may be limited if the price of all goods and services, including real estate, is also increasing. In other words, real income, rather than monetary income, deserves primary consideration.

Real estate resources are in competition with other goods and services for a portion of the consumer's income. The real estate market is not isolated from other markets; it is an integral part of the entire economic system. Real estate market changes must always be considered in relation to other developments in the local or national economy.

Housing Market Analysis

The factors discussed above refer to all types of real estate markets. In making an analysis of the single family residential market, the following are considered in detail.

Housing Demand

Expanding economic opportunities will encourage growth and stimulate the demand for housing. Rising incomes, even without expansion of employment, may also lead to heavier housing demand. Thus economic base and similar types of analyses are often helpful in housing market studies.

In relating incomes to housing demand, income must be related to house prices. As a rule, families cannot afford to pay more than two to three times their annual income for housing. Consequently, a good housing market analysis requires that an income distribution of the families in the area be secured. Data of this type is available by census tracts in metropolitan regions and for cities, towns and counties. Such census reports also indicate the number of owner-occupied and rental units by price in rent brackets.

Closely related to income, cost and price factors are financing considerations. If financing is available on easy terms, demand may be maintained even though incomes are not advancing. Conversely, if financing terms are not favorable, housing demand may be reduced rapidly even though incomes are steady or advancing. Changes in the terms of financing may have an even greater impact on the market than changes in incomes because of the large proportion of borrowed funds that go into most purchases of single family residences.

Housing Supply

The supply of new dwelling units can be estimated on the basis of new building permits and the number of water or electric meters added. Data of this type can be broken down by districts and related to base periods such as those for which census materials are available.

A long period of strong building activity may point toward a weakening market, especially if vacancies are increasing and new houses are selling slowly. Also, construction costs must be studied in relationship to current prices to determine whether it is profitable to continue high volumes of construction activity.

Efficiency of building and low sale prices stimulate demand. Larger builders, both those with large-scale, on-site operations and prefabricators, have been able to stimulate demand in this way.

However, whenever market prices fall below the cost of construction, regardless of scale or methods used, few new housing starts are initiated.

Changes in design or style may appeal to changing taste and preference of consumers, thus affecting demand.

Summary

An appraiser must possess a thorough understanding of the real estate market before estimating accurately the market value of any parcel of real estate. This comprehension may be based on studies by specialists in the field or by the appraiser. All real estate transactions take place in the real estate market, a term that refers to the activity of the transactions, not to a specific marketplace.

Competition from both supply and demand must exist to have an effective market. Demand in excess of supply creates a seller's market; supply in excess of demand creates a buyer's market.

The restrictions on the open and effective functioning of the real estate market are caused by the uniqueness of each different parcel of real estate and the involvement of legal rights in each transaction. The economic characteristics particularly applicable to the single family residence are: (1) fixity of location; (2) long life; (3) large economic units, and (4) interdependence of private and public property.

Factors that influence market operation are generally dependent upon supply, demand, price, legal procedures and complications, subjective values of both buyers and sellers and the overall economic climate.

The objective of any market analysis influences how it is conducted and what information or data is used in the analysis. Major topics for analysis can be divided into supply factors, demand factors or a combination of both. The analysis of a housing market involves applying factors that are pertinent to the residential sector of the real estate market.

Review Questions

1. What is the objective of market analysis?
2. Define "market" and "marketplace."
3. What features should a market have for maximum efficiency?
4. How does the single family residential market differ from the typical market?
5. How and why do markets vary?
6. Explain and relate how changes in supply and demand affect the single family residential market.
7. What is the relationship between the volume of single family residential activity and the level of the local economy?
8. Which is more volatile in the single family market—demand or supply? Explain.
9. List and explain the major factors to be considered in making an analysis of the single family residential market.

6

Neighborhood Analysis *

A house is an integral part of its neighborhood and its community; its market value is affected substantially by the neighborhood in which it is located. Therefore, the primary purpose of neighborhood analysis is to identify the geographic area which is subject to the same influences as the property being appraised. Prices paid for comparable properties in the defined area theoretically reflect the positive and negative influences of the particular neighborhood. Two houses with similar physical characteristics may have significantly different market values, attributable to location in different neighborhoods.

In the appraisal process neighborhood analysis precedes and provides background for valuation. Information that has no bearing on value is irrelevant and may mislead the reader who can rightfully assume everything in the appraisal report is related to the appraisal process and final estimate of value. Misuse of neighborhood analysis can lead to double counting and false conclusions.

Assume, for example, that after complete neighborhood analysis, the appraiser delineates the neighborhood and obtains an indication of value based on recent prices received for similar properties in the same neighborhood. In such a case, it would be incorrect to adjust value for neighborhood influences, because these influences can be assumed to be reflected in the observed market prices.

The depth of analysis varies according to the need, but a neighborhood must be defined in terms of some common characteristics and trends in order to interpret market evidence fairly. The appraiser should avoid reliance on the racial, religious or ethnic characteristics of the residents. Racial and other ethnic factors are not reliable predictors of value trends and use of such factors by the appraiser in neighborhood analysis can be misleading. People's

---

* The authors have incorporated in this chapter material on neighborhood analysis from The Appraisal of Real Estate, 7th Edition (Chicago: American Institute of Real Estate Appraisers, 1978).

reactions and preferences are so diverse and variable that they are not readily quantifiable in the course of the appraisal process.

Definition of Neighborhood

The word *neighborhood* is difficult to define precisely.[1] In fact its meaning has been changing. Neighborhoods previously were defined as a segment of a community that gave a noticeable impression of unity. This unity might have been similar uses of the properties within the neighborhood such as mostly industrial plants, retail stores or multiple or single family housing. It also might have been a unity of structural appearance such as mostly colonial or contemporary style buildings. It sometimes was a unity based on the economic, religious, racial or ethnic status of most of the residents of the neighborhood. For example, some neighborhoods would be occupied predominantly by workers from a local industry or by persons of a particular national origin, race or religion.

Neighborhoods that can be defined on these bases are becoming less common. Often industrial, commercial and residential uses all exist in the same neighborhood. Likewise, people with a variety of economic, ethnic, racial and religious backgrounds now often live compatibly together in the same neighborhood.

The criteria for neighborhood analysis are clearly changing, reflecting changes in our social structures and attitudes. Obsolete standards of conformity have no place in modern neighborhood analysis. Broad federal and state fair housing laws have made discrimination on the basis of racial, religious or ethnic factors unlawful in the sale, rental and financing of housing. These laws and changing social standards have contributed to the establishment and maintenance of many stable, integrated residential areas.

Today *a neighborhood tends to be any separately identifiable cohesive area within a community with some community of interest shared by its occupants. Some neighborhoods may have recognizable natural or man-made boundaries.* Neighborhoods sometimes have their own names, such as Old Town or Pigeon Hills, but fre-

---

[1]An intriguing definition by Dr. Robert O. Harvey is "a neighborhood is the area around a lot to a point where changes in land use have no direct effect on the value of the lot." ARES Course Instructors' Manual, Real Estate Certification Program, Indiana University, Revised Edition, August 1977.

quently neighborhoods of this size actually consist of many sub-neighborhoods with different characteristics. A neighborhood may be as large an an entire community but it may be as small as a one- or two-block area.

Neighborhood Analysis

The first step in the study of a neighborhood is to identify its boundaries. Sometimes they are natural, physical barriers such as lakes, rivers, streams, cliffs, swamps and valleys. They also can be highways, main traffic arteries, railroad tracks, canals and other man-made boundaries. The boundary of a residential neighborhood may also be a change of land use to commercial, industrial, institutional or public park. Some boundaries are clearly defined and others more difficult to identify precisely.

The analysis of the neighborhood continues with a description of the properties within the neighborhood. In addition to single family housing, a typical residential neighborhood may contain multi-family dwellings, retail stores, service establishments, schools, churches, theaters, municipal buildings, institutions and sometimes industrial and commercial buildings.

Part of this analysis is the consideration of discernible patterns of urban growth that will influence the neighborhood. Careful analysis can reveal the general trends in the surrounding community area and the directions of growth, decay and renewal that will affect the neighborhood.

Few neighborhoods are fixed in character. Most are dynamic in nature and are changing at various rates of speed. What is happening in one neighborhood in a community often affects other neighborhoods in the same and nearby communities. As new neighborhoods in a community are developed, they compete with existing neighborhoods. An added supply of new homes also tends to induce shifts from old to new. New neighborhoods may have the advantage of new housing stock. Older neighborhoods may have the advantage of closer location to places of work and other community facilities. Educational facilities, utilities, services, historic significance, parks and recreational facilities affect the competitive position of a neighborhood. All these things being equal, a new house usually has an advantage over an older one.

The Importance of Objectivity in Neighborhood Analysis

Consideration of observable neighborhood conditions and trends is an important aspect of neighborhood analysis and typically includes observation of factors that enhance or detract from property values. In identifying and discussing these conditions, trends or factors, objectivity is essential. For instance, general reference to a presumed "pride of ownership" (or the lack thereof) may be too vague and too subjective to be indicative of an actual contribution to or detraction from property values. The presence of special amenities or detrimental conditions should be noted and described with particularity.

The appraiser's findings with respect to neighborhood conditions and the effects of these conditions on property values are considered by buyers, sellers, brokers, lenders, courts, arbiters, public officials and other decision-makers or advisors. Because of this broad influence, the appraiser is often called upon to provide specific evidence of neighborhood conditions and trends and to elaborate the findings in a written appraisal report. The use of photographs and detailed field notes enables the appraiser to recall important evidence and verify the facts considered in the analysis.

The appraiser should avoid generalization with respect to the desirability of particular types of neighborhoods. Older urban neighborhoods, as well as newer suburban subdivisions, can attract a wide range of residents. Neighborhood trends do not necessarily depend upon the age of the neighborhood or the income of neighborhood residents.

Neighborhood Life Cycles

Neighborhoods are established when new buildings are constructed together with streets, utilities and other services. Sometimes a new neighborhood is established where an old neighborhood existed. This transition is most common where a residential neighborhood changes into a commercial or industrial neighborhood. With the help of urban renewal, an industrial or commercial neighborhood can be changed into a residential neighborhood.

The first stage of a new residential neighborhood is the growth period. This growth period may last for a year or so or it may spread over many years. It may continue until all the available land is used or it may stop when the demand for new houses diminishes or when acceptable financing is not available. If the neighborhood is successfully developed, there will be active building. New construction will attract new inhabitants and usually the neighborhood gains public recognition and favor.

When the growth period ends, the neighborhood enters a period of relative equilibrium. Changes rarely stop completely but in this stabilizing period they may slow down considerably. New construction may continue on a limited basis as demand increases or financing terms improve and make building profitable. The period of stability is characterized by the lack of marked gains or losses. Many neighborhoods are stable for long periods of time. There is no preset life expectancy for a neighborhood and decline is not imminent in all older neighborhoods.

The period of decline starts when the neighborhood is less able to compete with other neighborhoods. During this period, prices may be lowered to attract buyers to the neighborhood. Among the characteristics of a declining neighborhood are properties in a poor state of maintenance, conversions to more intensive uses and a lack of enforcement of building codes and zoning regulations.

The period of decline may end when the neighborhood changes to another land use and a new neighborhood is developed or when it moves into a renewal period. This may be caused by a change in one or more of the economic, social, physical or governmental forces. For example, expansion of commercial activities in the community may increase the demand for housing in the neighborhood.

Neighborhood rejuvenation can also be the result of organized community activities such as redevelopment programs, organized rebuilding and historical renovation. The rebirth of an older neighborhood often is caused by a combination of these factors, some of which are a result of planning and outside aid and some simply because of changing preferences and lifestyles.

After the rebirth of an older neighborhood the life cycle may be repeated in which a period of stability and eventually a period of decline may occur unless, again, a change in the forces that affect desirability and marketability takes place.[2]

[2]There are many interpretations regarding cycles of residential neighborhoods. An interesting concept is presented in a report entitled, "The Dynamics of Neighborhood Change," prepared by Public Affairs Counseling, a division of Real Estate Research Corporation, San Francisco, for HUD, under Contract #H-2151R, dated December 1975.

Factors Affecting Value

To understand these life cycles and how neighborhoods change involves understanding the relevant physical, social, economic and governmental factors that affect value. The following is an outline of these factors, together with their various considerations. After the outline each of the considerations is developed in more detail.

PHYSICAL OR ENVIRONMENTAL

1. Location within the community
2. Barriers and boundaries
3. Topography
4. Soil, drainage and climate
5. Services and utilities
6. Proximity to supporting facilities
7. Street patterns
8. Pattern of land use
9. Conformity of structure
10. Appearance
11. Special amenities
12. Nuisances and hazards
13. Age and condition of residences and other improvements

SOCIAL

1. Population characteristics
2. Community and neighborhood associations
3. Crime level

ECONOMIC

1. Relation to community growth
2. Economic profile of residents
3. New construction and vacant land
4. Turnover and vacancy

GOVERNMENTAL

1. Taxation and special assessments
2. Public and private restrictions
3. Schools
4. Planning and subdivision regulations

Physical or Environmental Factors

These factors cover conditions of the natural and man-made environment that physically define and limit the neighborhood.

● *Location within the Community.* The location of a neighborhood in relation to the larger community is important. A neighborhood adjacent to the central business district, for example, may benefit from the convenience of local shopping and municipal services, or it may suffer from exposure to a high crime rate and heavy traffic. Locations in the direction of growth may benefit but those away from the growth may suffer.

• *Barriers and Boundaries.* Both natural and man-made boundaries can effectively protect and define a neighborhood. These boundaries frequently help to reinforce the neighborhood identity, particularly when they are prominent landmarks such as a large park, super highway or river. Explicit boundaries are usually a favorable sign.

• *Topography.* Like barriers and boundaries, topography may be natural or man-made conditions of terrain. Typically, considerations as to the desirability of various topography depends upon the nature of residential development. For large-lot, high-value properties, hillside or wooded sites are often at a premium; tract developers, however, usually seek a level or a plateau which is more conducive to subdivision construction. The proximity to a lake, river, swamp or salt marsh may constitute a topographical advantage or disadvantage. Good topography can contribute protection from wind, fog or flood as well as provide an attractive view. The preferred topography is a rolling terrain at a slightly higher elevation than surrounding neighborhoods. Values tend to rise with the elevation of the land in many areas. Values are penalized where the land is very flat or excessively rugged without reasonable access.

• *Soil, Drainage and Climate.* The natural quality of the soil directly affects the cost to build and the value of residences in the neighborhood. Its bearing quality, its ability to support landscaping and lawns and the absorption rate for waste disposal must be considered.

Drainage of surface water and the neighborhood susceptibility to flooding also affect values. Flood maps are now available for many communities and the appraisal report should indicate if the neighborhood and residence being appraised are subject to flooding (see Appendix F on flood insurance). Even in neighborhoods that are not subject to flooding, the disposal of storm water is an important consideration.

Sometimes because of proximity to water, mountains or other natural conditions, a neighborhood has a different climate than nearby neighborhoods which affects its competitive position.

• *Services and Utilities.* The availability of services and utilities such as electricity, city water, sanitary sewers and natural gas affect the relative desirability of a particular neighborhood. Large price differentials for obtaining these services would also be detrimental to values.

• *Proximity to Supporting Facilities.* In analyzing a neighborhood, an appraiser must consider the proximity and accessibility of major supporting facilities such as public transportation, places of worship, schools, shopping areas, recreational facilities and centers of employment. Some people prefer to live within reasonable walking distance of convenience stores and service establishments, yet such supporting facilities should not inflict a commercial atmosphere on the residential neighborhood. Convenience and ease of access to these supporting facilities often add to the desirability of a neighborhood and to the values of homes in the area.

• *Street Patterns.* Streets are an important man-made physical element which can affect value. They are the entrances and exits of a neighborhood. The physical plan of a neighborhood is strongly influenced by its street pattern. The attractiveness of individual settings depends on the effective use of natural contours, wooded areas, ponds and other features. Contemporary planned neighborhoods make use of curving streets, cul-de-sacs with generous turn-around space and circular drives. These act as deterrents to through traffic, which can be a hazard in older neighborhoods where streets run in grids or square blocks. Curvilinear and dead-end streets reduce such traffic hazards, make a neighborhood more aesthetically attractive, and help to preserve the communication and unity of the area. Ideally, expressways and boulevards should be outside the immediate residential neighborhood but should offer easy access from local streets. Traffic within the neighborhood should move easily and slowly.

• *Patterns of Land Use.* The pattern of land use within a neighborhood often helps an appraiser estimate the stage in the life cycle of that neighborhood. A stable neighborhood has clearly defined areas for various uses, well-buffered areas between uses, and respect for zoning and deed restrictions which maintain the neighborhood's integrity.

• *Conformity of Structure.* The character of a neighborhood is partially set by its "average" house. The class of ownership, structural nature of the house and its architectural style, combined with its age and condition, are physical considerations that have important impact on the desirability of the neighborhood. Widely diverse styles and levels of care often indicate a transitional period within a neighborhood heading towards change or possibly towards redevelopment.

• *Appearance.* Maintenance of individual homes and their architectural compatibility influence the general appearance of a neighborhood. Landscaping, plantings and open space preservation also directly affect the appearance of a neighborhood. Neatly kept yards and houses as well as community areas reflect ongoing care by their owners.

• *Special Amenities.* In neighborhood analysis, the consideration of amenities is of major importance. People tend to live in the best housing they can afford, and a major factor in higher priced housing is amenity value. The homebuyer in the lowest income group purchases "shelter level" housing—that is, the bare necessities exclusive of most amenities. The more prosperous can afford to pay for the availability of external amenities such as parks, beaches, pools, tennis courts, country clubs and libraries. Amenities strongly improve a neighborhood's competitive position in attracting new residents.

• *Nuisances and Hazards.* Noise, traffic congestion, smoke and other nuisances directly affect the desirability of a neighborhood. The extent of tolerance of nuisances and hazards tends to be directly related to the income level of the residents. Values of properties tend to be higher in neighborhoods that have accepted standards of public health, comfort and safety than those that do not. A nearby factory complex or the flight path of an adjacent airport can have a marked negative affect on the property values in a residential neighborhood. Effective barriers against such disturbances tend to create a premium.

• *Age and Condition of Improvements.* The age and condition of residences in a neighborhood can affect the marketability of a house located in that neighborhood. Age alone may not be an indication;

however, it is recognized that buildings do wear out even with good maintenance or become obsolete and therefore less marketable, or that their location in relation to community growth may cause economic obsolescence. Regardless of age, delayed building maintenance may cause rapid loss of marketability in a residence. Several neglected houses in a neighborhood may not cause the entire neighborhood to decline in attractiveness, but as the percentage of neglected houses increases, there is a tendency that the entire neighborhood will begin to follow the same pattern. The presence of community and neighborhood associations (which will be discussed further in the following section) often spur maintenance and repair programs, thereby preserving market value and preventing decline among residences in the neighborhood.

Social Factors

Social factors include population characteristics, community and neighborhood organizations and the crime level.

• *Population Characteristics.* Population trends and characteristics indicated by U. S. Census figures or statistics compiled by local agencies are important tools in estimating the trend of a neighborhood.

It was once common practice by some appraisers to examine the racial composition of a neighborhood in an effort to detect signs of change which were assumed to be indications of a trend toward lower values. Such an approach is now regarded as misdirected. This evolution in appraisal practice reflects a corresponding evolution in social attitudes and public policy. The old applications of the principle of conformity have no place in current neighborhood analysis techniques. Changing social standards supported by broad federal and state fair housing laws have made it possible for the racial or ethnic composition of a neighborhood to change without values decreasing. They have also encouraged the establishment and maintenance of many stable, integrated residential areas. There is no factual support for the outdated assumption that racial or ethnic homogeneity is a requirement for maximum value.

Changing social standards and lifestyles now show a growing preference on the part of many people for social heterogeneity in their neighborhoods. In these areas the traditional social groupings are changing to conform to these new social preferences. Analysis based on traditional, outdated social groupings has no relevance in current appraisal process.

In our changing society there is no longer any universal set of social standards. Factors that are relevant in one neighborhood may be irrelevant in another. Many of those factors are subjective and difficult to isolate. The appraiser recognizes the difficulty of accurately measuring the effect on value of subjective factors, such as changes in population makeup, and that no mathematical or empirical allocation method should be relied on to estimate the effect of such subjective considerations on value.

• *Community and Neighborhood Associations.* A variety of community and neighborhood associations exist. Some are legal entities formed by the original developers of an area, with a membership including all the owners within defined boundaries. Many of these organizations were started before World War II, often in coastal communities or around lakes or other recreational areas. The developer would deed the beach, lakefront or other desirable natural area to the association, which in turn would maintain and control it for the benefit of its members.

Associations were also formed to maintain and guard exclusive subdivisions having common grounds, parks, courts and limited access. In addition to maintenance of common facilities, a major function of the association was to hire guards to keep uninvited guests off the association property. Some of the typical functions of this type of homeowners' association were:

1. Maintaining common owned land, beaches, courts, pools, club house and golf course.
2. Collecting rubbish and garbage, removing snow, sweeping streets.
3. Providing and maintaining sewer disposal systems and water supply systems.
4. Providing police and fire protection.
5. Providing lifeguards on beaches, waterfronts and pools.

These groups often tried to exercise considerable control by enforcing private covenants and restrictions that gave them the right to approve the transfer of title or rental of property and to approve the style and size of any new buildings. They were also empowered to (1) establish an annual charge to be paid by the association members; (2) put a lien on the property of owners who did not pay their charges; (3) borrow money on behalf of the members; and (4) buy and sell property.

After World War II, the planned unit development became popular. Common land was deeded by the developer of a PUD to the local community. When the community accepted the common land, it incurred a financial obligation to maintain it and also lost tax revenue on it. Because of these reasons and also because the land became usable by the whole community, many communities refused to accept such common land. Developers then formed private homeowners associations to accept the land and maintain it. They found this was a good way to provide recreational facilities and often constructed swimming pools, tennis courts and golf courses on the common land as an added inducement to potential purchasers.

Other types of neighborhood organizations have been formed on a voluntary basis by the residents in a neighborhood or segment of a neighborhood (for example, a block club). The purposes of these organizations are usually neighborhood preservation and enhancement and social interaction among the residents. Common activities include political lobbying efforts to prevent zoning changes the community believes to be detrimental to the neighborhood. Such groups also maintain contact with community officials to obtain services, facilities and improvements within the neighborhood. They may also become involved in political activities, supporting local candidates and parties. Neighborhood improvement projects with the members doing all or some of the work themselves, social gatherings, block parties, fairs, parades, etc., are sponsored by such community groups. Membership is voluntary and usually open to everyone within the neighborhood.

Some associations have little or no effect on the value of the property of the members; they have limited functions, few activities and low dues or assessments. Other associations have a substantial impact on the value of property of their members. Often they are a whole neighborhood themselves. Houses that are in the association may have higher values than nearby houses that are not in the association. These associations usually control important recreational facilities and/or provide substantial needed services, security and other amenities.

The appraiser must investigate the association to determine the facilities or services provided and the additional costs to individual property owners. When these services appear to be substantial or their cost is high, it is usually best to select comparables from within the association membership. It is often difficult to make a location adjustment to reflect the difference in value between houses in the association and those outside of its membership. (The subject of adjustments is covered in detail in later chapters.)

• *Crime Level.* Unfortunately, the crime level in many communities and neighborhoods continues to increase and so the appraiser must consider the impact of the crime level as part of the neighborhood analysis. When a neighborhood obtains the reputation of having an excessively high crime rate, some residents may leave and potential new residents are discouraged from buying homes there. Increased street lighting and police protection as well as vigilance on the part of residents in reporting suspicious activities to the police may help reduce the crime rate.

Economic Factors

These are factors that are the result of economic forces affecting a neighborhood.

• *Relation to Community Growth.* Property values in a neighborhood are directly affected by the growth pattern of the surrounding community. Houses in the path of an expanding community are usually marketable and tend to increase in value. Other neighborhoods less accessible to newly developing community centers or places of employment may be less desirable as sites for new homes.

• *Economic Profile of Residents.* The income and employment profile of the residents of a neighborhood, and the corresponding price levels and rents these support, are important economic parameters in the analysis of a neighborhood. The type, stability and location of employment have a strong impact on the value of residential property, since employment determines to a large degree the ability of individuals to purchase or rent in a particular area. Income levels tend to set a value range for a neighborhood. The influence of neighborhood is often obvious; a superior house will be penalized for its location in a neighborhood that does not support its value.

Changes in purchasing power result in changes in property values. Therefore, substantial change affecting the available income

of people living in the area as well as of those who constitute the
market for property in the neighborhood must be considered. A
downward trend in available income for shelter usually previews a
dip in property values.

• *New Construction and Vacant Land.* Vacant land suitable for the
construction of additional houses within a neighborhood may exist
simply because the owners, for personal reasons, do not wish to
develop or sell the land. It may forecast additional future construction activity or indicate a lack of effective demand.

If only a few vacant lots remain in a neighborhood, residential
construction on them usually will not substantially affect values in
the neighborhood. However, if they are spot-zoned nonresidential,
or if variances are granted permitting nonresidential construction,
the nonconforming uses may have an adverse effect on the surrounding properties.

What is constructed on the larger parcels of vacant land may substantially affect values in the neighborhood. Available information
about proposed future development of these parcels is an integral
part of neighborhood analysis.

• *Turnover and Vacancy.* The rate and duration of vacancies is
another statistical indicator of the economic health of a neighborhood. Some turnover of properties within a neighborhood is usually
a sign of a healthy market. At the same time, a neighborhood that is
stable and attractive continues to hold a majority of its residents.
High rates of long-term vacancy may signal decline or the
necessity of changes in use. A large number of "For Sale" signs
may be a warning that the neighborhood is experiencing a down-
turn in popularity. Conversely, a scarcity of vacant houses is a sign
of stability in a neighborhood. Reviewing newspaper ads offering
available rental and sale units helps the appraiser estimate the
strength of housing demand and the extent of the supply.

Governmental Factors

These are based on the activities of government, including taxation, restrictions, schools, planning and building regulations.

• *Taxation and Special Assessments.* Neighborhoods are competitive with one another and the level of taxation can be an important
deciding factor for potential residents. Taxation is often a signifi-

cant variable in making comparisons from one neighborhood to another. Special assessments should be directly related to the extra services or advantages they provide, such as private beach association or extra fire protection. When special assessments become high compared to other houses in the market, they may seriously reduce the value of the highly taxed house. An unpaid special assessment lien often will reduce the value of the house by approximately the amount of the lien. This value reduction may be offset by the enhancement that results from the special improvement or service that is the basis of the special assessment.

• *Public and Private Restrictions.* Zoning regulations and building codes are important guardians of stability for a neighborhood. They provide legal protection against adverse influences, nuisances and hazards. When special exceptions or variances are easily obtained without consideration for their effect on surrounding houses, the value of those houses may be decreased. A breakdown in the enforcement of existing zoning and building regulations may also cause a decrease in value. Such violations often start with illegal signs, use for businesses and conversion to higher density use than permitted by zoning.

Deed restrictions can protect properties from the negative impact of incompatible use and breakdown of their enforcement may lead to lower values. Some deed restrictions written years ago, however, may be now obsolete or unenforceable. For example, deed restrictions setting the minimum cost of construction may be meaningless based on today's costs. The courts have ruled that deed restrictions based on race, religion, or national origin are not enforceable. Generally, any deed restriction that is against the public interest is not enforceable.

• *Schools.* Educational facilities may be a strong attraction for prospective homebuyers. Families may be attracted to a neighborhood, at least in part, by its schools. Schools are of immediate interest to all families with children. Even homeowners with no children may consider the availability of educational facilities when purchasing a house, because future buyers of their home may have children. Neighborhood schools may be of less importance where children are bussed to schools outside the area.

• *Planning and Subdivision Regulations.* Planning for the future development of a community is an important task of government. Such planning should include protection of the integrity and character of existing neighborhoods, while providing for anticipated future uses of undeveloped areas. Poor planning for recreational facilities, schools, service areas and other needs of residents may lead to neighborhood disintegration.

Requirements imposed on developers and subdividers influence the types and quality of basic services available to homeowners in the neighborhood and have a strong effect on the value of existing structures. The protection of open space areas, such as wetlands, for example, will act as a deterrent to developers who may attempt to sacrifice the character of a neighborhood in order to build a maximum number of units.

Sources of Neighborhood Data

Much neighborhood data must be gathered in the field through close observation and analysis of existing conditions, but other sources of information are needed for population statistics, income and employment profiles and vacancy information. In addition to census data, local utility companies and community-level government organizations frequently have pertinent data available. Other sources of information include real estate brokers, local lending institutions, other appraisers and the residents of a neighborhood.

Redlining and the Appraiser

Because the attitudes and decisions of lenders and insurers may affect the marketability of homes within a particular neighborhood, an understanding of redlining is helpful for many types of neighborhood analysis problems.

Redlining refers to the reluctance of lenders, investors or insurers to make loans, invest or issue insurance on usual terms in a particular geographic area because of some feature or characteristic that is perceived to affect adversely the utility or security, and hence the value, of individual parcels of property in the area. The term originated many years ago to describe a practice, once engaged in by both private and government organizations, of drawing a red line on a map around the borders of areas considered to contain such adverse features and regarded as unsuitable for lending, insuring or investing purposes. The term is now applied figuratively whether or not an actual map or red pencil is used. The word *greenlining* is sometimes used to describe a policy on the part of a lender, group of lenders or other organizations to affirmatively seek loans in specific neighborhoods. It also is used sometimes to characterize strategies employed by homeowners or activist groups to protect a neighborhood from the effects of redlining.

Redlining can be a rational response to a real risk that exists in an area. For instance, property located in a flood plain, slide area or in close proximity to a geologic fault may present a level of risk that would be unacceptable to a mortgage lender or insurer. However, when the perceptions of risk are based on unrealistic, inaccurate or arbitrary assumptions, or when the boundaries of affected areas are overly broad, such practices may result in negative decisions being made with respect to whole neighborhoods that may contain many sound properties and might otherwise be stable and viable.

The term *racial redlining* refers to the practice of basing loan, insurance or investment criteria on the racial characteristics of the people who live in a particular neighborhood, presumably because of a perception of risk arising from the racial or social composition of the population or changes in this composition. Racial redlining has been held to be unlawful by the courts and by several federal agencies that have regulatory authority over lending institutions, including the Federal Home Loan Bank Board, the Federal Reserve Board and the United States Department of Housing and Urban Development. In addition, the major secondary market organizations that purchase home loans (Federal Home Loan Mortgage Corp. and the Federal National Mortgage Association) have stipulated on their forms that the racial composition of areas must not be considered in appraisals for home loans submitted for their purchase.

Summary

A neighborhood today tends to be any separately identifiable area of a community, usually having recognizable natural or man-made boundaries. Sometimes they are clearly defined and other times they are difficult to identify precisely. The old concepts of unity and conformity no longer apply.

Most neighborhoods are changing at various rates; what happens in one neighborhood affects surrounding neighborhoods. An added supply of new houses tends to induce a shift from older houses to the new ones. However, other factors such as location, community facilities, educational facilities and parks also influence the rate of shifting.

The analysis of a neighborhood starts with a description of the area and the properties it contains. It also describes the growth pattern around it.

Neighborhoods go through life cycles that start when the neighborhood is developed. This is called the growth period. When construction slows down or stops, a period of stability follows. This period ends either because the housing stock deteriorates or changes occur in the economic, social, physical and governmental forces that affect the neighborhood. Decline may cease when these forces change again or when there is an organized effort to rejuvenate the neighborhood. This renewal period is comparable to the original growth period. The life cycle is then repeated with another period of stability and a period of decline. If the period of decline is not reversed, the neighborhood will come to the end of its economic life and usually will change to another use.

To understand neighborhood cycles, one must understand the relevant physical, social, governmental, and economic forces that affect its value.

Information about the neighborhood and the factors that make up the four great forces must be gathered in the field by close observation and interviewing information sources and local residents. This information is reconciled to determine what effect the neighborhood has on the value of the house being appraised. The form and depth of this analysis depends on the particular appraisal problem. It always must be objective, supported by facts and based on current social standards.

Review Questions

1. What besides the property's own physical characteristics affects its value?
2. How may the term "neighborhood" be defined?
3. What are the stages of a neighborhood's life cycle?
4. Of what may a neighborhood's boundaries consist?
5. What is the preferred topography for a residential property?
6. How does soil quality affect a single family residence?
7. What is an amenity as related to the single family market?
8. Give examples of several nuisances and/or hazards that may tend to decrease value.
9. What is the purpose of zoning regulations and building codes?
10. In addition to zoning regulations, private restrictions and building codes, what other type of regulations now affect development of vacant land?

7

Residential Site Data
and Analysis

According to tradition, when an appraiser is asked to name the three most important factors affecting value, the answer is, "Location, location, location." More specifically, the answer might be stated: "Community location, neighborhood location and site location."

Because of the fixed nature of real estate, location contributes more than any other single factor to wide variations in value among similar improvements. Therefore, good appraisal practice requires that the exact location of the property being appraised be clearly and definitively established. An accurate description of the legal boundaries and a detailed review of the physical features are combined with a thorough analysis of the site's location in the neighborhood and community.

Land and Site

In the specialized vocabulary of the real estate professional, *land* and *site* are *not* synonymous. *Land* means the surface of the earth, which is unimproved by man, plus a wedge-shaped subsurface piece that theoretically extends to the center of the globe and air rights extending upward to the sky. In practice, the use of air rights is limited in the United States by an act of Congress, which holds that navigable air space is public domain. In some areas of the country, subsurface mineral rights are owned by the government or someone other than the owner of the rest of the fee. All natural resources in their original state are also considered to be part of the land, including mineral deposits, fossil fuels, wildlife and timber. In the appraiser's definition, everything that is natural and within the property boundaries is part of the land.

Site is the land plus improvements that make it ready for use, including streets, sewer systems and utility connections.

Many appraisers include such items as the cost of clearing the site, grading and landscaping, drainage, water and sewer connections (or septic systems), electric and gas service, private access streets, alleys, drives and sidewalks as part of the site analysis. Occasionally, local custom dictates that some of these items be treated as building improvements rather than site improvements. It is important in making an appraisal to indicate this distinction clearly and treat the comparable market data in a consistent manner. Proper appraisal terminology states that "improvements *to* the site" are those described above and that "improvements *on* the site" are house, garage and other out buildings.

Purpose of Separate Site Valuation

The purpose of site analysis is to provide a solid framework of information and insight for highest and best use analysis, the major theoretical basis of the appraisal (see Chapter 8).

It has been argued that once the site is improved with a house a separate site valuation is difficult—if not impossible and unnecessary. The claim is that only a total property valuation is possible in such cases and that the two units are inseparable. In spite of the theoretical merits of this argument, however, many practical reasons exist for making separate site valuations even when the property is already improved.

Separate site valuations are required by statute in most states for ad valorem (real estate) tax purposes. The assessed value is almost universally split between the land (or site) and the improvements. Special assessments for public improvements, such as streets, water lines, sewers, etc., are often based on their estimated effect on land or site values. Income tax preparation also requires that the cost of a property be split between the improvements and the site. The first step of the cost approach is to estimate a separate market value of the site. Separate site value estimates are also commonly used for establishing condemnation awards, adjusting casualty losses, deciding whether to raze existing improvements to use the site for a new structure and establishing site rentals.

No single accepted manner exists in which to organize and present the necessary data; the following example groups the four categories of material in the order they would normally be collected.

1. Title and record data.
2. On-site physical characteristics.
3. Relationship to surroundings.
4. Economic factors.

A form such as shown in Fig. 7-1 may aid in assembling the data required.

Title and Record Data

A legal description of the site plus data relating to taxes, special assessments, zoning, easements and other restrictions are covered in this section.

Every appraisal must describe the property so that it is easily and accurately identified and cannot be confused with any other parcel. The best way to establish the exact location of a property is to incorporate a deed description and survey into the appraisal. In addition, a location map showing the site in relation to the surrounding neighborhood should be provided. A reliable way to identify the property is by street name and number if the parcel is within the limits of a defined community. Rural areas also have improved identification systems.

Legal Descriptions

Often the appraiser decides that the use of street address numbers does not provide the required positive identification of the property. In such cases, an accurate legal description of the property must be obtained from the deed, mortgage or other land record sources in the community. Legal descriptions found in these documents are prepared in one or a combination of four ways: (1) lot and block; (2) metes and bounds; (3) geodetic survey; and (4) government survey system.

• *Lot and Block System.* This system, derived from the rectangular survey system, applies in most urban communities. It originated in the manner in which these communities grew. The early developers had their tracts surveyed and platted in rectangular blocks and lots. Each was numbered and the numbers were entered on a plat map. Copies of the plat were filed in the local government record office for permanent reference. Identification by use of lot and block numbers is usually sufficient in subdivisions where each lot is clearly distinguished from its neighbors. An example of this system is shown in Fig. 7-2.

FIG. 7-1: Site Analysis
Title & Record Data
Identification _____

_____

Assessment _____ Special assessment _____
Taxes _____ Comparison of taxes _____
Zoning: Permitted uses _____ Prohibited uses _____
   Setback, sideyard, rear yard requirements _____
Building code restrictions _____
Easements, encroachments _____ Party wall agreements _____
Environmental restrictions _____ Riparian rights _____
Probability of future change in permitted use _____

On-site Physical Characteristics
Width and frontage _____ Depth _____
Shape _____ Size _____
Excess area _____
Corner or cul-de-sac influence _____
Surface soil (lawn & landscaping support potential) _____
Subsoil _____
Landscaping _____
Surface and storm water disposal _____
Water (source, quantity, quality) _____
Waste disposal _____ Gas _____
Telephone _____ Electricity _____
Street improvements: Paving _____ Width _____
   Sidewalks _____ Curbs _____
   Gutters _____ Street lights _____
View _____ Hazards _____
Nuisances _____
Site improvements: Fences, walls _____
   Sidewalks _____ Driveways _____
   Patios/pool _____ Courts _____
Climate or meteorological conditions _____

Relationship to Surroundings
Abutting and nearby street and traffic flow _____
Use of nearby lots _____
Orientation of improvements _____

Access by Car		Public Transportation
_____	To shopping	_____
_____	To place of work	_____
_____	To recreation	_____

Safety of children from vehicular traffic _____

Economic Factors
Prices of nearby lots _____
Tax burden as compared with competitive lots _____
Utility costs _____ Service costs _____

FIG. 7-2: Lot and Block System

SEC. 18, T. 38, R. 14.

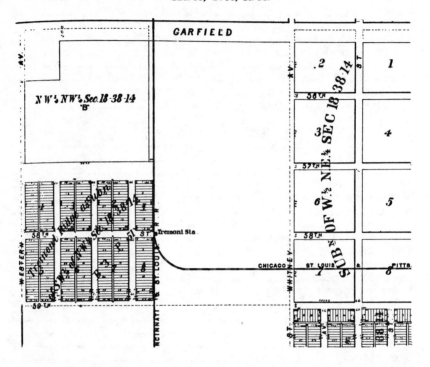

- *Metes and Bounds System.* Originally used in colonial America, this system identifies property by delineating its boundaries in terms of a series of directions and distances, starting at a fixed point. Typical points referred to in old deeds are large trees, rocks, streams, etc., which today in some cases have become difficult, if not impossible, to locate positively. Each boundary line is described in succession, using a compass bearing and distance, until the entire parcel has been enclosed; for example, "Starting at the old oak tree known as Grand Dad's Oak, South 63 degrees 35 minutes for a distance of 185 feet ..." (see Fig. 7-3).
- *Geodetic Survey.* A land survey that was initiated to identify tracts of land owned by the federal government gradually has been extended throughout the nation. These survey maps are prepared by

FIG. 7-3: Metes and Bounds System

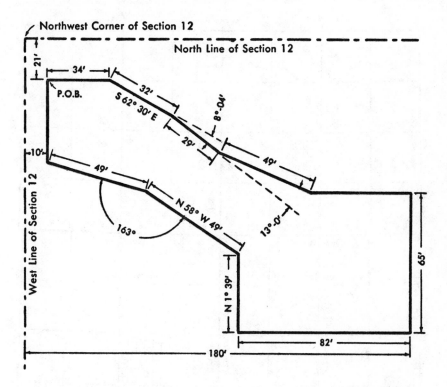

the United States Geological Survey Division, Department of the Interior. They show, among other things, height contours, latitude and longitude, existing rivers and streams, buildings and railroads. They are available on various scales by named quadrangles. The skeleton of this survey is a network of "benchmarks," which cover the entire country, each of which is located by its latitude and longitude.

• *Government Survey System.* This system also developed during colonial times; it provides for a unit of land approximately 24 miles square, bounded by base lines running east and west and meridians extending north and south. Because of the curvature of the earth, the north boundary of the square is slightly shorter than the south. The 24-mile square unit is divided into areas six miles square, called townships. A "tier" is an east/west row of townships between two

FIG. 7-4: Government Survey System

24 Miles — Correction Line — 24 Miles

24 Miles · Meridian West · 24 Miles

T.4N.

Principal Meridian · T.3N.

Township Line

6	5	4	3	2	1
7	8	9	10	11	12
18	17	16	15	14	13
19	20	21	22	23	24
30	29	28	27	26	25
31	32	33	34	35	36

Range Line · T.2N.

Meridian East · 24 Miles

T.1N.

R.4W. R.3W. R.2W. R.1W. R.1E. R.2E. R.3E. R.4E.

Base Line   Initial Point   Base Line

T.1S.

Township Line

T.2S.

24 Miles · First Guide · Range Line · Principal Meridian · T.3S.

6	5	4	3	2	1
7	8	9	10	11	12
18	17	16	15	14	13
19	20	21	22	23	24
30	29	28	27	26	25
31	32	33	34	35	36

First Guide · 24 Miles

T.4S.

24 Miles   Correction Line   24 Miles   A. W. O'Bosla

SOURCE: John S. Hoag, *Fundamentals of Land Measurement* (Chicago: Chicago Title Insurance Company).

parallels of latitude six miles apart. A "range" is a north/south row between two meridian lines also six miles apart. Ranges and tiers are assigned numbers from principal meridians and base lines. A township is divided into 36 sections, each one mile square. The sections are numbered consecutively, beginning with the northeast corner and continuing, east to west and west to east, down to Section 36 in the southeast corner. Discrepancies pertaining to the north boundary, and others due to errors in measurement or alignment, are allowed for in the most westerly half mile of the township (see Fig. 7-4).

Assessment and Taxes

Traditionally, a substantial portion of the funds needed by a community to provide services to its citizens is raised by taxes levied on real estate, based on the value of the property, hence the term ad valorem taxation.

Taxes are intended to pay for services that make ownership more desirable, but net benefits obviously decrease when taxes are out of proportion to income. Therefore, the appraiser compares the tax status—assessed values, tax rates, and tax burdens—of the appraised site with that of competitive or comparable sites. In some communities the assessed value of land for taxes bears a reasonable relation to market value, particularly when a recent reassessment has been made; but in other communities the assessed value does not have a realistic relation to value.

The first step the appraiser takes in considering taxation is to report the actual assessment and tax rate of the community as it applies to the appraised property. The assessment is often divided between the land and the improvements. Sometimes the site improvements are assessed separately. There may be a single tax rate or a series of separate tax rates to provide segregated funding for education, utilities, etc.

Usually the assessment is some percentage of market value. In communities with efficient assessors and frequent revaluations that reflect changes in the value of property, there is a good relationship between assessments and values. In many communities, however, where the assessor is unqualified, understaffed or not motivated, or where revaluations are infrequent, there may be little relationship between assessments and market values.

Two longstanding traditions exist in the assessment and taxation process. One is that assessments are often a percentage of market value; the second is that the tax rate is expressed in mills rather than as a percentage of assessment. A mill is a tenth of a cent. The mill rate is the number of mills per dollar of assessed value. For example:

Assessment	$1.00
Mill rate	100 ($1.00 x .100)
Taxes	$.10

Assessment	$1,000
Mill rate	90
Taxes	$90

This system sometimes is confusing to both the public and the appraiser because it is difficult to compare readily the taxes in one community with those in another. For example, a lot that has a value of $8,000 might be assessed at 70% in one community with a tax rate of 40 mills. Taxes would be calculated as follows:

Market value	$8,000
Assessment ratio	70% (.70 x $8,000 = $5,600)
Assessment	$5,600
Tax rate	40 mills
Taxes	$224 (.040 x 5,600)

A similar lot valued at $8,000 in another community might be assessed at 35% with a tax rate of 80 mills.

Market value	$8,000
Assessment ratio	35% (.35 x $8,000 = $2,800)
Assessment	$2,800
Tax rate	80 mills
Taxes	$224 (.080 x 2,800)

In some states tax rates are expressed in terms of dollars per $100 of assessed value. The above example for this system is:

Assessment	$ 2,800
Tax rate	$ 8
Taxes	$ 224 (28 x 8)

Widely varying assessment ratios and mill rates can produce the same tax burden on a property, depending on their combined influence. A major problem, however, is that far too often a community's supposed assessment ratio (for example 60% of market value) is actually not in effect. Although legally set at 60%, actual relationship to market value may be markedly different among similar properties or among different classifications of property.

The second step the appraiser takes is to compare the tax burden on the appraised property to that on competitive properties both in the subject community and in competing communities. One way to accomplish this is to compare the dollars of taxes directly with the market value. This is done by dividing the actual dollar amount of the tax burden on a property by the market value of the property, to give an effective rate of taxes on the property.

Market value $8,000
Taxes $224
Effective rate   .028 or 2.8% ($ 224 ÷ $8,000)

By using this direct comparison method, the appraiser finds how consistent the taxes within a community are and also how taxation in one community compares with competitive communities.

Unit-foot depth and corner premium tables are often used to establish uniformity between assessments in valuations made by assessors for tax purposes. The purpose of such tables is to express equivalent values for one foot of frontage applicable to sites of varying depth. The standard area of land represented has one foot of frontage, in a uniform lot width, and a specified depth. For a lot of any stated type or location, a standard depth is established. It originally was fixed in most localities at 100 feet. For example, if the adopted standard depth is 100 feet, a lot 50 by 100 feet worth $2,175 would have a unit-front-foot value of $43.50. Another lot, 50 feet wide and 150 feet deep, might be worth $2,500, or $50 per front foot, with the same unit-front-foot value of $43.50—that is, it would be equivalent in value to $43.50 per front foot for a depth of 100 feet, multiplied by a depth factor of 115%. The percentages are designed to provide a uniform system of measuring the additional value that accrues because of added depth.

One of the first depth rules was the 4-3-2-1 rule, which described a system where the front quarter of a lot contributed 40% of the value; the second quarter, 30%; the third quarter, 20%; and the fourth quarter, 10%. Because this left too wide a margin for assessment purposes, the deficiency usually has been overcome by the establishment of more specific depth tables expressed in percentages for every foot, or at least for every 10 feet of depth, to reflect the conditions applicable in a certain locality or to certain types of property (residential, business, industrial, commercial).

Similarly, corner influence (premium) tables have been developed for ad valorem tax purposes, to establish the amount by which the market value per unit foot of an inside lot is increased for a lot with a corner location. Such tables are also related to localities and types of land for which they are prepared.

Appraisers should use extreme caution in using any standard depth or corner influence (premium) table. The use of such tables is a major cause of nonuniform assessments. To apply a table established for one neighborhood or community to another area is not good appraisal practice. The only depth tables that might be useful would be those specifically constructed for the community and neighborhood in which the appraised property is located. Assessors are required in some communities to use them to provide equalizations.

• *Special Assessments.* These are levied by a specific district taxing authority for a definite period of time, usually for a public improvement such as sewers, street paving, sidewalk construction, etc. Usually the assessment is based on the benefits derived by the property from the improvement, rather than the cost of providing the improvement to a specific property. For example, it might cost $3,000 to provide sewers for one lot, and $1,000 to provide sewers for another lot in the same project area. The amount of the special assessment, however, should be equal, based on the assumption that the lots would be equally enhanced in value.

When a property is sold subject to a special assessment, adjustment must be made if comparable properties are not subject to the same special assessment. When a property is subject to special assessments that are greater than the value of the benefits derived, the property is reduced in value by the special assessment burden.

• *Zoning.* A part of the police power of the government, zoning gives the public the right to control the uses of private property for the benefit of the entire community. Zoning as it is known today did not exist during the 19th century, which was the major development period for most American cities. As a result of this lack of control and planning, cities developed with congested streets, overcrowded buildings, poor light and air, and a mixture of uses, each negatively affecting the others. From this disorganization came the deteriorated commercial areas, slums and urban blight of today. Uncontrolled social pressures increased the population density still further, resulting in the construction of large apartment houses that were built to the boundaries of their lots. People with enough money fled the cities into newly developing suburbs, a pattern that still exists today.

In the early 1900s, Los Angeles and Boston passed laws that controlled the use of land. In 1916 New York City passed the first truly comprehensive zoning law. Included in it were use districts, control of building heights and area coverage regulations. Shortly thereafter other cities passed zoning ordinances that stood up against many court challenges. By the middle of the 1920s the constitutionality of zoning laws, based upon the government's right to use its police power to regulate private property, was well established in legal precedent.

The zoning regulations of the 1920s were primarily concerned with height regulations and front, side and rear yard requirements, to ensure that the population had adequate light and air. By the late 1920s, zoning regulations began to emphasize the separation of residential neighborhoods from commercial and industrial uses. Also, high density apartments were segregated from low density single family areas.

Since World War II a new thrust in city zoning has occurred. These newer zoning regulations emphasize direct control of development and design in an effort to prevent further spread of urban congestion and decay. Zoning often restricts the use of a site that would be physically possible and economically feasible. In such cases, a change in zoning to permit such uses would change the highest and best use of the site. The highest and best use must always be a use that is legally permitted (see Chapter 8), but an appraiser must be alert to potential zoning changes. If there is a *reasonable probability* that the applicable zoning may be changed in the near future, the appraiser must consider how the market will react. Care must be taken not to anticipate changes that are only speculative. Residential properties are often bought and sold subject to the success of an application for zone change, such as from residential to more intensive apartment use or from residential to industrial or business use. The potential rezoning of nearby property may have a substantial effect on the value of the property being appraised.

Some suburban communities have attempted to use zoning as a method of preventing further growth, which is accomplished by increasing the minimum lot requirements to sizes greater than that necessary for orderly growth. Other requirements making it economically impossible to develop vacant land have been imposed in some areas, but growing social and legal pressures are being applied to stop the use of punative (or "exclusionary") zoning to restrict community growth. Ideally, zoning should be used to regulate and promote orderly and consistent development but should not be used to stop expansion. Good zoning fosters sound values, sufficient municipal services such as schools and parks and a climate of orderly growth without the stagnation of highly restrictive regulation.

A new type of zoning classification increasing in popularity is the planned unit development (PUD). Residences are grouped in clusters, with part of the land dedicated to open space for use by everyone. Ownership in the common land may be held by an owners' association or by the community. In its most advanced form, the PUD can actually be an entire city, where some of the nonresidential land is used for commercial and industrial development as well as recreational and open space use.

Not every community has resorted to zoning to control its development. There are vast areas of the country that are not governed by zoning regulations. Many of these areas are rural or sparsely populated and developed. However, one of the best anti-zoning arguments in the country is the metropolitan center of Houston, Texas. Without zoning, Houston has developed into one of our most modern, exciting cities. Several times the citizens of Houston have been asked to vote on the zoning question, and in every test, they have voted to remain an unzoned community.

The key to Houston's orderly development has been the use of deed restrictions and the enforcement of a rigid building code that includes control of density. By a special act of the Texas legislature, the enforcement of deed restrictions is the responsibility of the city attorney rather than the individual property owners. The deed restrictions are also enforced by the local lending institutions, which refuse to loan money for purposes that violate deed restrictions. In addition, Houston's civic clubs help enforce and police deed restrictions. There are problems, of course. Federal funds for urban renewal were withheld for a time, and in many areas the mixture of uses has caused severe losses in value for adjoining properties.

Older residential areas tend to be hastened through the last phase of their life cycle. Still, advocates of nonzoning make a strong case that land values and land uses should depend on the natural highest and best use of property, and not on the misguided whims or outright self-interest of local political appointees.

• *Building Codes*. These are specific restrictions that, like zoning regulations, are based on the police power. They provide design control of permitted buildings and delineate the types of materials that may be used. In addition to a general building code, many communities have separate electric and plumbing codes.

• *Deed Restrictions*. These limitations may be placed on the use of land by a property owner and will run with the title to the land as it passes on to future owners. Deed restrictions are contractual and are usually imposed by the deeds used to convey title. Sometimes deed restrictions are imposed on an entire tract by the developer of the land. Usually, the goal of such restrictions is to protect the value of all property in the development.

At one time, racial and religious restrictive covenants were not unusual in single family subdivisions. In the 1930s and early 1940s, the Federal Housing Administration sometimes required such restrictions as a condition of granting mortgage insurance. Restrictions of this kind have been unlawful for many years following a 1948 decision of the Supreme Court[1] and now violate many federal, state and local fair housing laws. Occasionally, deeds containing such racially restrictive covenants still appear but they are not enforceable.

• *Easements*. These are rights extended to nonowners of the fee for ingress and egress over property usually for specific purposes, such as access to a roadway or beach. Other easements give nonowners the right to use the air over the property or subsurface rights for utility installations, soil removal, flood control or mineral deposits. Appraisers must consider the effect of an easement on the value of the property and report this effect in the appraisal report. Normally, the value estimated includes the assumption that the property is free and clear of all easements. If this is not the case, the appraiser must take special care to evaluate and report the nature

---

[1]*Shelley* v. *Kramer*, 334 U.S.1, 68 S.Ct. 836

and effect of any easements so that the report will not be misleading.
• *Encroachments.* Two types of encroachment exist. Either the improvement may extend over the property line onto abutting properties or the improvements on abutting properties may encroach onto the subject site. The appraiser is not expected to make a survey to determine if there are any encroachments. Normally, a statement in the "limiting conditions" section of the report declares that the assumption is that there are no encroachments. However, as with easements, if an encroachment is evident, it must be reported in the appraisal and care must be taken not to mislead a potential user of the appraisal as to the effect of such encroachment.
• *Party Wall Agreements.* A party wall exists when improvements are so erected that one common wall is used by two abutting property owners. Many party walls exist without any written agreement. When such an agreement is part of a deed, the appraiser should ascertain whether it imposes any unusual requirements upon the owner of the property being appraised and include this in the report.
• *Environmental Restrictions.* Controls on land use are becoming more common and more important to appraisers. Like zoning regulations, they appear to be based on the police power of government, although some of the laws are still being tested in the courts. Appraisers must be familiar with current environmental developments that affect value, including wetland controls, flood hazard area designations and other land use restrictions.
• *Riparian Rights.* These deal with the rights of owners whose land abuts a body of water (lake, river, stream, ocean) with respect to the use of the water. These rights may include the right to construct piers, boathouses and other improvements over the water or may be for use of the body of water for fishing and recreational purposes or for irrigation. Riparian rights may have a substantial effect upon the value of the land and must be carefully considered where they apply.

The Physical Site

Every appraisal must contain an accurate, physical description of the site being appraised. Although much of the data can be obtained easily, some of it may prove to be more difficult to find or be totally unavailable. The appraisal report must state the assumptions that have been made about the nature of the property or site in the absence of precise information. For example, in the case of an un-improved lot, a soil test is usually desirable. In the absence of such a test, the appraiser should carefully point out that assumptions have been made as to the physical characteristics of the soil, and that the value estimate as given may be substantially different if these as-sumptions are not consistent with the actual conditions of the site.

Characteristics

• *Width and Frontage.* Although *width* and *frontage* are often used synonymously, they have two distinct meanings. *Width* is the distance between the side lines of a lot. When a lot is ir-regular in shape, the term *average width* is often used. Another important measurement is width at the building line. Many zoning regulations specify a minimum width at this point, which is required in order to permit the use of the site for construction of a particular type of improvement. *Frontage* refers to the length of one or more boundaries that abut a thoroughfare or accessway the lot faces. In the valuation of residential lots, "front feet" are often used as units of comparison (see Chapter 9, "Site Valuation"), but the importance of frontage appears to vary from one location to another. Care must be exercised in using front footage as the unit of comparison for resi-dential lots. Once a lot meets the standard size acceptable in the neighborhood, excess frontage does not always add proportionately to the value of the lot.

• *Depth.* Depth is always considered together with the width and frontage of a lot. Most residential neighborhoods have a standard acceptable lot depth so that lots with less depth sell for less, and lots with excess depth sell at a premium. The penalty or premium paid for depth considerations, however, is rarely directly proportionate to the actual footage involved.

The problem of varying and disproportionate increases or de-creases in value relative to changes in depth may be analyzed by constructing a table or formula to reflect these value changes. These depth tables are popular with assessors and other mass appraisers who staunchly defend their use, claiming that the tables can be con-structed and adjusted to work in different neighborhoods. Theoreti-cally, this may be possible; nevertheless, depth tables have been so widely misused and misunderstood that most professional appraisers avoid using them altogether, unless they are absolutely convinced that a particular table truly applies to the neighborhood of the property being appraised. Some rules of behavior do apply to many residential lots, which the appraiser should know about when considering the influence of depth:

1. As the depth of a lot decreases from that of the typical lot in the neighborhood, its value per front foot decreases, but its value per square foot or per acre increases.
2. As the depth of a lot increases beyond that of the typical lot in the neighborhood, the value per front foot increases, but its value per square foot or per acre decreases.

• *Shape.* The shape of a lot affects the value of the lot differently from one neighborhood to another. In some areas, irregularity of shape may decrease value; in other areas, as long as the lot is suitable for a house, little difference appears to exist between the value of regularly and irregularly shaped lots. If the irregular lot shape results in increased construction costs, however, it would probably decrease the value of the lot. The value of irregularly shaped parcels is usually indicated in dollars per square foot of area or in dollars per acre.

• *Size.* If value were directly related only to size, the unit of comparison (such as square feet or acre) for lot values would always be value per square foot or value per acre. However, frontage, width, depth and shape interplay with size and together affect value.

Plottage value is the increase in unit value resulting from improved utility when smaller plots are combined to form a larger one. To accommodate a substantial building development, small plots may be assembled, often from different owners. This procedure usually entails extra costs, and key parcels may need to be purchased for more than their individual land value, either because they are already improved or because of a negotiating disadvantage.

After assembly, the project must support the excess costs of the land in addition to other capital costs involved. It is not the cost of assembly that creates plottage value. Size itself is no guarantee of a plottage increment in value. For plottage value to be realized, there must be the potential of a higher and more profitable use. Otherwise, the whole could not be worth more than the sum of its parts, as is the case with plottage.

The area of a lot can also be divided into its effective area and its excess land. Usually the excess land (particularly if it cannot be used) is worth substantially less per unit of measurement than that part of the lot within the effective (usable) area.

• *Corner and Cul-de-Sac Influences.* Historically, because a corner location provides more light and air and may afford more prominence on a particular street, it was thought to have more value. However, a corner lot also has less privacy and often is taxed at a higher rate. It also may be subject to more noise and more passing traffic. The appraiser must make a judgment, based on the specific lot and its market, if a corner location adds or detracts from the value when the property is compared with other lots in the neighborhood. Lots located at the end of dead-end streets that have cul-de-sacs for turnarounds also may have different values from similar lots without the cul-de-sac influence. Again, no universal rule applies, and the appraiser must look to the market for evidence of the effects of location on value.

• *Contour and Topography.* Probably the most desirable residential lot is one that slopes up gently from the street to where the house is located, and then slopes downward steeply enough so that there can be a walkout basement door leading directly to the rear yard recreation area. Again, what is true for one neighborhood is not necessarily the case for other areas. Sites tend to have lower value if they are costly to improve because of extreme topographical conditions. A lot higher or lower than the abutting street level may create additional costs to correct poor drainage, erosion, or accessibility problems. Sometimes, however, difficult conditions are offset by advantages recognized in the market, such as a scenic view or extra privacy. Another factor to be considered is the amount of site work required to make the site buildable. If there is bedrock, excess excavation costs may be incurred. In some cases a site may require fill, or it may have excess fill that can be sold.

• *Surface Soil.* In many areas the soil's ability to support a lawn and landscaping is an important factor in the marketability of the property. An appraiser should note whether the soil appears to be suitable and typical of the surrounding neighborhood. When appraising a new subdivision, the appraiser should determine if the natural surface soil (topsoil) will be replaced at the end of the construction process or whether it is being stripped during site preparation. A trend today among developers is to disturb as little as possible the natural growth and topsoil during the building process. A naturally sandy or rocky soil may require the extra expense of purchased topsoil to support future lawns and landscaping.

• *Subsoil.* The character of subsoil definitely affects the cost of preparing a site for building; it can also influence the design of the structure that can be erected on the site. If bedrock must be blasted, or if the soil is unstable, the cost of improvements is increased. Soil conditions are usually determined by an engineering study of the bearing quality of the soil and its suitability for foundations. Extra expense is entailed for foundation walls and the sinking of piles if a site must be filled in. Underground tunnels can present a hazard in mining districts. The appraiser must include a consideration of such possibilities in a thorough site analysis.

• *Landscaping.* Natural trees and shrubs are usually considered part of the land itself. Landscaping is treated separately by most appraisers as a site improvement. Lawns, shrubbery, gardens and plantings in general improve the appearance and desirability of residential properties. However, because plantings are a matter of individual taste and will deteriorate rapidly without good care, typical buyers are inclined to discount the cost of replacing such plantings. Although such improvements are usually regarded as an asset, their contribution to the value of a property will vary with location and character.

• *Surface and Storm Water Disposal.* Some method must be provided to drain the site of surface and storm water. It may be a simple swale that channels the water off the surface of the lot to the street or into some natural drainage. When the lot is level or slopes away from the water disposal area, storm sewers must be constructed. In some areas, the leaders or downspouts that collect rain falling on the house may be connected into the storm water disposal pipes. When a house has a basement, footing drains are needed to carry the water from under the basement to prevent leaks from developing. When the house is built on a slope, special care must be taken to keep the surface water away from the sides of the house.

• *Water.* Every house requires an adequate supply of water of acceptable quality. Water can be obtained from a municipal or private company or from a well. Common sense and the FHA Minimum Property Standards require that when a public water supply is available, it should be used. Some houses still obtain water directly from rivers, streams, lakes and even rain water collected from the roof and stored in tanks. None of these systems is considered satisfactory, since they will not consistently supply an adequate quantity of safe water. When water is supplied by a public or publicly regulated company, the appraiser usually need only check on its availability at the site, including whether there is sufficient pressure. When the water is supplied by a smaller, unregulated company, this must be reported and the dependability of the supply must be analyzed. Wells, either artesian or shallow, should be capable of delivering a sustained flow of five gallons per minute. The water should meet the standard bacteriological and chemical requirements of the local health authorities.

When appraising vacant land not on a public water supply, the appraiser should check surrounding properties where wells have been dug to determine the probability of an adequate water supply being found for the property being appraised.

• *Waste Disposal.* Few will argue the substantial advantage of being connected to a municipal sewer system. It is estimated, however, that almost 50 million people in 15 million homes depend on septic systems for their waste disposal and that 25% of new houses being constructed do not connect to municipal systems. If no public sewer exists, a percolation test must be made to determine if the soil can absorb the runoff from a septic system.

A typical septic system consists of a large concrete tank buried in the ground. One end accepts waste materials from the house drainage line. Once inside the tank, wastes tend to separate into three parts. The solid wastes (only about 1% of the total) sink to the bottom. The grease (also less than 1% of the total volume) rises to the top. The rest is liquid. Bacteria in the tank decompose the solid wastes and grease, and a relatively clear liquid flows from the opposite end through the drain line, either to a distribution box, which directs the liquid into a network of buried perforated pipes called a leaching field, or into a seepage pit. From here the liquid runs off into the ground and is absorbed.

• *Installation of Public Utilities to the Site.* Included in the value of a site is the cost of bringing water, electricity, gas, telephone, and storm and sanitary sewers to the site. A recent addition to this list is cable television. The site may have additional value because of the availability of these utilities even if they are not connected to the subject house. It is not unusual to find a house still using a well or septic system even where public water and sanitary sewers are available.

• *Access (Streets and Alleys).* A site cannot be used unless there is some type of usable access. It may be a right-of-way over abutting property or a private driveway or street. Access may also take the form of a public street or alley. When access is not by public street, special attention should be given to who maintains the street and if lending institutions servicing the neighborhood give mortgages on houses without public access.

• *Street Improvements.* The description of a site should also include information about street improvements, such as the width of the street, how it is paved, and the condition of the pavement. In some areas, lenders require substantial details about private streets when they represent the only frontage for a property. Also to be reported are details about the sidewalks, curbs, gutters and street lighting.

• *Site Improvements.* In addition to utility connections, which sometimes are classified as site improvements, a variety of other site improvements are typically found on an improved residential lot. These include fences, walls, sidewalks and driveways, pools and patios, tennis courts and other recreational facilities. These all must be described in the appraisal report, and an analysis must be made as to their contribution to the value of the property.

• *View.* The view enjoyed from a property may substantially affect its value. Lots in the same neighborhood that are identical in all respects except location and orientation have markedly different values which are directly attributable to the effect of the superior view one enjoys. The most popular views are of water, mountains and valleys. Conversely, a poor view reduces value.

• *Hazards.* Sometimes hazards exist in the neighborhood that reduce the value of a property. The most common hazard is heavy traffic, and the market will definitely recognize and penalize this problem. The awareness of flood hazards has become quite important in many parts of the country now that many lenders cannot issue a mortgage in a flood hazard area without flood insurance (see Appendix F). An appraiser must learn whether the site is in an identified flood hazard area, and if so, if flood insurance is available and at what cost. The effect on value must also be considered and reported in the appraisal. Other hazards that should be investigated include potential slides, earthquakes, dangerous ravines and bodies of water, or any unusual fire danger.

• *Nuisances.* A variety of services contribute to the value of a site when they are in the neighborhood but detract from value when they are too close. For example, a fire house, public school, stores, restaurants, hospital, medical offices and gas station are desirable nearby but not immediately adjacent. Industries, large commercial buildings and offices, noisy highways, utility poles and high tension wires, motels and hotels, funeral parlors and vacant houses all generally detract from property values when they are located in a residential neighborhood.

• *Climatic or Meteorological Conditions.* Generally, climate affects the whole region or community and should be reported and analyzed in that section of the appraisal report. Sometimes these conditions specifically affect the value of the site being appraised. In some regions there may be an increase in the value of lots that face a certain direction. For example, if prevailing winds are consistent, lots may be favorably or adversely affected by their relation to the direction of the wind.

Relationship to Surroundings

Because the location of a site is fixed, its surroundings have a significant effect on value. Much of this location effect has been covered in the region, community and neighborhood analyses. To be considered here is the relationship of the specific site to its immediate environment.

Considerations

• *Use of Nearby Lots.* The use of the immediately adjacent lots is of great importance to the value of a property. The principle of conformity states that to obtain maximum value, the improvements of the property being appraised should reasonably conform to those on surrounding lots. For example, if neighboring lots are improved with medium-value, colonial-style, multi-story houses, the appraiser might seriously question the appropriateness of plans for construction of a high-priced, extremely contemporary, split-level on the site being appraised. However, it is not always necessary to conform to obtain maximum value.

• *Orientation of Improvements.* Again, the principle of conformity applies in the orientation of the improvements. If the abutting houses are set back 75 feet from the street and face out towards it, it will probably be difficult to orient the house on the subject lot differently, even if such orientation (such as with the living/social zones facing towards the rear yard) would seem preferable.

• *Abutting and Nearby Streets and Traffic Flow.* Abutting and nearby streets may be in the older grid pattern or the newer style of dead-end or limited-access streets. Some streets in a neighborhood will become thoroughfares and suffer from heavy traffic flow. Access by a back alley or a special service road adds to or detracts from value.

• *Public Transportation.* The value of a residential lot is affected by the availability of public transportation. Most important is the availability of such transportation to places of work and to shopping and recreational areas. Changes in the availability of public transportation can affect the value of property. New systems, such as San Francisco's BART rapid transit system, increase values in the area but deteriorating systems tend to decrease values. The quality and quantity of public highways leading from the property being appraised to places of work, shopping and recreation also have an effect on property values.

• *Access by Car.* Automobile access to work, shopping and recreation areas substantially affects value. Lots that slope steeply upward toward the street are less desirable than level lots or lots that slope downwards. It is dangerous to have to back into traffic or be forced to enter on a curve or hill where visibility from oncoming cars is limited; and the market will penalize a site for these problems.

• *Safety of Children from Vehicular Traffic.* The sheer volume of traffic is not the only safety consideration of parents with smaller children. Traffic and speed controls and sidewalks from the site to places such as schools and parks are also important factors. Another important point is the availability of places away from the streets for children to play.

Economic Factors

Many economic factors have already been discussed in the regional, community and neighborhood analyses. Some economic factors apply specifically to the individual site under appraisal rather than to larger areas.

Considerations

• *Prices of Nearby Lots.* The price of nearby lots offered for sale has at least a short-range effect on the value of a site. The principle of substitution would limit the price paid for the lot being appraised to that for which similar lots in the neighborhood could be purchased, at least until the supply was exhausted.

• *Tax Burden Compared to Competitive Lots.* If assessments are not uniform, lots with excessive tax burdens are depressed in value at least temporarily by the excess levy. The reverse would also be true; lots that are underassessed might be expected to bring a premium.

• *Utility and Service Costs.* If location necessitates incurring extra costs to bring utilities to a site, the market may recognize a parallel decrease in the value of the lot.

• *Service Cost.* Some lots are not eligible for municipal services such as garbage collection because they are not on public streets. These services must be purchased privately, which would decrease the value of the site.

Summary

The site data and analysis portion of the appraisal should first positively identify and describe the property being appraised. A deed description and survey, together with a neighborhood and community map, is the ideal way. Other shortcut methods are acceptable only if the property being appraised is positively identified.

Data is gathered and organized into four categories: (1) title and record data; (2) on-site physical characteristics; (3) relationship to surroundings; and (4) economic factors.

All of the data is carefully considered and analyzed in relation to the appraised site. Relevant material is reconciled and processed for use in the highest and best use analysis, which forms the basis of the appraisal.

Review Questions

1. Define the terms "land" and "site" and explain how they differ.
2. Give three reasons why a separate site valuation may be needed.
3. Into what four categories is site data organized?
4. How might the exact location of a property be established?
5. What is ad valorem taxation?
6. What is the best way to compare the taxation of two competing properties?
7. Why does the appraiser analyze tax rates of the property being appraised?
8. What is a special assessment?
9. What is an easement? an encroachment? riparian rights? party wall agreements?
10. List at least 10 physical characteristics the appraiser should consider when describing a site.
11. What are some of the factors of a site's immediate environment that should be considered by the appraiser?

8

Highest and Best Use Analysis

This chapter discusses the highest and best use analysis of the two major elements of a residential property—the site and the improvements thereon. Appraisal theory has long supported the concept of the highest and best use of the site. Only recently has the concept been developed of the highest and best use of improvement on the site—the house or other major buildings "as improved."

For a site to have value, it must have utility and be in demand. In highest and best use analysis, the appraiser considers that use among all options that most fully develops a site's potential utility. Highest and best use analysis should form the base on which the appraiser builds the three traditional approaches to value.

Definition

Highest and best use is defined as "that reasonable and probable use that will support the highest present value, as defined, as of the effective date of the appraisal."[1] Alternatively, it is "that use, from among reasonable, probable and legal alternative uses, found to be physically possible, appropriately supported, financially feasible, and which results in highest land value."[2] Simply stated, the highest and best use of a site is "the perfect improvement that can be constructed on the site which will produce the maximum rate of return on the capital invested."[3]

Highest and Best Use "As if Vacant"

Highest and best use analysis is always done in two steps. First the

---

[1] *Real Estate Appraisal Terminology, op. cit.*, p. 107.
[2] *Ibid.*
[3] Henry S. Harrison, "The Residential Appraiser: 'Highest and Best Use Analysis of a Single Family House,'" *The Real Estate Appraiser*, March/April 1975, pp. 48-49.

site is analyzed as if vacant. After the highest and best use of the site has been estimated, the property is analyzed considering the existing improvements.

The Four Tests

To estimate the highest and best use of a site, the appraiser utilizes four tests. The projected use must meet all four of these tests:

1. Legally permitted.
2. Physically possible.
3. Economically feasible.
4. *Most* profitable.

Each potential use of a property is considered by the appraiser in terms of these four tests. If a proposed use fails to meet any of the tests, it is discarded and another use is reviewed. The highest and best use meets all four tests.

• *Legally Permitted.* Each use must be tested first to see if it is legally permitted on the site. Public legal restrictions consist of zoning regulations, building codes, environmental regulations and other applicable ordinances. Private restrictions are limitations that run with the land and are passed from owner to owner. Generally they are imposed by the developer of the tract who attempts to preserve the value of the entire development by restricting what can be done with individual lots. Easements, encroachments, party wall agreements and the like also restrict the development of a site.

A gasoline station, for example, may appear to be the highest and best use for a level corner lot at the intersection of two major traffic arteries. The appraiser cannot consider this to be the highest and best use of this site unless it is legally permitted by the zoning regulations in effect or unless there is a high degree of probability that existing zoning can be changed within the near future to permit such development.

Occasionally a site is clearly not being utilized to its highest and best use, not because of any lack of market demand or physical suitability but solely due to legal restrictions. Since the land is usually zoned according to a political-social scheme rather than an economic one, zoning frequently does not conform to current market requirements. In such cases, the land remains economically under-utilized until the prescribed limitations are lifted. If the land manifests more valuable potential use than allowed by law and if there is reasonable probability that a change in use will be permitted at some point in the near future, this must be considered by the appraiser.

In such a situation, the appraiser must be extremely careful that the value estimate is not speculative, but rather that the market "would widely recognize the strong possibility of a zoning change,"[4] and that "a high degree of probability (exists) that the zoning can be changed within the very near future."[5] The effect of probable change on market value is the added premium that prospective purchasers (the market) would pay after giving due consideration to time and expense factors involved in obtaining the change.

● *Physically Possible (Suitable).* The use of a site must be physically possible. Uses might be limited by the physical characteristics of a site, such as size, frontage, topography, soil and subsoil conditions and climatic conditions. Despite the need for single family residential housing, an area of severe terrain with poor subsoil characteristics cannot be considered appropriate for such development. For example, sites along earthquake fault lines in California are not considered safe for house construction. Flood plains are also considered unsuitable for house construction. A corridor in the Palm Springs, California, area is considered undesirable because prevailing winds from the coast carry smog and fog.

● *Economically Feasible.* A realistic assessment of market demand for a proposed use is a critical factor.

For example, acreage may be available that is zoned for single family residential use of a certain concentration, served by all utilities and with good proximity and access; however, similar subdivisions already in the market have remained unsold for some time. There is no need for the addition of such lots and so even though the property meets the first two tests, it fails economic feasibility. Thus, market demand acts to create highest and best use. In reviewing alternative uses, therefore, the appraiser must consider the demand for each use and the other available competitive land suitable for that use,

___

[4]Harrison, *op. cit.*, p. 48-49.
[5]Ibid.

which constitutes the supply. These factors must be weighed in the economic analysis. All physically possible and legal uses that fail to meet the test of economic feasibility are discarded. The remaining uses produce some net return to the property.

• *Most Profitable.* The fourth test is essentially a test for maximum return. The appraiser is seeking the most profitable among all legally permitted, physically suitable, and economically feasible uses.

Because change is constantly occurring, the existing use of land is often no longer the highest and best use. If the land alone has a higher value under an alternative physically suitable, legally permitted use than the whole property as currently improved and utilized, the proposed use becomes the highest and best use. The existing improvement is at the end of its economic life but it still will be the highest and best use during the transition period. For example:

Market value of site zoned for commercial use (highest and best use, as if vacant)	$23,000
Market value of property as currently improved, for residential use	20,000
Contribution of improvement	None

The highest and best use of this property is no longer the existing use, except during the transition period.

Use as Single Family Residence

Once the decision has been made that single family residential use is the highest and best use of a property, the appraiser must describe the "perfect" improvement that should be built on the site. Such a house would take advantage of all the factors analyzed in the community, neighborhood and site sections of the appraisal report. Also considered are the structural type and architectural style of this "ideal" house, its size, number of rooms, layout, quality of construction, kinds of material, mechanical systems and special features.

The principle of conformity tends to set the size, price range and other characteristics of the ideal improvement since houses that are similar to others in the neighborhood will normally have the highest ratio of value to cost. Once the house size has been determined, the structural type should be considered. Generally, single family houses can be classified into one of eight major types.

These include 1-story; 1-1/2-story; 2-story; 2-1/2-story; 3 or more stories; bilevel or split entry (raised ranch) houses, split levels and mansions. Two- and three-story houses were popular before 1900 but are not as common today as the split entry or one-story house.

Once the ideal size and type of house have been chosen, the architectural style should be decided. The neighborhood may call for a traditional colonial look, or one of the popular French or English styles, with special window treatments and exposed half-timbering. In Santa Fe, New Mexico, modern homes in some neighborhoods conform to the highest and best use *only* if they are built in the accepted pueblo or adobe style. In general, good design produces maximum value, regardless of whether the structural configuration or architectural style of a house is traditional or contemporary.

The next step in highest and best use analysis is to consider the market preferences for interior design. The number of bedrooms, baths and types and sizes of various auxiliary rooms in the ideal improvement vary greatly from neighborhood to neighborhood.

By completing this type of detailed improvement analysis, the appraiser describes the perfect improvement that should be constructed on the site, if it were vacant. If the appraisal is of a piece of unimproved residential land, this would conclude the highest and best use analysis.

Theory of Consistent Use

The theory of consistent use is basic to appraisal practice and highest and best use analysis. A property nearing transition to a new use *cannot* be valued on the basis of one use for land and another for improvements. The improvements must add to the value of the land to have value attributed to them.

The land is always valued first and as if vacant. If the buildings existing on the site add to the value of the overall property, even if their presence restricts it to a less intensive use, the existing use continues to be potentially the highest and best use. Only when no value may be attributed to such improvements, or they represent a negative value (burden) to the property, does an alternative use become the highest and best use.

An illustration of the violation of the consistent use theory in valuing a site is shown in the following example. A turn of the century house is located on a corner lot, where both main thoroughfares are moving to nonresidential uses. Recent rezoning permits business use and the corner being considered is so classified to permit the construction of a service station. The house converted to apartments is still being used. An uninformed appraiser learns from the market that such corners have been selling for service station sites for $70,000. Then, in violation of the consistent use theory, the appraiser adds to site value a value for the building of $30,000, totalling $100,000. The correct consideration is to accept the $70,000 for the site "as if vacant." To make it vacant, demolition costs of $5,000 are estimated. The market value of the site in its highest and best use, therefore, is $65,000 ($70,000 − $5,000).

Highest and Best Use "As Improved"

Often the appraisal is of an existing house that has not reached —or appears to be reaching—the end of its economic life. It may be an older house in an established neighborhood of older homes, conforming substantially to the houses in the neighborhood. Again, as with the analysis of the site as if vacant, the appraiser must determine what is the perfect improvement for the site. However, the appraiser must consider utilization of the existing improvements to obtain the maximum profit. If there is a house on the site, the appraiser must estimate what can be done to make it the most profitable use of the site. Any improvement that will add more value than the cost to produce it should be considered in this analysis. These improvements might range from simple repairs to major remodeling, modernization or rehabilitation.

An existing use may be nearing the end of its economic life but still be the highest and best use of the site at this point in time. If the existing house still contributes to the overall value of the total property, it continues to have utility; for example:

Market value of property as currently improved for residential use	$26,000
Market value of a site zoned for commercial use (highest and best use, as if vacant)	23,000
Contribution of the structure	$ 3,000

Although the highest and best use of this property, as if vacant, is different from the existing use, the old residential structure continues to add to the total value of the property. Thus, the existing residential use is the best use of the site for the remaining economic life of the structure.

Frequently, a site is improved with a building that is at the extreme end of its economic life. Such use is often an "interim use," a temporary use of the property until the time when the ultimate highest and best use can be attained. A downtown property utilized as a residence may not appear to be the highest and best use of the land, but it may still contribute enough additional income to the owner to justify its continuation as a "tax payer" while plans and financing arrangements are completed for more profitable development in the future. In an area where demand has not created an active market, an interim use may be necessary to hold the property until a more favorable market response is noted. A parcel of land suitable for a residential subdivision, for example, may be marginally farmed until such time as the residential housing market will support the conversion to several new building lots.

The appraiser must realize that the highest and best use of a property *as improved* often differs from the highest and best use of the site *as if vacant.*

Summary

To determine highest and best use, the appraiser first analyzes the site as if vacant and determines what the perfect improvement for such a site would be. Four tests are applied to the proposed uses. Only the use that meets all four tests (legally permitted, physically possible, economically feasible and most profitable) is the highest and best use.

Next the appraiser analyzes the property as improved. If the value of the site and its improvements, maintained in its present use, is *less than* the value of the site if vacant and available for alternative use, the present improvements are no longer potentially the highest and best use. If the present improvement in its existing program of utilization produces a higher value for the property than if the site were vacant, the current use is the potentially highest and best use.

The appraiser must analyze the existing improvements to see what rehabilitation, modernization or remodeling is needed to produce the maximum profit (see Chapter 10). The improvements as they would be when renovated would be the highest and best use of the property "as improved."

Review Questions

1. Define "highest and best use" in your own words.
2. What four tests are applied to estimate the highest and best use of a site?
3. When may a use not permitted by existing zoning regulations be considered the highest and best use?
4. Can the highest and best use of a property as improved differ from that of the site as if vacant? Explain.
5. Will existing use always be the highest and best use? Explain.
6. After the appraiser estimates the highest and best use of a site is a single family residence, what description is then developed?
7. Explain the term "interim use."
8. Explain the theory of consistent use.
9. Explain why land (site) is always valued first and as if vacant.

9

Site Valuation

The only source of market values for sites is the market itself, inasmuch as land cannot be produced or built like improvements. Sales and other market information about similar, comparable sites provide a basis for estimating the market value of the site being appraised. Thus site values are primarily a reflection of market activity. The interaction of supply and demand produces prices that are the source of market value of sites.

Two basic procedures for estimating market value of individual residential sites are:

1. *The Comparative Procedure,* which involves comparison and contrast of similar sites with the site being appraised.
2. *The Allocation Procedure,* which requires the appraiser to divide the overall price or market value of a residential property between site and site improvements (including structures).

The Comparative Procedure

The comparative procedure is based on comparing and contrasting pertinent data of comparable sites that have actually sold with the site being appraised. It is the most popular and practical site valuation procedure. The appraiser may also consider offering and listing prices and other market information, but primary attention is given to actual sales of like sites, consummated under typical market conditions as close to the date of the appraisal as possible. Sellers may offer a property at any price they choose, and potential purchasers may bid any price they like; but it is the actual selling price of a site (a figure acceptable to both buyer and seller) that best reflects market conditions.

As discussed in Chapter 2, market value is intended to describe the results of the interaction of buyers and sellers operating in an *open* market, all parties being knowledgeable, willing and able. Thus, having exposed the real estate in the open market for a reasonable period of time, the result is an agreed upon price that is recognized as market value. The comparative procedure results in the development of market values of sites by converting sale prices (and sometimes other evidence) into market value for the site being appraised.

Appraisers are cautioned to consider and, if possible, adjust for any unusual pressures present in sales being used as market data. Obviously, the threat of foreclosure, the need to sell or buy rapidly or changes in local zoning regulations resulting in different potential uses all have a strong effect on selling price. Also, prices paid by federal or local governments usually are not acceptable as open market transactions because of the possibility that compulsion was involved, which eliminates the willing buyer-willing seller concept.

Classification and Analysis of Data

All pertinent market data regarding comparables should be organized so that it can be retrieved quickly in a format that promotes easy and accurate comparison with the residential lot being appraised. To qualify as an acceptable comparable sale, the details of each transaction must be verified. Hearsay evidence is not sufficient since the bona fide nature of each comparable used must be unquestioned. The use of key-sort record cards is a practical and efficient technique. A more expensive method is the computer which produces instant and comprehensive recall of all stored facts. Many professional appraisal organizations are moving toward the development and use of elaborate computer systems.

The process of comparing the property being appraised with others in the market always involves two components — *elements of comparison* and *units of comparison*. To organize better the comparison process, a standard format is recommended. In this process, the appraiser is more exact and efficient by following guidelines that have been developed by practicing appraisers.

Elements of Comparison

Appraisers use four elements of comparison when considering the comparability of like sites; they are:

1. Time or date of sale.
2. Physical characteristics.
3. Location.
4. Conditions of sale.

Professional appraisers generally accept that these four encompass every possible consideration necessary to extract market value from market prices.

• *Time or Date of Sale.* The process of comparing the date of the appraisal with the date of sale of the comparables recognizes that market conditions do change from time to time. This process determines if the comparable sale took place under the same or similar market conditions prevailing on the date of the appraisal. Sometimes market conditions remain relatively stable for a year or more; at other times they may change within a three- to six-month period, or even less.[1] The interaction of demand and supply affects prices; if one or the other or both change, prices adjust accordingly. In either a seller's market or a buyer's market, price changes occur. This is the type of phenomenon that the appraiser must investigate, identify and compensate for in this step of the comparative procedure.

Judgments regarding the element of time of sale are made by a close study of market conditions prevailing at the time of the appraisal, compared and contrasted with those prevailing at the time of the sale of the comparable. If the comparable was sold in a market similar to that prevailing at the time of the appraisal, no adjustment need be made. If, however, the appraiser recognizes that market conditions varied considerably between the two dates, an adjustment must be made.

---

[1] In the process of analyzing the differences in the market from the time of the appraisal to the time of the sale, strange phenomena may be encountered. One may tend to think that market prices and costs are even and steady in their change—that is, going up 4% per year, or remaining the same throughout a year, or declining 2% per year. This, however, may not be realistic. Markets are known for their erratic activity in short periods of time; such activity may be cyclical, seasonal or a combination of both. There may be short periods of time in an annual market period that will have very erratic activity, but the average for the whole year would not identify it as such. For example, average increase for the last calendar year may be 6%; however, a closer scrutiny reveals that all of this was experienced in the last quarter of the year. Use of sales data from the first three quarters would have to be adjusted accordingly. Thus the monthly average increase is *not* 1/2% nor is each quarterly average increase 1½%.

Although probably not adequate in itself to justify a difference between two markets, the simplest example is the situation in which a residential site sold one year ago in an open market situation after a reasonable listing period. Then for justifiable reasons, it sold again just two months ago for $1,200 more than the earlier price. This illustrates a singular example of the change in the market between two time periods expressed by the difference in the two sales prices. It also illustrates the kind of process the appraiser must apply to identify dollar or percentage adjustments between markets. An intimate knowledge of the market is necessary to establish the amount of the adjustment and a continuous collection and storing of data is essential to reach a defensible conclusion.

• *Physical Characteristics.* In this comparison process only major physical similarities and differences are identified and considered. A physical inspection of each comparable is desirable. The. appraiser must be reasonably well-informed about the basic soil conditions and physical characteristics of the comparable sites being used so that justifiable adjustments can be made between them and the property being appraised.

If a great number of physical differences exist between the properties, the sale probably should not be used as a comparable. If there are none or only a few such differences, it may be a justifiable and usable comparable.

The same procedure for determining the amount of adjustment for differences in physical characteristics is followed as for the other elements of comparison. Professional appraisers rely heavily on the local, active market from which to extract dollar (or percentage) amounts. The "matched pair" technique may be used.

If there are two lots which are comparable in all respects except depth, one lot having 20 extra feet of depth, which sold for $250 more than the other lot, it is reasonable to conclude that the market paid $250 more for the extra depth of 20 feet. Such conclusions, however, should be supported by more than one pair of sales. The greater the number of sales to support dollar (or percentage) adjustment figures, the more convincing the appraiser's conclusions.

When necessary, pairs of sales can be used to extract adjustments from the market even when there are two or more differences between the sales. One sale is selected as a base sale and all known differences between it and the other sale are adjusted for. The remaining difference is then attributed to any remaining unadjusted difference between the sales. (This technique is explained in greater detail in Chapter 13, starting on page 248.)

Among other items to be considered are such things as:

1. Inside lot compared to a corner lot.
2. A rectangular lot compared with an odd-shaped lot (five- or six-sided).
3. Difference in storm water disposal (one area has no facilities, another is well-drained by storm sewer; the market probably would adjust for this difference).
4. Difference between a lot which is flat and relatively easy to build on and one which drops 20 feet below the street level.

• *Location.* The third element of comparison to be considered is that of location. Much emphasis has already been made of the importance of neighborhood influence on marketability of sites. Chapter 6 outlined in detail the physical, social, economic, and governmental factors to be considered in analyzing neighborhoods.

If a comparable site is in the same neighborhood as the appraised site, then there is a likelihood that no neighborhood adjustment would be made. In rare instances, if it were on the edge of a neighborhood and subject to either some beneficial or undesirable elements, neither of which affected the site being appraised, an adjustment must be made. If, however, the neighborhood has been properly identified, it is unlikely that differences in schools, parks, and other kinds of important neighborhood considerations will exist.

In the event a site being considered as a comparable is located in a different neighborhood from the property being appraised, a more thorough analysis must be made of possible differences between the two neighborhoods. It should be recognized, however, that two separate neighborhoods may be very similar in all respects and no adjustments need be made. On the other hand, if there are major differences between the two neighborhoods, appropriate adjustments must be calculated.

For example, the neighborhood of the appraised site may be served by excellent schools in close proximity to the site. In contrast, the comparable may be located in a neighborhood with less desirable schools much farther away. The market typically would recognize both factors and pay accordingly. To estimate the difference in price for these two variations, the matched pair system can be used again. That is, the comparable in a different neighborhood is compared with an identical site that has sold in the subject's neighborhood. If the former has a lower sale price, this is an indication of the difference the market recognizes in the two neighborhoods because of the school situation.

Many other kinds of neighborhood differences, such as variations in deed restrictions, zoning and building codes, must be considered and if they are major, an adjustment must be made.

• *Conditions of Sale.* This element of comparison is probably the most difficult to extract from the market and for which to make adjustment. It refers to the circumstances under which both buyer and seller make their decisions to purchase and sell a specific residential site. By definition, market value requires a willing, informed and able purchaser and a willing and informed seller. Quite often, however, and probably more frequently than is generally realized, there are more than normal compulsions to buy or sell. An obvious situation of unusual pressure is a condition of bankruptcy.

Financing conditions are also considered in this element. If conventional financing is typical for the purchase of the type of site in question, comparables that have sold with 100% financing, on conditional sales contracts or with a type of financing other than conventional require special analysis and judgment. If such special conditions produce a price different from that which would have been paid with conventional financing, an adjustment must be made. The conditions of financing, which include the amount of interest charged, the length of the mortgage and the ratio of loan to value, must be analyzed for every sale. When there are substantial differences between the comparables and the property being appraised, either a percentage or dollar adjustment must be made. This again must be extracted from the market and requires thorough and complete analysis of the circumstances involved.

The conditions of sale element is often difficult to prove in the market. Even if certain conditions are recognized, it may be difficult to apply an appropriate or justifiable dollar or percentage adjustment

FIG. 9-1: Site Sale Adjustment Grid

Element of Comparison	Site Being Appraised	Comparable Lot Sale 1		Comparable Lot Sale 2	
		Description	Adjustment	Description	Adjustment
Time (date) of sale[1]					
Physical characteristics[2]					
Location[3]					
Conditions of sale					
Total adjustments					

[1]Date of appraisal for the site being appraised.

[2]A listing of *major* physical characteristics that are different between the property being appraised and comparable sales, such as depth of lots or terrain characteristics.

[3]Identification of the neighborhood by subdivision or other acceptable area description.

for the differences between the property being appraised and the comparable in the market. Some professional appraisers feel strongly that if the conditions of the sale are different from those applying to the property being appraised, the sale should not be used as a comparable. Others feel that if reasonable adjustments can be made for conditions of the sale, it is permissible to use it in this procedure to reach an indication of the market value of the residential lot being appraised.

The analysis of pertinent data about the site being appraised and comparable sales can be facilitated by developing a grid that lists the four elements, comparing those of the site being appraised with comparables (Fig. 9-1).

Making Adjustments Using Units of Comparison

Adjustments for differences between the site being appraised and the comparables may be made in dollars or in percentages (see Figures 9-2 and 9-3). If dollar adjustments are used, they may be based on either total price of the whole property or on other units of comparison, such as price per square foot, per front foot (designated F/F) or per acre. Depending on local custom and practice, units of comparison may be used rather than total price of the whole site. A reference to $100 per F/F for a site is more specific and understandable than $10,000 for the site. It sometimes is easier to make adjustments using units of comparison than the whole price of a lot.

A front-foot unit of comparison can be used appropriately even if the front footage of the site being appraised and that of the comparable are not identical. This system automatically takes care of this difference as long as the two lots have basically the same utility. In such circumstances where major frontage differences exist, the square-foot unit of comparison may be preferable. Another unit of comparison for residential lots is an acreage unit for larger estate-type sites.

Percentage as well as dollar adjustments may be used. Like dollar adjustments, percentages may be used to recognize differences in market conditions from one time to another. If it is evident from empirical evidence that single family lot prices increased by 10% from last year to this year, a 10% adjustment is applicable to the lot being appraised in comparison with the sale of a year ago.

**FIG. 9-2: Portion of Site Sales Adjustment Grid
Using Dollar Adjustments**

Elements of Comparison	Site Being Appraised	Comparable Site Sale 1	
		Description	Adjustments
1. Time (date) of sale	Current	1 year ago	+ $500 (10% in one year)
2. Physical characteristics a) Size	60′ x 150′¹	50′ x 165′¹	−$250 (lot 15 ft. deeper)²
b) Shape	Rectangular	Rectangular	None
c) Streets, curbs and walks	Yes	Yes	None
d) Utilities	All	All	None
e) Terrain	Level	Level	None
3. Location a) Subdivision/neighborhood	Jones addition, Sec. 1	Jones addition, Sec. 3	$250 (better parks and schools in Sec. 1)
4. Conditions of sale	Open market	Open market	None
Total net adjustments			+ $500

¹This relatively small range of 10 feet in frontage in this example is considered to be within reasonable range for this kind of lot. If the differences in frontage were considered to be unreasonable, such as 40 feet, then this unit of comparison could not be used.

²Note that adjustment was made only for depth. Appropriate adjustment is made for difference in frontage by using the front foot unit of comparison. Assume the sales price of #1 was $5,000. If the market did, in fact, recognize a difference between frontages of 50 feet and 60 feet, then it would be necessary to reduce the adjusted sales price of #1 to a front foot unit as follows: $5,000 plus $500 = $5,500 ÷ 50 FF = $110 per FF. Applying this adjusted market price to the sale being appraised ($110 FF × 60 FF) indicates a market value of $6,600.

FIG. 9-3: Portion of Site Sales Adjustment Grid Using Percentage Adjustments

Elements of Comparison	Site Being Appraised	Comparable Site Sale 1	
		Description	Adjustments
1. Time (date) of sale	Current	1 year ago	+10% (market up 10% in one year)
2. Physical characteristics a) Size	60' x 150'[1]	50' x 165'[1]	—5% (lot 15 ft. deeper)[2]
b) Shape	Rectangular	Rectangular	None
c) Streets, curbs and walks	Yes	Yes	None
d) Utilities	All	All	None
e) Terrain	Level	Level	None
3. Location a) Subdivision/neighborhood	Jones addition, Sec. 1	Jones addition, Sec. 3	+5% (better parks and schools in Sec. 1)
4. Conditions of sale	Open market	Open market	None
Total net adjustments			+10%

[1]This relatively small range of 10 feet in frontage in this example is considered to be within reasonable range for this kind of lot. If the differences in frontage were considered to be unreasonable, such as 40 feet, then this unit of comparison could not be used.

[2]Note that adjustment was made only for depth. Appropriate adjustment is made for difference in frontage by using the front foot unit of comparison. Assume the sales price of #1 was $5,000. If the market did, in fact, recognize a difference between frontages of 50 feet and 60 feet, then it would be necessary to reduce the adjusted sales price of #1 to a front foot unit as follows: $5,000 + 10% is $5,000 + $500 = $5,500 ÷ 50 FF = $110 per FF. Applying this adjusted market price to the sale being appraised ($110 FF × 60 FF) indicates a market value of $6,600.

Typically, adjustments are made on a plus or minus base. In Figure 9-3, the sale price of the comparable lot would be adjusted upwardly by 10%. Other adjustments might result in minus percentages.

Reconciliation of Adjusted Site Sale Prices

The next step is to reconcile all the adjusted comparable sale prices into an indicated value of the site being appraised. Use of a simple arithmetic average of the value indications is not acceptable appraisal practice. Averaging small groups of numbers produces a meaningless measure of central tendency, which may or may not reflect actual market value. The accepted procedure is to review each sale and judge its comparability to the property being appraised. The final value is based on all the information available to the appraiser.

When a unit of comparison is used, two extra steps are needed. First, the adjusted unit sale prices are reconciled into a single or range of adjusted sale prices per unit. Then the number of units in the site being appraised is multiplied by the value or range of values per unit to give an indicated value or range of values of the site.

For example, assume the indicated value of the site being appraised is $100 per F/F, based on the reconciled adjusted sale prices of comparable sites. If the site being appraised had 75 front feet, its total value is $7,500 (75 F/F x $100 per F/F). If the indicated value of the site appraised was $ .10 per square foot and the site was 80,000 square feet, its indicated value is $8,000 (80,000 sq. ft. x $ .10 per sq. ft.)

For both dollar and percentage adjustments, the amount of adjustment should be extracted from the market in a valid manner. In some instances, adjustment amounts may not be available from the market. If so, either a logical judgment must be made regarding the amount of the adjustment or the sale must not be used as a comparable in developing the market value for the site being appraised.

Techniques of Making Adjustments

There are two basic techniques in making adjustments for differences between the comparable site and the site being appraised. No unanimous agreement exists as to whether one is better than the other. Practicing appraisers use both techniques, and as long as they are used properly, they produce the same results. The first is considered by some to be more logical and understandable than the second. It follows this rule: if the property being appraised is better than (+) the comparable, a plus adjustment is made; if poorer than (−) the comparable, a minus adjustment is made. For example, a lot being appraised is considered to be $500 better than Comparable A because of physical terrain. If Comparable A sold for $6,000, the adjustment would be made as follows: The lot being appraised is $500 better than (+) the Comparable. Indicated market value of the appraised property is $500 + $6,000, resulting in a figure of $6,500.

Now consider the situation in which the property being appraised is poorer than the comparable. The comparable lot sold for $7,500 and is served by a sanitary sewer; the lot being appraised is not served by a sanitary sewer. The market indicates a preference in the amount of $750 for sanitary sewer. Therefore, the appraised property is poorer than (−) the comparable by $750. The indicated market value of the lot being appraised is $6,750 ($7,500 − $750).

A second technique for making adjustments used by many appraisers is described on the joint FHLMC/FNMA single family appraisal form. It states: "If a significant item in the comparable property is superior to, or more favorable than, the subject property, a minus (−) adjustment is made, thus reducing the indicated value of subject; if a significant item in the comparable is inferior to, or less favorable than, the subject property, a plus (+) adjustment is made, thus increasing the indicated value of the subject." In the example used above, if a significant item in a comparable is inferior—that is, the lot is $500 less favorable than the lot being appraised—a plus adjustment of $500 is made to the reported sales price of the comparable, increasing the indicated market value of the property being appraised to $6,500 ($6,000 + $500). In this technique, it is necessary to remember that a favorable element of the comparable property becomes a minus and an inferior element of the comparable property becomes a plus in the adjustment process.

In the use of both techniques, however, it is essential to remember that adjustments are being made to the property being used as a comparable for the justifiable difference between the comparable and the property being appraised. In this manner, the

FIG. 9-4: Average Improved Lot Value as a Percentage of Average Sale Price of Home

Year	Sale Price	Market Price of Site	Site Value as % of Sale Price
1955	$12,113	$1,626	13.5
1960	14,662	2,477	16.7
1965	16,825	3,442	20.0
1970	23,056	4,982	21.2
1975	32,342	6,382	18.8
1976	34,608	6,954	19.2

Source: *1976 Statistical Yearbook of the U.S. Department of Housing and Urban Development* (Washington, D.C., 1977), p. 106.

comparable is being made as much like the property being appraised as possible. It is not the appraiser's desire to change the characteristics of the site being appraised; rather, the comparable is adjusted to make it as similar as possible to the site being appraised.

The Allocation Procedure

A relationship exists between the application of the agents of production and the market value of a site. This is confirmed by the application of the principles of balance, contribution, surplus productivity and increasing and decreasing returns. Therefore, site value can be estimated by allocating the total sale price of a comparable between its two utilitarian and productive parts—the lot and the improvements. The appraiser determines what portion of a property's sale price typically may be allocated between the lot and the improvements, estimating the market value of the house and other improvements first. The balance (residual) then is allocated to the site.[2]

Statistics shown in Figure 9-4 from the U.S. Census demonstrate the relationship between sale price and site value of residential properties. The statistics are presented on a national and regional average. The older the improvements; the higher the ratio of land value to total value. The typical ratio can be affected by a lot of unusual size or characteristics and by building costs.

---

[2]The National Association of Home Builders reports that land cost, which was about 11% of the cost of a new home after World War II, has nearly a 22% share today (1977).

To estimate the value of unimproved property in an area where vacant land sales are lacking, the appraiser can allocate from the total sale price of a comparative property the part that could reasonably be assigned as building value. The remainder, except for intangibles, is the site value.

For example, assume that a property with a 1,500-square-foot house sold for $35,000. The appraiser estimates the depreciated cost of the house at $20 per square foot, or $30,000. The remainder ($5,000) is the residual price of the site, assuming that the house represents typical or highest and best land use and that no extraneous considerations were involved in the transaction.

The advantage of this procedure is that a sense of proportion is retained. If a neighborhood is typically improved with certain types of properties that can justify only a certain land value, the typical vacant lot probably will not be improved to a higher and better use. Where no vacant site sales are available, this method does afford an indication of site value. However, the results may sometimes be inconclusive and need collateral confirmation.

Variations in the Problem: Value Factors

The same fundamental principles underlie all site valuation procedures; however, the key factors that influence the utility and value of a given site vary with the type of property being appraised. For example, heavy pedestrian traffic would tend to increase value in a retail business site but would lower value in a residential area. The aesthetic considerations and amenities that are important in establishing the value of a residential site might have little relevance to the value of a commercial site.

Value factors differ according to the type of land use. For instance, in a residential area the primary value factors may include convenient location to schools and shopping, amenities available in the neighborhood, or the beauty of the site. In an industrial development the key value factors may be availability of raw materials, zoning regulations or proximity of transportation. In other words, the major factors influencing value of a site vary with the highest and best use of the land.

Sources of Data

The sources of market data are varied and differ by community and the character and location of specific properties. The most direct and thorough approach is to interview the parties involved in the transaction—the seller, buyer, and broker. By talking directly to individuals, the appraiser can gain information about conditions surrounding the sale that may have influenced the transaction. A good deal of information may be revealed in the recorded instruments of conveyance and other public records on file with the local record office. Such records may identify the buyer, seller, mortgagee and trust deed holder and provide an accurate and legal description and other data such as sale price, encumbrances and approximate date of sale. In some circumstances, deed restrictions and other limits on the use of the property are found as part of these records.

Often real estate professionals other than appraisers can provide valuable background material as well as market data. Bankers, savings and loan executives, real estate brokers and mortgage bankers may be able to provide a clear picture of local real estate market activity and can contribute information reflecting the conditions surrounding specific sales which have been chosen for use in the comparative procedure.

A large number of publications and professional information services are available, serving as another excellent data source. Multiple listing systems (MLS), for example, usually contain records of all the activities of members in a local real estate board. Valid information on listings, offers and final sales prices is available from most MLSs. Certain government agencies (FHA, VA) often maintain records of the prices, conditions, sizes and other pertinent information about the housing stock and sales in their jurisdiction.

Summary

Of the two procedures for site valuation, the comparative process is basic. If the comparative sale is typical, the appraiser compares it with the site being appraised in terms of time, location, physical characteristics and conditions of sale. Adjustments are made to develop an indicated market value of the site being appraised.

Other procedures can be used when comparable sales data are lacking or when circumstances limit their application. The allocation procedure is helpful in existing neighborhoods and as an aid to the comparative process. The development procedure can be used in estimating value of land available for improvement, usually in large tracts.

The highest and best use of the land or site determines the crucial value factors for consideration in each individual case.

Techniques for making adjustments for differences between the site being appraised and comparables illustrated in this chapter show that adequate support from the marketplace is essential in developing such dollar or percentage figures.

Review Questions

1. What are the basic procedures for estimating site value? Explain how each is applied.
2. Why are actual sales preferable in the comparative procedure to offerings or listings?
3. Why is the date of sale of a comparable important to consider?
4. What are the four elements of comparison?
5. Why do appraisers use units of comparison?
6. Explain the technique of adjusting a comparable.
7. How is the allocation procedure used to value a site?

10

Improvement Description and Analysis*

The description of the appraised property starts with an analysis of the region, community, neighborhood and site being appraised. The next step is to describe and analyze the improvements. This description is based on a physical inspection of the property by the appraiser. A major portion of this chapter presents details on house construction and components to guide the appraiser in making this inspection. The assumption is that the appraiser makes a complete inspection of the exterior and interior of the property. If this is *not* done, the appraisal report must prominently state that complete inspection was not made by the appraiser and cite the reasons for this omission.

A requirement of AIREA Canon 5, Regulation No. 10, is that every appraisal contain "a clear and reasonably complete description of the property." This includes both a written description as well as graphic illustrations, such as photographs, sketches and a plot plan. In addition to the description of the region, community, neighborhood and site, a typical residential appraisal includes a description and analysis of the following:

1. Site improvements.
2. Relationship of the improvements to the site.
3. General description and classification of improvements.
4. Exterior.
5. Interior.
6. Mechanical systems and equipment.

---

*Portions of this chapter are based on *Houses,* first revision, by Henry S. Harrison, copyright 1976 by REALTORS National Marketing Institute®.

7. Items requiring immediate repair.
8. Deferred maintenance items.
9. Overall condition of improvements.
10. Design and layout (functional utility).
11. Renovation: rehabilitation, modernization and remodeling.

If the structure is partially constructed or a renovation program is proposed, the appraiser may have to obtain the details of the work to be done from a set of house plans. Basic information about how plans are drawn and the symbols used by architects to illustrate proposed construction work are given later in this chapter.

Site Improvements

In the chapter on site data and analysis, it was discussed that the term "land" implies no improvements of any kind and that "site" is land plus those improvements which make it ready for use. In the typical appraisal some of these improvements are included as part of the site value and other improvements are valued separately. Because there is no universally accepted way to treat site improvements, the appraiser must be familiar with local customs. The appraisal report must indicate clearly which items are included in the site value and which are treated as site improvements. One suggested treatment, according to *Real Estate Appraisal Terminology*, is:

Improvements Included in the Site Valuation

1. Clearing.
2. Grading.
3. Draining.
4. Landscaping (often valued separately).
5. Installation of public utilities to the site.
6. Access (streets and alleys).
7. Lighting.
8. Sidewalks and curbs (often valued separately).

Site Improvements Valued Separately

1. Septic system (often included in site valuation).
2. Utility connections.
3. Well (often included in site valuation).
4. Driveways and parking spaces.

5. Patios.
6. Pools and courts.
7. Fences and walls.
8. On-site lights and poles.

One of the advantages of valuing site improvements separately is that they can be depreciated according to current IRS codes; improvements that are part of the site may 'not be depreciated. The appraiser considers each of the site improvements in the description and analysis sections of the report. The final value estimate is the same regardless of whether the improvement is considered part of the site or a separate improvement.

Placement of Improvements on Site

In addition to being the wrong improvement for the site (in terms of size, design, quality of construction, etc.), many houses are poorly located on their lots. As long as the public will buy houses lined in a row facing the street—in spite of the proven advantages of alternate methods of site planning—that is what developers will continue to build. A lot, like a house, should be divided into zones for good planning. There are three zones in a house lot: the public zone, the private zone and the service zone.

The public zone is the area visible from the street, which preferably should be kept small by bringing the house as far forward on the lot as possible. If this is not possible, some sort of screening, such as fencing or shrubbery, should be considered. The service zone consists of sidewalks and driveways plus trash storage and clothes-drying areas. Like the public area, this zone should be kept as small as is practical and convenient. The private zone is where the children play, the patio or family porch is located, and the vegetable gardens grow. This zone should be as large as possible.

A well-designed house takes advantage of the fact that during the summer the sun rises in the northeast, travels in a high arc across the sky and sets in the northwest. In the colder winter months, it rises southeast, travels in a low arc and sets in the southwest. As a result, the south side of the house, when protected by a large roof overhang, will receive much more sun in the winter than in the summer. The opposite is true of the east and west sides of such a house. All other factors being equal, such as street location, topography and view, the best direction in which to face a house is with the broad side containing large windows toward the south.

General Description and Classification of Improvements

The description of the improvements should start with a general summary, including the architectural style of the house (see Fig. 10-1); type of car storage; number of rooms, baths and lavatories; and gross living area. This is followed by a detailed description of the exterior and interior of the structure.

Exterior

A detailed description of the exterior includes information about the major construction details, including:

1. Footings and foundation walls.
2. Framing.
3. Insulation.
4. Ventilation.
5. Exterior wall covering.
6. Masonry walls.
7. Windows.
8. Storm doors and windows
9. Weatherstripping.
10. Screens.
11. Gutters and downspouts.
12. Roofs.
13. Flashing.
14. Chimneys.

The condition of these items and any needed repairs or modernization should also be reported in this section of the report.

Construction Details

• *Footings and Foundation Walls.* The objective of the footing is to provide support for the dwelling without excessive differential or overall settlement or movement. It is the perimetric base of concrete on top of which all foundation walls are poured or laid. Block foundations walls must be properly laid and well-mortared, then filled with concrete and made watertight with cement plaster or other waterproofing compounds. Cinder blocks are inferior to cement blocks for a solid foundation because they are porous. Brick and tile,

FIG. 10-1: The CTS System of House Description

The CTS System is designed to provide a uniform method of describing residential construction. Class denotes the number of occupants per dwelling; type refers to the structural nature of the house; and style relates to the decorative design of the house based on historical or contemporary architecture.

THE CTS SYSTEM
(CLASS, TYPE, STYLE)
A UNIFORM METHOD FOR DESCRIBING HOUSES

# CODE	DESCRIPTION	ABBREVIATION
	CLASS	
1	One-family, detached	1 FAM D
2	Two-family, detached	2 FAM D
3	Three-family, detached	3 FAM D
4	Four-family, detached	4 FAM D
5	One-family, party wall	1 FAM PW
6	Two-family, party wall	2 FAM PW
7	Three-family, party wall	3 FAM PW
8	Four-family, party wall	4 FAM PW
9	Other	OTHER
	TYPE	
1	One-story	1 STORY
2	One-and-a-half story	1½ STORY
3	Two-story	2 STORY
4	Two-and-a-half story	2½ STORY
5	Three-or-more Stories	3 STORY
6	Bi-level	BI-LEVEL
6	Raised ranch	R RANCH
6	Split entry	SPLT ENT
7	Split-level	SPLT LEV
8	Mansion	MANSION
9	Other	OTHER
	STYLE	
100	COLONIAL AMERICAN	COL AMER
101	Federal	FEDERAL
102	New England Farm House	N E FARM
103	Adams	ADAMS CO
104	Cape Cod	CAPE COD
105	Cape Ann	CAPE ANN
106	Garrison Colonial	GARR CO
107	New England	N E COL
108	Dutch	DUTCH CO
109	Salt Box	SALT BOX
109	Catslide	CATSLIDE
110	Pennsylvania Dutch	PENN DUT
	Pennsylvania German Farm House	GER FARM
111	Classic	CLASSIC
112	Greek Revival	GREEK
113	Southern Colonial	SOUTH CO
114	Front Gable New England	F GAB NE
114	Charleston	CHARLES
114	English Colonial	ENG COL
115	Log Cabin	LOG CAB
200	ENGLISH	ENGLISH
201	Cotswold Cottage	COTSCOT
202	Elizabethan	ELIZ
202	Half Timber	HALFTIM
203	Tudor	TUDOR
204	Williamsburg	WILLIAMS
204	Early Georgian	E. GEORG
205	Regency	REGENCY
206	Georgian	GEORGE

# CODE	DESCRIPTION	ABBREVIATION
300	FRENCH	FRENCH
301	French Farm House	FR FARM
302	French Provincial	FR PROV
303	French Normandy	FR NORM
304	Creole	CREOLE
304	Louisiana	LOUISIA
304	New Orleans	NEW OR
400	SWISS	SWISS
401	Swiss Chalet	SWISS CH
500	LATIN	LATIN
501	Spanish Villa	SP VILLA
501	Italian Villa	IT VILLA
600	ORIENTAL	ORIENT
601	Japanese	JAPAN
700	19th CENTURY AMERICAN	19th CTY
701	Early Gothic Revival	E. GOTH
702	Egyptian Revival	EGYPT
703	Roman Tuscan Mode	RO TUSC
704	Octagon House	OCTAGON
705	High Victorian Gothic	HI GOTH
706	High Victorian Italianate	VIC ITAL
707	American Mansard	MANSARD
707	Second Empire	2nd EMP
708	Stick Style	STICK
708	Carpenter Gothic	C GOTH
709	Eastlake	EAST L
710	Shingle Style	SHINGLE
711	Romanesque	ROMAN
712	Queen Anne	Q. ANNE
713	Brownstone	BROWN S
713	Brick Row House	BR ROW
713	Eastern Townhouse	E. TOWN
714	Western Row House	WEST ROW
714	Western Townhouse	W. TOWN
715	Monterey	MONTEREY
716	Western Stick	W. STICK
717	Mission Style	MISSION
800	EARLY 20th CENTURY AMERICAN	EARLY20C
801	Prairie House	PRAIRIE
802	Bungalow	BUNGALOW
803	Pueblo	PUEBLO
	Adobe	ADOBE
804	International Style	INTERNAT
805	California Bungalow	CAL BUNG
900	POST WORLD WAR II AMERICAN	POST WW2
901	California Ranch	C RANCH
902	Northwestern	NORTH W
902	Pudget Sound	P SOUND
903	Functional Modern	FUN MOD
903	Contemporary	CONTEMP
904	Solar House	SOLAR
905	"A" Frame	A FRAME
906	Mobile Home	MOBILE
907	Plastic House	PLASTIC

although good foundation materials, are costly and require substantial skill for proper laying. Stone, which was once very popular in the northeast United States, has the same disadvantage.

The three basic design types are slab-on-ground, basement and crawl space. Slabs are constructed by first building footings for support, although some slabs (known as "floating slabs") are built without them. The excavation is then covered with gravel and a vapor barrier and insulation are installed around the edge. A basement floor is constructed similarly to a slab. The height between the basement floor and the bottom of the joists is usually 7½ to 8 feet. Crawl spaces are constructed similarly to basements except that the distance from the floor to the joists is 3 to 4 feet. They provide flooding protection and also a convenient place to run heating ducts, plumbing pipes and wires that must be accessible for repairs.

• *Framing.* Most houses built in the United States are of wood frame construction. This includes many homes that have brick veneer siding. Platform frame construction is the most common type. Balloon framing was popular for multi-story brick veneer houses, but because of poor fire resistance it does not comply with many building codes. Plank and beam framing was used for barns and colonial houses; it is used today for contemporary designs where the framing members are left exposed (as in exposed beam ceilings). Panelized construction, a new method of framing, is becoming more popular.

After a house is a few years old, visible signs of defective framing, such as bulging exterior walls, can often be detected. Window sills that are not level are a sign of settling, defective framing or original sloppy carpentry. A careful house inspection should include opening and closing every window. Sticking windows may be a sign of settling or defects in framing. All doors should be checked, including a look at their bottoms to detect if they have been resawed. Sagging and sloping floors may be detected visually or by putting a marble on the floor and watching if it rolls. Other signs of defective framing include large cracks developing on the outside of the house between the chimney and the exterior wall or cracks running outward at an angle from the upper corners of window and door frames.

Cracks in the walls other than these may be cause for concern but in themselves are not conclusive evidence of framing problems. All houses settle unless built upon solid rock; it is a rare house that doesn't develop some wall and ceiling cracks. These should be of concern only when accompanied by some of the other signs of defective framing. If framing defects are suspected, professional consultants may be called in to confirm this opinion.

• *Insulation.* Almost any house without adequate insulation is substandard today. Insulation is as important in warm climates to keep the heat out as it is in cold climates to keep heat in. Prior to World War II, many houses were constructed without insulation, many of which have since been insulated. Residential insulation falls into the following five categories: loose, blanket and bat, sprayed-on, foil and wallboard.

Among loose insulation materials are rock wool, glass wool, slag wool, perlite, vermiculite, wood fiber, paper, cotton fiber paper and macerated paper. All of these products may be blown or poured into the hollow spaces between the studs on the exterior walls and above the ceiling or below the roof rafters. Their major disadvantage, however, is that they tend to settle, eventually leaving uninsulated spaces. Blanket and bat insulation is loosely felted and glued between two sheets of treated paper or foil and quilted. When installed, it is stapled, clipped or nailed with lathing between the studs and under the rafters or over the ceiling. Sprayed-on insulation is a hot, viscous mixture that is sprayed onto the inside of the sheathing. When it cools and solidifies, it becomes a porous layer one to two inches thick. Foil, usually aluminum several thousandths of an inch thick, is installed in up to four layers. It is especially effective in keeping out heat. Wallboard insulation, which is used successfully under siding and roofs, is made of a variety of synthetic or vegetable fibers.

The two primary benefits of insulation are fuel economy and occupancy comfort. Its secondary benefits are the reduction of noise transmission and of fire hazard since insulation will impede fire from spreading. The difference between fuel costs for an uninsulated house and for an otherwise identical one with storm windows and doors and good insulation can be 50%. The standard measurement for the effectiveness of insulation is its R value (resistance to heat flow). The higher the R value the better the insulation. Over-the-ceiling or under-the-roof insulation should have an R rating from R-13 (in mild climates with no air conditioning and with gas or oil heat) to R-24 or higher (in cold or very hot climates or where there is electric heat or air conditioning).

Exterior wall insulation ranges from R-8 to R-11. Floor insulation, if a house is built over a crawl space, should be at least R-9 and preferably R-13. When the house is built on a slab, only edge floor insulation is needed.

• *Ventilation.* To prevent water condensation, a flow of air is necessary in the attic, behind the wall covering and through the basement or crawl space. When water condensation collects in unventilated spaces, it promotes rot and decay. This air flow will also reduce attic heat in the summer. Ventilation can be accomplished by providing holes ranging in size from one inch to several feet in diameter; these holes should always be covered with screen to keep out vermin. The use of attic, basement, kitchen and bathroom fans also is part of the ventilation system.

• *Exterior Wall Covering.* The construction of an exterior wall on a frame house starts with the attachment of sheathing to the wall framing studs. Common sheathing materials are wood boards, plywood, fiberboard and gypsum board panels. Next the sheathing is covered with waterproof sheathing paper (often asphalt-saturated felt). A wide variety of house wall finishes and exterior wall coverings exist; many houses have more than one type of siding. Some common types of wood siding are bevel, bungalow, colonial, rustic, shiplap and drop siding. Shingles are another common siding material. Stucco is still used in dry climates on wood frame construction but it is more commonly used over solid masonry walls.

A masonry veneer wall is built by attaching the masonry (clay or concrete bricks, split blocks or stone) to the sheathing. In houses with masonry veneer walls, all the structural functions of the walls are performed by the framing and not by the masonry. When the walls are constructed, three-quarters to one-inch air spaces are left between the masonry and the sheathing, and weep holes are installed at the base to let moisture escape.

A variety of other types of siding materials are available, including aluminum, stone, hardboard, gypsum board, fiberglass and metals.

• *Masonry Walls.* Masonry walls are either solid or hollow. Solid masonry walls, if well constructed, are durable and easily maintained. They should be insulated and require a larger foundation than a wood frame wall. Such walls can be either one or two units thick. Single-unit walls are most commonly made of eight-inch concrete. Multiple-unit masonry walls are constructed of either two layers of brick, tile or cement block or of a combination of materials, with the higher grade material on the outside and the cheaper unit as the back-up.

Hollow masonry walls have two wall units separated by a two- to four-inch air space and bonded together with metal ties of joint reinforcement. These cavity walls are used mainly in northern sections of the United States for protection against severe outside temperature and storms. Masonry bonded walls are similar to cavity walls. Although they are economical to construct, their insulation qualities are inferior to cavity walls and they are used primarily in the Southwest.

• *Windows*. Among window types commonly found in houses are single and double hung windows, casement windows, horizontal sliding (traverse) windows and jalousie windows.

During the inspection, dust streaks or water stains around the window may be noticed, which can be evidence of leakage. Missing locks and window lifts or counter balance weights also may be discovered. Window placement should be noted. For example, a double-hung window over a kitchen sink may be difficult to open, or a window in the bathroom over the tub or toilet may let in uncomfortable drafts.

• *Weatherstripping*. The purpose of weatherstripping on windows and doors is to provide a seal against drafts and dust. A common kind of weatherstripping used today is the "spring tension" type made of bronze, aluminum, rigid vinyl, stainless or galvanized steel or rigid plastic steel. Other types are woven felt, compression sash guides and compression bulbs.

• *Storm Doors and Windows*. These serve as a means of insulation and may provide a fuel saving of between 10% and 20%. Today they are often made of aluminum and permanently installed, together with screens. The wooden type, which are removed and stored during the summer, are becoming obsolete. In many markets, it is difficult to estimate how much storm windows and doors add to the value of a house, but the principle of conformity is helpful in this determination.

• *Screens*. Screens are needed in almost every part of the country. The old-fashioned wood frame is becoming obsolete. Most screens today have aluminum frames and screening material and are combined with storm windows. The appraiser should count all window and door screens, noting if any are missing (a common occurrence).

• *Gutters and Downspouts.* These provide the means for controlling water runoff from the roof to prevent property damage and unsightly exterior wall stains where roof overhangs are not provided. Gutters or eave troughs carry rainwater off the roof to downspouts or leaders. Metal gutters of aluminum, copper or galvanized iron, which are attached to the house with various types of metal hangers, are the most common type of gutter now in use. Wood gutters are attached to the house with noncorroding screws bedded in elastic roofers cement to prevent leakage. Built-in gutters are made of metal and set into the deeply notched rafter a short distance up the roof from the eaves. Pole gutters consists of a wooden strip nailed perpendicular to the roof and covered with sheet metal.

Downspouts or leaders are vertical pipes that carry the water from the gutter to the ground and into sewers or dry wells. They should be large enough to carry the water away as fast as it flows from the roof. The junction of the gutter and downspout should be covered with a basket strainer to hold back leaves and twigs, especially if the gutter connects to a storm or sanitary sewer, to prevent clogging.

• *Roofs.* The roof must be constructed to support its own weight, plus that of snow, ice and wind, and also to act as a base for the application of the roof finishing materials. The most common systems of roof construction found in houses are trusses, joists and rafters, joists alone, plank and beam roofs and panelized construction. A truss is made up of a number of individual boards usually arranged into a framework of triangles. These trusses are suspended between load-bearing walls so that each truss acts as a unit to support the roof loads. Joists are horizontal boards suspended from exterior walls, with their narrow sides parallel to the ground, and often supported by interior load-bearing walls. Plank and beam construction consists of boards that are "tongue and grooved" so that they fit into a structural ridge beam. Panelized roof systems consist of preframed, precut and sheathed panels usually made of boards covered with plywood.

Roof sheathing provides support of roof loads and a backing for the attachment of roofing materials. The most common types of sheathing are plywood, fiberboard and roof boards (planks).

A majority of house roofs consist of shingles and shakes made of wood, asphalt, asbestos, cement, slate or tile. Metal, clay tile and built-up or membrane roofs can also be found. Since roof covering rarely lasts to the end of a house's economic life, the appraiser should carefully observe the roof and report its condition, age and estimated remaining life.

Water may leak through the roof for a variety of reasons. Asphalt shingle roofs may leak in a high wind if light-grade shingles are used. As these shingles get older, they curl, tear and become pierced with holes. Wood shingles may curl, split, loosen, break and fall off the roof, and asbestos shingles may crack and break. Metal roofs can rust, become bent and pierced with holes. Roll and built-up roofs may loosen, tear, and become patched and worn through.

• *Flashing*. Flashing is needed whenever a roof is intersected by two different roof slopes, adjoining walls or projections through the surface by chimneys, pipes or vents. Flashing is a process by which metal strips, impregnated felt or a combination of both are nailed across or under the intersecting point; a waterproofing compound or cement is then applied and finally the roofing or siding materials are applied over the edges to hold the flashing in place permanently.

• *Chimneys*. The efficiency of any heating system (except electric) depends upon the chimney or vent. A good chimney is safe, durable and smoketight. Defective chimneys and vents may constitute serious fire hazards. A chimney may be a simple flue or an intricate masonry construction consisting of heater flues, ash pits, incinerators, ash chutes, fireplaces and fireplace flues. Whatever its construction, the chimney is the heaviest portion of the house and must be supported by its own concrete footings, which must be designed so that it will not settle faster than the rest of the building. Masonry chimney walls should be eight inches thick when they are exposed to the exterior of the house and must be separated from combustible construction. A two-inch air space must extend at least two feet above any part of the roof, roof ridge or parapet wall within 10 feet of the chimney. At the bottom of the chimney should be an ash pit with a clean-out door, into which run the flues from the fireplaces.

The heart of the chimney is the vertical open shaft, called a flue, through which smoke and gas pass to the outside air. A rough surface retards this outward flow of smoke or warm air; a flue lining will overcome this problem. A single flue should not be used for more than one heating device. The flue should extend out a few inches above the top of the chimney wall, which should be capped with concrete, metal, stone or some other noncombustible, waterproof material, sloped from the flue to the outside edge. Flues from the furnace and hot water heater should not run into the ash pit, because cold air below the smoke pipe connection will interfere with the draft in the flue.

The furnace and hot water heater are connected to the chimney by a smoke pipe, which for fire safety should be at least 10 inches below the floor joists. The joists should be further protected with plaster or a shield of metal or asbestos.

Prefabricated chimneys that are assembled off the premises are now available. Many of these units consist of a flue liner encased in a concrete wall.

Interior

The description of the interior rooms should provide information about their location in the house, size of each room, number of closets, and floor, wall, and ceiling coverings or finishes. Special features should also be described and any needed repairs or modernization should be reported. Some appraisers describe general construction details and mechanical equipment on a room-by-room basis. However, unless such materials vary significantly from room to room, it is better to describe them just once.

Typical items included in a description of the general interior construction (exclusive of the mechanical systems and equipment, which are described separately) are:

1. Basement construction and finishing.
2. Main bearing beam and columns.
3. Subflooring.
4. Floor covering.
5. Interior walls and ceilings.
6. Stairs.
7. Doors.
8. Molding and trim.
9. Cabinets.
10. Fireplaces.
11. Termite protection.

The condition of these items and any needed repairs or modernization should be reported in this section of the report.

Construction Details

• *Basement Construction and Finishing.* The basic construction of the basement consists of the footings and foundation walls previously described; a basement floor, which usually is poured concrete over a vapor barrier and gravel; and the ceiling, which often is the unfinished underside of the first floor subflooring. Dirt floors are obsolete.

Basements can be finished in a variety of ways. Simple finishing consists of some type of floor and wall covering over the concrete and foundation walls and a simple ceiling finishing. In contrast, some basements are finished with the same materials as the rest of the house. There is a trend to raise the basement part way out of the ground to provide better natural light and ventilation and direct access to the outside. In raised ranch and hillside ranch-type houses the basement often is finished so as to be an integral part of the house. When a basement is half above ground and heated and finished like the rest of the house, it is included in the gross living area measurements (see pages 217-218).

A main problem with basements is dampness, which may be caused by poor foundation wall construction, excess ground water not properly carried away by ground tiles, poorly fitted windows or hatch, a poorly vented clothes dryer, gutters and downspouts spilling water too near the foundation wall or a rising ground water table. A basement that is wet or damp only part of the year can usually be detected any time by the presence of a powder-white mineral deposit a few inches off the floor. Stains along the lower edge of the walls and columns and on the furnace and hot water heater are indications of excessive dampness, as is mildew odor.

• *Main Bearing Beam and Columns.* Most houses are too large for the floor joists to span foundation walls. Bearing beams resting on columns are used to support the house. Steel beams, because of their high strength, can span greater distances than wood beams of the same size. Wood beams, however, are often used. Most beams are supported by wood posts, brick or block piers or metal Lally columns, which are concrete-filled steel cylinders.

• *Subflooring and Bridging.* Subflooring provides safe support of floor loads without excessive deflection and also adequate underlayment for the support and attachment of finish flooring materials. Plywood is the most common material now being used for subflooring, but panelized floor systems are increasing in popularity. Plank and beam floor systems serve as the subfloor and working platform; they transmit the floor loads to fewer but larger members than in wood joist floor systems. Bridging is used to stiffen the joists and prevent them from deflecting sideways.

• *Floor Covering.* Flooring made of strips of hardwood was the standard in many markets for over 50 years. Before that time planks of hard and soft woods were used. Soft woods continue to be used in low-cost houses. Hardwood strip flooring is installed directly over the joists or the subflooring. Wood block flooring is similarly installed. Both types of flooring may also be installed by attaching them to a suitable underlayment with special adhesives.

Wood floors that have been exposed to water may warp and bulge upward. Wide cracks between the floorboards are a sign of poor workmanship or shrinkage caused by improperly dried or stored wood prior to installation. Rough, discolored, blemished, burned or gouged floors can usually be cured by refinishing.

Carpeting, installed over either finished flooring or subflooring, is rapidly gaining in popularity as a floor covering. Carpeting, however, tends to depreciate very rapidly and often does not add value equal to its cost, especially when it is laid over another floor covering. Ceramic tile is still popular for bathrooms and lavatories. It can be laid in a bed of plaster (called a mud job) or attached with a special adhesive to the subflooring.

Concrete slabs may be used for floor covering with no further treatment, painted with special concrete paint or covered with other flooring coverings. Resilient tile, glued with special adhesives, must not be installed directly over a board or plank subfloor; a suitable underlayment must first be installed. Terrazzo flooring is made of colored marble chips mixed into cement; it is ground to a smooth surface after being laid.

• *Interior Walls and Ceiling.* Most interior walls are made of wood covered with a variety of materials. The purpose of wall and ceiling finishes is to provide both a decorative and waterproof finish in spaces subject to moisture. The materials now most commonly used include plaster, gypsum, plywood, hardboard, fiberboard, ceramic tile and wood paneling.

A well constructed plaster wall provides a high degree of soundproofing. Its main disadvantages, however, are high cost and susceptibility to cracking. As long as cracked plaster is tight to the wall, it may be sufficient to patch and redecorate a crack. Bulging ceiling plaster is dangerous and should be repaired. This defect often can be detected by pressing a broom handle against the ceiling, noting if there is any give to the plaster.

Gypsum and other wood composition walls can be installed directly to studs or masonry, eliminating the drying time needed for plaster walls. Ceramic tile walls are installed similarly to ceramic tile floors, either by cement plaster or special adhesives. Tile around the bathtub may cause problems. Defective grout will permit water to seep behind the tile and loosen the glue. New types of waterproof adhesives help eliminate this and tiles set in plaster also are less likely to present problems.

• *Stairs.* A well-planned stairway provides safe ascent and adequate headroom and space for moving furniture and equipment. A simple check for adequate design includes noting: headroom, width clear of handrail, run, rise, winders, landings, handrail and railings. Railings should be installed around the open sides of all interior stairwells including those in the attic and basement.

• *Doors.* There are seven basic types of doors: batten, sliding glass, folding, flush solid, flush solid core, flush hollow core, and stile and rail doors. Batten doors, consisting of boards nailed together in various ways, are used where appearance is not important, such as for cellar and shed doors. Flush solid core doors are made with smooth face panels glued to a core that is made of either a composition material, glued-together wood blocks or glued-together wood pieces. Solid doors are often used as exterior doors. Flush hollow core doors are also perfectly flat. They have a core that consists mainly of crossed wooden slats. These doors are light and are used for interior doors. Stile and rail doors consist of a framework of vertical boards (stiles) and horizontal boards (rails). The hanging of doors is difficult. If the door is improperly hung, it will stick. Pre-hung doors are now available.

• *Molding and Trim.* Molding is made from a variety of hard and soft woods that are cut, planed and sanded into desired shapes. A general rule is that the thicker the molding and the more intricate the design, the more expensive it is. Although in the past architects would design a special molding for custom houses, most molding used today is standardized in size and shape.

The use of interior molding in a modern house may be limited to simple casing around the doors and windows, baseboards and ceiling. In more elaborate houses extensive or elaborate molding may be used. When the upper portion of a wall is finished with a different material than the lower portion, the lower portion is called the wainscot and the finishing material is called wainscoting. Older houses may have horizontal strips of wood nailed to the wall at chair height to prevent marring of the walls.

• *Cabinets.* Prior to World War II most cabinets were made of wood. Factory-made metal cabinets are often used today. Drawers, adjustable shelves, backs, sides and fronts are of enameled pressed steel sheets. Doors are usually hollow steel. Cabinets must be installed level, plumb and true to ensure proper operation. They should be screwed, not nailed, to the wall studs and the screws should go through the framing members.

• *Fireplaces.* In most American homes a fireplace is an amenity rather than a primary source of heat. There is no rule of thumb as to how much value one adds, and it is a mistake to assume—without market evidence—that it adds value equal to its cost.

Fireplaces are usually constructed of masonry but metal ones are becoming common. They must be well-designed and constructed to work properly. The hardest parts to design and build are the smoke shelf and smoke chamber, both of which are not accessible to routine inspection. Many fireplaces allow smoke to back up into the house, especially when it is windy outside. The owner should be asked how the fireplace works, which should be recorded in the appraisal report (clearly indicating the answer is that of the owner and not the appraiser). For fire safety, the hearth should extend at least 16 inches from the front and eight inches beyond each side of the opening.

• *Termite Protection.* The subterranean termite (see Fig. 10-2) is becoming more common in parts of the United States that historically have been free of such pests. As the problem of termite damage increases in an area, the demand for termite protection increases. The appraiser must be aware of possible termite damage in the area and how much protection is expected.

Termites live in the moist earth, not in wood; they travel from the ground into the wood only to feed. They do not like light and will travel above ground through cracks in masonry foundation, through wood or in mud tunnels they construct on masonry surfaces.

FIG. 10-2: Differences between Winged Adult Ants and Termites

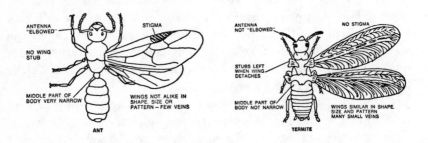

Termite protection is provided by (1) controlling the moisture content of the wood used; (2) providing effective termite barriers and (3) using naturally durable or treated wood. Most appraisers are not qualified to make a complete termite inspection; however, they can make a preliminary examination which should report the following:

1. Wood that is not at least six inches above the ground. Joists, sills, and girders should have even more clearance.
2. Soft wood that may be termite infested.
3. Cracks in masonry that could be termite pathways.
4. Mud termite tubes that are signs of termites.
5. Insects that appear to be termites.
6. Termite shields and other special termite protection.

If there is any sign of termites, inspection by a professional termite inspector should be recommended in the appraisal report.

Mechanical Systems and Equipment

A house cannot provide adequate shelter and comfort unless its mechanical systems are in good working order. Each system must be inspected by the appraiser and described in the appraisal report. There is no standard way to categorize the mechanical systems and equipment; the following is a summary of the major systems described in this chapter:

1. Heating system.
2. Cooling system.
3. Plumbing system.

4. Hot water system
5. Electrical system.
6. Miscellaneous systems.

Heating Systems

Heating systems are based on warm air, water, steam or electricity. Warm (or hot) air heating systems utilize either the natural force of gravity or some type of pressure blower to push heated air through the ducts. Filters can be installed to clean the air and a humidifier is often added to increase the moisture content. All the air systems distribute the heated air into the rooms through registers. Most gravity systems are old and obsolete and ready for replacement; however, gravity floor furnaces are still being installed in small houses. A space heater is another type of low-quality gravity system.

In hot water systems (also known as hydronic systems) water is heated in a cast iron or steel boiler. Some old systems depend on gravity to circulate the water through radiators located throughout the house; most modern systems use one or more electric circulators to pump the heated water through pipes into either baseboard panels or convectors, radiators or tubes embedded in the floors, walls or ceilings. These units depend on both convection (air being warmed as it passes over the heated metal and then circulated into the room) and radiation (heat waves being transferred directly from the heated metal to the object being heated by radiant energy). There are also combination systems in which the heat is brought to the radiator by warm water. A fan in the radiator blows air over the radiator fins, heating the room by convection.

Steam heat is produced by a furnace that is a boiler with a firebox underneath it. As the water boils, steam is created that is forced by its pressure through pipes into radiators.

Electricity may be considered as either a fuel to heat air or water in a furnace or a source of heat in itself. Its use with resistance elements produces heat at the immediate area to be heated. These resistance elements, which convert electricity into heat, are embedded in the floors, walls and ceilings to provide radiant heat. The advantages claimed for electric radiant heat are the lack of visible radiators or grilles and its ability to maintain adequate air humidity levels. Electric heat also provides the advantage of individual room temperature control. Its acceptance by the public, however, is not universal.

Electric heating panels, also with individual resistance elements, are often used for auxiliary heat in bathrooms, additions to the original house and summer houses.

The type of fuel used in any heating system must be considered as world fuel markets and prices change from day to day. Fuel needs and supplies have become a major factor in international economics and politics. Each fuel has its own significant advantages and disadvantages which change from time to time and differ from one region to another.

Coal was once the most popular fuel but most coal systems are now obsolete; however, new systems are again being manufactured as a return to coal from oil and gas is being suggested.

Fuel oil is still the least expensive fuel in the Northeast and Northwest sections of the United States and is competitively priced in many other areas as well. It may be stored in the basement of the house in free-standing tanks not more than 275 gallons in size (larger or more than two tanks in a basement are considered unsafe). Outside tanks buried in the ground commonly have 550- or 1,000-gallon capacities.

Natural gas offers the convenience of continuous delivery via pipeline without the necessity of storage tanks. In most areas of the country (the major exceptions being the Northeast and Northwest), gas has been the most economical fuel. Liquid petroleum gas is used in many rural areas. It requires on-premises storage tanks and is usually more expensive than natural pipeline gas. In other respects it is similar to natural gas.

Electricity appears to be the fuel of the future. Electric systems are the least expensive to install, since they require no furnace, furnace room, ducts, flue or plumbing. They do require, however, a much larger electric service into the house and wiring to each unit. To date, in spite of advertising to the contrary, electric heat costs remain high except in lower-cost power areas.

The least developed source of heat to date comes directly from the sun. Solar heat is still in the experimental stages. A variety of solar heating systems are on the market today and appraisers will have to stay current on solar heat developments to appraise a house with solar heating.

Cooling Systems

Until the late 1940s, most home cooling was done with fans. Even today, the fan in a warm-air heating system can be used to bring cooler basement air into the house. In some areas of the West, where the humidity is low even in periods of high heat, a simple system which blows air across wet excelsior or some other water-absorbing material is used to cool the air. Such package units are manufactured for home installation in windows.

Many homes today, however, have some type of air condition- ing system. Window (or sleeve) air conditioning units are sold by the millions each year. Small 4,000- to 5,000-BTU units usually can be self-installed and plug into a regular duplex outlet. Larger units (up to 12,000 BTUs) often require a separate power line, since they work better on 220 volts. New units gaining in popularity are those no longer requiring a sleeve or window mounting. The unit is split into two parts; the compressor hangs or stands on the outside of the house and the fan is hung on the interior wall. Only a small hole in the wall is needed for the connecting tube and wire. The appraiser must determine whether by custom or law window air conditioners are classified as real or personal property, and the appraisal report should clearly indicate which case applies.

Ducted central air-conditioning systems may be custom-made or prewired, precharged, factory-assembled packages that are con- nected at the home site. The condensor portion is set outside the house or on the roof. It is connected by pipe to the evaporator air-handling unit inside the house. The air-handling unit, consisting of the evaporator and a fan, is connected to a system of ducts that distributes cool air to areas of the house to be cooled. If the house has a warm forced-air heating system, the air-conditioning system can use the same fan, filter and duct work. However, the ducts may not be suitable for air conditioning because cooling generally requires double the duct size than heating, and the cooling system works much better if the registers are high on the wall or are the type that direct air steeply upward.

Heat pumps are another device for both heating and cooling a house. The heat pump is actually a reversible refrigeration unit. In the winter, it takes heat from the outside air or ground or well water and distributes it in the house. Its efficiency decreases when it is very cold outside and it must be supplemented with resistance heating. In the summer the system cools by extracting heat from the inside of the house like a typical air-conditioning unit. Heat pumps constitute only a small percentage of systems being installed.

Plumbing Systems

The plumbing system is an integral part of any house; the materials used for this system determine its ability to supply adequate clean water and remove wastes over a long period of time. The pipes carrying clean water should work without leaking, making noise, reducing pressure or imparting any color or taste to the water. Brass was used for many years but is now expensive. Older brass pipes tend to crystallize and become coated inside in areas where the water is corrosive. Galvanized steel is used in some areas; like brass, it is easy to work and is connected with threaded joints and fittings, but it is easily attacked by corrosive water. Galvanized wrought iron is similar to steel but more resistant to corrosion. Copper and lead are also used; lead is still used for the pipe from the water main to the house. Plastic is the newest material for pipes. Although plastic piping is gaining acceptance, it is still not permitted in many cities.

Water pipes must be strong to withstand the pressure necessary for water to flow through them. Because there is no pressure in a waste drain line, the pipes must be slanted so that waste will flow from each fixture through the main lines into the sewer or sewage disposal system. Pipes for the drainage system are made of cast iron, copper, plastic, tile, brass, lead or fiber. Special fittings are often used, especially on cast iron pipes, to aid the flow of sewage.

Standard bathroom fixtures consist of lavatories (wash basins), bathtubs, showers, and toilets (water closets). The best material for lavatories is cast iron covered with acid-resistant vitreous enamel. Newer ones are made of fiberglass. Bathtubs are the most expensive bathroom fixture. The most common materials are ceramic tile, steel or cast iron covered with vitreous enamel or fiberglass. Standard size is 5-1/2 feet long by 16 inches deep. Many tubs also have a shower unit because they are less expensive to build than a separate tub and shower stall. Separate shower stalls are often prefabricated steel or fiberglass units. The appraiser should be alert for possible leakage problems with such units. Leaking usually takes place through the walls, at the joint between the wall and floor pan and around the seam at the edge of the floor pan and drain. In older houses, inspection of the ceiling under the shower usually will show if there has been any leakage.

Most residential toilets consist of a bowl and a tank that stores sufficient water to create proper flushing action. The toilet can be rated by its self-cleaning properties, its flushing action, the amount of noise during flushing, and the ease of cleaning around the exterior.

Kitchen plumbing fixtures include a single or double sink, generally installed in a counter. The sink drain should have a removable crumb cup or a combination crumb cup and stopper. Kitchen sinks may be made of acid-resistant enameled cast iron, enameled steel, stainless steel or Monel metal. A garbage disposal unit and/or a dishwasher may be connected to kitchen plumbing.

Both bathroom and kitchen fittings include a series of faucets, spigots and drains, which require repair and replacement many times during the life of a house. The most common type of faucet arrangement has two separate valves, one each for hot and cold water. In older or very cheap installations, there also is a separate spout for each valve. Most faucets now being installed feed into a single spout and a further refinement is a single control valve that controls both the water temperature and volume. A shower should have an automatic diverter control that switches the flow of water back to the tub after each shower so that the next user will not accidentally get wet or scalded. Most modern kitchen sinks have a combination faucet with a swing spout. A separate spray on a flexible tube is also common. Another attachment now available for a kitchen sink provides boiling water instantly.

Specialized plumbing fixtures, such as laundry tubs or a wet bar, may also be found in laundry and family or recreation rooms.

Hot Water System

An adequate supply of hot water is essential. Houses with inadequate hot water systems suffer from functional obsolescence. This supply is usually generated in a hot water heater, with optional storage tanks as a supplement. The heater may be powered by electricity, gas or oil as a separate unit; or hot water may be supplied from furnace heat. The latter system supplies only a small amount of hot water, which may be exhausted too quickly; another disadvantage is the need to run the furnace all year.

The recovery rate (the time it takes to heat water) determines the size tank needed. Standard gas hot water tanks range from 30 to 80 gallons. Because the recovery rate of an oil hot water heater is faster than gas or electricity, a 30-gallon tank provides enough hot water for the needs of most families. They are not popular, however, because of the initial high cost and installation, especially if no flue or oil storage tank is already available.

In many areas of the country, large amounts of minerals such as calcium, magnesium, sulphates, bicarbonates, iron or sulphur are often found in the water. These minerals react unfavorably with soap, forming a curd-like substance which is difficult to rinse from clothing, hair and skin. A water softening system can be installed in the home to eliminate these mineral deposits.

Electrical System

In most houses electrical service begins at a "service entrance" which brings power from outside utility wires through an electric meter to a distribution panel in the house. The service entrance may be designed to bring in 30, 60, 100, 150, 200, 300, or 400 amperes of electricity. In smaller and older houses 30- or 60-ampere service may still be found but in most houses this would be considered obsolete. A 100-ampere service is the standard today for most small and medium-sized homes that do not have electric heat or central air conditioning. It provides 23,000 watts of power. A typical panel box has 12 to 16 fuses or circuit breakers. In larger houses and where electric heat, central air conditioning or a large number of appliances are used, 150- to 400-ampere service is needed. Most homes today are served by a three-wire, 220- to 240-volt service.

The distribution box has a switch that cuts off all electric service in the house when manually pulled in the event of an emergency. It also must contain either a master fuse or circuit breaker that will automatically disconnect the entire system if the system overloads. A fuse is a piece of wire that will melt when more than the prescribed amount of electricity flows through it. A circuit breaker is a special type of automatic switch that switches off when excess electricity passes through it. The distribution box divides the incoming electric service into separate branch circuits that lead to the various areas of the house. Each individual circuit must also be protected by a fuse or a circuit breaker. If an overload or short circuit occurs on the line, it automatically shuts off without tripping the main fuse or circuit breaker.

General circuits run to each area of the house. Receptacle outlets and permanently installed lighting fixtures are connected to them. These general circuits are protected with a 15-ampere fuse or circuit breaker. Special circuits for small appliances are protected with 20-ampere fuses; they provide 2,400 watts of 110- to 120-volt power. Large appliances such as clothes dryers, water heaters, ranges, dishwashers, freezers and large window air-conditioning units often require 220- to 240-volt power. These circuits are protected with 30- to 60-ampere fuses or circuit breakers.

The most preferred type of wiring is through rigid steel pipe, which looks like water pipe. It is also the most expensive method. Wires are pulled through the pipe after it is installed. A less expensive system that has code approval in most cities makes use of armored (BX) cable which consists of insulated wires wrapped in heavy paper and encased in a flexible, galvanized steel covering wound in a spiral fashion. Surface raceways made of metal or plastic are sometimes used in houses, mostly for repairs and in solid-core walls and partitions. Flexible steel conduit is constructed like BX cable except that it is installed without the wire, which is drawn through the conduit after installation.

Nonmetallic cable systems are prohibited in many cities. In this type of wiring each wire is wrapped with a paper tape and then encased in a heavy water- and fire-resistant fabric. A similar system has cable with a thermoplastic insulation and jacket; the cables are attached to the joists and studs with staples. A now obsolete system involves running two parallel exposed wires from the panel box to outlets and fixtures. The wires are attached to the house with white porcelain insulators, called "knobs." When the wire passes through a wall or joist, it is placed through a white porcelain tube—hence the name "knob and tube wiring." This type of system should be replaced.

Telephones and doorbells use low voltage wiring that does not present a safety hazard and therefore can be run loose throughout the walls and along the joists. Intercommunication, central music and burglar alarm systems also use low voltage, hazard-free wiring.

Until 1960 the duplex receptacle was the most common type of household outlet used. It accepts a two-prong plug, the type most often found on lamps and small appliances. In 1960 the National Electric Code required that all receptacles be of the grounding type, designed to accept a three-prong plug, to reduce shock hazard. Special waterproof receptacles with caps for outside use and other special purpose outlets are available. Outlets should be conveniently located throughout the house; in all habitable rooms, no point along the floor line should be more than six feet from an outlet.

Wall switches control permanently installed light fixtures and wall outlets. The simplest and most common switch is a two-way snap switch. Three-way switches are used to control a fixture or outlet from different locations, which is useful, for example, for a light in a stairwell.

Some houses are controlled by a low-voltage switching system. Instead of the switch directly opening and closing the circuit, it controls a relay which in turn operates the switch. The advantage of this system is that many lights and outlets can be controlled from one place. Control panels are often located at the main entrance or in the master bedroom. Dimmer switches are used to vary light intensity, which allows for better light distribution and decorative effects.

A good indication of an adequate switching arrangement is to be able to walk anywhere in the house and turn on a path of light and then turn it off without having to retrace steps or walk in the dark.

Miscellaneous Systems and Equipment

A variety of mechanical systems and special equipment is being installed in houses today. Many reflect fads or the special interests of the homeowner. They include such items as intercommunication and sound systems, burglar and fire alarms, automatic doors, elevators, incinerators, laundry chutes, and central vacuum cleaners. The appraiser must judge each situation for how much value these specialized items add to a house. A further consideration in some cases is whether the items are realty or personalty.

Items Requiring Immediate Repair

Except for homes in an exceptional state of maintenance, there will almost always be items needing repair as of the date of the appraisal. The repair of these normal maintenance items should add more value to the property than the cost. In the cost approach, these items fall under "physical deterioration-curable." The repair list should include conditions observed by the appraiser that constitute a fire or safety hazard. Many clients request that these items be listed separately in the report. Sometimes the appraiser is requested to estimate the cost of each repair (cost to cure). Some of the most commonly found items of immediate repair are:

1. Touching up exterior paint.
2. Minor carpentry repairs to stairs, molding, siding, trim, floors, porches.
3. Redecorating interior rooms.
4. Fixing plumbing leaks and noisy plumbing.
5. Loosening stuck doors and windows.
6. Repairing holes in screens and replacing broken windows or other glass.
7. Rehanging loose gutters and leaders.
8. Replacing missing roof shingles and tiles.
9. Fixing cracks in pavements.
10. Making minor electrical repairs.
11. Replacing rotted floor boards.
12. Exterminating vermin.
13. Fixing cracked or loose bathroom and kitchen tiles.
14. Repairing septic system.
15. Eliminating all fire and safety hazards.

Deferred Maintenance Items

Although the paint, roof, wallpaper, etc., may show some signs of wear and tear, it may not be ready for replacement on the date of the appraisal. The test is whether its repair or replacement will add more value to the property than its cost. For example, if a house has an exterior paint job that is three years old in an area where this type of paint lasts five years, the paint has suffered some depreciation. Repainting, however, probably would not add value to the property *equal to its cost* if it were done at the end of three years. (The treatment of deferred maintenance is discussed in more detail in Chapter 12.)

The following items normally have to be repaired or replaced before the end of the economic life of the house. They are known as short-lived items:

1. Interior paint and wallpaper.
2. Exterior paint.
3. Floor finishes.

4. Shades, screens and blinds.
5. Waterproofing and weatherstripping.
6. Gutters and leaders.
7. Storm windows.
8. Roof covering and flashing.
9. Hot and cold water pipes.
10. Plumbing fixtures.
11. Domestic hot water heater.
12. Electric service entrance.
13. Electric wiring.
14. Electric switches and outlets.
15. Electric fixtures.
16. Furnace.
17. Ducts and radiators.
18. Air conditioning equipment.
19. Carpeting.
20. Kitchen appliances.
21. Kitchen counters and cabinets.
22. Well pump.
23. Water softener system.
24. Laundry appliances.
25. Ventilating fans.
26. Fences and other site improvements.

The appraiser should note any of these or other short-lived items whose condition is better or worse than the overall condition of the house.

Overall Condition of Improvements

This section of the report is substantially completed when all items requiring immediate repair and all deferred maintenance are described. One last step, however, is to report the condition of items that should last the normal economic life of the house. Their condition is affected by abnormal wear and tear, and they can be damaged accidentally. They also may have been poorly made or installed when the house was built. It would be a very unusual house where all the long-lived items were in exactly the same condition. For example, the clapboard siding on a house may show signs of warping because of a roof leak; the condition may not be bad enough to warrant replacing the siding now. This case is a form of "physical deterioration-incurable." Observations of this type are used to estimate the effective age of the house (see Chapter 12).

Design and Layout (Functional Utility)

The perfect house is one that is the exact size, shape and design to produce the maximum profit. It would be the theoretical highest and best use of the site. Most houses are *not* the perfect or ideal house for their neighborhood. Room sizes, their number and type, and the design and layout of a typical home differ from the idealized highest and best use house. In fact, many things could be improved in the design and layout of a typical home. The appraiser is not on a quest for the perfect house but is trying to identify design elements that adversely affect value. These items constitute "functional obsolescence" in the cost approach (see Chapter 12).

Since most appraisers have little or no training in house design, they tend to rely on their own likes and dislikes as a basis for making design judgments, an inappropriate basis on which to rely. It is better to learn what is generally accepted in the market as good design. The appraiser can judge then how a particular market reacts to houses that do not meet standard design criteria.

House Zones

A good way to consider the interior layout of a house is to divide it into zones. The private/sleeping zone contains the bedrooms, bathrooms and dressing rooms. The living/social zone consists of the living room, dining room, recreation room, den and enclosed porch. The working/service zone consists of the kitchen, laundry, pantry and other work areas. In addition to these three zones are circulation areas consisting of halls and stairs plus guest and family entrances (see Fig. 10-3).

The three zones should be separated from each other so that activities in one zone do not interfere with those in another. The private/sleeping zone should be located so that it is insulated from noise in the other two zones, and it should be possible to move from the bedrooms to the bathrooms in this zone without being seen from the other areas of the house.

The working/service zone is the nerve center of the house; from here the household activities are directed. From the kitchen, it should be possible to control both guest and family entrances, act-ivities in the private/sleeping zone and living/social zone, plus activities in the porch, patio and backyard areas.

The guest entrance should lead into the center of the house. From here should be direct access to the living areas, guest closet and guest lavatory. A noise and visibility barrier should exist between the guest entrance and the private/sleeping zone.

Ideally the family entrance should be from the garage, carport or breezeway into the kitchen or from a circulation area directly con-necting to the kitchen. Traffic from this entrance should not have to pass through the work triangle of the kitchen to enter the other rooms of the house. Circulation should be such that one may move from the working/service zone to the private/sleeping zone without going through the living/social zone.

If the house has a basement, it may have a separate outside en-trance. The inside basement entrance should lead into a circula-tion area that has access to the private/sleeping zone, the living/social zone and both the guest and family entrances, without going through the living room or the kitchen work triangle.

According to a national survey of homeowners, some of the most common floor plan deficiencies include the following items. These will vary depending on the geographic region and the size and value of the residence.

1. Front door entering directly into the living room.
2. No front hall closet.
3. No direct access from front door to kitchen, bath or bedroom without passing through other rooms.
4. Rear door not convenient to kitchen and difficult to reach from the street, driveway and garage.
5. No comfortable area in or near the kitchen for family to eat.
6. A separate dining area or room not easily accessible from the kitchen.
7. Stairways off of a room rather than in a hallway or foyer.
8. Bedrooms and baths that are visible from the living room or foyer.
9. Recreation or family room poorly located (not visible from kitchen).
10. No access to the basement from outside the house.
11. Walls between bedrooms not soundproof (separation by a bathroom or closet accomplish soundproofing).
12. Outdoor living areas not accessible from kitchen.

FIG. 10-3: Zones of a One-Story House

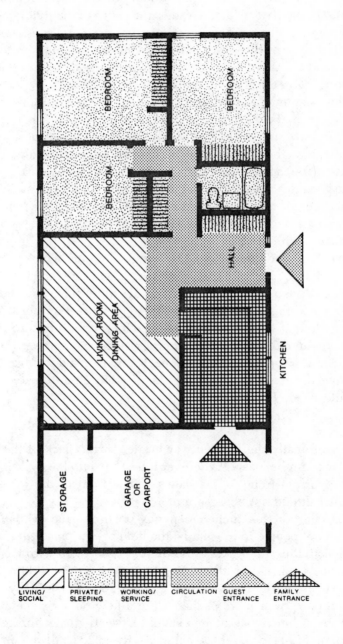

BEDROOM

BEDROOM

BEDROOM

HALL

LIVING ROOM
DINING AREA

KITCHEN

STORAGE

GARAGE
OR
CARPORT

LIVING/
SOCIAL

PRIVATE/
SLEEPING

WORKING/
SERVICE

CIRCULATION

GUEST
ENTRANCE

FAMILY
ENTRANCE

Living Room

Until World War II, the living room was the living center of the house. In the past several decades, the status of the living room has undergone a change. Today, the family room, patio and kitchen are more likely to be the locations for relaxing, socializing and entertaining. As these areas have grown and developed, the size and the importance of the living room has diminished.

The location of the living room may be in the traditional front of the house or, if view or access to outdoor living areas is better, in the back or on a side of the house. The room should be positioned to supplement the dining and outdoor entertainment areas in the house. Often one end of the living room is the dining area, so it must have good juxtaposition with the kitchen/service areas as well. The living room should not be a traffic-way between other rooms. The following are some guidelines for judging the size of the living room compared with the rest of the house.

In a three-bedroom house, the living room should have minimum dimensions of 11 by 16 feet, or at least 170 square feet. The recommended dimensions are 12 by 18 feet. If a dining area is at one end of the room, dimensions may go up to 16 by 26 feet or more. A maximum width of 14 feet is recommended for proper furniture arrangements around the room. Where traffic is necessary through the room, a width of 15 or 16 feet could conceivably be used to advantage by routing the traffic outside the conversation circle created by the furniture (see Fig. 10-4).

Kitchen

Traditionally the kitchen was located at the back of the house. Today it can be located wherever it best fits into the overall design and a current trend is to locate it at the front of the house. The kitchen should not be a main thoroughfare.

The size of the kitchen depends on the space available, the number of people in the family, the kind of equipment desired and what activities other than those directly associated with food preparation are carried on there. The minimum size for a kitchen in a small house is 8 by 10 feet. Better sizes are 10 by 10 and 10 by 12 feet.

Ten percent or more of the cost of a new home is spent on the kitchen. A functional kitchen should have adequate storage space, appliance space, counter and activity space, all arranged for

FIG. 10-4: Minimum Size Living Room Layout

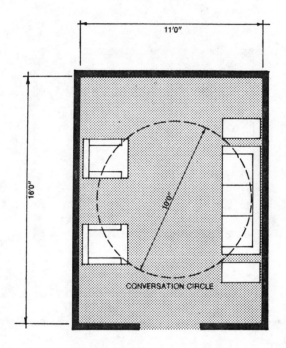

maximum efficiency. The term *triangle* has become fashionable to describe the essential work zone of the kitchen, since there are three key work areas of use and activity: the refrigerator area, sink/wash/ preparation area and range/serving area. They can be arranged in any logical way, determined by the space available and the personal preference for one particular center over another (see Fig. 10-5).

However the kitchen is arranged, work should flow in a normal sequence from one center to another. Ideally, no traffic should move through the triangle in the main kitchen work area. Properly establishing the location of windows and doors will help to ensure a traffic pattern that does not interfere with efficient use of the kitchen. Most building standards require that the window area should equal at least 10% of the floor area of the room. At least one section of a work

FIG. 10-5: Typical Kitchen Layout

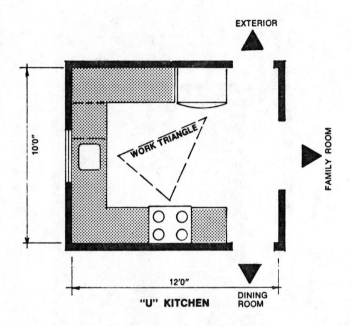

The total of the three sides of the Work Triangle should not exceed 22 feet.

counter should have a window over it with provision for controlling direct sunlight. Many people prefer to have a window located over the sink. (For reasons of both safety and good housekeeping, the range should never be located under a window.)

Many kitchens suffer from one or more of the following inadequacies (listed in order of most common occurrrence):

1. Insufficient base cabinet storage.
2. Insufficient wall cabinet storage.
3. Insufficient counter space.
4. No counter beside the refrigerator.
5. Not enough window area.
6. Poorly placed doors that waste wall space.
7. Traffic through the work triangle.
8. Too little counter space on either side of the sink.
9. No counter beside the range.

10. Insufficient space in front of cabinets.
11. Distance between sink, range and refrigerator too great.
12. Range under a window.

Dining Rooms and Dining Areas

A dining room was included in most pre-World War II homes. Now many houses have dining areas that are part of another room. The space requirements for dining rooms probably no longer apply to many markets. A minimum size dining room is 9 by 11 feet with 12 by 12 being preferable. In some markets an acceptable alternative to the dining room or area is an extra large "eat-in" kitchen. The appraiser must determine what the market wants and judge if the appraised house meets the requirements.

Bedrooms

The number of bedrooms in a house is an important design consideration. Three bedrooms is most common today. Houses with only two bedrooms are often constructed at the direction of an owner who does not need the third room; however, many markets do not accept only two bedrooms without a substantial discount. A fourth bedroom is appealing to many families, but in many markets the additional price a four-bedroom house brings is not as great as the cost of the extra bedroom. Of course, luxury homes may have five or more bedrooms. One bedroom homes are usually substandard in any market, except for recreational homes.

Two key factors in the location of bedrooms are that they be isolated from the noise generated in the rest of the house, and that one should be able to get from each bedroom to a bathroom without being seen from the living/social zone of the house. The minimum size bedroom for a single bed is 8 by 10 feet; this size is satisfactory only if the layout is good and no space is wasted. The minimum size room for a double bed is 10 by 11½ feet. Some markets expect bedrooms to be more than minimum size; other markets will not pay the extra cost for the larger space (see Fig. 10-6).

Each bedroom should have at least one closet with a minimum depth of two feet, a width of three feet and a height sufficient to allow five feet clear hanging space. It should also have a shelf not over 74 inches above the floor of the room with at least eight inches clear space over the shelf.

FIG. 10-6: Minimum Size Bedroom Layouts

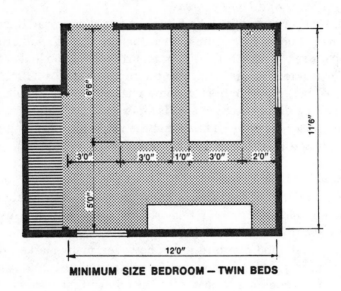

MINIMUM SIZE BEDROOM — TWIN BEDS

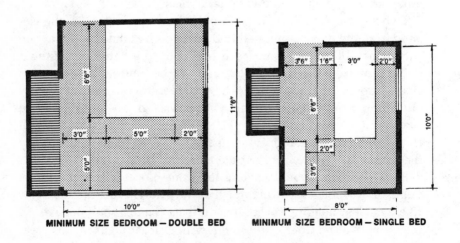

MINIMUM SIZE BEDROOM — DOUBLE BED   **MINIMUM SIZE BEDROOM — SINGLE BED**

Bathrooms and Lavatories

Houses with only one bathroom are obsolete in many markets; 1½ baths is becoming a minimum standard, except in low-priced and recreation homes. The older minimum standard for two-story houses of one bath upstairs and a lavatory downstairs also is being replaced in many markets with a standard of two baths. The minimum size for a bathroom containing a five-foot tub/shower combination, basin and toilet is 5 by 7 feet. This allows for the toilet to be on the wall opposite the tub rather than between the tub and basin, which is unsatisfactory; it also allows the door to swing in without hitting a fixture (see Fig. 10-7). A bathroom should not be located between two bedrooms with a door leading directly into the bathroom from each bedroom.

The terminology used to describe bathrooms and lavatories varies around the country. In most areas a full bath consists of a room with a toilet (also known as a water closet), wash basin (also known as a sink, lavatory or vanity) and a tub. A 3/4-bathroom has a toilet, wash basin and stall shower (called a full bath in some areas). A half-bath (also known as a lavatory, lavette, or powder room) has a toilet and washbasin.

The bathroom requires the most heat and the best ventilation of any room in the house. A bathroom or lavatory with or without a window is equally acceptable. Ventilation of an interior bathroom or lavatory is essential. A ventilation fan, ducted to the outside, should be wired to the light switch so that it goes on automatically when the

FIG. 10-7: Minimum Bathroom Layouts

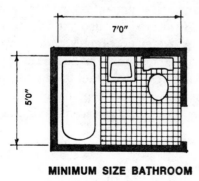

MINIMUM SIZE BATHROOM

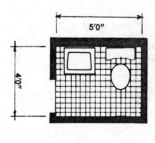

MINIMUM SIZE HALF BATH

room is in use and turns off automatically when the lights are turned off.

Family and Recreation Rooms

Before World War II attics, dens and finished basements generally were used as additional recreation space. Today the family room is used as a den, study, guest room, nursery, library, TV room, or hobby entertainment center. The key to the successful location of this room is to have it visible from and easily accessible to the kitchen. It also should be accessible to the outdoor living area, such as the backyard or patio. A good size for the recreation room in a small house is 12 by 16 feet. Appraisers should remember that many family or recreation rooms are overimproved or too large for their particular market.

Patios and Porches

In some areas patios are very elaborate and an integral part of the house. They can be described as part of the improvements rather than a site improvement. Porches have been decreasing in popularity and importance for many years except in a few areas of the country. The exceptions seem to be sun and side porches on more expensive homes, the Hawaiian "lanai" (a covered or open porch) and screened-in porches in beach and summer homes.

Garages and Carports

Every market has identifiable standards for car storage; houses that do not meet or exceed this standard suffer from functional obsolescence. A garage in an area that accepts carports is a superadequacy. Likewise, a carport in an area that demands a garage is a deficiency. Heated, three-car or oversized garages, though appealing, are often superadequacies. The minimum standard size for a one-car garage is 10 by 20 feet, and 18½ by 20 feet for a two-car garage. Many older garages are less than 20 feet deep, making them too short for some cars. Detached garages have decreased in popularity in some areas of the country.

Laundry Rooms and Storage Areas

A growing trend has been to bring the washing machine and clothes dryer out of the basement. These appliances are being installed in the kitchen, a separate laundry or utility room, the garage, or even in hallways or closets on the first or second floors.

Anyone who has lived in a house with a basement finds it hard to understand why they are not more universally accepted. A house without a basement may suffer from a lack of adequate storage space, which will be penalized by the market. Alternate acceptable storage areas are attics, closets, storage rooms, garages, storage sheds, etc.

Renovation: Rehabilitation, Modernization and Remodeling

Often the appraiser finds that substantial renovations are necessary if the existing improvement is to achieve the highest and best use of the site. These alterations and improvements go beyond the normal curable physical deterioration and functional obsolescence (see Chapter 12). The owner of the property may have come to a similar conclusion before the appraisal and may already have done some or all of the work.

These substantial changes can be described by the terms rehabilitation, modernization and remodeling. Each term, as defined in *Real Estate Appraisal Terminology*, has a specific meaning with which the appraiser should be familiar:

1. *Rehabilitation.* The restoration of a property to satisfactory condition without changing the plan, form or style of a structure. In urban renewal, the restoration to good condition of deteriorated structures, neighborhoods, and public facilities. Neighborhood rehabilitation encompasses structural rehabilitation and in addition may extend to street improvements and a provision of such amenities as parks and playgrounds.[1]
2. *Modernization.* Taking corrective measures to bring a property into conformity with changes in style, whether exterior or interior or additions necessary to meet standards of current demand. It nominally involves replacing parts of the structure or mechanical equipment with modern replacements of the same kind and hence seldom includes capital improvements.[2]
3. *Remodeling.* Changing the plan, form or style of a structure to correct functional or economic deficiencies.[3]

Rehabilitation

A growing trend in many cities throughout the country is the

[1]*Real Estate Appraisal Terminology*, op. cit., p. 174.
[2]Ibid., p. 142.
[3]Ibid., p. 175.

restoration of older neighborhoods and homes. People are moving back into city neighborhoods, and older homes in center city locations are now attracting young professionals, business people and white-collar workers. Some older homes are not much more than four good walls and sturdy ceilings; more often the interior floors and walls are usable. The woodwork can be restored and although the mechanical systems usually have to be replaced, some parts of the original systems may be usable. The appraisal of this type of property often requires the appraiser to help plan the rehabilitation.

Modernization

Modernization implies replacement or remodeling specifically designed to offset the effect of obsolescence or making additions necessary to meet current design standards. The replacement of old radiators and lighting or plumbing fixtures with new items of fundamentally the same type is nothing more than improving the condition of the old installation. However, the substitution of convectors for cast-iron radiators, of built-in bathtubs for tubs on legs, or of modern lighting fixtures for old-fashioned types would not necessarily reflect on the physical condition of the items being replaced and therefore would constitute an improvement of the property. These expenditures offset obsolescence and may be classified as modernization. Modernization may cost more than simple renewal but can be economically justified where it offsets the obsolescence inherent in the older equipment.

Modernization usually extends the economic life of property. To be justified, a modernization program must be economically feasible. Sometimes modernization is done because the owner desires the convenience it creates. The installation of a modern kitchen at a cost of $10,000 may add only $5,000 in value to the house. This is an example of a superadequacy or overimprovement.

Remodeling

Remodeling becomes practical when the use of part of the house can be changed. Common examples are finishing a basement or attic or adding a bathroom to an existing room. Considerable remodeling is often done to suit the needs of a specific owner without much thought given to what the market in general expects and will pay. The expenditure of $6,000 to finish a basement playroom may add only $3,000 in value in some markets.

Costs

It is much more difficult to estimate renovation or rehabilitation costs than that of new construction. Unit-in-place costs for new work, plus an additional allowance for the normally higher cost of repair work, aid in making renovation estimates. Rehabilitation estimates frequently may be based upon actual recent costs for the same or equivalent work performed in the property or in similar properties. Management records may even include bids for specific rehabilitation items that have not been accomplished, such as exterior painting, roof repair, or interior decorating.

The cost of some rehabilitation work may approximate that for similar work in new construction. However, the cost of modernization or remodeling work is almost invariably higher than that for new construction, for several reasons. Although the quantity of material may be the same as for new work, more labor is involved and the conditions are different. The alteration of a structure usually involves tearing out old work and performing small portions of new work under conditions not conducive to the degree of efficiency attainable on new construction. If the estimate made by the contractor is on a flat-fee basis, the charge may be substantially higher than the cost of identical work in new construction, so the contractor can protect himself against complications that may develop as the remodeling progresses. Such unforeseen complications may involve the placement of existing conduits, pipes, and structural load-bearing members.

Other costs to be considered are those that may be incurred by the owner rather than the contractor. These include the architect's fee, the owner's cost of supervision and loss of use of the house while the work is being done.

Feasibility of Renovation

Whether rehabilitation, modernization or remodeling is involved, the justification for any renovation program depends on what constitutes the highest and best use of the property. The study that the appraiser gives to this question produces the cost estimates necessary for a program to achieve such use, which in turn provide the basis for a decision as to its economic justification.

If the property is old but in sufficiently sound condition for remodeling, if the neighborhood standards and trends are materially
higher than the property's present status, and if the prospective
value increase is substantial, a comprehensive program may be feasible. A wide range of potential programs may justify consideration,
but there is only one satisfactory way to select the final plan. This is
to explore the alternatives, estimate the cost and potential value
increases and then be guided by the results of a comparison of the
data.

Assume that a brownstone townhouse is available in a neighborhood going through a period of redevelopment. The house can be
purchased for $15,000. It is estimated that it will take about $10,000
to rehabilitate the house to meet the minimum code requirements.
The estimated value when the rehabilitation is completed is
$30,000. Based on these figures, the rehabilitation to meet minimum
standards is feasible. A second possibility is to restore the house to its
original historical appearance and do a much more elaborate renovation. The estimated cost of this renovation would be $30,000, but the
final value would be $55,000.

Example 1:	Acquisition price	$15,000
	Renovation cost	10,000
	Total cost	$25,000
	Estimated value after renovation	$30,000
	Estimated profit	$ 5,000
Example 2:	Acquisition price	$15,000
	Renovation cost	30,000
	Total cost	$45,000
	Estimated value after renovation	$55,000
	Estimated profit	$10,000

Both the above programs are feasible. However, Example 2
represents the highest and best use of the property since it produces
the maximum profit. In some cases where the profit potential due to
a program of rehabilitation, modernization and remodeling is
substantial, the "as is" value estimate for the property being appraised should be modified upward. In many cities properties have
been purchased at relatively low prices by imaginative investors

who have undertaken programs of selective modernization, some-times involving new exterior ("skin") treatment and other major expenditures. Modernized and attractive properties thus created have become marketable at levels substantially higher than the investments involved. Whether this is practical in any specific situa-tion can be ascertained only on completion of a before-and-after feasibility analysis.

In the final analysis, the appraiser's estimate of a renovation pro-gram is part of the process used to arrive at a value estimate for the property. Whether or not the owner actually carries out such a pro-gram, the value of the property in its existing state may be influenced by its potential for increased value under a feasible renovation program.

Graphic Aids
Photography
Use of photographs has become an important part of the ap-praisal report. Out-of-focus, over or underexposed amateur photos are no longer acceptable as part of a professional appraisal report. Instant photography methods are acceptable to some clients. Others require more professional pictures taken with a conventional camera. A 35mm camera is the choice of many experienced apprais-ers, because of the rectangular shape of the photographs, the versa-tility of the equipment, the availability of film and low cost for color reproduction. The use of color photographs has become standard in many parts of the country.

There is no absolute rule as to what the photographs should in-clude. However, as a minimum, photographs of all sides of the house and any major site improvements, plus a shot of the street in both directions showing the house in the foreground, may be required. When the assignment warrants the extra expense, photographs of construction details and of the interior of the house may also be included.

Plot Plan
A plot plan shows the lot boundaries, important topograph-ical features and the location of the improvements. A well-drawn plot plan is made to scale, with lot dimensions indicated on the boundary lines. In addition to the house and garage or carport, it should show the position of sidewalks, driveways, patios, pools, etc.

Any abutting rights-of-way, known easements or apparent encroachments should also be shown. An appraiser is not expected to be a professional draftsperson but the plot plan should be neat and carefully drawn.

Sketch of the House

Often a simple sketch of the exterior walls of the house (and garage or carport, if any) or a more complete drawing showing the location of doors, windows and interior walls is included as part of the report. Many appraisers take special pride in their ability to produce professionally drawn sketches. Such drawings are not required for a typical house appraisal; a simple, neatly drawn sketch to approximate scale, showing the important dimensions, will usually suffice. The dimensions that appear on the house sketch should be the same ones used to calculate the gross living area.

Reading a House Plan

The appraiser who is appraising a house planned for construction, under construction or being considered for a program of renovation must be able to read the plans that detail the proposed construction. Architects use orthographic projections to picture the proposed work rather than perspective drawings. An orthographic projection permits proportional reduction of the drawing while maintaining the size and spatial relationships of the completed house. Lines drawn parallel in an orthographic projection represents walls that are parallel in the finished house.

A complete set of house plans consists of:

1. Orthographic projections of each floor and the basement.
2. Electrical plans.
3. Plumbing plans.
4. Wall sections.
5. Elevations of all sides.
6. Plot plan.
7. Door and window schedules.
8. Specifications.

The dimensions of an actual house may not appear to agree with those indicated on the house plans. It is impossible to tell from looking at the plans what the actual points of measurement are. An actual measurement read on the tape may be from one inch to more than five inches *less* than the dimension indicated on the plan. Architects seldom indicate dimensions from one wall surface to another. On drawings of frame houses, they prefer to indicate the dimensions between the surface of the studs of opposite walls or from the center of the opposite wall studs. When stud-surface-to-stud-surface is used, the actual tape measurements are about one inch less than the indicated dimension line measurement, which is the thickness of the sheetrock. When the center of the stud is used as the point of measurement, the tape reading is about five inches less, since half the thickness of the stud is usually two inches plus the thickness of the sheetrock.

The techniques for dimensioning masonry construction are different from those for frame construction. Dimension lines on masonry construction plans usually run from one masonry surface to another, rather than to the surface of the sheetrock or other wall coverings.

To read house plans, it is necessary to know the many symbols architects use to represent the materials, electric switches and outlets, plumbing fixtures and pipes, some of which appear on the following pages.

FIG. 10-8: Construction Material Symbols

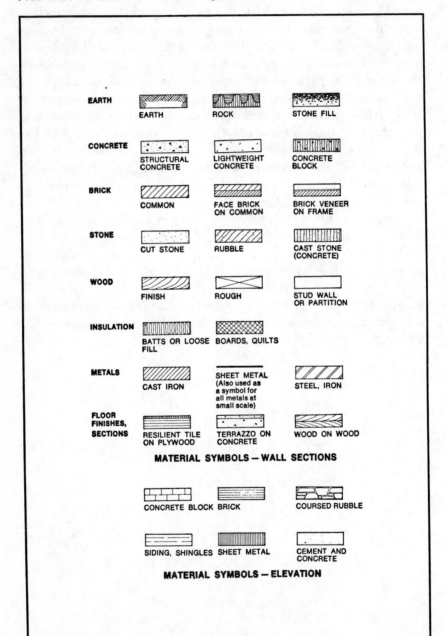

FIG. 10-9: Plumbing Symbols

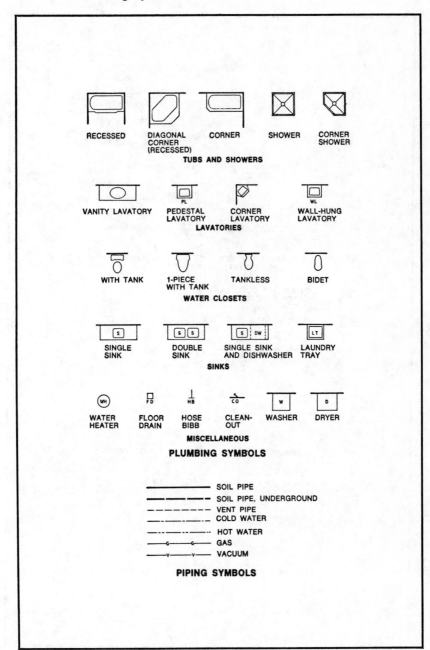

FIG. 10-10: Electrical Symbols

○	CEILING OUTLET	Ⓕ	FAN OUTLET
⊢○	WALL OUTLET	▲	SPECIAL PURPOSE OUTLET (DESCRIBED IN SPECS)
○PS	CEILING OUTLET WITH PULL SWITCH	⊙	FLOOR OUTLET
⊢○PS	WALL OUTLET WITH PULL SWITCH	▬	LIGHTING PANEL
⊖	DUPLEX CONVENIENCE OUTLET	▨	POWER PANEL
⊖WP	WEATHERPROOF DUPLEX CONVENIENCE OUTLET	▭	FLUORESCENT FIXTURE
⊖1, 3,	CONVENIENCE OUTLET (NUMBER INDICATES RECEPTACLES)	CH	CHIMES
⊖R	RANGE OUTLET	Ⓣ	THERMOSTAT
⊖S	SWITCH AND CONVENIENCE OUTLET	▣	PUSH BUTTON
▭▷	BELL	S_3	3-WAY SWITCH
TV	TELEVISION	S_4	4-WAY SWITCH
◀	TELEPHONE	S_P	SWITCH WITH PILOT LAMP
S	SINGLE-POLE SWITCH	S	WIRE TO OUTLET OR FIXTURE
S_2	DOUBLE-POLE SWITCH		

Summary

The description of the improvements is an important part of the appraisal report. It provides the information used in the three approaches to value. It includes a description of all the improvements to the site as well as a complete description of the residence and any ancillary improvements. Information about all the physical components including their design, quality and condition is included. A list of items requiring immediate repair, plus a list of items that will require repair in the near future, should also be given. When appropriate, any feasible renovations should be specified.

Review Questions

1. Must the appraiser make a personal physical inspection of the property? Explain.
2. What is a plot plan?
3. The description of the improvements is often broken into what two parts?
4. List several items described in the report relating to the exterior of the house.
5. What is the most popular type of framing used in houses built in the U.S.?
6. What are some of the signs of defective framing and how can they be detected?
7. What are the benefits of insulation?
8. What are the major mechanical systems of a house?
9. What is the most preferred type of electrical wiring for a house?
10. List five common floor plan deficiencies.
11. What is a major element in determining the feasibility of a remodeling program?

11

The Income Approach (Gross Monthly Rent Multiplier)

The income approach, applied to single family residences, is also called the Gross Monthly Rent Multiplier (GMRM), Gross Rent Multiplier (GRM), Gross Income Multiplier (GIM) or Gross Annual Multiplier (GAM). When used for income-producing properties (apartments, offices, retail stores), the multiplier is used primarily as a part of the market data approach. It sometimes is used in the cost approach to estimate obsolescense and in the market data approach to estimate adjustments.

The use of the income approach in valuing residential real estate is based on the assumption that value is related to the rent (income) the real estate can be expected to earn. This approach has its greatest application in areas where there is a substantial rental market. In neighborhoods that are predominantly owner-occupied, rental data may be too scarce for use of this approach.

Rarely does one refer to the annual income of a residence; it is more common to refer to the monthly income—usually the rental unfurnished without utilities—such as $200 per month, rather than $2,400 per year.

Steps in the Income Approach
When sufficient data is available, the appraiser follows these steps to derive an indication of market value from the income approach:

202

1. Calculates the Gross Monthly Rent Multiplier.
    a. Finds houses that have recently sold and were rented at the time of sale that are comparable to the property being appraised in the same or similar neighborhoods.
    b. Divides the sale price of each property by its monthly rental to derive a monthly rent multiplier, known as the Gross Monthly Rent Multiplier (GMRM).
    c. Reconciles the multipliers developed above to obtain a single multiplier or a range of multipliers that are applicable to the appraised property. This is *not* an average; it is a judgment of comparability and applicability.

2. Estimates the market rent of residence being appraised.
    a. Finds comparable rentals in the neighborhood.
    b. Analyzes each rental, comparing its features with those of the residence being appraised.
    c. Estimates the adjustments required to obtain an indicated market (economic) rent for the residence being appraised.
    d. Considers each comparable carefully, with emphasis on the need for adjustments, and formulates an opinion of the market rent of the residence being appraised, based upon the actual rents of the comparables.

3. Develops an indicated value of the residence being appraised.
    a. Multiplies the estimated market rent of the residence being appraised by the estimated monthly multiplier (or range of multipliers) to obtain its indicated market value via the income approach.

The multiplier is relied on as an indication of market value because it tends to express a constant relationship between the gross monthly rental income of a single family residence and its sale price. Practicing appraisers rely on this indicator as a direct application of market data and income information, which expresses the relationship between sale price (or market value) and rental income.

The multiplier is a whole number— that is, it is not a percentage or a fraction. The whole number is produced by dividing the monthly rental income into the sale price of a comparable property. For example, if the sale price of a residence were $20,000 and it had been rented for $200 a month, $20,000 is divided by $200 and the multiplier is found to be 100. The system is used by practicing appraisers because it is straightforward and simple. Its reliability, of course, rests on the dependability of the data used.

Most appraisers believe that no adjustments can or should be made in the development of the multiplier. They feel that if comparable sales are *not* reasonably similar, they should be dropped from consideration. A few appraisers still feel that under some circumstances adjustments can be made in the data collected, on the same basis as in the market data approach, using the four elements of comparison. This process is not recommended.

Limitations of the GMRM

The multiplier, like any other approach, can produce excellent results if the data used is reliable and appropriate. However, it can be misleading and produce indefensible conclusions if the technique used or the information applied is inappropriate. The situations under which the results are most desirable include:

1. The properties from which the multiplier is developed have common characteristics (size, age, physical condition, neighborhood, etc.) with the residence being appraised.
2. The multiplier is extracted from properties for which there is an active market. If there is not an active market (that is, many recent sales), information on which to base a conclusion will be inadequate. The rationale of the multiplier is that with a large number of sales, the ones that are out of line will automatically be displayed and the like ones will tend to cluster together in an array.[1] This illustrates the application of the law of large numbers—that the extreme of the ranges will be obvious to the analyst and will be disregarded.
3. The market information is correct and rentals have been verified.

When the appraised property is in a neighborhood where rentals are uncommon or nonexistent, it would be necessary to estimate the market (economic) rent without good data, which would substantially reduce the reliability of the approach. Also, if there are unusual situations or conditions of sale, the results will not be representative of market value. In some instances, properties may be rented for substantially above economic rent, while in others they may be

---

[1] An array is a statistical term that describes the listing of a series of figures in order from low to high or high to low, depending on the use of the data.

rented far below the market. If the conditions of the sale do not reflect an open market transaction, then the application of such sales will not be an appropriate basis for the appraiser's market value decision.

Calculating a GMRM

The following example illustrates how a GMRM is derived from the market, which is based on using actual sales and dividing them by their actual rentals at the time of the sale, without making any adjustments. The multipliers in Fig. 11-1 range from 107 to 112, with 110 as most common multiplier. It is the multiplier for properties that appears to be closest to the value of the property being appraised. Therefore, 110 was selected as the appropriate multiplier.

Fig. 11-1: Finding the GMRM Without Adjustments

Comparable Property	Verified Sales Price	Verified Actual Gross Income at Time of Sale		Indicated Gross Monthly Rent Multiplier (GMRM)
1	$39,900	$373	=	107
2	41,200	380	=	108
3	42,500	380	=	112
4	42,950	385	=	112
5	44,000	400	=	110
6	44,500	405	=	110
7	44,450	405	=	110
8	44,900	405	=	111
9	44,000	400	=	110
10	45,500	410	=	111
11	44,000	400	=	110
12	41,200	378	=	109

Estimating Market Rent of the Appraised Residence

Following are two illustrations that show how to derive the market rent of the residence being appraised from the market. The first is based on the actual rental of the residence being appraised, which has been ascertained to be the market rent. The second is based on comparing it with other rental residences and adjusting for any differences. The adjusted comparable rentals are used as indicators of rental value for the residence being appraised.

Example One

If the appraised property is rented, the monthly rental can be used as an indication of the market rent. It is not acceptable appraisal practice, however, to use this contract rent without checking it against other rents in the market. In this illustration the appraised property is rented for $400 per month. Based on information obtained from the owner and tenant, it appears to be an arm's length arrangement, with both parties believing the rent is what the property should be getting. This is a good indication that the market rent for such a property is $400. To check this rental in the market, other rented houses similar to it should be located.

FIG. 11-2: Estimating Market Rent Without Adjustments

Comparable Property	Monthly Rent
1	$395
2	400
3	405
4	400
5	400
6	390
7	410
8	400

Based on the array shown in Fig. 11-2, and considering the reported rent of the appraised residence, its market rent appears to be about $400. Some appraisers would consider this sufficient data on which to base the estimate of market rent. Others feel it is better to adjust the rental of each of the residences and then make the estimate, especially when the comparables differ to a certain extent from the property being appraised.

Example Two

In this example, the property being appraised has one bathroom, a one-car garage, an unfinished basement and is rented without utilities included. Some comparable rentals have two bathrooms, two-car garages, finished basements and/or are rented with utilities included. Adjustments may be needed to reflect the rental differences attributable to these differences.

Because it is difficult to tell if differences affect rents in similar or opposite ways just by looking at them, the "matched pair" technique is used to abstract adjustments from the market. When more than one difference exists, one rental is designated as the base rental, which is adjusted for all known differences except the one being sought. Then it is compared with the other rental in the pair and any remaining difference in rent is attributed to the remaining element of comparison. This technique is illustrated in Fig. 11-3.

FIG. 11-3: Estimating Market Rent With Adjustments

<u>Rental #1</u>: 83 Maple Street — a nearby house similar to the house being appraised; one bathroom, unfinished basement, one-car garage; was recently rented unfurnished and without utilities for $405/month. No special conditions.

<u>Rental #2</u>: 64 Pine Street — a nearby house similar to the house being appraised, with a one-car garage and unfinished basement, but two bathrooms. It was recently rented unfurnished and without utilities for $425/month, with no special conditions.

<u>Rental #3</u>: 18 Elm Street — a nearby house similar to the house being appraised, with an unfinished basement, two bathrooms and two-car garage. It was recently rented unfurnished and without utilities for $440/month, without special conditions.

<u>Rental #4</u>: 21 Oak Street — a nearby house similar to the house being appraised, with two-bathrooms, a two-car garage and a finished basement. It was recently rented unfurnished and without utilities for $465 per month, with no special conditions.

<u>Rental #5</u>: 14 Hemlock Street — a nearby house similar to the house being appraised. It was rented unfurnished with utilities supplied by the owner for $470. Like the house being appraised, it had only one bathroom, a one-car garage, and an unfinished basement. No special conditions.

Adjustments		Monthly Rental
Rental 1 (Base—one bathroom, one-car garage)		$405
Rental 2 (two bathrooms, one-car garage)		425
Difference attributable to number of bathrooms		$ 20

* * *

Rental 1 (Base—one bathroom, one-car garage)		$405
Rental 3 (two bathrooms, two-car garage)	$440	
Adjustment to Rental 3 to reflect difference in bathroom size (based on Rentals 1 and 2)	− 20	
Adjusted Rental 3		420
Difference attributed to garage size		$ 15

Rental 1 (Base—one bathroom, one-car garage, unfinished basement)		$405
Rental 4 (two bathrooms, two-car garage, finished basement)	$465	
Adjustment to Rental 4 to reflect difference in bathroom size (based on Rentals 1 and 2)	− 20	
Adjustment to Rental 4 to reflect difference in garage size (based on Rentals 1 and 3)	− 15	
Adjusted Rental 4		430
Difference attributable to basement finish		$ 25

* * *

Rental 1 (Base—one bathroom, one-car garage, unfinished basement, no utilities)		$405
Rental 5 (one-bathroom, one-car garage, unfinished basement, utilities paid by owner)		470
Difference attributable to inclusion or exclusion of utilities as part of rent		$ 65

Each comparable rental is adjusted to give an indication of the market rental of the appraised property. If an element of comparison in the comparable rental results in a higher rental than what the property being appraised would rent for, a *minus* adjustment is made. For example, if the only difference is that the appraised property has three bedrooms and a comparable rental has four bedrooms, with the extra bedroom contributing $25 to the monthly rental, then a *minus* $25 adjustment is made to the comparable rental. These adjustment techniques are identical to those used in the market data approach (see Chapter 13).

A rating grid may be used to display information about the appraised property and the comparable rentals, along with adjustments for each difference between them (see Fig. 11-4).

Applying the GMRM and Market Rent to Estimate Value

The third step of the income approach is to estimate the indicated market value of the residence being appraised, which is done by multiplying the estimated market rent of the residence by the GMRM selected. For example, if the GMRM selected were 110, based on market data, and the estimated market rent of the residence being appraised were $405 per month (unfurnished and without utilities), its indicated market value is calculated as follows:

1. Estimated market rent of house being appraised $ 405
2. Gross Monthly Rent Multiplier × 110
3. Indicated value of the residence being appraised via the income approach $44,550

FIG. 11-4: Comparable Rental Grid

Item	Appraised House	Comp. Rental 1	Comp. Rental 2	Comp. Rental 3	Comp. Rental 4	Comp. Rental 5
Rent		$405	$425	$440	$465	$470
Bathrooms	one	one / -0-	two / -$20	two / -$20	two / -$20	one / -0-
Garage size	one-car	one-car / -0-	one-car / -0-	two-car / -$15	two-car / -$15	one-car / -0-
Basement	unfinished	unfinished / -0-	unfinished / -0-	unfinished / -0-	finished / -$25	unfinished / -0-
Utilities Payment	tenant	tenant / -0-	tenant / -0-	tenant / -0-	tenant / -0-	owner / -$65
Net adjustment		-0-	-$20	-$35	-$60	-$65
Indicated rent of appraised house		$405	$405	$405	$405	$405

Actual data would rarely work out this precisely. Often both plus and minus adjustments would be made and the indicated rents for the house being appraised would vary, requiring reconciling into a final indicated rental value.

Summary

This chapter illustrates the use of the income approach as it applies to the single family residence. It is also referred to as the Gross Monthly Rent Multiplier and is considered a reliable approach to market value if the data used is verified and representative of the market.

There are three steps in the income approach:

1. The GMRM is selected by finding residences similar to the residence being appraised in the same or nearby neighborhoods that were rented at the time they were sold. The whole number, which is obtained by dividing the sale price by the monthly rent (usually unfurnished and without utilities included), is known as the Gross Monthly Rent Multiplier and expresses the relationship between rental income and value.
2. The market rent of the residence being appraised is estimated. Either the actual rent of the residence is used (after confirming that it is typical of the market) or the market rent is estimated by comparing the residence to other rented, comparable properties in the market and adjusting for any significant differences.
3. The indicated value via the income approach is obtained by multiplying the GMRM selected in Step 1 by the estimated market rent of the residence being appraised (Step 2).

Review Questions

1. What is a gross monthly rent multiplier and how is it used in the income approach?
2. What is the basic premise of the multiplier?
3. Why is monthly rather than annual rent used for single family residences?
4. When may adjustments be made to market data gathered to develop the GMRM? Explain why they should not be made.
5. What is the formula for extracting a multiplier from the sale price of a residence and its monthly rental? Using the formula, make up appropriate figures to produce a multiplier.
6. Having established a GMRM, show how it is applied to obtain an indicated market value for the residence via the income approach.
7. What are the advantages of using a GMRM? Its limitations?
8. What proper statistical methods and techniques may be applied to the data collected in order to assure correct conclusions?
9. List several situations under which the results of use of the GMRM will be most applicable.

12

The Cost Approach

The cost approach historically has been known as the summation approach — that is, the sum of site (land) value plus improvement value equals property value — but that term is rarely used anymore. The concept of the cost approach is based on the principle of substitution. It states that no rational person will pay more for an existing house than the amount for which he or she can obtain, by purchase of a site and construction, without undue delay, of a house of equal desirability and utility.

The philosophy in the cost approach to market value is unique compared to the other two approaches. The approach uses the sales of comparable sites to develop a market value estimate of the site as if unimproved, to which is added a market value estimate of the improvements based on "cost new" less any and all depreciation (loss in value). The procedure for the development of market value of the improvements is the conversion of "cost to construct" figures to market value figures. Cost is not necessarily or automatically the equivalent of market value. The process of making such a conversion requires care, caution and great skill.

A separate valuation of the improvements is needed for a variety of reasons, and the cost approach is one of the ways to obtain such valuation estimates. These reasons include tax purposes (where ad valorem tax laws dictate this separation in value), accounting (where it is desired to reflect the depreciation of buildings) and to obtain the value of the land by the land residual method. The cost approach is especially useful to estimate the value of special purpose properties where there is no market.

Steps of the Cost Approach

There are five basic steps to the cost approach. Essentially they provide for an estimate of the site (land) value, to which is added the depreciated reproduction cost or replacement cost (new) of the improvements as of the date of the appraisal. The appraiser:

1. Estimates the value of the site (land) in its highest and best use as if vacant.
2. Estimates the reproduction cost or replacement cost new of all the improvements (excluding any that were included as part of the site value).
3. Estimates accrued depreciation from all causes.
4. Deducts the total of accrued depreciation (Step 3) from the cost new of the improvements (Step 2) to arrive at a depreciated value of the improvements recognized as the market value. Steps 2, 3 and 4 are the process of converting cost to value.
5. Adds the site (land) value (Step 1) to the depreciated value of the improvements (Step 4) to arrive at a market value of the property indicated by the cost approach.

Estimating the Value of the Site (Land)

Estimating the value of the site (land) in its highest and best use as if vacant on the date of the appraisal has been covered previously. The appraiser must take care in the treatment of site improvements. If the figure arrived at in Step 1 is strictly land as provided by nature and totally unimproved, then all site improvements must be included in Step 2. Often appraisers elect to include some improvements such as grading, utility connections, and paving in Step 1. This step then becomes a site valuation rather than a land valuation. When some improvements are included in Step 1, they must not be included again in Step 2. The report should state clearly which procedure the appraiser follows.

Estimating the Reproduction or
Replacement Cost New of Improvements

Either reproduction cost or replacement cost may be used. The estimate is as of the date of the appraisal, *not* when the improvements were constructed. There is an important distinction between reproduction cost and replacement cost:

Reproduction cost is the cost of creating a replica of the house and other improvements based on current prices for labor and materials. The materials should be as similar as possible to those originally used; however, they do not have to be exactly the same.

Replacement cost is the cost of creating a house and other improvements having the same or equivalent utility, using current standards of material and design, based on current prices for labor and materials.

Theoretically, reproduction cost is easier to use but as a matter of practicality, it becomes quite difficult to estimate for older houses, because identical materials are not always available and construction methods and design are constantly changing. The use of replacement cost provides a practical alternative. It represents the funds required to build an equally desirable substitute house, not necessarily with similar materials or to the same specifications.

For example, reproduction cost for an older house erected with solid brick walls would be computed on the basis of identical design erected today. On the other hand, an estimate of replacement cost would not necessarily imply a structure with solid brick walls. Quite possibly current design and construction standards in the neighborhood for a house of this type, style and value would be frame construction with brick veneer walls. Accordingly, by using replacement cost instead of reproduction cost, some of the obsolescence or "inutility" present in the house with solid masonry walls would be eliminated from the estimate before deductions for accrued depreciation are made.

Care must be exercised not to take double depreciation. In the above example the solid masonry walls have already been treated by using replacement cost of a frame house with brick veneer walls. A penalty should not again be deducted as functional obsolescence.

Methods of Cost Estimating

There are a variety of acceptable ways for the appraiser to estimate the reproduction cost of a house. They range from the comprehensive quantity survey method, used by contractors, to the simpler unit-in-place method and the most popular method called the square foot method. (A similar method, called the cubic foot method, is rarely used for houses today.)

For analysis, the costs of a house can be divided into direct and indirect costs:

1. Direct costs
   a. Materials
   b. Equipment
   c. Labor
   d. Contractor's or subcontractor's overhead and profit (sometimes classified as an indirect cost)
2. Indirect costs
   a. Professional services
      i. Architect's fees
      ii. Engineer's fees
      iii. Surveyor's fees
      iv. Legal fees and expenses
      v. Appraisal fees
   b. Developer's overhead
   c. Building permits and licenses
   d. Insurance premiums
   e. Interest
   f. Taxes
   g. Selling expenses (commissions, advertising, promotion)
   h. Carrying costs from time of completion to sale or occupancy

Quantity Survey Method

This comprehensive method used by many contractors requires preparation of a detailed inventory of all the materials and equipment used to build the house. To this list is applied the cost of each item as of the date of appraisal. Also estimated is the amount of labor hours needed to install each item, using current labor rates. Finally the indirect costs, overhead and profit items are added to the cost of material, equipment and labor.

An example of part of a contractor's cost breakdown of a typical house is shown in Fig. 12-1. To prepare this breakdown using the

FIG. 12-1: Section of Contractor's Cost Breakdown

Item	Material			Labor			Total cost
	Units	Price	Total	Hours	Rate	Total	
Cabinet work base-finished w/formica top	16	$ 22	$352	14	$ 7.30	$102.20	$454.20
Plumbing: 60-gal. hot water heater	1	$325	$325	30	$15.40	$462.00	$787.00

quantity survey method, the contractor first lists all the material and equipment and estimates the amount of labor required to install each item. Then the material, equipment and labor are priced out per unit and extended to give the total cost of installing each item.

Except for unusual appraisals, this type of breakdown is beyond the scope normally required. When such a breakdown is required, the services of a trained cost estimator should be obtained.

Appraisers often use a summary of the contractor's cost breakdown; Fig. 12-2 (page 216) shows a typical cost breakdown for a house. The specifications and general description of the house used for this example are as follows:

General Description

One-family, one-story, ranch-style, seven rooms (living room, family room, dining room, kitchen, three bedrooms, two full baths), full unfinished basement. No porches. Gross living area: 1,422 square feet. Two-car, attached garage.

General Construction

Concrete footings and foundation walls. Exterior walls: cedar shingles. Roof covering: cedar shingles. Wood, double-hung windows, combination aluminum storm windows and screens. Aluminum gutters and downspouts. Batt type insulation. Wood platform framing, plywood subfloors, oak floors, except kitchen (vinyl asbestos) and bathrooms (ceramic tile wainscot).

Mechanical Systems

Plumbing: copper water and waste pipes connected to municipal services in street. Electric, 60-gal. domestic hot water heater. One double, stainless steel kitchen sink. Each bathroom has standard water closet, lavatory and tub with shower. Laundry tub in basement and washer/dryer hook-up.

Heating: Oil-fired, hot water furnace; two circulators; baseboard radiators.

Electrical: 100-ampere service; 16 circuits protected with circuit breakers; BX cable; adequate outlets and features.

Built-in Appliances: gas oven and range, hood with exhaust fan in kitchen.

General Quality

House is average quality throughout and meets FHA minimum standards.

FIG. 12-2: Example of a Cost Breakdown for a Single Family House*

Component	% of Total	Cost
Survey & Engineering	½	$ 200
Plans & Plan Checking	½	200
Site Preparation	½	200
Excavation	1	400
Footings & Foundation	4	1,600
Basement	6	2,400
Framing	7½	3,000
Interior Walls & Ceilings	3½	1,400
Exterior Siding	3	1,200
Roof Covering & Flashing	5	2,000
Insulation	2	800
Fireplaces & Chimneys (no fireplace)	2	800
Leaders & Gutters	1	400
Exterior & Interior Stairs	1	400
Doors, Windows & Shutters	2	800
Storm Windows, Doors & Screens	1	400
Main Floor Covering (Carpeting)	3	1,200
Kitchen Flooring	½	200
Bathroom & Lavatory Floors	½	200
Hardware	½	200
Water Supply	1	400
Waste Disposal	1	400
Heating	4	1,600
Cooling (no central air conditioning)	—	—
Domestic Hot Water	1	400
Piping	4	1,600
Plumbing Fixtures	3	1,200
Kitchen Cabinets & Counters	3	1,200
Built-In Appliances	1½	600
Shower Doors	½	200
Bathroom Accessories	½	200
Vanities, Medicine Cabinets & Counters	½	200
Electric Service	2	800
Electric Wires & Outlets	2	800
Lighting Fixtures	1	400
Painting & Decorating	4	1,600
Porches (None)	—	—
Patios	½	200
Finish Grading	½	200
Landscaping	1	400
Garages & Carports	5	2,000
Clean Up	½	200
Interest, Taxes & Insurance	1	400
Contractor's Overhead & Temporary Facilities	4	1,600
Professional Services, Permits & Licenses	1	400
Selling Expenses, Carrying Costs	5	2,000
Contractor's Profit	7½	3,000
Total Cost	100%	$40,000

*These are not actual costs but just an illustration of how costs might be approximately allocated in a $40,000 house.

Based on the summary in Fig. 12-2, an appraiser would estimate the reproduction cost new at $40,000. Note that this example is not in itself a complete quantity survey breakdown but represents a recapitulation of the cost estimater's quantity survey analysis.

Unit in Place Method

Many house contractors use numerous subcontractors, who have special expertise in certain areas and often can do the work better and cheaper than a general contractor. Typically, general contractors who use a substantial number of subcontractors figure the cost of a house by breaking it down into components corresponding to the work done by the various subcontractors. Popular cost services (which will be described later in this chapter) also use this technique, calling it the segregated cost method. It is based on the use of unit prices for the various building components, using workable units such as the square foot or lineal foot or other appropriate basic unit.

In Fig. 12-3 a typical list of house construction components is given. The cost estimates for these components are made in terms of standardized unit costs for installation. Providing that the units accurately reflect costs, this estimate is a short cut to an actual quantity survey. The resulting figure should correspond in accuracy with that derived from a quantity survey.

Square Foot Method

The comparative method is widely used by residential appraisers. It is a simple, practical approach to cost estimating, based on unit figures applicable to the gross living area of the house. It involves a comparison of the known costs of similar houses which have been reduced to units per square foot of gross living area. In applying this method, the number of square feet of gross living area in the house being appraised is first computed.

• *Gross Living Area.* Historically, there have been many different ways to measure a house. Although various systems are used by cost services and according to local definition, the increased acceptance of the FHLMC/FNMA appraisal forms and guidelines suggest following their method. They call for the calculation of total gross

FIG. 12-3: Estimated Costs of House Construction Components*

Component	Unit	Quantity	Unit Cost	Total
General expense (engineering, plans, survey, site)	sq. ft./GLA	1,442 sq. ft.	$ .69	$ 1,000
Foundation	sq. ft./GLA	1,442 sq. ft.	1.11	1,600
Basement	sq. ft./GLA	1,442 sq. ft.	1.66	2,400
Floors	sq. ft./GLA	1,442 sq. ft.	1.88	2,600
Exterior walls & insulation (including windows & exterior doors)	lin. ft./wall	1,450 lin. ft.	3.24	4,700
Roof	sq. ft./GLA	1,442 sq. ft.	2.08	3,000
Roof dormers	lin. ft. across face	None	—	—
Interior walls, ceilings, doors, cabinets, trim and accessories	sq. ft./GLA	1,442 sq. ft.	3.26	4,700
Stairways	each	2 outside	200.00	400
Attic finish	sq. ft./fin. area	None	—	—
Heating	sq. ft./GLA	1,442 sq. ft.	1.11	1,600
Cooling				
Electric system	sq. ft./GLA	1,442 sq. ft.	1.39	2,000
Plumbing system	sq. ft./GLA	1,442 sq. ft.	2.77	4,000
Fireplaces & chimneys	each	1 chimney	800.00	800
Built-in appliances	each	2	300.00	600
Porches	sq. ft./porch	None	—	—
Patios	sq. ft./patio	144 sq. ft.	1.39	200
Other	doors & windows	22	18.18	400
Site improvements (not included in land value)	each lump sum	—	600.00	600
Garage	sq. ft./garage	460 sq. ft.	6.09	2,000
Indirect costs**	sq. ft./GLA	1,442 sq. ft.	5.13	7,400
Total				$40,000

*These are not actual costs but an illustration of how costs might be approximately allocated in a $40,000 house.
**May be added to each component (rather than shown separately, as in this example).

living area, which is a measurement taken around the outside of the house and includes finished and habitable above-grade living area only. Finished basements or attic areas are calculated and shown separately for use in the cost estimate but are not included in the total gross living area.

The square foot unit cost varies in inverse proportion with the size of the house. It reflects the fact that plumbing, heating systems, doors, windows and similar items do not necessarily cost proportionately more in a large house than in a small one. If a similar cost is spread over a larger area, the unit cost is obviously less.

The apparent simplicity of the square foot comparison method can be misleading. Dependable square foot cost figures require the exercise of care and judgment in the process of comparison with similar or standard houses for which actual costs are known. Inaccuracies may result from selection of a square foot cost that is not properly related to the house under appraisal. However, correct application of this procedure will provide estimates of reproduction or replacement cost that are reasonably accurate and entirely acceptable in appraisal practice.

Sources of Cost Figures

Several reliable sources for obtaining cost data exist.

• *Cost Data File.* The use of square foot cost estimates involves assembling, analyzing and cataloging data on actual house costs. An appraiser should have available comprehensive current cost information for the types of houses and other improvements, including data on current material and labor costs. A system of grading quality of construction may also be used to refine the data further. This data can often be obtained from local builders, lenders, material suppliers and trade associations.

A file of this kind provides a check against costs of reproducing or replacing an existing residence, as well as against known or projected costs for existing or proposed houses of varying grades of construction. It also provides a check against the probable cost of different components of a house and of the various trades or work involved.

• *Cost Services.* Several recognized cost reporting services are also available to the appraiser. Some include illustrations of typical structures and provide adjustments to tailor the standard example to differently shaped or equipped residences. Some provide adjustment for individual cities or areas. Some show cubic foot costs, some square foot, and some are designed for unit-in-place information. (A listing of some of these cost services appears in Appendix H.)

• *Cost Indices.* A cost index service reflecting the relative cost of construction over a period of years is also useful. When the actual cost of a residence constructed some years ago is known, application of the index will indicate the present construction cost (provided the actual cost was a typical figure). For example, assume that a house cost $53,000 to build in January 1955 and that a 1955 cost index, from a national service, was 284.4. The April 1977 cost index was 596.3. Based upon this data, in April 1977 the building cost 2.097 times its January 1955 cost (596.3 ÷ 284.4), or an indicated cost of $111,141.

Building Cost Estimates

Building cost estimates should include all materials, equipment and labor. The contractor's overhead and profit, architect's fees and other outside professional services, taxes, insurance, administrative and interest on borrowed funds during the period of construction may or may not be included. Some appraisers elect to allocate these costs proportionately across the direct costs; others estimate and report them separately.

For example, assume as a benchmark house a two-story, brick residence that cost $23,600 to build three years ago, exclusive of detached garage or other site improvements. The quality of construction is roughly comparable to that of an average mass-produced home with asphalt shingle roofing, ½-inch drywall, good average finish and equipment with combination forced-air heat and air conditioning, plus a dishwasher, disposal and fireplace. Included are three bedrooms, 2½ baths and full basement. This residence contains 1,496 square feet, thus costing approximately $15.77 per square foot of gross living area.

Assume that the appraiser is preparing a cost estimate for a house roughly comparable to the above. In contrast to the benchmark house, the house being appraised has a concrete block foundation in lieu of poured concrete, no fireplace and a good grade of wood siding instead of brick exterior walls. The appraiser makes downward adjustments for these differences: $1,600 for wood siding; $125 for the block foundation; and $900 for lack of fireplace. (Note that these were the adjustments applicable three years ago.) The adjusted unit cost is now $14.02 per square foot. If indirect costs are not included in these unit cost adjustments, their total may be increased by an additional 15% to 20%.

Assume that the cost of construction has risen 12% in the last three years, which increases the $14.02 per square foot to $15.70. The house under appraisal contains 1,648 square feet of gross living area. Application of the derived current square foot unit costs to this property results in a current cost estimate of $25,874, rounded to $25,900 (see Fig. 12-4).

FIG. 12-4: Estimating Reproduction Cost

Cost of benchmark house 3½ years ago	$23,600
Adjustments to benchmark house	
Wood siding	− 1,600
Block foundation	− 125
Fireplace	− 900
Adjusted cost of benchmark house as 3½ years ago	$20,975
Gross living area of benchmark house	1,496 sq. ft.
Adjusted cost of benchmark house per sq. ft. 3½ years ago ($20,975 ÷ 1,496)	$14.02
Time adjustment to present	+ 12%
Estimated present reproduction cost per sq. ft. ($14.02 x 1.12)	$15.70
Estimated present reproduction cost of house (1,648 x $15.70 rounded)	$25,900

The difficulty inherent in this procedure is that the reported original cost may not represent a typical cost. It may also be difficult to ascertain which components are included and which are omitted in the reported original figure. Updating a historical cost provides a useful method of confirming a cost estimate, but it is not necessarily a substitute for other methods. Capital expenditures for improvement, subsequent to original construction, must also be taken into consideration insofar as they represent additional construction. They also may affect the separate estimate of accrued depreciation.

Estimating Accrued Depreciation

Estimation of accrued depreciation is the third essential step of the cost approach and probably the most difficult. To estimate it properly, it is helpful to understand the nature, components and theory of depreciation.

A simple definition of accrued depreciation is "the difference between the value of the land plus the reproduction or replacement cost of all the improvements and the market value of the property."

More formally, it has been defined as:

> A loss of utility and hence value from any cause. An effect caused by deterioration and/or obsolescence. Deterioration or physical depreciation is evidenced by wear and tear, decay, dry rot, cracks, encrustations, or structural defects. Obsolescence is divisible into two parts, functional and economic. Functional obsolescence may be due to poor plan, mechanical inadequacy or overadequacy, functional inadequacy or overadequacy due to size, style, age, etc. It is evidenced by conditions within the property. Economic obsolescence is caused by changes external to the property.[1]

Only improvements are subject to accrued depreciation, which is derived from causes both within the property (physical deterioration and functional obsolescence) and without (economic or environmental obsolescence). By definition it is the measure of the difference between the cost to reproduce or replace all the improvements on the date of the appraisal and their value as of that date.

Depreciation begins to accrue upon construction of the improvements; they immediately begin to age physically and to suffer from functional obsolescence caused by their design. Negative environmental forces cause immediate economic obsolescence.

When the improvements are constructed, their economic life begins. During this period, they should contribute value to the property. If they are the "perfect improvement," the amount of value they contribute would be their total cost. Since few, if any, perfect improvements are constructed, a difference exists between their total cost and their value, which represents some form of depreciation. At the point when an improvement cannot be profitably utilized, or when it no longer contributes to the value of the property, it is at the end of its economic life and depreciation has reached 100%.

Replacement cost may be used instead of reproduction cost in the cost approach but the distinction between these two terms must be clearly understood. The use of replacement cost in lieu of reproduction cost does not change the principle of estimating physical deterioration. However, some calculations may be eliminated in estimates of certain types of functional obsolescence often encountered in outdated structures (such as overadequacy of construction). Con-

---

[1]*Real Estate Appraisal Terminology, op. cit.,* p. 63.

sequently, accrued depreciation for an outdated building is frequently estimated in relation to the estimated replacement cost of a more modern structure rather than to the reproduction cost of a building identical in all respects to the original (see discussion of functional obsolescence-incurable on page 234). In eminent domain appraising, the use of reproduction cost is sometimes preferable, avoiding the necessity to explain the rationale of replacement cost.

Definition of Terms

Economic life is the period over which a house may be profitably utilized. It is the total period of time that the improvements contribute value to the property. As soon as the site alone is worth as much as the site and the improvements combined, the improvements have reached the end of their economic life.

Physical life is the time period during which the house may be expected to remain physically in existence. Since over 90% of the houses ever built in the United States are still in existence and since houses in Europe have lasted hundreds of years, it is almost impossible to forecast the estimated physical life of a house. Caution must be exercised in the use of tables that purport to estimate the total physical life of different types of houses. They are of limited use to the appraiser.

Effective age is how old the house appears to be, based on observation, considering its condition, design and the economic forces that affect its value. To paraphrase an old saying, "If it has the physical condition and design of a 13-year-old house and market conditions affect it as if it were a 13-year-old house, then for appraisal purposes it should be treated as a 13-year-old house (effective age: 13 years), even if it is 10 or 20 years old." The chronological age of the house should be noted in the appraisal (if known) but it normally has little use in the value estimation.

Generally if the house is of average condition and design *and* conforms to the other houses in a neighborhood that is not subject to unusual economic influences, its effective age and chronological age will be about the same. If the house has had better than average maintenance, rehabilitation or modernization, its effective age probably will be less than its chronological age. If it is in a poorer condition than typical houses of the same age or has not been modernized or rehabilitated as other similar houses in the neighborhood, or if some offsite economic environmental factor is negatively affecting the value, the effective age will be greater than the chronological age.

Remaining economic life is the period of time from the date of the appraisal to the end of the house's economic life. It is that period of time the house will continue to contribute value to the property. This is the period the appraiser attempts to estimate. The assumption should not always be that the property will continue to deteriorate at its present rate. Often rehabilitation, modernization or remodeling will extend the life of the property; lack of normal maintenance will shorten the economic life. Changing economic conditions and public tastes will also affect the remaining economic life. The estimate must be based on the assumption there will be no significant changes in the house or neighborhood, and be qualified to recognize that any changes may extend or shorten the remaining economic life.

The relationships between effective age, remaining economic life and total economic life are shown in Fig. 12-5.

Techniques of Estimating Depreciation

Accrued depreciation may be estimated directly through observation and analysis of the components of depreciation affecting the property or through use of a formula based on physical or economic age-life factors. It may also be estimated indirectly by use of the income or market data approaches.

Three techniques used by appraisers to measure depreciation are:

1. The abstraction, or market, method extracts depreciation directly from the market.
2. The age-life method is accomplished by estimating the typical economic life of the improvements and their effective age.
3. The breakdown method separates charges on the basis of origin or cause of loss (physical deterioration, curable and incurable; functional obsolescence, curable and incurable; and economic obsolescence). Each component is estimated separately, using the engineering method of observation techniques.

Abstraction Method

This method involves the use of market data to obtain an indication of the amount of depreciation existing in the property being ap-

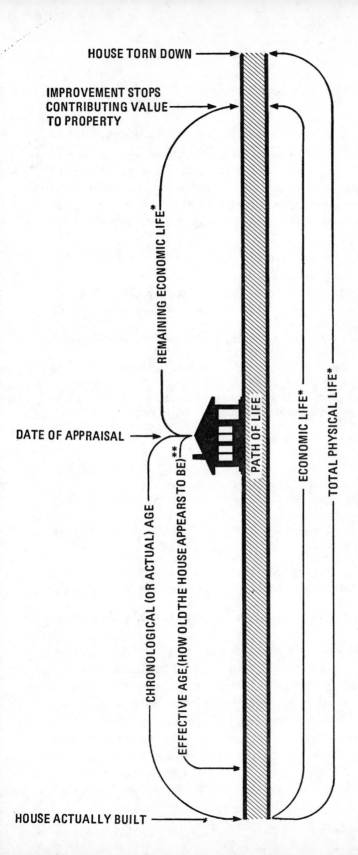

HOUSE TORN DOWN

IMPROVEMENT STOPS CONTRIBUTING VALUE TO PROPERTY

REMAINING ECONOMIC LIFE*

DATE OF APPRAISAL

PATH OF LIFE

ECONOMIC LIFE*

TOTAL PHYSICAL LIFE*

CHRONOLOGICAL (OR ACTUAL) AGE

EFFECTIVE AGE,(HOW OLD THE HOUSE APPEARS TO BE)**

HOUSE ACTUALLY BUILT

*MAY BE EXTENDED BY REHABILITATION, REMODELING OR MODERNIZATION OR CHANGING CONDITIONS.

**MAY ALSO BE GREATER THAN ACTUAL AGE.

FIG. 12-5: Life Span of a House

praised. An analysis of current sales indicates the amount of depreciation the market has penalized each sale. By analyzing sales of residential properties similar to and in the same neighborhood as that being appraised, the amount and annual rate of depreciation can be calculated. The assumption is that residential properties of similar age, construction, size, condition and location depreciate at the same annual rate.

The following steps are used to analyze the sales of comparable houses to obtain an indication of depreciation:

1. Select recently sold houses that are comparable to the one being appraised and obtain all the data necessary to estimate their reproduction cost.
2. Estimate the value of the site (land) of the comparables. Use the market comparison if sales data is available.
3. Deduct the site (land) value from the comparable sale price to obtain an indicated depreciated value of the improvement.
4. Estimate the reproduction cost new of each comparable sale as of the date of the appraisal. Use any of the appropriate techniques described in the first part of this chapter.
5. To obtain the *total amount of depreciation* the market has indicated in each of the sold properties, subtract the depreciated value of the improvements (Step 3) from the reproduction cost of the improvements (Step 4).
6. Estimate the age of the comparable property. (Effective age should be used.)
7. To obtain the *average annual amount of depreciation* indicated by each of the sold properties, divide the total depreciation by the effective age.
8. To obtain the *average annual rate of depreciation,* divide the annual amount of depreciation by the reproduction cost of the improvements.
9. Convert the rate to a percentage (multiply by 100 and add a percent sign).

The process shown in Fig. 12-6 should be performed for several comparable sales in the neighborhood. As with the market data approach, the more sales that are used and the closer they are in similarity to the property being appraised, the more accurate the estimate of depreciation will be. Fig. 12-7 is a more specific example. Assume a 20-year-old (actual and effective age), two-story colonial style house, with 2,200 sq. ft. of gross living area, including living room, dining room, kitchen, recreation room, four bedrooms and two full baths. There is also a two-car garage with an estimated reproduc-

FIG. 12-6: Estimating Accrued Depreciation by Abstraction—Example A

Step 1:   Select a house that has sold and obtain the needed data to estimate its reproduction cost new. Sale Price $55,000

Step 2:   Estimate the value of the site (land) from the market. Less site (land) value   −12,000

Step 3:   Depreciated value of improvements $43,000

Step 4:   Reproduction cost of comparable sale as of date of appraisal $69,000

Step 5:   Less depreciated value of improvements ments (Step 3) equals: −43,000

       Total amount of depreciation indicated by the market $26,000

Step 6:   Estimated effective age   13 years

Step 7: $\dfrac{\text{Depreciation (Step 5)}}{\text{Effective age (Step 6)}} = \dfrac{\$26,000}{13} = \$\,2,000$ (average annual amount of depreciation)

Step 8: $\dfrac{\text{Annual depreciation (Step 7)}}{\text{Reproduction cost}} = \dfrac{\$2,000}{\$69,000}$ .0289   (average annual rate of depreciation)

Step 9:   Convert to percentage .0289 = 2.89%   (average annual percentage of depreciation)

FIG. 12-7: Estimating Accrued Depreciation by Abstraction—Example B

Step 1:   Sale Price $45,500

Step 2:   Less site (land) value (from market)   −9,000

Step 3:   Depreciated value of improvements   36,500

Step 4:   Reproduction cost
    House (2,200 sq. ft. x $27.25) $59,950
    Garage   3,300
    Site improvements   1,200
    Total reproduction cost $64,450

Step 5:   Less depreciated value of the improvements (Step 3) equals: −36,500

    Total amount of depreciation indicated by market $27,950

Step 6:   Effective age   20 years

Step 7: $\dfrac{\text{Total Depreciation}}{\text{Effective Age}} = \dfrac{\$27,950}{20} = \$1,397.50$ (average annual amount of depreciation)

Step 8: $\dfrac{\text{Annual depreciation}}{\text{Reproduction cost}} = \dfrac{\$1,397.50}{\$64,450} = .0217$ (average annual rate of depreciation)

Step 9:   .0217 = 2.17% (average annual percentage of depreciation)

tion cost of $3,300 and site improvements with an estimated cost of $1,200. Lots are estimated to be worth $9,000 from the market. The estimated reproduction cost of the house is $27.25 per sq. ft. of gross living area. The house sold for $45,500.

In this example the reproduction or replacement cost of the site improvements, such as stone walls, fences, driveways, landscaping, etc., is difficult to estimate. Under these circumstances an alternate acceptable method is to deduct the estimated value these items contribute to the sales price first and then proceed to abstract the depreciation of the improvements (see Fig. 12-8).

FIG. 12-8: Estimating Accrued Depreciation by Abstraction—Example C

Step 1:	Sale price		$60,000
Step 2:	Less site value	−$15,000	
	Less contribution of site improvements	− 4,500	
	Value of site and improvements		− 19,500
Step 3:	Depreciated value of the house and other improvements		40,500
Step 4:	Reproduction cost		
	House (3,000 sq. ft. x $29.00)	$87,000	
	Garage	6,000	93,000
Step 5:	Less depreciated value of improvements		40,500
	Total amount of depreciation		$52,500
Step 6:	Effective age		15 years

Step 7: $\dfrac{\text{Total depreciation}}{\text{Effective age}} = \dfrac{\$52,500}{15} = \$ 3,500$ (annual amount of depreciation)

Step 8: $\dfrac{\text{Annual depreciation}}{\text{Reproduction cost}} = \dfrac{\$ 3,500}{\$93,000} = .0376$ (average annual rate of depreciation)

Step 9: .0376 = 3.76% (average annual percentage of depreciation)

A single type of depreciation can also be calculated by the abstraction method. This is done by first calculating the total depreciation as done in the above examples. Then two of the three forms of depreciation (physical, functional and economic) are estimated by observation and subtracted from the total depreciation; what remains is depreciation attributed to the remaining form of depreciation. For example:

Total Accrued Depreciation by Abstraction
Less: Physical Deterioration and Functional Obsolescence
Gives: Economic Obsolescence

Total Accrued Depreciation by Abstraction
Less: Functional and Economic Obsolescence
Gives: Physical Deterioration

Total Accrued Depreciation by Abstraction
Less: Physical Deterioration and Economic Obsolescence
Gives: Functional Obsolescence

Application of this technique appears as follows:

Total depreciation estimated by abstraction		$27,950
Estimated physical deterioration	$16,500	
Estimated functional obsolescence	7,300	
Total physical deterioration and functional obsolescence		23,800
Depreciation attributed to economic obsolescence		$ 4,150

This technique is limited by the accuracy of the observed estimates of physical deterioration and functional obsolescence. Care must be taken not to attribute to economic obsolescence what is actually an error in estimating physical and functional obsolescence, land value or cost new. The possibility of error is reduced when a number of properties is used.

Age-Life Method
This method of estimating depreciation is based primarily upon observation. The basis is that the percentage effective age is of the typical economic life is the same percentage the accumulated depreciation is of total reproduction cost. Both of these are as of the date of the appraisal. This concept can be stated as a formula:

$$\frac{\text{Depreciation}}{\text{Reproduction Cost}} = \frac{\text{Effective Age}}{\text{Typical Economic Life}}$$

An example of this formula is as follows:

$$\frac{20\% \text{ Depreciation}}{100\% \text{ Reproduction Cost}} = \frac{10 \text{ Years Effective Age}}{50 \text{ Years Typical Economic Life}}$$

The formula can also be expressed as follows:

$$\frac{\text{Effective Age}}{\text{Typical Economic Life}} = \% \text{ Depreciation of Reproduction Cost}$$

Some appraisers prefer to use the following ratios to estimate the depreciation:

$$\frac{\text{Actual Age}}{\text{Actual Age + Remaining Economic Life}}$$

or

$$\frac{\text{Effective Age}}{\text{Effective Age + Remaining Economic Life}}$$

No matter which technique is used, if the estimates are correct and the assumptions are the same, the estimate of depreciation will be correct and the same.

The age-life method can be used to estimate either depreciation from all causes or a single form of depreciation. Care must be taken to define clearly in the appraisal what is being estimated. The following examples show how the estimates are made.

A house has an estimated typical economic life of 50 years. Its chronological age is 20 years. Its effective age, based on its condition, design, and environment, is 25 years because it is in poor condition and is located near a gasoline service station.

$$\frac{25 \text{ years (Effective Age)}}{50 \text{ years (Typical Economic Life)}} = .50 \text{ or } 50\% \text{ depreciated}$$

Another house in the same neighborhood also has an estimated typical economic life of 50 years. Its chronological age is also 20 years. Its effective age, based on its condition, design and environment, is 20 years because it is in average condition and there are no unusual adverse environmental influences.

$$\frac{20 \text{ years (Effective Age)}}{50 \text{ years (Typical Economic Life)}} = .40 \text{ or } 40\% \text{ depreciated}$$

Still another house in the same neighborhood has an estimated economic life of 60 years. This longer economic life is forecast because it is of superior design and construction. Its chronological age is 20 years. Its effective age, based on its superior construction, modernization and lack of negative environmental influences, is 12 years.

$$\frac{12 \text{ years (Effective Age)}}{60 \text{ years (Typical Economic Life)}} = .20 \text{ or } 20\% \text{ depreciated}$$

These examples show how three houses in the same neighborhood, all the same chronological age, can suffer from substantially different amounts of depreciation. All of these estimates considered the effect of all three forms of depreciation.

When the estimate of effective age considers only one form of depreciation — say, physical deterioration — then the result is the amount of depreciation caused by physical deterioration. For example, a house has an estimated typical physical life of 75 years. The effective age, based only on the physical condition of the house, is 25 years.

$$\frac{25 \text{ years (Effective Age)}}{75 \text{ years (Typical Physical Life)}} = \frac{.333 \text{ or } 33.3\%}{\text{physically depreciated}}$$

The age-life method is an easy-to-understand, simple-to-use method based primarily upon the appraiser's observations, research and judgment. Therefore, its accuracy is dependent heavily upon the appraiser's knowledge and experience. It is an effective way to estimate the depreciation accumulated to the date of the appraisal but has proved to be a very poor way to estimate the rate of depreciation the property will suffer in the future.

For example, if by the age-life method it is estimated that a 25-year old residence has depreciated at the rate of 2% per year and is now 50% depreciated, it is incorrect to say that the remaining economic life is 25 years. This will only be true if:

1. The present rate of depreciation continues into the future on a straight line basis.

2. There are no changes in the forces that affect the value of the property.
3. There is no modernization, rehabilitation or remodeling.
4. The property is "normally" maintained through its remaining economic life.

A forecast that is based on a series of assumptions that most likely will not all be true serves a limited purpose. This kind of forecast has been misused by lenders to limit the term of mortgages. If an estimate of remaining economic life is required, it must be made considering all the above factors and qualified to recognize that any changes may extend or shorten the remaining economic life.

The Breakdown Method

The breakdown method is accomplished by dividing depreciation into its three separate components: physical deterioration, functional obsolescence and economic (environmental) obsolescence. Physical deterioration and functional obsolescence may be further broken down into curable and incurable types. A grasp of this procedure's underlying principles is essential to an overall understanding of depreciation.

• *Physical Deterioration-Curable.* These are all the items of maintenance that a prudent owner would accomplish on the date of appraisal to maximize the profit (or minimize the loss) if the property were sold. Almost any item of physical deterioration can be corrected at a price. However, to be classified as curable, the cure normally must contribute more value than it costs. Items of normal maintenance usually fall into this category, including paint touch-ups and minor carpentry, plumbing and electric repairs (leaking faucets, squeaking or tight doors and windows, etc.). Interior and exterior painting and redecorating may also be included.

The ultimate test is whether the market will recognize as additional value at least the cost of the repair. Realtors® have long recognized that minor repairs do add value equal to or in excess of their cost and they try to have an owner make these repairs before a house is offered for sale. The measure of physical deterioration-curable is the cost to cure. Many appraiser clients require that an itemized list of the curable items be part of the report together with an estimate of the cost to cure.

• *Physical Deterioration-Incurable.* As soon as a house is constructed, it begins to age and suffer from wear and tear. Physical deterioration-incurable is based on the physical life of the components of the house. The total physical life of the house would equal its total economic life if no other forms of depreciation were present. One of the practical problems in estimating the percentage of physical deterioration-incurable is estimating the physical life of the components. There is a tendency to assign too much depreciation to physical deterioration-incurable by using estimates of 50 to 100 years for items such as footings, foundations, framing, wall and ceiling covering, etc; some of these items may last hundreds of years.

To measure physical deterioration-incurable, items are divided into two categories: long-lived and short-lived. Long-lived items, such as footings, foundations, etc., can be depreciated as a group by making an estimate of their effective age and remaining physical life based on their condition. The engineering method, in which items are separately listed and their reproduction cost estimated, can also be used (see Fig. 12-9). By observation a percentage of depreciation is estimated and extended into a dollar estimate for each component. Indirect costs must be either allocated proportionately to each component or listed separately, and depreciation for them also estimated.

Fig. 12-9: Component Physical Life Engineering

House Component	Reproduction Cost New	Estimated % Deterioration	Accrued Depreciation
Survey & engineering	$ 200	20%	$ 40
Foundation	800	20%	160
Plumbing	1,000	30%	300
Electrical system	2,000	35%	700
Total	40,000		$22,000

Short-lived items are components whose remaining physical life is shorter than the total estimated remaining economic life of the house. Typically they include roof, gutters and downspouts, kitchen cabinets and counters, painting and decorating. Sometimes these items are classified as physical deterioration-curable-deferred.

Again, the technique for estimating depreciation is to make a list of components, estimating the reproduction cost of each as well as a percentage of depreciation, based on the appraiser's observations. These estimates are extended into a dollar estimate for each component and totaled. The process may be shortened by estimating a total reproduction cost of all the short-lived items and using an average percentage of depreciation; this may decrease the accuracy of the estimate.

• *Functional Obsolescence-Curable.* Most functional obsolescence-curable in residential properties is caused by some kind of deficiency. In other types of properties some superadequacies would also be considered curable but they are rare in residential properties. Typical items that fall into this category are kitchens that need new counters, cabinets, fixtures and floor coverings; inadequate electrical service and hot water systems; and need of an additional bath or powder room where adequate space exists. Again, the test is whether the value added by correcting the obsolescence is greater than the cost to cure as indicated in the market.

The measure of functional obsolescence-curable is the difference between what it would cost on the date of appraisal to reproduce the house with the curable item included and to reproduce the house on the same date without it. Only the excess cost of adding the item to the existing structure over the cost of incorporating the item as part of a total house construction process represents the measure of accrued depreciation. It is neither proper nor logical to deduct accrued depreciation from reproduction cost of an item that has not been included in the reproduction cost estimate for the existing house.

For example, assume that in light of current market expectations, the house being appraised lacks a second bath where room exists to install one. The estimated cost to include this bath as part of the total house construction program as of the date of appraisal is $2,000. The estimated cost to do it as a separate job as of the same date would be more because it generally costs more to build parts of a house separately as compared to building the whole house at one time. If it would cost $2,500 to build the extra bath as a separate job, the measure of depreciation would be the $500 excess cost. To deduct the additional $2,000, it first would have to be added to the reproduction cost of the house.

• *Functional Obsolescence-Incurable.* These items can be divided into two categories: loss in value caused by a deficiency or by an excess or superadequacy. Deficiencies are caused by exterior or interior design that does not meet current market expectations. This can be measured by the rent loss attributable to the deficiency multiplied by the gross monthly rent multiplier applicable to the property (see Fig. 12-10).

FIG. 12-10: Estimating Incurable Functional Obsolescence by Capitalizing Rent Loss

Monthly rental, House A with 3 bedrooms	$ 285
Monthly rental, House B with 2 bedrooms	265
Difference	$ 20
GMRM for neighborhood	130
Difference in value between A and B ($20 monthly rent loss x 130 GMRM)	$2,600

Consider a house with only one bath and a lavatory in a market that requires two baths and lavatory. Comparable rentals in the market indicate that a house with two baths and lavatory rents for $10 per month more than similar houses with one bath and a lavatory. The GMRM indicated for this neighborhood is 135. The loss of value caused by the lack of a second bath is $1,350 ($10 monthly rent loss x 135 GMRM). The amount of functional obsolescence is the difference between the cost of a house with and without the missing item, minus all other depreciation and the value loss indicated by the market. Therefore, if the cost of a house with a second bath is $1,500 more, less $300 of other forms of depreciation ($1,500 − $300 = $1,200), the functional obsolescence is $150 ($1,350 value loss − $1,200 = $150).

The amount of functional obsolescence to be deducted is the difference between the cost of the missing item, less all other forms of depreciation, and the value loss indicated by the market. For example, if House B cost $3,000 less to construct and there is $400 of physical deterioration and economic obsolescence because it has only two bedrooms, no additional deduction would be needed. If the house cost $2,000 less to construct and there is $300 of physical deterioration and economic obsolescence because it has only two bedrooms, a $900 deduction would be made.

This same depreciation might also be derived directly from the market. Sales of two separate houses might be found where a difference in sale price can be attributed to the variance in the number of bedrooms after other adjustments are made. For example, House C, a one-story, contemporary style house with living room, dining room, kitchen, three bedrooms and two full baths, sold for $47,200. Similar House D sold for $49,000. The significant difference between the two houses is that D has a two-car garage and only a bath and a lavatory. In this market, houses with a two-car garage sell for $3,000 more than houses with no garage. The value of the difference between a full bath and a lavatory can be calculated as shown in Fig. 12-11. The measure of functional obsolescence in this example is the difference between the cost of the extra half bath, less all other forms of depreciation, and the value difference indicated by the market.

FIG. 12-11: Estimating Incurable Functional Obsolescence Using Matched Pair of Sales

Sale price, House C with 2 full baths, no garage	$47,200
Sale Price, House D with 1 bath, lavatory, 2-car garage	49,000
Difference	$ 1,800
Value of 2-car garage indicated by market	$ 3,000
Indicated difference in value between 2 full baths and 1½ baths	$1,200

The second type of incurable functional obsolescence is caused by superadequacy. Probably only a small percentage of houses exist that do not have some such obsolescence. The number of superadequacies tends to increase as a house gets older and the occupants improve it with features suited for their individual living style. Superadequacies are not only improvements made after construction but also anything initially built into the house that does not add value at least equal to its cost. For example, a builder elects to install in a new house an intercom system, central air conditioning, stainless steel kitchen sink and vinyl kitchen floor, the cost of which might be $5,000 totally. If they only add $4,000 value to the house, the lost $1,000 would be functional obsolescence-superadequacy, assuming no forms of depreciation.

Another example is a master bedroom, 16 by 18 feet, which cost $500 more to build than a bedroom 14 by 16 feet. If the extra size only adds $300 value, the lost $200 is functional obsolescence, superadequacy (again, assuming there are no other forms of depreciation).

Almost all superadequacies are incurable in houses. (In commercial and investment properties sometimes it pays to remove them because of excess operating costs.) For example, a new house suffering from no physical deterioration or economic obsolescence has a swimming pool that cost $10,000 to install. It adds only $6,000 value, so $4,000 is functional obsolescence-superadequacy.

Superadequacies are measured in the same manner as deficiencies, by finding a matched pair of sales from the market. If a rent differential can be attributed to the superadequacy, it can be capitalized to indicate the value of the superadequacy. The difference between this value and the cost, less other forms of depreciation, would be the depreciation classified as functional obsolescence-superadequacy.

• *Economic Obsolescence.* Also called locational or environmental obsolescence by some appraisers, it is the loss of value caused by factors outside the property boundaries. It is unique to real estate, caused by its fixed location. The value of a house is directly affected by the neighborhood, community and region in which it is located. In analyzing the location and environment of the property, the appraiser must consider governmental actions, economic forces, employment, transportation, recreation, educational services, taxes, etc.

Consideration must also be given to factors in the immediate vicinity that detract from value. Unattractive natural features such as swamps, polluted waterways, and obstructed views are examples of items that will detract from value. Poorly maintained nonconforming houses, numerous houses for sale, increasing ratio of rented houses, and uncollected junk in yards are all indications of possible existence of economic obsolescence. Although facilities such as fire stations, schools, stores, restaurants, hospitals, and gas stations are advantageous nearby, if they are too close to the house, they may detract from its value. Nearby industry, highways and airports may be another type of nuisance, especially if they are unattractive, noisy or smoke and odor-emitting. Economic obsolescence can also be caused by factors that affect the supply or demand (such as an unusual number of houses for sale) of houses competitive with that being appraised.

The list of factors causing economic obsolescence is almost endless and the appraiser should carefully search for and evaluate anything off the property that detracts from the value of the house.

Economic obsolescence like functional obsolescence can also be measured by the rent loss attributable to the factor causing the obsolescence. However, a different method is used because part of the rent loss caused by economic obsolescence often is allocated to the land. For example, the market indicates that houses next to gasoline stations rent for $10 less than other houses. The GMRM for the neighborhood is 130. The land-to-improvement ratio in this neighborhood typically is land, 15%, improvements, 85%. Some of the rent loss must be allocated to the land, which in this case is 15% (see Fig. 12-12).

FIG. 12-12: Estimating Economic Obsolescence

Total rent loss	$10.00
Loss allocated to land ($10 x 15%)	1.50
Loss allocated to improvement	$ 8.50
Economic obsolescence ($8.50 x GMRM 130)	$1,105

Economic obsolescence can also be calculated by finding matched pairs of sales. The pair must consist of one sale that is affected by the influence causing economic obsolescence and another sale that is not so affected. First all other differences are adjusted for and any remaining difference is attributed to economic obsolescence. For example, House E is a new, one-story, ranch-style house with a two-car garage. It is two blocks from the local school. House F is very similar to House E except that it has a one-car garage and is next door to the school. House E sold for $48,000. House F sold for $44,500. Two-car garages in this market add $3,000 value to houses in this neighborhood and one-car garages add $1,000 value. Lots in this neighborhood are about 20% of total value of typical property (see Fig. 12-13).

FIG. 12-13: Estimating Economic Obsolescence
Using Matched Pair of Sales

Sale price, House E with 2-car garage, away from school	$48,000
Sale price, House F with 1-car garage, next to school	− 44,500
Difference	$ 3,500
Difference between value of 2-car garage and 1-car garage	− 2,000
Indicated difference in value caused by school	$1,500
Value loss allocated to improvements ($1,500 x 80%)	$ 1,200
Percent of depreciation caused by location next to school	2.5%

$$\left(\frac{\$\ 1,200}{\$48,000} = .0250 \text{ or } 2.5\% \right)$$

Summary

The cost approach is based on the principle of substitution. It holds that value tends to be set by the cost of a reasonable substitute improvement that could be built without undue delay. The steps of the cost approach are:

1. Estimate the value of the site (land) in its highest and best use as if vacant.
2. Estimate the reproduction cost (or replacement cost) new of all the improvements.
3. Estimate accrued depreciation from all sources.
4. Deduct the accrued depreciation (from all causes) from the cost new of the improvement to derive the depreciated value of the improvement.
5. Add the site (land) value to the depreciated value of the improvements to derive an indicated value of the property by the cost approach.

Site (land) value is estimated in its highest and best use as if vacant from data found in the market.

Reproduction cost is the cost of creating a replica of the house and other improvements. Replacement cost is the cost of creating improvements with the same or equivalent utility using current design and materials. Estimating reproduction cost can be done using the quantity survey, unit-in-place or comparative method.

Accrued depreciation is the difference between reproduction cost new of the improvements and their value as of the date of appraisal. It is the loss of value from all causes, which may be broken down into physical deterioration, functional obsolescence and economic obsolescence. There are three principal methods to measure accrued depreciation. The abstraction method uses sales from the market to indicate the depreciated value of the improvements. The age-life method is based on observation, in which estimates of economic life and effective age are converted into percentages of depreciation. The breakdown method divides depreciation into three categories (physical deterioration, functional obsolescence and economic obsolescence). Each one is estimated by whatever technique is most applicable to the property being appraised.

The accuracy of the cost approach depends on the appraiser's accuracy in estimating on the date of the appraisal the value of the land, reproduction cost new of all the improvements and all forms of depreciation. Without market data to make these estimates, the possibility of significant error is substantial.

Extreme caution should be practiced when the cost approach is used alone or as the most significant indicator of value. The report should contain valid justification as to why the appraiser has elected to do so.

Review Questions

1. What does it mean when one states the cost approach is based on the principle of substitution?
2. What are the steps of the cost approach?
3. Define reproduction cost and replacement cost. Explain the difference between the two terms.
4. As of what date is either reproduction cost or replacement cost estimated? Why?
5. Give two ways of estimating the reproduction cost of a house.
6. Define depreciation in your own words.
7. What three types of depreciation does the appraiser consider? Give an example of each.
8. Define the terms "remaining economic life," "chronological age," "effective age," and "total physical life."
9. What is a superadequacy?
10. What factors can create economic obsolescence?
11. Describe what physical deterioration-curable normally consists of in a single family residence.
12. By definition, accrued depreciation is applied only to what? Explain.

13

The Market Data Approach

The market data approach, also called the direct sales comparison approach, involves making a direct comparison between the property being appraised and other single family residences that have been sold (or listed for sale). All three approaches to value are based on market data, but the cost and income approaches depend on a less direct comparison than does the market data approach.

When carefully collected, analyzed, verified and reconciled, market data usually provides the best indication of market value for a house. The price that a typical buyer pays is often the result of a shopping process, in which many residences being offered for sale have been examined and evaluated. Buyers often base their value conclusions primarily on residences that are being offered for sale. Appraisers use this information plus information about residences that have sold and rented.

The principle of substitution states that when several commodities or services with substantially the same utility are available, the one with the lowest price attracts the greatest demand and the widest distribution. It is important to understand how this principle specifically applies to the theoretical framework of the market data approach. In single family residence markets, this means that when a residence is replaceable in the market (which it usually is), its value tends to be set by the cost of acquiring an *equally desirable substitute* residence. The assumption is that there will be no costly delay encountered in making the substitution. Experienced real estate brokers know that most buyers will accept more than one house in the market in which they are shopping and will accept only a short delay in negotiating the purchase of any specific house.

A popular myth is that one can sell a house at almost any price if one is willing to wait long enough for the one buyer who wants only that particular house and will pay substantially above its market value to obtain it. Houses that are listed substantially above market value generally remain unsold no matter how long they are offered for sale. The principle of substitution provides the basis for the premise that the market value of a house is the value indicated by active and informed buyers in the market for comparable houses offering a similar quality of shelter, amenities and other considerations characteristic of each market.

Individual sales often deviate from the market norm because of individual motivations, knowledge and/or conditions of sale; but in sufficient numbers, they tend to reflect market patterns. When information is available on a sufficient number of comparable sales, offerings and listings in the current market, the resulting pattern is the best indication of a house's market value.

Steps in the Market Data Approach

In applying the market data approach, the appraiser takes five steps:

1. Studies the market to select sales and listings of properties most comparable to the residence being appraised.
2. Collects and verifies data regarding these properties in regard to their selling and listing prices, date of transaction, physical and locational characteristics and any special conditions.
3. Analyzes and compares each comparable property with the residence being appraised as to time of sale, location, physical characteristics and conditions of sale.
4. Adjusts the sale or listing price of each comparable property for dissimilarities between it and the residence being appraised. The adjustments are derived from the market whenever possible, using "matched pairs," regression analysis and other adjustment techniques.
5. Reconciles the adjusted prices of the comparable properties into an indicated market value of the appraised residence.

Studying the Market

A market study is made to find those comparable sales and listings that are similar to the property being appraised. Generally, the more current the comparable sale and the more similar it is to the property being appraised, the better it will be as an indicator of the value of the property being appraised. Often more sales and listings are considered than are finally used in the appraisal.

Collecting the Data

Accuracy of the value indication from the market data approach depends heavily upon the quantity and quality of sales, offerings and listings data for competitive properties.

Through a sound collection program, a large bank of market data can be accumulated in the appraiser's own files and should be organized to serve the appraiser's needs most effectively. Only some of the data may be immediately pertinent; the remainder may be collected, filed and cross-indexed for future use. Records should carry the address, a file number, and additional salient information. Sales information often is collected and recorded on a standardized sheet, such as the accompanying form (Fig. 13-1), which may be adapted to the area in which the appraiser is working. As the system grows, an indexing system must be devised to facilitate data retrieval as necessary. Many offices are using computers for data storage, retrieval and analysis.

In addition to the appraiser's own research, numerous other sources are available for market data.

• *Multiple Listing Services.* These can be a bountiful source of data because they often require a detailed description of the listed property. There can be pitfalls in using this information, however. Adjectives used by brokers and salespeople to describe property conditions are sometimes different from those used by appraisers. "Average" to an appraiser should mean a house that is typical of its market; one whose effective age is approximately the same as its actual age (see Chapter 12). A broker or salesperson might describe the condition of the same house as "good" or "very good." They may say a substandard house is "fair," and one that is not even habitable may be called "poor." Houses rated by an appraiser as "above average" may be called "like new," "excellent" or "A-1" on the MLS card. Another problem with MLS information is that functional and economic obsolescence rarely is accurately described. Square foot measurements, if shown, may prove to be inaccurate or may not be the gross living area figure used by appraisers. Finally, conditions of sale are rarely indicated. Once the MLS is used to locate a sale, the property should be personally viewed by the appraiser to obtain needed information.

• *Deed Records.* Deeds are a traditional source of sales information

FIG. 13-1: Comparable Sales Data Sheet

Address: _____

Class: _____ Type: _____ Style _____

Date of Sale: _____ Grantor: _____

Sale price: _____ Grantee: _____

Financing: _____ Data source: _____ Verification: _____

Lot Dimensions: _____ Lot size: _____

Site improvements/landscaping/topography: _____

_____

Zoning: _____ Conforming: _____ View _____

Neighborhood life cycle: _____ Improvement conformity_____

No./Rooms: _____ No./Bedrooms: _____ No./Baths: _____

Other rooms: _____

Car storage: _____

Functional utility: _____

Assessment	**Services & Mechanical Equipment**	

Land: _____ Water: _____ Type of heat: _____

House: _____ Sewage: _____ Fuel: _____

Other: _____ Electricity: _____ Hot Water: _____

Total: _____ Gas: _____ Plumbing: _____

Construction	**Extra Features**

Type: _____ Air conditioning: _____

Quality: _____ Storm windows/doors/screens: _____

Kitchen style: _____ Pool: _____ Other: _____

Bath style: _____

Condition: _____

Effective age: _____ Appeal: _____

Basement % of 1st flr.: _____ Sq. ft./finished space_____

Rent & GMRM: _____

Sq. ft. of GLA: _____ Sale price (sq. ft./GLA): _____

Special considerations: _____

Date Inspected: _____

but their main contribution is in reflecting the existence of a sale. They usually contain only the address of the property, a legal description (this is part of a good positive identification), names of grantors and grantees, and the date of title transfer (which is sometimes a substantially different date from the actual date of the closing). In some areas, deed records also show the sale price (or have tax stamps affixed, which indicate the sales price) and the terms of the financing, but it is imprudent to rely upon this data alone as comparable sales data.

● *Title Companies.* Title company data ranges from complete descriptions of houses to information similar to that found on deeds. Even companies that have nothing more than deed information may be helpful if they file information by street rather than chronologically, as is done in most deed recording offices.

● *Transfer Tax Records.* Some communities keep separate records of transfer taxes. The main advantage of this information is its accuracy and ease of use, particularly if filed by street.

● *Assessment Records.* A cooperative, knowledgeable assessor with up-to-date records can be a major asset for the appraiser. A good set of assessor's records contains an accurate description of the property. Many assessors, however, inspect properties at intervals of 10 years, and the descriptions may not include recent improvements. Many assors' measurements are quite accurate. Although they may not use gross living area calculations, their measurements can usually be converted to such figures. Appraisers must resist the temptation, however, to depend on assessor's description and measurements without personally viewing the property.

● *Mortgage Loan Records.* An excellent source of information, often overlooked by appraisers, are records of lending institutions. They usually include appraisals of nearly every property for which a loan application has been made. Many lending institutions make this information available to bona fide appraisers.

● *Real Estate Brokers Files.* In areas where other sources are not available, the appraiser may elect to use the files of individual brokers, which are often elaborate and accurate. Brokers are a particularly good source of rental data and information about listings and unsold houses.

● *Government and Private Mortgage Insurers.* The FHA and some

private mortgage insurers are good sources of data. Like lending institutions, they often have appraisals in their files for recent sales, which contain good, accurate information.
• *Atlases and Survey Maps.* These give data on lot size, relate legal descriptions to street numbers and frequently show building locations and dimensions to scale.
• *Other Appraisers.* Sharing sales data is traditional among appraisers. Working with other professionals saves considerable duplication of effort and time and increases the quality of everyone's work. Some appraisers charge each other for exchanged sales data. Exchanges of data should not be viewed as a substitute for personal research.
• *Real Estate Newspapers.* Real estate newspapers concentrate on people making real estate news, major sales and leases and new construction; however, they often have information about subdivisions, condominiums and other developments that would be difficult to obtain elsewhere.
• *Commercial Publications.* In some areas, special commercial publications give sales and rental information along with other business news. Although they usually report only the information available from the recorded deeds and leases, they are an excellent source of locating comparable sales.
• *General Circulation Newspapers.* Daily newspapers often publish information pertaining to real estate transfers as well as about proposed developments, zoning changes and other general real estate news. Many weekend papers carry special real estate supplements or sections. The classified advertisements are a good source of information about properties for rent and for sale.
• *SREA Market Data Center.* The Data Center is an independent, nonprofit organization, sponsored by the Society of Real Estate Appraisers. It is a good source of data particularly when it represents a sufficient percentage of the sales in the market. Data is collected on a standardized form (primarily from lending institution appraisers), processed through a central computer and displayed in printouts prepared at regular intervals. Because input is made by appraisers, the description of condition is in appraisal terminology, with at least some functional and economic obsolescence identified. There may be an indication of unusual conditions of sale. This service assists

appraisers in identifying comparable sales. When a sale is selected, it should be inspected and the data verified by the appraiser.

● *Miscellaneous Sources.* There is a variety of other data available from cost services, libraries, universities, consumer organizations, public housing bureaus and company relocation offices.

Verifying the Data

Each sale used as a comparable in an appraisal report should be personally inspected and the data confirmed with the buyer, seller or broker. The appraiser must be assured that such considerations are factual—that is, that all depreciation has been considered, the measurements are correct and the reported price and terms are accurate.

Verification and inspection processes do more than confirm the accuracy of the data gathered. They also provide for exploration of motivating forces involved in a sale, such as: Were both buyer and seller acting without financial pressure? Was the sale an "arms-length" transaction, or were the parties related in some way? Other matters to be investigated include: Were both buyer and seller knowledgeable about the property and market in which the sale took place? Did the seller have a reasonable time to sell and the buyer to buy? Were there any special concessions granted by either party? Was financing typical of the market, or was there a purchase money mortgage, second mortgage, assumed mortgage or other unusual situations? Were there any other special sale conditions such as inclusion of personal property in the sale (furniture, above-ground pools, boats, automobiles, sports equipment, etc.)? Was there any special government program involving a subsidy, attractive financing terms or guarantee of payment?

Sometimes an owner sells for less than expected if allowed to occupy the property for a substantial period of time after the transfer of title. Sometimes a sale is the result of an option granted in the past when different market conditions prevailed, resulting in a sale price that may not be typical of the current market. These are only some of the possible conditions that might make the reported sale price different from the market value. Only by personally interviewing the buyer and seller or broker can the appraiser gain knowledge about such conditions.

Analyzing and Comparing the Data

Comparison of sales, offers and listings provides a basis for estimating market value of the property being appraised. When comparable properties are similar to the property being appraised; have sold very recently; and have few if any physical, locational and conditions of sale adjustments, such information is helpful to the appraiser in reaching a market value figure. On most assignments, however, the appraiser recognizes substantial differences between the appraised property and the comparable sales. As described in Chapter 9, two analytical tools are used by appraisers: elements of comparison and units of comparison. Each element of comparison (date of sale, physical characteristics, location, and conditions of sale) *must* be considered; the units of comparison provide a means for making these considerations.

Adjusting the Comparables

Once all of the elements of comparison between the comparable sales and the property being appraised are described in the appraisal report, they must be analyzed and adjustments must be made to reflect the dollar or percentage value of the dissimilarities noted.

Matched Pairs of Sales

In the past many adjustments were based on nothing more than educated guesses. Good appraisal practice requires that adjustments be supported with data from the market. The best technique is to extract the amount of the adjustment from the market by utilization of "matched pairs." This is often the only acceptable technique to many sophisticated purchasers of appraisals. It involves the selection of two sales in the market, one having the item for which the adjustment is sought, and the other not. The theory behind this technique is that if this is the only difference between the two sales, the difference in sale price can be attributed to the item. Although generally reliable where only one difference is present, the technique may be less reliable where there are several differences.

The following is an example of an adjustment based on only one difference between matched pairs. Each of the comparable sales used in these illustrations is assumed to be very similar to the house being appraised and to each other except as noted. They are also assumed to have sold recently so that no time adjustments are needed.

Comparable Sale 1 (Similar to the others except as noted)
1-acre lot
1-car attached garage
Sold recently for $38,000

Comparable Sale 2 (Similar to others except as noted)
1-acre lot
2-car attached garage
Sold recently for $40,000

The only significant difference between these sales is the garage size. From this information, it appears that the market recognizes a $2,000 difference between one- and two-car garages. The indicated adjustment for this item, therefore, is $2,000.

Usually more than one difference exists between two sales. In such cases, adjustments can be made for each of the differences. Any remaining difference in sale price, after all other adjustments have been made, is attributed to the item for which adjustment is being sought. Continuing the above example:

Comparable 3 (Similar to the others except as noted)
1-acre lot
1-car attached garage
Next to gasoline service station
Sold recently for $35,000

This sale can be directly paired with Comparable 1. The $3,000 difference in sale price between 1 and 3 can be attributed to the gasoline service station. Comparable 3 could also be paired with 2. There is a $5,000 difference between the sale prices of Comparables 2 and 3, of which $2,000 is caused by the difference in value between a one-car and two-car garage (based on pairing Comparable 1 with Comparable 2).

When there are two or more differences between the matched pairs, the differences may affect the sales in the same or opposite ways. In this example they both affect the sales in the same way. Comparable 3 is $5,000 less valuable than 2 because 2 has a larger garage and is not affected by the gasoline service station.

Because it is difficult to tell if the differences affect the sales in the same way or opposite ways just by looking at them, it is necessary to estimate the effect from the market. This is done by designating one sale as the base sale and then first adjusting the other sale for all the differences between it and the base sale, except for the one being sought. When all the adjustments have been made, the remaining difference between the base sale and the other sale of the pair can be attributed to the one difference being sought.

Paring Comparable 2 with 3 illustrates how the process works.

Comparable Sale 2 (Base—similar to the others except as noted)
1-acre lot
2-car attached garage
Sold recently for $40,000

Comparable Sale 3 (Similar to the others except as noted)
1-acre lot
1-car attached garage
Adverse influence from nearby gasoline service station
Sold recently for $35,000

Adjustment of 3 to base sale 2 to reflect
    difference between 1-car and 2-car garage
    (based on comparing 1 with 2)   +   2,000
Adjusted Sale Price 3 $37,000

Abstraction for remaining difference attributable to adverse influence of nearby gasoline service station:

Sale price 2 (base) $40,000
Adjusted sale price 3   − 37,000
Amount attributable to adverse effect of
    location near gasoline service station $ 3,000

This process can be extended still further. Comparable Sale 4 is also similar to the other sales and sold recently for $45,000.

Comparable Sale 4 (Similar to the others except as noted)
2-acre lot
2-car garage
Adverse influence from nearby gasoline service station
Sold recently for $45,000

This sale cannot be compared directly with any of the other sales to extract an adjustment for the two-acre lot. In each case, there is at least one other difference:

Comparable 1: 1-acre lot, 1-car garage, away from gasoline service station.

Comparable 2: 1-acre lot, away from gasoline service station.

Comparable 3: 1-acre lot, 1-car garage.

Even though there is more than one difference in each matched pair, Comparable 4 can be paired with each of the others by first adjusting for the other differences.

Pairing Comparable Sale 4 with 1 works out as follows:

Comparable Sale 1 (Base—similar to the others except as noted)
1-acre lot
1-car garage
Sold recently for $38,000

Comparable Sale 4 (Similar to the others except as noted)
2-acre lot
2-car garage
Adverse influence of nearby gasoline service station
Sold recently for $45,000

Adjustment of 4 to base sale 1 to reflect
   the difference between 1-car and 2-car garage
   (based on comparing 1 with 2)   − 2,000

Adjustment of 4 to base sale 1 to reflect
   adverse influence of gasoline service station
   on 4 (based on comparing 3 with 1 and 2)   + 3,000

Adjusted Sale Price 4 $46,000

Abstraction for remaining difference attributable to lot size:

Adjusted Sale Price 4	$46,000
Sale Price 1 (base)	− 38,000
Amount attributable to difference between 1-acre and 2-acre lot	$8,000

Pairing Comparable Sale 4 with 3 works out as follows:

Comparable Sale 3 (Base—similar to the others except as noted)
1-acre lot
1-car attached garage
Adverse influence of nearby gasoline service station
Sold recently for $35,000

Comparable Sale 4 (Similar to the others except as noted)
2-acre lot
2-car attached garage
Adverse influence of nearby gasoline service station
Sold recently for $45,000

Adjustment of 4 to base sale 3 to reflect
   the difference between 1-car and 2-car garage
   (based on comparing 1 with 2)   − 2,000

Adjusted Sale Price 4 $43,000

Abstraction for remaining difference attributable to lot size:

Adjusted Sale Price 4	$43,000
Sale Price 3 (base)	− 35,000
Amount attributable to difference between 1-acre and 2-acre lot	$ 8,000

Figure 13-2 summarizes the data analyzed in the preceding example.

FIG. 13-2: Comparable Sales Grid

Item	Appraised House	Comp. Sale 1	Comp. Sale 2	Comp. Sale 3	Comp. Sale 4
Sale price	—	$38,000	$40,000	$35,000	$45,000
Time of sale	Date of appraisal	Recent —0—	Recent —0—	Recent —0—	Recent —0—
Physical Lot size	1-acre	1-acre —0—	1-acre —0—	1-acre —0—	2-acre −$8,000
Car storage	1-car attached	1-car attached —0—	2-car attached −$2,000	1-car attached —0—	2-car attached −$2,000
Location Adverse influences	None	None —0—	None —0—	Next to gas station +$3,000	Next to gas station +$3,000
Conditions of Sale	None	None —0—	None —0—	None —0—	None —0—
Net adjustment	—	—0—	−$2,000	+ $3,000	−$7,000
Indicated value appraised house	—	$38,000	$38,000	$38,000	$38,000

In actual sales analysis calculations would rarely work out as precisely as in this example, due to two major factors. First, even active, informed markets produce different buyer and seller opinions of the value of *each* comparison item considered by the appraiser; thus for each property there may be a range of price considered reasonable for its market. Second, the adjustment for one item of difference may already include a partial adjustment for another item of difference.

To illustrate, in the above example, the price per acre may differ for locations near service stations. This may be true in a situation in which the market might require a larger lot to better buffer against the adverse influence, yet not pay more for the extra land. Adjustment for both adverse influence and lot size may overstate the actual difference because an adjustment for location near the service station may already include a partial adjustment for lot size.

The appraiser must be cautious to avoid the conclusion that apparent precision of adjustment processes provides a more accurate estimate of value. In many situations that accuracy may be reduced by adding more adjustment factors. Unless aided by properly applied adjustment processes such as regression analysis, the appraiser should generally make the fewest adjustments possible and should reflect the uncertainties of multiple adjustments in final reconciliation of the value estimate. This is particularly true in making multiple adjustments for physical differences.

Likewise, the appraiser should avoid the temptation to use cost estimates as a basis for market adjustments. While relationships between cost and value contributions of components may exist, they may be supported only by market data. Thus comparison of market data should be used to support the adjustments used.

Regression Analysis

In recent years, attention has been drawn to methods of analyzing market data through use of regression analysis and other mathematical techniques. Stepwise multiple regression routines, like more traditional methods, are based upon the concept that certain identifiable characteristics of residential markets (called independent variables) may each be studied for their individual and joint contributions to value. Unlike traditional methods however, the mathematics of analyzing comparable sales is more complex and generally requires more powerful computing equipment. An example of the use of multiple regression analysis in the valuation of residences is included in Appendix E.

A major contribution of these newer techniques has been to focus attention on the adjustment process in sales analysis. Where more than one set of matched pairs is used to extract adjustment factors, the possibility of "doubling up" on adjustments exists. This is due to the interdependence or interaction of many comparison elements (often referred to as their "collinearity"). Traditional comparison methods have generally overlooked these relationships and do not provide a means for measuring interdependence of data.

For example, if adjustments are made for both square footage of living area and number of bedrooms, either variable is likely already to include some consideration of the other. Regression techniques (particularly stepwise) can serve to reduce this problem and provide a means of measuring where significant interdependence is present.

Regression techniques also permit a measure of reliability and significance of both data used and results produced.

Another reason for the growing use of regression analysis and similar techniques is that they often allow use of more market information and provide a better analysis and understanding of markets for market value estimates than traditional methods. In simple terms, traditional application of the market approach has usually taken the mathematical form of:

1. $Y_c = bX$

   Where Y_c means calculated value, b is a multiplier as a unit of comparison, and X is measured data for a property appraised. Example: market indicates a price of $27.38 per square foot, and property appraised has 1,738 square feet.

   $Y_c = (\$27.38)(1,738) = \$47,586$ or $\$47,600$

2. $Y_c = bX \pm a \pm b \ldots \pm n$

   Where a, b, . . . n are plus and minus adjustment factors. Example: In addition to data already given, appraiser considers property appraised to be $1,500 superior as to condition but $750 less as to location:
   $Y_c = (\$27.38)(1,738) + \$1,500 - \$750 = \$48,336$ or $\$48,300$

3. $Y_c = a \pm b \pm c \pm \ldots n$

   Where a is lump sum amount, and b, c . . . n are various adjustment factors. Example: An appraiser estimates a base market value of $47,500 before adjustments (or is dealing with a comparable which sold for that amount) and then considers the condition and location adjustments already mentioned:
   $Y_c = \$47,500 + \$1,500 - \$750 = \$48,250$ or $\$48,300$

4. $Y_c = X(a \pm b \pm \ldots n)$

   Where a,b, . . . n are percentage adjustment factors that are added and subtracted; alternatively each may be applied independently to X, the base for calculations. Example: A property appraised is considered 3% superior as to condition, but 2% inferior as to location to a base of $47,500:
   $Y_c = \$47,500 (100\% + 3\% - 2\%) = \$47,975$ or $\$48,000$

These basic methods and relationshps have other variations in common use. Each should be understood in applying the market data approach to avoid commonly encountered abuses and errors.

Particularly important is recognition that the model used for final application of market adjustments must also be used as the model for original extraction of adjustment factors from market data. It is improper to extract adjustment factors using one method and apply them using another.

Where sufficient data for analysis is available, many appraisers have found that use of simple linear regression analysis may provide more accurate use of available data—and an application of more market information—than traditional methods. This is particularly true in situations where a simple price per square foot unit of comparison is used. To illustrate, assume that an appraiser has collected sales data for 10 nearby properties which have recently sold, as shown in Fig. 13-3.

FIG. 13-3: Comparable Sales Data Set for Simple Regression Analysis

Sale No.	Gross Living Area	Total Sale Price	Sale Price per Sq. Ft./GLA
1	1,000 sq. ft.	$29,000	$29.00
2	1,100	27,500	25.00
3	1,200	29,000	24.17
4	1,400	29,000	20.71
5	1,500	31,000	20.67
6	1,600	30,000	18.75
7	1,650	32,000	19.39
8	1,750	30,500	17.43
9	1,850	32,000	17.30
10	1,950	31,500	16.15

Several situations are found in common practice:

1. In appraising 1,100 square foot dwelling, the appraiser might consider Sales 1, 2, and 3, which have a mean price of $26.06 per square foot, as the three prices per square foot do not form an applicable pattern.
2. In appraising a 1,500 square foot dwelling, the appraiser might consider Sales 4, 5, and 6, which have a mean price of $19.86 per square foot, as the three square foot prices again do not form a regular pattern.
3. In appraising an 1,800 square foot dwelling, the appraiser might consider Sales 7 through 10, which have a mean price of $17.57 per square foot, as the pattern is once again inconclusive.
4. In appraising any property for which these sales are considered comparable, it will be extremely difficult through traditional

means of analysis to apply more than three or four of the sales in any one sales comparison process. Thus, the concept of market is reduced because of the simple mathematical inadequacies of traditional analysis methods.

Particularly distressing is the tendency of many brokers (and some buyers and sellers) to generalize, based on these 10 sales, that "the market indicates about $20.00 per square foot for properties in this area," (the arithmetic mean of the 10 sales is actually $20.86). Such a generalization is potentially meaningful only for sales near the middle of the group and is severely misleading for those not near the middle.

Often overlooked is the fact that *any* use of a simple unit of comparison such as price per square foot is an application of simple linear regression analysis. Each of the square foot prices discussed ($26.06, $19.86, $17.57, and $20.86) may be substituted for b in the relationship $Y_c = bX$ where X is square footage, and a simple linear regression model is implicit with any such use of comparison units. Unfortunately, this application is an oversimplification of a more accurate form of simple linear regression which adds a constant "a" to the equation: $Y_c = a + bX$

Fig. 13-4 illustrates the difficulty of applying the traditional unit of comparison relationship $Y_c = bX$ and one of the advantages of the more extensive form $Y_c = a + bX$. By plotting the price/square foot relationship, it can be seen that a regular pattern of price increase with increase in square footage exists. Alternatively, prices per square foot could be illustrated. If the $20 per square foot generalization is used, a 1,500 square foot dwelling would be expected to sell for $30,000. Likewise, a 0 square foot dwelling would be expected to sell for $0. While the latter is ridiculous, the expectation establishes the slope of the price expectations at any reasonable square footage. Thus the traditional method forces a price per square foot slope to pass through the intersection of the X and Y axis (the zero intercept) regardless of the actual slope of price to square foot relationships.

This zero intercept fallacy may be overcome by application of the $Y_c = a + bX$ relation which can be calculated by simple linear regression techniques (see Appendix E). Figure 13-4 shows that this formula provides a much better explanation of the market data than

FIG. 13-4: Comparison of Y_c = bX and Y_c = a + bX as Descriptors of a Residential Sales Data Set

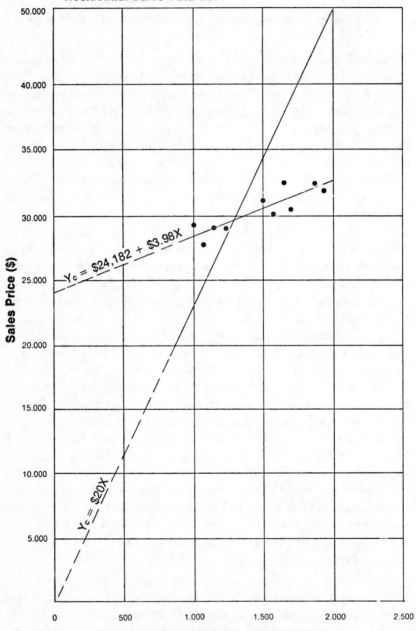

Square Feet of Living Area

Note: the formula for a straight line is Y = a + bX

the traditional method and allows the use of all 10 sales in this instance. While the mathematics of this calculation can be handled by even simple calculators, it is also possible to approximate the relationships by freehand drawing on graph paper once the basic data is plotted.

This same example also illustrates the hazard of inadvertently "doubling up" on adjustments in the traditional market approach when there is an interdependence of comparison units. Fig. 13-5 includes data for both square footage and bedrooms for each of the 10 comparable sales. Use of both comparison units is common in applying the market approach. However, analysis shows that a high interdependence between square footage and bedrooms is present in this data.

FIG. 13-5: Comparable Sales Data Set for Simple Regression Analysis

Sale No.	Living Area	Bedrooms	Sale Price
1	1,000 sq. ft.	2	$29,000
2	1,100	2	27,500
3	1,200	2	29,000
4	1,400	2	29,000
5	1,500	3	31,000
6	1,600	3	30,000
7	1,650	3	32,000
8	1,750	4	30,500
9	1,850	4	32,000
10	1,950	4	31,500

Analysis of this data through a stepwise multiple linear regression model produces the following "correlation matrix," which measures the amount of correlation among variables:

Square Feet	Bedrooms	Price
1.00000	.92768	.84687
	1.00000	.81088
		1.00000

These results indicate that over 84% of the price variance among the sales may be explained by square footage and that about 81% is explained by bedroom data. Thus either variable *used alone* is capable of explaining a great deal about price. The almost 93% correlation between square feet and bedrooms is particularly significant because it indicates a very high level of interaction or interdependence between the two variables.

Other analysis by the multiple regression model produces standard error of the estimate measures, which indicate the precision of regression estimates. Standard errors were calculated for square footage and bedrooms where each was used as a single independent variable and then for their combined use as joint predictors of value, with the following results:

Independent Variable(s)	Standard Error
1. Square footage only	$851.80
2. Bedrooms only	937.35
3. Square footage and bedrooms	903.22

Use of square footage alone is shown to be a better predictor of value in this instance than either bedrooms alone or a combination of both variables. Bedrooms would seldom be used alone as a unit of comparison in traditional market data methods (except in the paired sales concept), but both bedrooms and square footage would frequently be used.

This example shows that addition of the data regarding bedrooms actually reduces the capability of the units of comparison to predict value because of the high interrelationship between square footage and bedrooms. Without the multiple regression calculation, effects of this interrelationship would possibly be overlooked and a doubling of adjustments would occur. Although the dollar amount here is minimal (due to the simplicity of this example), substantial effects can often be seen in grid analysis techniques, which commonly use numerous independent variables simultaneously.

Simple examples such as these raise at least three questions about contemporary application of the market approach:

1. Can appraisers afford to continue use of *only* three or four comparables where more market data factually exists and is available?

2. When using only one unit of comparison, can the traditional concept of $Y_c = bX$ continue to be used in favor of the linear regression concept of $Y_c = a + bX$ or similar nonlinear relationships?

3. When using more than one unit of comparison, can the appraiser continue to ignore the interdependence of data that is generally present in grid analysis techniques (or to ignore the multiple problems of combining series of adjustments extracted by the paired sales technique)?

Appraisal methodology is still in transition, but the weaknesses of many traditional methods in the market approach can be overcome by collecting more data and using study methods which analyze larger amounts of data, such as those illustrated.

Although a full exposition of regression analysis is beyond the scope of this discussion, these examples illustrate the complexity of market comparison processes and point out both the basis for common errors and the possibility of overcoming these errors with newer analytical techniques.

Other Adjustment Techniques

Another commonly used indirect technique for adjusting the comparables is to estimate the cost new, less depreciation, of the item for which adjustment is needed. The accuracy of this technique depends on the relationship of the cost less depreciation estimates and value differences in terms of market recognition. Depreciation is especially difficult to estimate, because the market may recognize only a small portion of the cost, and substantial functional obsolescence may have to be deducted to obtain the actual value contributed by a specific item.

The appraiser should be familiar with other ways of making adjustments, even though they are usually not used for residential appraisals. Percentage adjustments are based upon a percentage of value for each comparable sale. For example, the adjustment for condition might be 3%. If the comparable sale price was $40,000, this adjustment would be equivalent to a $1,200 adjustment.

When percentage adjustments are used, they are usually added and subtracted to give a net adjustment percentage, which is applied to the comparable sales price to yield an indication of value for the property being appraised. For example, if the time adjustment is +5%, the location adjustment is +3%, the adjustment for physical characteristics is −2%, and no adjustment for conditions of sale, the net adjustment is +6%. The comparable sale price is then increased by 6% to give an indicated value for the appraised property.

In the past some appraisers felt that it was not proper to add these percentages together; it was more accurate to convert them to decimal form and multiply them by each other to get the net adjustment figure. Using the figures given in the above example, they would calculate the adjustment as follows: $1.05 \times 1.03 \times .98 = 1.0598$. This figure, known as a "composite adjustment," would then be multiplied by the comparable's sale price to give an indicated value of the appraised property. The composite adjustment derived by multiplication is generally considered no longer valid.

Up to this point adjustments have been discussed on the basis of the whole property, resulting in a comparable sale price of the property as a whole to give a direct indication of value for the appraised property. Adjustments on a unit basis may also be applied. A good technique is to work in units, which for single family residences is most commonly square feet of gross living area. If this unit is used, the sale price of each comparable is converted into a price per square foot before the adjustments are applied. The adjustments are then made in unit figures. For example, the adjustment for condition might be $.75 per square foot.

The final value indication would be value per square foot of gross living area. This figure can be converted into an indicated value for the appraised property by multiplying its number of square feet of gross living area by the adjusted value per square foot of each comparable. This procedure could be done at this point or later in the reconciliation.

Comparison or Rating Grid

In the market data approach, each comparable property is analyzed and compared to the property being appraised, based on the four elements of comparison. A comparison or rating grid may be used on which information about the appraised property and the comparable sales is displayed and adjustments for each difference between them are shown. Fig. 13-6 is an example of such a rating grid.

Each comparable sale is adjusted so that its sale price is converted to an indication of the market value of the appraised property. There-

FIG. 13-6: Sample Rating Grid

Item	House Being Appraised	Sale 1	Sale 2	Sale 3
Sale price				
Time (date) of sale (Time adjustment)				
Physical characteristics Lot size, shape, etc. Encroachments & easements View Landscaping Site improvements House size General construction Design & appeal Age & condition Basement Plumbing Heating & cooling Electrical system Kitchen equipment Baths & lavatories Family & rec rooms Other rooms Rehab/modernization/ remodeling				
Location				
Conditions of sale				
Net adjustments				
Indicated value of house being appraised				

fore, if an element of comparison in a comparable is more valuable than those found in the appraised property, a *minus* adjustment must be made. For example, the only difference between the appraised property and Comparable Sale 1 is that the first has no porch and the latter has an open porch, which contributes $1,500 additional value to the comparable in this market.

	House Being Appraised	Comparable Sale 1
Sale Price		$45,000
Porch	none	− 1,500
Indicated value of appraised property		$43,500

In the above example, Comparable Sale 1 is *more valuable* than the appraised property, so a *minus adjustment* is necessary to produce an indicated value for the property being appraised.

In the following example the property being appraised has an in-ground swimming pool and the comparable has none. In-ground swimming pools add $4,000 value in this market, making the appraised property *superior* to the comparable house.

	House Being Appraised	Comparable Sale 1
Sale price		$40,000
In-ground swimming pool	yes	none
		+ 4,000
Indicated value of appraised property		$44,000

In this example the comparable was *less valuable* than the property being appraised, so a *plus* adjustment is made.

Reconciliation of Market Data Approach

After the best comparable sales have been selected and each one is adjusted to give an indicated value of the appraised property, the indications must be reconciled to produce a final estimate of value via the market data approach. It is not acceptable appraisal practice to use a simple arithmetic mean of the value indications. Averaging small groups of numbers produces a meaningless measure of central tendency, which may or may not reflect actual market value.

The accepted procedure is to review each sale and judge its comparability to the property being appraised. Generally, the fewer and smaller the adjustments used on a comparable sale to produce the indicated value estimate, the more weight the sale is given in the final reconciliation. However, consideration should also be given to the basis for the adjustments.

The final value selected is a judgment made by the appraiser based on all the information available. It is not always necessary to select a single figure at this point in the appraisal process; some appraisers believe that the use of a range is more helpful. The use of such a range to describe market value is becoming more common, most likely a result of greater awareness of statistical techniques on the part of appraisers.

Summary

The market data approach to value is generally the preferred approach to estimate the market value of single family residences. Appraisals that depend primarily upon the cost or income approach have a strong possibility of being subject to substantial error.

The key to the market data approach is market abstraction of adjustments and the use of an appropriate unit of comparison. Typically, in the appraisal of single family houses, the unit of choice is square feet of gross living area.

Each comparable sale is compared with the appraised property. Adjustments are made to the comparable sales price to reflect significant differences between them. Traditionally, the elements of comparison are divided into the four categories of time, location, physical characteristics and conditions of sale.

In order to obtain all of the information needed to use a comparable sale, the appraiser should inspect each comparable property and verify the nature of the sale with either the buyer, seller or broker. These are the people who can tell the appraiser about the conditions of sale and the actual physical condition of the property at the time of sale.

New techniques using more sales are available as alternatives to the above techniques. They do not depend upon adjustments based on limited market information but rather on statistical treatment of many comparable sales.

When the market data approach is based upon a sufficient number of carefully chosen sales similar or adjustable to the appraised property, the value indication is usually persuasive.

Review Questions

1. Which approaches to value are based on market data?
2. For the single family residence, which approach is usually the best indication of value?
3. How does the principle of substitution relate to the market data approach?
4. What, in your own words, are the steps of the market data approach?
5. Besides sales, what other market information can be used in the market data approach?
6. What two required items of information regarding a comparable sale must be verified by either the buyer/seller or broker?
7. What are the three most common ways to make market adjustments?
8. Why is averaging not an acceptable appraisal technique to obtain a final estimate of value?
9. Besides dollar adjustments, what other ways of making adjustments are available to the appraiser?

14

Financing and the Valuation of Single Family Residences

The relationship between financing and the valuation of single family residences is probably the most difficult to recognize, explain and understand in the process of making an appraisal. All who have studied valuation theory and applied the appraisal process know that there is some intangible relationship between financing and price, cost or value of residences. The market reflects this relationship in some manner, but it is difficult to "tie down." It is essential that the influence of financing be considered in the appraisal process, from which value figures (whether selling or offering price, cost figure or one of many kinds of value) are developed.

Financing terms are always present in the market and affect decisions of both buyers and sellers. The intangibility of the effects of financing does not lessen its importance in the market; it plays a major role in home buying decisions. The question the appraiser must solve is: how much of an impact do special and unusual conditions of finance have on price, cost and value?

To assist in analyzing the relationship between financing and value, it is necessary to recall the major economic characteristics of real estate. In Chapter 5 these characteristics were described as fixity of location, large economic units, long life and interdependence of private and public property. These characteristics, which are peculiar to real estate, must be recognized as causal factors for the type of financing typically involved in a real estate purchase. Because of fixity of location, the commodity is excellent security for a large, long-term loan. The long life and large economic unit characteristics make the mortgage type of financing feasible; risk tends to be diminished for the mortgagee when the collateral is likely to exist and be useful for many years.

The fourth economic characteristic of real estate is the interdependence of public and private areas. The public sector spends much of its budget and time on facilitating single family home ownership and in providing adequate protection, utilities and access. This reliance upon the public sector and the protection that results also makes the home good collateral for a large, long-term loan.

The Mortgage Instrument

Because long-term financing arrangements are necessary in most cases when a home is purchased, the mortgage instrument has been developed to fit these needs. It is a legal document comprised of two parts — the mortgage and the note. The use of the mortgage instrument has been commonplace in this country for many decades.

The traditional first mortgage is categorized as a conventional mortgage. Nonconventional mortgages are those which are insured or guaranteed by an agency of the federal government (Federal Housing Administration or Veterans Administration) or a private insuring company. Since the 1930s, the FHA has been insuring loans to persons who require assistance because of their lack of financial capacity or reliability. The VA provides a similar service to veterans. Both FHA and VA interest rates tend to be lower than conventional loans and usually have longer terms and a higher loan-to-value ratio.

Other types of financing include deeds of trust, private insured and guaranteed loans, cash, second mortgages and contract purchases.

Legal restrictions and requirements applying to a mortgage vary from state to state. Such legal considerations and impacts on the mortgage instrument are two-sided: The homeowner is given as much protection and encouragement as possible, and the risk to the lender also must be considered. The best examples of this are foreclosure laws of the various states. A state having foreclosure legislation most favorable to the borrower may attract few funds from outside the state. Those states that give the greatest protection to the mortgagee, with short time periods for foreclosure, tend to attract more funds from around the country.

Sources of Mortgage Money

Funds for financing the purchase of a single family residence come from either primary or secondary sources. Primary sources are institutions that actually assemble the money from savers and loan it directly to the borrower. Individuals who make mortgage loans also fall in this category. Secondary sources are institutions that do not directly raise the money but facilitate financing opportunities by buying and selling mortgages and thereby increase the effectiveness of the lending market. Examples of the latter are the Federal National Mortgage Association and the Federal Home Loan Mortgage Corporation.

Savings and loans associations and mortgage companies are the leading sources of funds to the residential buyer. Life insurance companies provide some funds, but they tend to look more toward multi-family and other types of income property. Commercial banks provide a limited supply of funds, usually on much shorter terms. The following table, taken from HUD statistics, shows the distribution of mortgage funds by primary sources in 1975:

Loan Source	% of Loans
Savings & loan associations	50.6
Life insurance companies	4.0
Commercial banks	17.2
Mutual savings banks	10.3
Federally supported agencies	12.8
Other	5.1
Total	100

Competition for Funds

The availability of funds to single family home buyers is of great concern to the appraiser. Not only is the appraiser concerned with the amount of money available, but also with the interest rate at which loans are being made, the length of the term and the ratio of loan to value. Each of these variables or combinations thereof are critical to the buyer making a decision in the market. The appraiser's first concern, however, is the total amount of investment funds flowing to the single family housing market. In 1973 and 1974 this flow of funds was reduced sharply because this market was not as competitive as other markets for investment funds. When the prime lending rate reached 12% (plus an additional 4% in some cases), there was no way that savings in institutions would flow to the single family home buyer who was only able to pay a maximum of 9% or 10%. In other words, mortgage financing for residences declined substantially, thereby reducing effective demand, and so the demand for houses dropped. The fixed supply of housing did not change so there was a normal tendency for prices to drop.

The Money Market

To understand the competition for investment funds, it is necessary to comprehend to a certain extent the nature of the whole money market. Money is defined as all currency plus all deposits in private checking accounts and "near monies", which include time and savings deposits, savings and loan shares, mutual savings bank deposits and short-term U.S. government securities. All are cash or the equivalent to cash; that is, they are available for expenditure without delay.

These funds are regulated by the U.S. Treasury Department and the Federal Reserve System. It is their obligation to assist the economy by having adequate money available. Originally the "Fed" was charged with the primary responsibility for the money market. As described in *The Federal Reserve System: Purposes and Functions,* "the function of the Federal Reserve System is to foster a flow of credit and money that will facilitate orderly economic growth, a stable dollar, and long-run balance in our international payments. Its original purposes, as expressed by the founders, were to give the country a lasting currency, to provide facilities for discounting commercial paper, and to improve the supervision of banking." As the economy changed, broader objectives were outlined, namely "to help counteract inflationary and deflationary movements, and to share in creating conditions favorable to a high level of employment, a stable dollar, growth of the country, and a rising level of consumption."

The function of the Treasury is different from the Federal Reserve System. Although it has some monetary impact, it is more obligated to conduct and manage the fiscal policy of the United States government. It has been described as being the banker for the federal government, processing obligations and income. It plays some role in money management, but it is relatively small compared to the Fed.

The Federal Reserve System controls the money stock consisting of currency, notes, checking account balances and the like. The supply of actual money, including credit, on the market at any one time tends to be manipulated by the discount rate. All commercial banks participate in this activity. To "dry up" the supply of money, the "cost" of money is raised; when the Fed feels it is appropriate to make more money available to users, it lowers the "cost" of money, making it easier for consumers to acquire funds.

The money market in the United States operates on a quasi-open market basis. Official controls are enforced, but the market tends to revolve around the traditional supply and demand situation. The total supply of funds is distributed to those who are willing and able to pay the greatest amount for them. As an anti-inflationary measure, additional restrictions may be placed on the user who is willing to pay almost any amount to get money or credit.

The mortgage market, which provides the basic supply of funds for the homeowner, is in direct competition for these funds. At times the mortgage market is not competitive with other users. Then the supply of funds goes down, the cost of money goes up, or both occur. At other times, as reflected by the experience in 1976, slow decline in the cost of money takes place without a corresponding reduction in the supply of money. This rather unusual situation existed because other users of funds were willing to pay less than the mortgage market.

The Mortgage Market's Relation to the Economy

The mortgage market does not operate independently of the total money market or of the economy. When business conditions are good and the economy is strong and growing, savings usually accumulate more readily, thereby making funds more available for all borrowers. In some circumstances, the funds flow adequately to mortgage lenders, which in turn encourages the construction of new homes and the purchase of existing homes. When the economy faces a decline, is stabilizing, or is in a major recession, one of the earliest markets to be hit is housing. As a result, either the supply of money available is reduced substantially or the conditions under which it is available reduces effective demand. Whether it be cause or effect, the reaction of the consumer is the same.

The Secondary Mortgage Market

The financing of real estate has been facilitated greatly in recent years by the development of the secondary mortgage market. Many lending institutions formerly made home loans and held them; now they are able to sell loans in the secondary market and thus secure additional funds for home financing. A number of private investors and institutions purchase home mortgages. They are also purchased by the Federal National Mortgage Association, a quasi-government agency; by the Government National Mortgage Association and by the Federal Home Loan Mortgage Corporation.

Some mortgages are sold on a participation basis with the seller retaining an interest in the loan plus the servicing. Some mortgages are sold as whole loans. Discounts or points allow for adjustments to interest rate charges.

Pension funds have been attracted into the market by the use of mortgage-backed securities. Some private lenders make use of mortgage-backed bonds to attract additional funds into this field. Thus, recent years have seen a dramatic expansion of secondary mortgage market activities, and current trends suggest the continuing development of this important area.

Financing and Risk

Lending institutions, the source of mortgage money, analyze the risk in making residential loans very much like any other investment. The security of the real estate in the mortgage loan gives added incentive to many institutions and individuals to make mortgage loans. However, certain risks are involved, such as delinquencies and the need to foreclose, which are costly. Another risk is that at some point the loan will be greater than the value of the real estate (the amount for which the real estate can be sold under pressure), thereby resulting in a loss to the financial institution.

In analyzing the relationship of financing to real estate values, it is necessary to consider the mortgage lending system and the risks involved. The quoted interest rate for a mortgage loan is the cost of the money. The annual rate of interest tends to be commensurate with the risk involved in the specific investment; however, the range of the rates is in relation to the money market in general and the mortgage market specifically.

Interest rates may be different from the actual yield of an investment. The mortgage market has become active on a much broader than local basis and so the impact of the secondary market (and the national market in some respects) affects the yield which a mortgage may produce. The yield is the amount of return, expressed as a percentage, of the dollars of interest earned compared to the net dollars in the investment. A 10% interest rate on a $50,000 loan pays, on an annual basis, $5,000. If an individual or institution acquires the loan at a discounted price of $45,000, the yield per year would be $5,000 on a $45,000 investment — a rate of 11.11% ($5,000 ÷ $45,000), rather than the contract rate of 10%. Conversely if the investor paid $55,000, the yield is reduced to 9.09%.

To compete in the market, it is necessary at times to charge "points" or to use a discount rate. For example, if a loan were to be made in the amount of $10,000 at the going rate of 9%, the lender may feel that rate is inadequate under the circumstances and make one of the following adjustments. The borrower may be asked to pay points—say, four points—for the right to borrow the money, which on a $10,000 loan would be $400. Another technique is applying a discount rate. By discounting the loan 3%, the amount of money actually advanced at the time of closing is 3% less than the original $10,000; however, the borrower still pays 9% interest on $10,000. In other words, a 9% return would be earned on $10,000 even though only $9,700 was loaned. This increases the yield to the lender, providing compensation for what the lender perceives to be a higher risk or to meet yields in other types of investment opportunities. All such manipulations in the mortgage market must be understood to relate their impact on the market (the interaction of the buyers and the sellers) and relate such activities to market value.

Other Types of Financing

In addition to the first mortgage, a second or "junior" mortgage may be used to facilitate the purchase of a home. As its name implies, a second mortgage is secondary to the rights of the first mortgagee. It is used in circumstances in which the buyer is unable to arrange for adequate financing based on one mortgage and so requires a second mortgage. This technique provides additional funds for the borrower and facilitates the purchase of the home when the buyer may not be able to do so otherwise.

While the mortgage is a traditional means of financing the purchase of a house, some states provide vehicles to accomplish the same end but with different kinds of legal arrangements. In some western states, a deed of trust, which is similar to a mortgage, is used. It involves a third party who serves as a trustee. Money is borrowed in the same manner as with a mortgage but the trustee holds the title to the property until the borrower meets all obligations at which time the title is conveyed.

A relatively common means of financing a home is with a conditional sales contract (buying on contract). This device requires the seller to finance the sale of the property to the new buyer. Title does not pass from the seller to the buyer until the buyer has satisfied the contract—that is, paid it off. Quite often terms are different from those available with first mortgages; a conditional sales contract may have a shorter term or provide for a higher ratio of loan to value, but traditionally at a higher interest rate than a conventional mortgage.

A few buyers provide all cash for the entire purchase of a residence. Through the sale of other property or the accumulation of funds in some manner, they are able to purchase property with a lump sum cash payment. Such financial arrangements quite often expedite the purchase and affect the negotiating ability of the buyer.

A variation of FHA insured loans has been developed by private mortgage insurance companies for conventional mortgages. Such companies insure the risk to the lender of the top 10% above the amount traditionally loaned as a conventional mortgage. If an 80% loan-to-value were available, the next 10% (increasing the loan to 90% of value) is insured by the private mortgage company.

Practices vary by community and the appraiser-analyst must be constantly in touch with the market to interpret the financing trends and practices in the market.

Financing Impacts on Home Buying Negotiations

Each of the numerous methods of financing the purchase of a residence in one way or another creates its own little market with its special considerations. These markets include:

1. Conventional first mortgage loans.
2. FHA-insured loans.
3. VA-guaranteed loans.

4. Conventional financing with private mortgage insurance.
5. Cash purchase.
6. First mortgage plus second mortgage.
7. Purchase money mortgage.
8. Contract purchase.
9. Deed of trust.
10. Others or combinations of the above.

When comparing and contrasting comparable sales with the property being appraised, if the latter can be purchased with a conventional mortgage, the comparable properties should be those that have been purchased with the same type of financing. Comparables may be selected in which other than conventional financing was used but the conditions of sale must be applied and adjustments made accordingly if possible to do so.

The most common financing market is the conventional first mortgage loan. In the conventional market, if the going loan for a particular community is 8½%, 20-year term, with 80% loan-to-value ratio, sales used as comparables should have a similar type of financing. If financing varies by a quarter percent of interest, a few years difference in length or a few percentage points variation in loan-to-value ratio, these would not be considered adequate differences of conditions of sale to require adjustments. In the above example, however, if a comparable were financed (because of special arrangements) at a 7½% rate for 30 years with a 95% loan-to-value ratio, adjustments must be made before it could be used, on the assumption that such special and favorable conditions of financing affected the sale price. Similarly, a buyer required to pay 9½% interest with a maximum term of only 15 years and a 70% loan-to-value ratio would probably also have paid less for the property, and adjustment would have to be made.

FHA-insured and VA-guaranteed loans tend to be in a market by themselves and when such properties are being appraised, comparables should be those with FHA or VA loans. It is quite common today for investors to seek out subdivisions that have been predominantly FHA- or VA-financed. By doing so, financing terms are typically very favorable—sometimes interest rates are one-half or two-thirds of the going conventional rate. The length of the term may be greater and the original loan-to-value ratio may be very competitive with conventional mortgages as of the date of the purchase. These unique financing arrangements have a marked effect on sale prices. To compare the sale of a house having favorable financing arrangements with the sale of a house subject to conventional financing arrangements cannot be justified. Rather than attempt to make an adjustment for such differences, most appraisers feel that it is essential to restrict themselves to using comparable sales from a similar market.

Each kind of financing market tends to be different and special in its own way. It is essential for the appraiser-analyst to be constantly in touch with each of the markets and to recognize the differences, if any, in sale prices resulting from financing terms.

Summary

In this chapter an attempt has been made to point out the relationship or the impact of financing upon sale prices and therefore on market value. Financing terms are an intangible component affecting value; as such it is difficult and demanding to recognize the impact of financing when applying the appraisal process and to interpret it properly in terms of dollars.

The mortgage market is in competition for funds with all other money markets. The special characteristics of real estate both hamper and help in attracting funds to the mortgage market. The money market as a whole must be understood to comprehend the operation of the mortgage market.

A variety of ways exist for financing the purchase of a residence, including conventional first mortgages, FHA and VA loans and contract purchases. Each creates its own little market, which the appraiser-analyst must interpret to determine if the financing has an effect upon buyer-seller negotiations. If the financing either gave the advantage to the buyer, thereby lowering the price, or provided a special incentive to the seller, thereby increasing the price, the use of such comparable sales in estimating the market value of the property being appraised would have to be adjusted accordingly.

Financing must be considered under the conditions of sale, the fourth element of comparison in the market data approach. If financing conditions vary between the comparable and the property being appraised, the comparable property may not be usable in the comparison process. Under some circumstances, based on the collection and analysis of market data, such differences may be reflected in a dollar or percentage adjustment. If so, the comparable property can be used wisely.

Review Questions

1. Why is it difficult to "tie down" the relationship of financing to sales prices of residences?
2. Relate the four economic characteristics of real estate to the financing of single family residential real estate.
3. Name other types of house financing in addition to the conventional first mortgage.
4. Savings and loan associations were the source of slightly over one-half of mortgage funds in 1975. Why do savings and loans provide such a major proportion of mortgages for home ownership?
5. In the competition for funds, why is it difficult for the single family residential sector to compete against other uses of funds?
6. Explain the secondary mortgage market. How does it facilitate the flow of funds to the housing sector?
7. Relate interest rates, ratio of loan to value, terms and "points" to the degree of risk which the lender assumes when making a house loan.

15

Reconciliation and Final Value Estimate

The objective of an appraisal is to make a supported estimate of the defined value of an adequately described property as of a specific date. The reconciliation leading to a value conclusion takes place in each step of the appraisal process. There is also a final reconciliation which leads to the final value estimate. All the data and indicated values resulting from the three approaches to value are brought together and evaluated in a logical cause-and-effect analysis which leads to the final value conclusion.

Reconciliation is defined as "the process by which the appraiser evaluates, chooses and selects from among two or more alternative conclusions or indications. . . . "[1] It is an ongoing process throughout the appraisal, since an appraiser must constantly sort and evaluate a myriad of data which may or may not be applicable to the specific appraisal problem.

In the past, this process was known among appraisers as *correlation*. Since correlation has a different meaning in statistics and other academic disciplines, it has been replaced by the word *reconciliation*.

Definition of the Problem

Reconciliation starts at the very beginning of an appraisal, with the definition of the appraisal problem, the preliminary survey and the data collection program. The appraiser must ascertain the character and quantity of work to be accomplished and begin to weigh the relative significance and applicability of various data and approaches to the problem.

---

[1] *Real Estate Appraisal Terminology, op. cit.,* p. 173.

Identify Real Estate

The report must provide a positive identification of the residence being appraised. Regardless of the method of identification (street name and number, metes and bounds, etc.) the location and boundaries must be specified. All significant easements, encroachments and rights-of-way must be considered. If an owners' association exists or rights to use nearby facilities are involved, these rights must be completely identified. The appraiser should be sure the identification meets the requirements of the Code of Professional Ethics of the American Institute of Real Estate Appraisers, which requires a clear and complete description of the property.

Identify Rights

When the property is in fee simple, a plain statement to this effect should be sufficient. If a leasehold or a residence on leased land is involved, the terms of these leases must be described and their effect on the estimated value must be analyzed. Analysis of condominium or cooperative ownership rights requires a survey of the entire project in which the features (both good and bad) of the entire project are related to the ownership interest being appraised. A residence that has time-sharing rights requires other consideration. For example, are the rights to use the property for December and June equal to the rights to use the same property for January and July?

The ownership rights of the property being appraised must be compared to those of comparable sales and offerings. Any differences will require adjustment.

Date of Valuation

In a stable market the date of valuation and any time adjustments made to comparable sales, rentals, cost estimates and offerings present few problems. However, in unstable and rapidly changing markets any time differential is reviewed. Time adjustments often are averaged over a period of time when in reality the market has been moving both upward and downward during the period. Such adjustments based on average value changes in a community may not apply to the neighborhood or the price range of the property being appraised. Large time adjustments based on one or two matched pairs may contain substantial error caused by some unknown factor.

Objective of Appraisal

If the objective of the appraisal is to estimate the market value, the appraiser asks if it accomplishes this objective. Is the potential error in the appraisal within boundaries that are satisfactory to the user of the appraisal? Would more data and better analysis reduce the possibility of potential error? Does the appraisal state the degree of potential error that exists, or is its degree of accuracy misleading? Often the real objective of the appraisal is more than just a value estimate. For example, a potential buyer or lender also needs a forecast of the future value of the property. When such a forecast is made, is it based on solid facts obtained as a result of good research or is it based only on feelings and conjecture?

When the objective of the appraisal is to estimate value other than market value, the data collected and analyzed must be sufficient and proper to produce the required value estimate. For example, if the value estimated is insurable value, have all the items to be excluded such as footings, underground pipes and site work been properly treated?

Finally, the most important question is whether the value estimated is a sufficiently accurate estimate of the defined value.

Definition of Value

It is not satisfactory to put a stock definition of value into the appraisal report without carefully understanding its meaning.

For example, market value may be defined in part as the highest price the property will bring or as the most probable selling price. One definition may be more appropriate than the other after an analysis has been made of the data. Insurable value requires a definition that is acceptable in the locale or region for the type of property being appraised. Often a different definition of insurable value exists for residential and commercial properties.

A review of the definition of value should be made after all the data has been collected and analyzed to determine if it still applies or should be modified.

Preliminary Survey and Appraisal Plan

Before the appraisal is completed, a step-by-step review of the preliminary survey and appraisal is made to determine if all the data has been obtained and analysis has been provided to arrive at the value estimate. Often the initial estimate of the data needed to make the appraisal proves to be insufficient to arrive at a satisfactory value estimate. For example, the original plan may call for only the use of comparable sales. However, when the market analysis is made, it may indicate that the shifting market is being affected by the number of competitive listings available and therefore information about listings should be used in the market data approach.

Changing building costs and the availability of sites and new, competitive houses may indicate that a detailed application of the cost approach, based on actual costs of available sites and residences currently under construction, will provide a good value indication. The lack of current rentals and information about rented houses that have sold may indicate the abandonment of an original plan to include an income approach analysis.

As part of the reconciliation process, the data used in each section of the report must be carefully analyzed with emphasis on making a final judgment about whether sufficient data has been collected and which data should be used to make the final value estimate. It is poor practice to have inflexible rules about the type and amount of data used; this must be based separately on each appraisal problem.

Data Sources

After the initial data has been collected and analyzed, the data sources should again be reviewed to determine if additional sources may be available. For example, offerings of nearby comparable properties from an MLS may not show as sales because they were sold either by another broker or by the owner after the listing expired. By finding these particular properties where sales are recorded in the community, additional useful sales may be found. The search for comparables may disclose sales of residences that were recently completed by a local builder. This builder now becomes the potential source of cost data to be used in the cost approach.

Brokers, lenders, and others interviewed for information often supply leads to additional data sources. All data sources should be reviewed to determine if they have been properly used.

Personnel and Time Schedules

The initial estimate of needed personnel should be reviewed to see if they will be able to obtain all the necessary data within the prescribed time. If additional data is needed, extra personnel or additional time on the part of the original personnel will be required.

Often the time originally allocated to complete an assignment will have to be revised. Only when the special requirements of a specific assignment are known can a final estimate of the time schedule be made. Other considerations such as new assignments taking priority over existing assignments, unexpected illnesses of personnel, revised requirements of the client and personal needs of the appraiser often make scheduling revisions necessary.

The completion flow chart initially serves as a guide through the appraisal process. It can consist of simple notes on how the appraisal will be made or it may be a formal chart showing the progress of the appraisal on a step-by-step basis. Some appraisers use magnetic boards and movable pieces to plot the progress of each appraisal assignment. Whatever system is used, it should be reviewed to keep track of the progress of the assignment and altered to reflect the updated requirements to complete the assignment.

Data Collection and Analysis

Ongoing decisions must be made on how much data will be collected and whether the quantity and quality are sufficient to complete the appraisal assignment.

General Data

It is easy to collect masses of general data about the region, community and neighborhood in which the residence being appraised is located. It is very hard to cull from this mass of data the information that can directly describe the environment and explain the forces affecting the value of the property.

This reconciliation is probably one of the most difficult and one that tends to be downplayed in importance. "Window dressing"—an appraiser's term for unnecessary (merely decorative) figures, charts and displays—is *not* appropriate in a professional appraisal report.

The use of demographic information is a good example. There is little justification for simply presenting population figures. Rather, a comparison of population increase with the availability of housing stock, vacancy rates and a forecast of the rate of growth of new housing is more valuable. Raw figures cannot tell the story. All information pertaining to the region, community and neighborhood must be carefully analyzed and reconciled to produce a meaningful presentation.

Economic data, used to prepare market, financial and economic base analyses and to project future trends, also tends to be available in great masses. A visit to the local chamber of commerce will often supply the appraiser with pounds of this type of information. Usually one source, no matter how good, will be insufficient to provide all the needed data. As the data is sorted and analyzed, it is reconciled into a meaningful analysis that will be useful in making a value estimate of the property being appraised.

The economic base analysis of the region and community is based on information about employment in the community, which is analyzed to show the strengths and weaknesses of the region and community economic base. Basic and nonbasic activities are analyzed as to their projected stability and future growth. This is reconciled into a conclusion as to how the the economic base will affect the value of the property being appraised.

Specific Data

Information about the property being appraised is obtained at the community record source and at the property site. The goal is to accumulate all of the needed data during one trip to each of these places. This can be accomplished by careful planning and the use of checklists and fieldnote forms. A careful review of the data collected on location is the beginning of the specific data reconciliation.

An appraiser is not expected to be a title searcher. However, it is necessary to acquire enough skill to be able to find and use the needed documents. Title papers are examined to produce a positive description of the property; they also will reveal easements, rights-of-way and any private deed restrictions. Sometimes these items have a substantial effect on the value of the property.

Another item to be checked at the record source is the tax assessment. If possible, the assessor's field card should be examined. It often contains useful descriptive information about the property that may affect the final value estimate.

Zoning information can also be obtained at the municipal record source. A preliminary reconciliation may reveal whether the property conforms or if a reasonable probability of a zoning change exists. An initial reconciliation at the data source can determine whether additional record data pertaining either to the property being appraised or comparable properties is needed. Later when the data about the community, neighborhood, and property being appraised is reconciled, a more accurate judgment may be made.

Most of the information is usually obtained at the site. The use of checklists or fieldnote forms is helpful. Some clients will provide forms with their special informational requirements. Some clients require a complete list of all items of observed physical deterioration-curable, together with individual estimates of the cost to cure each item. These items may have to be checked even though the appraiser normally would not include them.

The final reconciliation of this information determines whether the property has been completely and accurately described and whether there is sufficient information to complete each of the three approaches to value.

Highest and Best Use

Estimating the highest and best use starts with an analysis and reconciliation of all the general and specific information collected about the property. It is done in two parts: first the site is analyzed as if vacant, and then taking into consideration any existing improvements. The information is reconciled with the four tests of highest and best use. First zoning information and private restrictions are reconciled to indicate what uses are currently legally permitted. Then the community and neighborhood information is reconciled with economic information to determine if a reasonable probability of change in zoning exists. The information is further reconciled into an estimate of the reasonable and probable permitted legal uses. Next the physical information about the site is reconciled to estimate which of the reasonable and probable legally permitted uses is also physically possible.

The community, neighborhood and economic data is again reconciled to estimate what uses would result in the production of a profit. Even if the legally permitted use is for a single family residence and such a residence can be built and can produce a profit, this is not sufficient to conclude that the highest and best use is for a single family residence. The type of residence, style, size, design and construction must also be estimated (see Chapter 8, "Highest and Best Use Analysis").

If after reconciliation of the available information it is estimated that the highest and best use is for something other than a single family residence, this should be stated. (Estimating highest and best use for other than single family residences is beyond the scope of this text.)

The final step is an estimate of the most profitable use. Again, all the information is reconciled. If additional information is needed, it is gathered and analyzed and again a reconciliation is made and a decision made about what the most potentially profitable, physically and legally permitted use of the site is, assuming it were vacant.

This analysis is then repeated to estimate the highest and best use of the property as improved. The information about the region, community, neighborhood, site and existing improvements is analyzed to estimate what renovation and repairs, if any, could be made to result in a greater potential profit (or smaller loss) by the owner if the property were sold on the date of appraisal. This estimate may range from a simple list of physical and functional curable items through major renovations and proposed additional improvements to the site.

The estimation of highest and best use is based on a thorough analysis and reconciliation of all the data collected. Again, it may be necessary to collect and analyze additional data before final reconciliation as to the highest and best use can be made. For example, the preliminary reconciliation may indicate that some renovation may be needed. At this point additional information about its cost and physical feasibility is necessary before a final determination can be made; the reconciliation process is continued after the needed information is collected and analyzed.

Information about sales of comparative sites and improved properties, comparative rentals and rented properties that have sold is initially reconciled to see if it is sufficient to proceed to estimate an indicated value by the three approaches to value.

The preliminary reconciliation reviews the sources of cost data to be used to estimate reproduction or replacement costs. If a cost service is used as one source, a second source should also be developed. The cost data should be reconciled preliminarily with the description of the improvements to see if material to estimate all of the costs is available.

A decision about the method of estimating depreciation based on the available data should be made. If the abstraction method is used, comparable sales are analyzed to see if they are sufficient in number and comparable enough to the property being appraised to produce a satisfactory depreciation estimate. If the age-life or breakdown method is used, a preliminary reconciliation is again needed to determine if sufficient data has been collected.

The income approach depends upon comparable rented residences to estimate both the market rent of the property being appraised and also to develop the GMRM. The rentals used to develop the GMRM must be of properties that have recently sold. The initial reconciliation again is to determine if sufficient usable data has been collected to make these estimates or whether additional rentals and sales are needed.

Since the final value estimate of most single family residential appraisals depends heavily on the market data approach, it is necessary to reconcile the comparative sales data continuously during the appraisal process. Initial reconciliations are needed to see if sufficient comparable sales data as well as data to make necessary adjustments has been collected to reflect the differences between the comparable sales selected and the residence being appraised.

It is not good appraisal practice to claim insufficient data is available to develop the market data approach unless a thorough search of the market has been conducted. If sales appear insufficient after the initial reconciliation, the search should begin again. This expanded search can be over a wider geographic area, wider price range or greater time frame. The process may be repeated several times, each time collecting and reconciling data to determine its usefulness until it is concluded either that sufficient data is collected for the market data approach or that further expansion of the search will not produce any additional useful data.

All of the reconciling done up to this point is of a preliminary nature, with the primary goal being to collect enough useful data to proceed through the three approaches to value.

Application of the Three Approaches

The reconciliation process continues as the collected data are further analyzed for use in each of the approaches.

Income Approach (GMRM)

The Gross Monthly Rent Multiplier technique used in the appraisal of single family residences includes the following eight steps:

1. *Find residences that have recently sold in the neighborhood that are comparable to the property being appraised and that were rented at the time of sale.* All comparable residences are reviewed and those most comparable are selected for final use. No fixed number of comparables is needed. Many appraisers try to find at least 12. If a large number can be found, they may lend themselves to analysis by statistical techniques (see Appendix E).

2. *Divide the sale price of each comparable by the monthly rental to derive the GMRM.* The resulting GMRM figures should be arranged in order to determine if they fall into a useful range and if extremes should be dropped or additional data is needed.

3. *Reconcile the multipliers to obtain a single multiplier or a range of multipliers that is applicable to the appraised property.* If a single GMRM is selected, it should not be an average of the multipliers obtained in Step 2. It should be a result of considering how comparable each of the properties that produced a multiplier was to the property being appraised or the result of statistical analysis of the range of multipliers.

4. *Find comparable rentals in the neighborhood.* Comparable rentals are reviewed and selected for final use. Again no fixed number is standard; however, less than three usually is not satisfactory. The reconciliation here emphasizes the comparability of the rental to the property being appraised and the identification of the existing significant differences for which adjustments are made.

5. *Analyze each of the comparable rentals by comparing them with the corresponding features of the house being appraised.* A

decision must be made on an item-by-item basis about whether the differences can be adjusted or if the rental must be rejected and replaced by a more comparable rental. If many rentals are rejected, it may be necessary to go back to the market and expand the search to find additional useful data.

6. *Estimate the required adjustments of each comparable rental property to obtain an indicated rental for the appraised property.* All the additional rentals needed to estimate the adjustments are analyzed and those that will produce indications of the needed adjustments are processed. These adjustments are reconciled with the comparable sales and data is added or eliminated as required.

7. *Consider each comparable rental carefully, with emphasis on the need for adjustments, and formulate an opinion of the market (economic) rent of the property being appraised, based on the adjusted rentals of the comparables.* Often the rentals are adjusted with the aid of a grid. The result is a group of adjusted rentals, each of which is an indication of the market rent of the residence being appraised. These adjusted rentals are individually compared to the property being appraised to estimate which are most comparable. Finally a decision is made as to the estimated market rent of the property being appraised. This estimate should not be an average but based on the results of the reconciliation.

8. *Multiply the estimated market rent of the appraised property by the estimated monthly multiplier (or range of multipliers) to obtain an indicated value of the appraised residence via the income approach.* This result should not be accepted without another reconciliation of all the data. The appraiser must be satisfied that the data used is of adequate quantity and quality to produce a useful estimate.

Cost Approach

The reconciliation process is applied to each step of this approach.

1. *Estimate the market value of the site as if vacant and available for development to its highest and best use* (see Chapter 8). The estimate of the site value actually requires all of the steps of the market data approach. First the comparable sites are reconciled, comparing their use with the estimated highest and best use of the site being appraised. For example, if the site being appraised were best suited for a house in the $80,000 to $100,000 range, sites for

houses of similar value would be the best comparables even if the house being appraised were in the $30,000 to $35,000 range and therefore not the highest and best use.

The best comparables are selected and individually compared to the site being appraised. Differences between the comparable sites and the site being appraised are reported. The data is further analyzed for information on which to base adjustments for all the significant differences. A decision is then made about each comparable as to whether it can be adjusted satisfactorily or rejected and replaced with a better comparable. If many sales are rejected, it may be necessary to go back to the market and expand the search for more comparable site sales and/or more data on which to base the adjustments.

When the appraiser is satisfied that the assembled data is adequate and all the needed adjustments are made, the adjusted sale prices of each of the comparables are analyzed and a final indicated value of the appraised site is made. This estimate is not an average of the adjusted sale price of the comparables; it is based on the results of the reconciliation.

2. *Estimate the reproduction (or replacement) cost new of the improvements.* This estimate can be based on data from construction cost services and/or from actual costs of similar residences constructed in the same market. The available data is reconciled to determine which method will be used. Both the description of the improvements and the data being used as a cost basis are analyzed to determine if everything needed to make the cost estimate has been gathered. The cost data is reconciled with the description of the improvements data to produce an estimated reproduction or replacement cost of the residence being appraised.

3. *Estimate the amount of depreciation the improvements have suffered.* A decision is made as to which method will be used to estimate the accrued depreciation. When the abstraction method is used, the sales selected from which to abstract the depreciation are analyzed and processed. The range of resulting amounts of depreciation or rates of depreciation are reconciled. The amount selected should be based on a reconciliation that considers the comparability of the data from which the amount or rate of depreciation is abstracted. The final reconciliation considers the amount

of data used, the degree of variance between the rates and whether additional data is needed to produce a satisfactory estimate.

If the age-life method is used, depreciation may be based entirely upon observation. To estimate the typical economic life of a residence, data about the region, community and neighborhood is considered, along with specific data about the residence being appraised. Each of the four great forces that affect the value and life of the residence is considered. All this is then reconciled by the appraiser, who relies heavily on personal knowledge and experience, into an estimate of typical economic life. Finally, the percentage of depreciation is calculated by dividing the effective age by the typical economic life. A final reconciliation of the results is made to judge how good the estimate is and how much weight it will be given in the appraisal process.

The breakdown method of estimating depreciation is done in five steps that correspond to the five types of depreciation identified by this method. First, the physical deterioration-curable is estimated by making a list of all the physical deterioration that is observed. Cost to cure these items is estimated either by the appraiser or by a local contractor who can provide the needed cost information.

Most items of normal maintenance are automatically classified as physical deterioration-curable without actually proving they add value in excess of their cost. However, it may be necessary to obtain market information to justify classifying large items of maintenance as curable. The list of items to be cured and the estimated costs to do the work are reconciled in an estimate of physical deterioration-curable.

Physical deterioration-incurable is divided into two groups. One group is items that are not ready to be cured on the date of the appraisal but will need to be cured before the end of the residence's economic life. Again, a list is prepared together with cost estimates to repair or replace the items. These items are reconciled into an estimate of physical deterioration-incurable (short-lived items). The other group of items includes those that have suffered some deterioration but will not be economically feasible to repair or replace during the remaining typical economic life of the improvements. This estimate is often made based on an engineering breakdown of the components of the residence against which percentage of depreciation estimates are applied to produce a total estimate of the physical deterioration-incurable. This estimate depends heavily on the appraiser's knowledge and judgment. All the data used should be carefully reconciled; based on this, the estimated reliability of the results is reported.

Items of functional obsolescence are listed and analyzed to estimate if a cure is possible and if so, if the cost to cure is less than the value added. Reconciliation of this information may require the use of additional data to support whether the value added will exceed the cost to cure. Data is also needed to estimate the cost to cure the items as part of a total construction program as well as the cost to do it separately on the date of the appraisal. In the reconciliation the reliability of this estimate is considered.

The loss from functional obsolescence-incurable may be based on comparison of recently sold or rented residences with and without the item causing the obsolescence.

The items off the premises that cause a loss in value (economic obsolescence) are listed, measured and estimated similar to the vay functional obsolescence-incurable is estimated.

In the past the breakdown method was a favorite method of nany appraisers. However, it is a very difficult method to use in actual practice because of all the data needed. There is usually a high probability of error.

4. *Deduct the depreciation from the reproduction (or replacement) cost new of the improvements to obtain the depreciated value of the improvements "as is."* If depreciation has been estimated by more than one method, the results are reconciled into a depreciation estimate. When sufficient data is available, the abstraction method usually produces the most accurate estimate because it is based directly upon market data. The age-life method usually is based primarily on the appraiser's judgment, supported more heavily by general knowledge than by specific data. Because it is easy to explain, it usually is the best method when insufficient data is available for the abstraction method. The results of the breakdown method tend to be deceiving because it is broken into five parts. Because it is not primarily based on the market, there is the potential for substantial error. When used, it should be carefully reconciled to eliminate

as much potential error as possible.

When more than one method is used, the results should be compared to each other. Reasons for differences should be sought and the estimates further refined, if possible, to reduce the discrepancy. The final depreciation estimate is deducted from the estimated reproduction or replacement cost to produce the depreciated value of the improvements.

5. *Add the site (land) market value obtained in Step 1 to the market (depreciated) value of the improvement to obtain an indicated value of the property.* After the estimated value is obtained, it is compared with the values indicated by the other approaches. A wide variance is indicative of possible weakness in the data, assumptions, or application of the cost approach or its validity and applicability to the specific appraisal problem.

Market Data Approach

The reconciliation process is applied to each of the five steps of the market data approach.

1. *Find the sales, listings and offerings of properties that are similar to the property being appraised.* When a group of sales, listings and offerings of properties similar to the property being appraised has been collected, a preliminary reconciliation is made for the purpose of deciding if enough usable data has been obtained. The setting of arbitrary numbers of sales, listings and offerings to be used without actually considering the quality of the data is poor appraisal practice.

2. *Verify each sale with the buyer, seller or broker to confirm the selling price, date of transaction, physical and locational characteristics and conditions of sale.* The only acceptable way to find out about the conditions of sale that affected a transaction is to interview the buyer, seller or broker. Only these people will know all the terms, motivations and whether the sale was bona fide in nature. The results of the interviews should be reconciled. If information developed indicates conditions of sale that will be difficult to adjust for, the sale should be rejected and replaced with additional data if possible and the reconciliation process repeated.

3. *Analyze the important attributes of each comparable and*

compare the corresponding features of the property being appraised. Use the elements of comparison such as time of sale, location, physical and other characteristics (see Chapter 13). The analysis of the important attributes of each comparable will identify differences between the comparable and the property being appraised. The available data is then reconciled to determine if it will serve as a basis for making the needed adjustment or whether additional data will be needed. The search continues for data until a sufficient number of sales, listings and offerings is found with differences that can be adjusted.

4. *Estimate the adjustments that will be required of each comparable's sales price to give an indicated value of the appraised property.* Adjustments should be supported with data developed from the market, which are reconciled to produce an adjusted price of each comparable.

5. *Consider each of the comparable sales and the accuracy of any and all adjustments required because of dissimilarities among these sales and the appraised property. Formulate an opinion of market value for the latter based on the comparable sales which have been analyzed.* The reconciliation of the adjusted price of each comparable into a final value estimate for the appraised property is the critical step in the appraisal process because this estimate will most likely be used as the main basis of the final value estimate. The reconciliation process considers the amount and support of each adjustment. When there is a substantial spread in adjusted prices, consideration should be given to expanding the data search and repeating the whole process to obtain better results.

In the final reconciling of the market data approach the quantity and quality of all the data is reviewed. Generally, the older the data, the further from the property being appraised and the more physically dissimilar, the less accurate the adjusted price will be. It is particularly difficult to adjust accurately for conditions of sale and economic influences.

Again, the market value obtained in the market data approach is compared with the value indications derived in the other two approaches. Wide discrepancies in indicated value usually suggest that further collection, refinement and analysis of the pertinent data is needed.

Final Reconciliation into Estimate of Value

The final step in reconciliation is to check all data used for accuracy, reliability and applicability. The purpose and objectives of the report are summarized and the characteristics of the property are reviewed. A decision is made regarding the most appropriate approach or approaches to value and the reliability of each value indication is obtained.

Advantages and Disadvantages of Each Approach

The income approach is mathematically simple and direct. It is most useful when the subject of the appraisal is located in a neighborhood where houses are frequently rented. Disadvantages of this approach are that the condition of comparables is not always reflected in rent differentials, many quality neighborhoods have few houses that are rented and subsequently sold, and a considerable volume of rental and sales data is necessary to estimate properly the market rent and appropriate multiplier for use in this approach.

The cost approach was traditionally the favorite approach to value for many appraisers. Its advantages include that it is simple to use and usually reliable for new improvements on properties developed to their highest and best use. One disadvantage is the difficulty of accurately estimating accrued depreciation when no sales are available from which to calculate the depreciation by abstraction. Another is that reproduction cost estimates may not reflect actual prevailing economic and market conditions.

The market data approach is usually the preferred approach in single family residential appraising. The value indication obtained is based on actual market transactions, is easily understood by laypeople and is most applicable in court testimony. It is not particularly useful when there is a lack of recent, reliable and highly comparable sales data.

Appraisal Report

The final step of the appraisal process is the preparation of a report of the value estimated. It is poor appraisal practice to give a value estimate without a report that meets at least the minimum reporting requirements.

All the data is again reconciled to select the material to be displayed in the appraisal report. Reports to be used for condemnation proceedings and other legal proceedings often must be very comprehensive, containing large amounts of data used to make the value estimate. Photographs, maps, sketches, charts and other graphics are often included to help the reader understand the analysis and reasoning that led the appraiser to the final estimated value. A lender who uses the services of an appraiser on a regular basis may require only a form report that displays the highlights of the data and reasoning used to arrive at the value estimate.

Summary

The accuracy of an appraisal depends on the appraiser's knowledge, experience, and judgment. Equally important are the quantity and quality of the available data that will be reconciled in the final value conclusion. A judgment is made as to the validity and reliability of each of the value indications derived from the three approaches to value. These indications are never merely averaged. To do so is substituting arithmetic for judgment. Rather, the appraiser reconciles the value indications, analyzing the alternatives and selecting from among them the indication of value that will be most defensible and truly representative of the property being appraised.

Review Questions

1. Define the term "reconciliation" in your own words.
2. What was the reconciliation process formerly called?
3. Where in the appraisal process does reconciliation occur?
4. What types of data must be considered when reconciling each of the three approaches? Give examples for each approach.
5. Which method of estimating depreciation is preferred when data is available?
6. List the advantages and limitations of each of the three approaches.
7. Which approach are most residential appraisals primarily based on?
8. What are some of the factors on which the accuracy of an appraisal depends?

16

Special Kinds of Residences

Many single family residences have unique characteristics that set them apart from the typical house. They often present special appraisal problems requiring special appraisal techniques. This chapter deals with such residences, including the special ownership forms of condominiums, cooperatives, time-sharing and residences built on leased land. It also discusses special purpose houses: resort and recreation homes, housing for the elderly, farm and ranch houses and mansions. Information is also included on planned unit developments, mobile homes, modular and prefabricated houses, log cabins, historic houses, experimental houses and solar homes. The special characteristics of each are discussed, together with suggestions as to how they might be appraised.

CONDOMINIUMS

Condominium is a form of ownership created by special real estate laws, which permit individual dwelling unit estates to be established within a whole, larger property estate. All 50 states have enacted condominium legislation. These acts vary from state to state but many are similar because they are patterned on a uniform condominium act.

Each condominium owner owns the fee to an individual unit and a percentage of the common areas of the land and improvements (entryways, corridors, elevators, drives, walks and green areas). In some instances owners may have exclusive use of some of the limited common areas, such as basement storage, patios, and parking areas; however, most condominium laws only permit the actual living area to be individually owned.

The location of each individually owned unit must be exact in terms of both the usual horizontal description found in the deed and also a vertical description. The physical horizontal boundaries of individual units for the exterior may be anywhere from the outside of the exterior wall to its inside surface and for the interior may be the wall surface, stud surface or middle of the wall. The vertical boundaries are usually the floors and ceilings within the unit.

The boundaries of the common property are described as they would be for any other type of property. Whatever is within these boundaries and not within an individual unit is common area. The exact boundaries of the common area and the individual units are also shown on a plat (also known as a plot plan) and on the architectural plans, both of which have to be publicly recorded in many states.

A condominium is formed when a master deed is recorded that complies with the requirements of the condominium laws of the state in which it is located. These documents must also establish an owners association that will control the use and maintenance of the common areas. The association (also called a condominium or homeowners association) is governed by a board of directors elected by the individual owners. It operates under a set of bylaws —recorded by the master deed—which in turn must always comply with the provisions of the condominium statutes of that state. Usually a 66% or 75% majority of the owners must vote to change the bylaws. It usually takes a 100% vote to change the master deed.

Condominiums can be new units or units in existing buildings that have been converted to condominium ownership. Either new or old, they can take the form of a highrise, townhouse, small groupings of party-wall units or free-standing units.

An in-depth study as to what people like and dislike about condominium living has been made by the Urban Land Institute.[1] Among favorable factors cited were:

1. Building up equity.
2. Lower cost than single family housing.
3. Freedom from house and yard maintenance.
4. Better environment.
5. Recreational facilities.
6. No rent.

---

[1]Carl Norcross, *Townhouses and Condominiums: Residents' Likes and Dislikes.* Urban Land Institute: Washington, D.C., 1973.

People were found to dislike:

1. Living too close together.
2. Noisy or undesirable neighbors and children.
3. Neighbors' pets.
4. Trouble with parking.
5. Poor association management.
6. Poor construction.
7. Dishonest salespeople who sold units.
8. Negligent builders.
9. Renters in other units.
10. Thin party walls.
11. Long identical rows of houses.

In spite of the problems some condominiums have faced, this form of ownership continues to play an important role in the housing market.

Special Appraisal Problems

The appraisal of an entire condominium complex is beyond the scope of this book; the following are considerations for the appraisal of individual condominium units.

The key to these appraisals is use of the market data approach, supported by the income approach if rentals of units similar to that being appraised exist. The cost approach will usually lead to the wrong value estimate. To use it, the costs (both direct and indirect) of the entire project would have to be estimated and then a portion allocated to the unit being appraised.

The best comparables are resales of similar units in the same condominium or similar condominium projects. Because many variables exist in common charges, design, recreational facilities and size, comparable sales from any but very similar complexes will prove extremely difficult to adjust accurately. Also, because of the unusual volatility in the market, time adjustments are often difficult to make. The price of new, similar units should be considered but resale prices in some projects are substantially lower than those of comparable new units.

Many lenders (and good appraisal practice) require an analysis of the whole project in order to estimate the value of an individual unit. Special attention should be paid to the common charges and their rate of increase. Similar units in different projects may have different common charges, which affect their value significantly.

COOPERATIVES

A cooperative apartment building is owned by a corporation, which sells shares to buyers who wish to occupy individual units. Along with the ownership of a cooperative share goes the exclusive right of occupancy of a portion of the space in the building and the nonexclusive right to use other areas of the property.

Technically, a share in a cooperative apartment is not a single family residence but because these shares are bought and sold in a manner similar to condominium units, the public is only vaguely aware of the difference between these ownership forms. Cooperative-owned buildings are financed with one mortgage whereas condominiums are financed with individual mortgages on individual units. The cooperative corporation owns everything while a condominium association owns nothing.

The shareowners (stockholders) of a cooperative elect officers and directors who run the affairs of the corporation. These officers have the power to assess shareholders for operating expenses.

Cooperative ownership was popular in New York City and some other markets around the country during the past decade. Changes in condominium and cooperative laws are reducing the differences between these two types of ownership.

Special Appraisal Problems

All of the approaches to value can be used to appraise the value of individual shares in a cooperative apartment. Resale of ownership shares provides the best evidence of value. The resales can be in the same cooperative or in similar buildings. In some markets, like New York, many sales of units may be available; in other markets, data may be more scarce. In some areas, a relationship may exist between the sale of condominium units and cooperative share values in the same markets.

Some confusion may exist regarding the sale price of a cooperative unit. For example, a share that entitles the owner exclusive occupancy of a three-bedroom apartment may be offered for $15,000, which appears to be a very low price. However, this is not the total price. The entire building might be subject to a $300,000 mortgage, of which unit's indirect portion might be $30,000, bringing the real price of the unit to approximately $45,000. Therefore, in addition to normal operating expenses, the owner of the share will be assessed for mortgage payments on a $30,000 share of the mortgage debt.

When comparable sales within the same corporation are used, no adjustment is needed to reflect the mortgage. The price of two similar units in two separate cooperative corporations may differ because of different mortgage obligations of the two corporations.

Some cooperative corporations permit rentals of individual units to tenants; others restrict use to actual shareholders. When rentals are permitted, there may be a relationship between rentals and value, making the income approach usable.

If cooperative apartments are still being built in the market, the cost approach can be used as a value indication. However, if new construction has stopped, it probably will not lead to an accurate value estimate.

TIMESHARING

Many resort housing units have been sold on the basis that if there were a loss to the owner, the burden of the loss was modified by possible tax write-offs. New tax regulations have generally limited the availability of such write-offs. More recently developers have sought other methods of attracting buyers and one that has emerged is known as *timesharing*.

The essence of timesharing allows one property to be purchased by several owners, each of whom has the right to use the property for a predetermined period of time. For example, 10 owners may buy a home at a ski resort. Each owner shares the cost of the property equally, and each has the right to use the property two weeks during the ski season and three weeks in the non-ski season. Other devices may be used, but the goal of all of these methods is to allocate the time equally among shareholders or proportionately to what each owner pays.[2]

Special Appraisal Problems

The first step of the appraisal process—identifying the rights being appraised—has special significance in this type of appraisal. These rights are divided into the type of ownership and the rights to

[2]See *Timesharing*, edited by Stuart Marshall Bolch and William B. Ingersoll, Urban Land Institute, Washington, D.C., 1977.

use the property. All the conventional types of ownership may be used, such as fee simple, tenants in common, joint tenants, condominium, cooperative, limited partnerships and real estate investment trusts. The use rights (which part of the property will be allocated for use by the shareholder) also must be established; these substantially affect value.

The best way to estimate the value of timeshared units is to look for resales in the subject complex or similar complexes. They are better evidence than new sales because the latter are often the result of heavy developer promotions which would not apply to resale properties. The income approach may also be applicable, if some of the units are rented during part of the year. The owners may use the property for part of the year and rent it for the remainder. Research into the market may reveal a relationship exists between the rental value and the resale value of this type of property. The cost approach may also be used if new units are being sold in the area and land is available for additional units as they are needed.

RESIDENCES ON LEASED LAND

Not all single family residences (which are not in condominium or cooperative forms of ownership) are held in fee simple. In some parts of the country, especially in Hawaii, it is quite common to build residences on leased land. Although many of the leases are for 99 years, others are for much shorter periods and leases for 50 years or less are quite common. To protect the mortgage, there is sometimes a provision in the lease that subordinates the fee owner's interest to that of the mortgagee's. More commonly, the lease gives the mortgagee the right to take over the land rent payments in the event that the owner defaults. The mortgagee usually also has the right to find a new owner who will continue the lease payments. At the end of the lease the improvements become the property of the landowner, who may extend the lease, modifying it to reflect current market conditions.

Special Appraisal Problems

Residences on leased land are appraised using the same techniques as for residences held in other ownership forms. An additional adjustment is required to reflect any difference in land rent. This, of course, is true only in areas where the concept of residences built on leased land is acceptable. Where the market is not used to this type of ownership, the principle of conformity comes into play and depreciation will result.

RESORT AND RECREATION HOUSES

Several million houses in the United States are second homes, occupied by their owners on a seasonal basis. Some of these homes are large, expensive mansions, more valuable than many primary homes. Such homes are found in communities like Newport, Rhode Island, and Palm Beach, Florida. However, the majority of second homes tend to be simpler, possibly located near a body of water or other recreation area. Prior to World War II, these houses tended to be developed individually or in small groups. After the war many large corporations went into the second home business, developing large tracts of land and many houses at the same time. Recreational facilities serving the site also were constructed.

Special Appraisal Problems

The second home market can be very volatile. Economic and weather conditions, gasoline shortages, and competitive developments may have a greater effect on the value of a second home than on a primary residence. One apparent trend in many areas is that properties on or near water tend to increase in value faster than similar properties without the water amenity.

Resales are better evidence than initial sales, which are often the result of heavy developer promotions. Where recreation homes are rented seasonally, a relationship may exist between rentals and value, which would make use of the income approach valid. The cost approach may be useful when land is still available and new homes are still being built in the area.

HOUSING FOR THE ELDERLY

Housing for the elderly may be single-family units or multi-unit buildings (which are beyond the scope of this book), with the same physical characteristics of conventional housing or they may be specially designed for elderly occupants, with emphasis on safety features, ease of egress, etc. They may be owned in fee simple or be part of a condominium or cooperative development.

Some housing becomes housing for the elderly simply because the developers elect to market it to that segment of the population. The courts have upheld the legality of restricting sales in "senior citizen" (usually defined as people over 55 years of age) developments. However, if these restrictions were ruled invalid, it might affect the value of projects marketed to the elderly.

Other units are designated for elderly occupants to receive government subsidies toward either mortgage payments or rent.

Condominium and cooperative units are popular to this segment of the population because they appeal to people who desire home ownership with "carefree" maintenance. The same is true for townhouse developments and free-standing units that have homeowners associations that perform some of the maintenance on a community-wide basis.

Special Appraisal Problems

The definition of the problem takes on special importance in the appraisal of housing for the elderly. The type of ownership and special age restrictions (both public and private) must be considered. When the project has special construction and facilities designed for the elderly, it becomes difficult using the market data approach to make the necessary adjustments with sales from outside the project. Housing for the elderly often costs more per square foot than conventional housing. Such things as higher fire ratings of materials and special equipment may raise the cost. However, housing units for the elderly tend to contain less square footage per unit than conventional housing. Market data from conventional housing is difficult to adjust for in appraisals of elderly housing units. The cost approach is useful for newer units in active areas, and the income approach is also used where there are rental units in the same or similar projects.

Housing for the elderly that is subsidized during construction or where the owners or tenants receive government aid present unique appraisal problems. The cost and income approaches rarely produce accurate indications of value under these circumstances. Comparable sales must be found even if it means looking over a wide geographic area.

FARM AND RANCH HOUSES

Although rural property appraisal requires special skills and experience, appraising farm and ranch houses used for residential purposes is similar to that for a single family residence in any other location.

Special Appraisal Problems

The appraisal of rural houses and acreage is based on the market data approach when most of the value is in the improvements and on the cost approach when most of the value is in the land. For example, if the property being appraised consists of 50 acres of land, with a value of $5,000 per acre, plus a 1,200-square-foot, six-room, one-story, ranch-style house with a depreciated cost of $15,000, the appraiser should look for comparable land sales and estimate the value of the land and then add $15,000 to arrive at the total value. This produces a more accurate value estimate than using as comparables sales of houses on small lots and making an adjustment for the excess land.

If the appraisal were of an eight-room, two-story farm house with a value of about $50,000 on two acres of land, it would be best to look for comparable sales of similar farmhouses and adjust for land size differences.

A careful highest and best use analysis is essential. Often excess land is present that could be separated from the part of the property that is improved with the house and outbuildings. This land could be valued separately and may have a different highest and best use.

PLANNED UNIT DEVELOPMENTS

Planned unit developments (PUDs) are a zoning alternative, not a type of housing. Housing built in PUDs can be in fee simple or condominium ownership in the form of single family residences, townhouses or multifamily buildings. PUD developments may also include commercial and industrial uses. In essence the PUD concept permits the grouping of housing units on lots smaller than usually allowed for residential construction. As a trade-off for being allowed to build on smaller lots, the developer sets aside some unused land to be dedicated to the community or to a homeowners association. PUD developments can provide for more flexible designs for streets, landscaping and public facilities than are possible in conventional neighborhoods.

Special Appraisal Problems

The appraisal problems and techniques for PUD residences are similiar to those for condominiums or fee-simple properties.

MOBILE HOMES

Although not considered real estate in many states, mobile homes account for nearly 10% of all the existing single family residences in the United States. The pre-World War II trailer has evolved into today's mobile home. The most popular size is 12 feet by 60 feet, known as a "12 wide." There are also "14-wides" (which are only permitted in a few states) and "double-wides," which may run from 24 feet by 47 feet to 28 feet by 60 feet. There are also smaller units but they are rarely used for year-round housing. Mobile home owners become insulted when their homes are called "trailers." Once settled on a pad or foundation, a mobile home is rarely moved and experienced mobile home owners claim a unit should never be moved off the original location.

Mobile homes are popular because they offer substantial living space at a cost much below comparable conventional housing. Many mobile home owners are senior citizens, young couples, students and military personnel. Studies show that a typical unit lasts about

15 years as year-round housing. At that time, the shell still is useful and has some value. Studies also have shown that with average maintenance the typical mobile home depreciates approximately 10% the first year (based on wholesale value) and between 5% and 6% per year thereafter.

Special Appraisal Problems

The best way to appraise a mobile home is to use conventional appraisal techniques with application of all three approaches.

Many mobile home appraisals are made using a valuation book. These books are prepared by national publishers who collect sales data from mobile home dealers all over the country; they are similar to the books car and truck dealers use to appraise used vehicles. They are a useful tool but are not a satisfactory substitute for a well prepared appraisal. The problem with their use is that their figures are derived by averaging sales in many markets. The assumption is that mobile homes can be moved. Surveys show that most mobile homes are not moved when they are sold in place, especially when they are only a few years old. Therefore, like a house, their value is affected by their individual environment, and like a house, they can suffer from economic obsolescence. An appraisal based solely on a valuation book would not reflect the environmental influence.

MODULAR AND PREFABRICATED HOUSES

Modular and prefabricated houses are a small part of the housing market. They are partially constructed off-site in a factory and then transported to the site for installation and final assembly. Some units are almost totally assembled off the site. There is little difference between a small modular house and a large mobile home. Larger modular houses consist of several segments, which are shipped to the site by rail and/or truck and joined together on the site. Prefabricated houses are shells that are factory-built and then shipped to the site for assembly. They usually have less mechanical equipment as part of the package than modular homes.

Modular houses and prefabs are used for a variety of reasons. The construction of single family houses has changed less than almost any other major item manufactured in this country. Theoretically, the efficiency of the assembly line and mass production methods should be applicable to housing, and the manufacturers of modular and prefabricated homes are trying to do this. Speed of construction is another reason for this system of producing housing units. The on-site assembly of a factory-produced modular or prefabricated home is often as little as a few days. Another advantage is that the owners of individual lots can see complete model houses. This is not possible if a house is constructed from a set of house plans unless the builder has a similar house available for inspection. Also lot owners may feel more confident they will get a house that is truly similar to the model they have seen when they buy from a large established company rather than buying from a confusing set of plans and specifications.

Some prefab companies have had problems with local building inspectors, electrical and plumbing inspectors and construction trade unions. The latter particularly object to products made in factories that do not have union employees. State and national building codes and standards have reduced some of these problems.

Special Appraisal Problems

Prefabricated and modular houses can be appraised in the same manner as conventionally built homes. In most markets, there is little, if any, value difference between these houses and conventionally built houses of the same size, design and quality. The speed of construction, cost differential and other advantages—if they exist —are enjoyed by the original owner, but they usually do not affect the resale value.

MANSIONS

Mansion or estates are vehicles for gracious living for those who can afford the high cost. With many extra rooms for recreation, entertaining, guests and servant quarters, they are usually individually designed to reflect the special tastes of the owner, whose goal often is to enhance family prestige. Some mansions may have historical value.

Special Appraisal Problems

Except for a few areas of the country, mansions are few in number and these are sold relatively infrequently.

The highest and best use analysis is an important part of a mansion appraisal. The appraiser must consider whether the land is now best utilized or if there is excess land that can be otherwise developed. Is the main building now suitable as a single family dwelling, or can it be converted into multi-family, institutional or other use? If the highest and best use is other than a single family residence, the appraiser should apply generally used appraisal techniques, which are beyond the scope of this book.

If the highest and best use of the property continues to be as a single family residence, only the market data approach is meaningful. The cost and income approaches will lead to erroneous conclusions in most cases.

When selecting comparable mansion sales, it is often necessary to look into other neighboring communities. The location adjustment is important but difficult to make. When the gross living area unit value is developed, some type of meaningful range of value may be produced. If possible, a final value estimate in terms of a range of value will emphasize the difficulty of estimating the value of this specialized type of housing.

HISTORIC HOUSES

Many houses built before the turn of the century and much earlier in the United States are still in habitable condition. Some are considered to be part of the country's national heritage, because of special architectural design or other historic note, and public interest groups have formed in many parts of the country to see that such houses are preserved. When appraising an older house, the appraiser must be aware of whether it has possible historic value.

Houses designated as historic landmarks are governed by special legislation, at either the national or state level or by the local municipality. Such legislation is concerned primarily with the control of the exterior appearance of these structures. There are also private easements and restrictions controlling the exterior appearance. Most of these regulations provide for an administrative body, which is charged with approving or disapproving any proposed exterior renovation. In the long run, such regulations and restrictions may enhance the value of such properties, although some property owners feel that they limit their ownership freedoms and thereby decrease the value of their property.

To encourage the preservation of historic homes, special tax legislation has been passed that benefits property owners who give historic easements, which restrict and control exterior and interior renovations. Most states have historic preservation organizations that are qualified to accept historic easements. The National Trust for Historic Preservation operates in the same capacity on a national level. The advantage to the property owner for granting such an historic easement is twofold. According to current Internal Revenue Service regulations, the property owner may be permitted to deduct the value of the easement as a gift for income tax purposes. Some communities have special provisions in their property tax laws that lower the property taxes when historic easements have been granted.

Special Appraisal Problems

It is difficult to appraise historic houses. Neither the cost approach nor the income approach is applicable. Because market data is scarce in many cases, appraisers try to apply the cost approach on the theory that historic properties should be appraised as special purpose properties. This is not good appraisal practice. The income approach is difficult to apply since there is rarely a relationship between the rental value of an historic house and its value. This leaves the market data approach, requiring that a much wider area must be screened for comparable sales than is normal for nonhistoric houses.

Two types of comparable sales may be used: nonhistoric houses in the neighborhood and historic houses wherever they can be found. Location is very important in the value of historic houses. For example, there may be two reasonably similar historic houses in a community. One is in a neighborhood that is part of a redevelopment program. A neighborhood association is being formed, houses are being renovated, exterior appearances are being controlled and the sidewalks and streets are being rebuilt. The other house is in a neighborhood that is reaching the end of its economic life. The exteriors of nearby houses are in need of carpentry repairs and paint, several houses have had serious fires and are unrepaired, the area is primarily tenant-occupied, and many nearby homes are for sale although few are sold. The first house would seem to be more valuable than the latter. A house of major historical importance, however, may be less affected by its neighborhood than a nonhistoric house in the same neighborhood. But even houses of major historical importance usually cannot completely escape the effect of its neighborhood.

Estimating the value of historic easements depends on seeking and analyzing relatively scarce market data. It may be possible to find properties granted historic easements where offers were made on the property prior to date the easement was given or where the property was sold and then resold after the easement was granted. It also may be possible to find two properties that have sold, one with an historic easement and another without the easement, where all other differences can be adjusted for (see Chapter 13, "Market Data Approach").

LOG CABINS AND OTHER COLONIAL REPRODUCTIONS

As colonial and other historic houses have gained popularity, a revival of interest in authentic reproductions has occurred. The advantage is that the owner hopes to enjoy the amenity value of the old style without the inconveniences associated with older homes. Log cabins are a good example of this trend. Several companies have developed a complete set of materials for the construction of reproductions of log cabins and are successfully marketing their product. Modern plumbing and heating systems are among the benefits of choosing a reproduction rather than an authentic original. In Santa Fe, New Mexico, there are many excellent reproductions of adobe houses constructed with synthetic adobe materials. Other examples of popular reproductions of regional historic styles exist throughout the United States.

Special Appraisal Problems

The appraiser has to explore the market to find evidence to estimate how much depreciation the house may suffer because it violates the rule of conformity and compare it with increased value caused by the amenity value created by the authenticity of the reproduction. Again, sales are the best evidence. The cost and income approaches must be used with extreme caution.

SOLAR HOUSES

Because of the growing concern with limited fossil fuel supplies, solar heating is being considered as an alternative, and solar houses are being designed with special materials and a particular orientation on the lot. Solar homes are still considered experimental by many people. In the future the additional costs of design and materials may be offset by future savings but no conclusive evidence of this possibility now exists. Even if and when successful solar application to housing is made, the results may not apply to many areas of the country.

In spite of their experimental nature and inherent higher cost as compared with similar nonsolar houses, solar houses are being constructed and it appears this trend may continue.

Special Appraisal Problems

The appraiser must first determine if value to be estimated is value-in-use to a special owner or actual market value. In some markets, part or all of the excess costs of a solar house may add value, although the experiment has yet to be proved successful. Some buyers are willing to pay a premium for the privilege of living in a solar house. They want to be part of this housing experiment and feel satisfaction and status is worth the extra cost. They feel that the solar house has an amenity value that raises its value.

Resales now are scarce but will increase with time. Matched pairs do exist in some markets, where developers have built solar and nonsolar models together. The builder of a solar house may create a house with some functional obsolescence that the market will recognize on resale. The appraiser must be cautious in making the value estimate. An objective analysis, backed with current market data, will lead to the correct value estimate.

EXPERIMENTAL HOUSES

A variety of experimental houses, which use new materials such as plastic, fiberglass, foams and other nonconventional building products, exist in the United States.

Special Appraisal Problems

Most experimental houses lose part of their cost to functional obsolescence because they violate the principle of conformity (see Chapter 2). The experiment may have been subsidized or created value-in-use but often the value-in-use is greater than market value.

Market data is the best evidence of value because the cost approach usually is based on a guess about depreciation and the income approach is rarely applicable. Location is an important consideration as is status and amenity value. For example, an experimental house designed by a nationally known architect may have more value than one designed by an unknown. In some markets unusual house designs have experienced special market reactions. The flat-roofed, modern or contemporary house appeals to a few buyers but usually not to the market generally. The appraiser must take special care to consider such special market reactions.

Review Questions

1. How does condominium ownership differ from cooperative ownership?
2. What is the document that establishes a condominium and what does it contain.
3. Why should comparable sales used in valuing a condominium unit preferably be within the same building?
4. Why is the "share price" of a cooperative unit not necessarily representative of its value?
5. What is "time-sharing"?
6. What elements may affect the second home market to a greater degree than for a primary residence?
7. What is an historic easement?
8. What is the best approach to value when appraising historic houses? Why?
9. Why is value-in-use an important aspect to consider when appraising experimental houses?
10. What is the significance of solar heating in the market currently?
11. What are the two methods of valuing farm houses?
12. Why is highest and best use analysis important when appraising a mansion?

Appendices

Appendix A: Model Narrative Appraisal

On the following pages is a narrative appraisal report of a single family residence. The report is based on an actual appraisal but it has been modified to illustrate the techniques described in the text. Rarely, if ever, would an appraisal contain data that works out as optimally as in this report. Although the appraisal does not give specific dates, the reader can assume all months shown for comparable sales and rentals fall within one year prior of the date of the appraisal (unless otherwise specified).

This report is not intended as an example of a demonstration appraisal applicable for credit toward the MAI or RM designation of the American Institute of Real Estate Appraisers.

Appraisal Report
Of A
Single Family Residence
Located At
33 North Road
, Typicaltown, Illinois

Prepared For
American Institute of Real Estate Appraisers
430 North Michigan Avenue
Chicago, Illinois 60611

By
Leslie E. Clinton, MAI, SREA
Chicago, Illinois

As Of
June 19, 197__

COSGROVE AND CLINTON, INC.

REAL ESTATE APPRAISERS · CONSULTANTS

182 NEW AVENUE. CHICAGO, IL 06104 ·
TEL. (312) 689 - 4123

June 25, 197_

American Institute of Real Estate Appraisers
430 North Michigan Avenue
Chicago, Illinois 60611

At the Institute's request I have prepared the attached appraisal of a single family residence located at 33 North Road, Typicaltown, Illinois, more specifically described in the accompanying report.

The purpose of the appraisal is to estimate the market value of the property in fee simple.

I personally inspected the property on June 19, 197_, and have gathered all the data I considered necessary to arrive at the value conclusion.

As a result of my investigation and my analysis of the information gathered, I estimate the market value of the property as of June 19, 197_, to be:

FORTY-ONE THOUSAND THREE HUNDRED DOLLARS

($41,300)

Respectfully submitted,

Leslie E. Clinton

Leslie E. Clinton, MAI, SREA

LEC:ee

ii

TABLE OF CONTENTS

PHOTOGRAPHS OF 33 NORTH ROAD

SUMMARY OF SALIENT FACTS AND IMPORTANT CONCLUSIONS

Type of Property: Single family residence

Location: 33 North Road
                           Typicaltown, Illinois

Zoning: Single Family Residential R-3

Objective of the Appraisal: To estimate the market value of fee simple ownership as of June 19, 197—.

Regional Highlights: The third largest metropolitan area in the country. It has a strong economic base and and has grown at about the same rate as the rest of the country. The growth has been in the suburbs.

Community Highlights: A residential suburb 18 miles northwest of Chicago with a population of about 80,000. Its economy is tied to metropolitan Chicago. The growth rate has slowed down due to the lack of additional available land for development.

Neighborhood Highlights: Stuart Acres is a subdivision of about 250 houses in the Wrightville neighborhood. It is located conveniently to transportation and shopping facilities. The houses are moderately priced and well-maintained.

Site: A level lot with 66-foot frontage on North Road and a depth of 132 feet with a total area of 8,712 square feet.

Improvements: A one-story ranch-style frame house built over a 4-foot crawl space with a living room, kitchen, three bedrooms, one bath and a one-car carport containing 1,056 square feet of gross living area.

Site Valuation: $9,000

v

Market Value Indicated by
  the Cost Approach: Site: $9,000
                                     Improvements: 32,400
                                     Total: $41,400

Gross Monthly Rent
  Multiplier: 130

Estimated Market Rent: $315 per month

Market Value Indicated by
  the Income Approach: $41,000

Market Value Indicated by
  the Market Data
  Approach: $41,300

Final Estimate of Market
  Value: $41,300

Date of Appraisal: June 19, 197__

PART TWO — DESCRIPTION, ANALYSIS AND CONCLUSIONS

OBJECTIVE OF THE APPRAISAL
AND
DEFINITION OF MARKET VALUE

The objective of this appraisal is to estimate market value as of June 19, 197_.

Market value as used in the report is defined as:

The highest price in terms of money which a property should bring in a competitive and open market under all conditions requisite to a fair sale, the buyer and seller, each acting prudently, knowledgeably and assuming the price is not affected by undue stimulus. Implicit in this definition is the consummation of a sale as of a specified date and the passing of title from seller to buyer under conditions whereby:

1. Buyer and seller are typically motivated.
2. Both parties are well informed or well advised and acting in what they consider their own best interest.
3. A reasonable time is allowed for exposure in the open market.
4. Payment is made in cash or its equivalent.
5. Financing, if any, is on terms generally available in the community at the specified date and typical for the property type in its locale.
6. The price represents a normal consideration for the property sold unaffected by special financing amounts and/or terms, services, fees, costs, or credits incurred in the transaction.

1

IDENTIFICATION OF THE PROPERTY

The property is located at 33 North Road, Typicaltown, Illinois. The deed is recorded in the Typicaltown land records in Volume 802, page 614. The legal description is as follows:.

Lot #222 in Richard M. Mullert's subdivision of the west 76 acres (except the south 25 ft. thereof) of the southwest quarter of section 19 in township 41 north, range 11, east of the third principal meridian, in Cook County, Illinois, recorded October 19, 1953. Document #15747614.

PROPERTY RIGHTS APPRAISED

The property rights being appraised are fee simple. Fee simple is defined as: An absolute fee without limitations to any particular class of heirs or restrictions, but subject to the limitations of eminent domain, escheat, police power and taxation. An inheritable estate.[1]

STATEMENT OF OWNERSHIP

The property is owned by John M. Freeman and Rose B. Freeman and is occupied by the owners and their family as their principal residence.

DATE OF VALUATION

The estimate of market value is as of June 19, 197_.

---

[1]*Real Estate Appraisal Terminology*, Byrl N. Boyce, ed., Ballinger Publishing Company, Cambridge, Mass., 1975, p. 87.

2

REGIONAL DATA

Greater metropolitan Chicago is the nation's third largest metropolitan area. It consists of eight counties located at the western foot of Lake Michigan.

Basic economic support is very diversified. Manufacturing companies employ over one million workers and produce a variety of durable goods, electrical and non-electrical machinery, fabricated and primary metals together with printing, publishing and food products. It is a major center for trade, commerce, services, finance and federal government offices.

Chicago is the railroad center of the nation. It is served by 15 of the major railroads who operate one-half of the nation's railroad mileage. Over 12,000 trucks provide extensive services with daily schedules to 54,000 communities. Airlines handle about 40 million passengers annually and 15 percent of the nation's air cargo. Being the connecting link between the St. Lawrence Seaway and the Mississippi River, it has become a major seaport.

The area population has grown from about 4.5 million people in 1940 to about 8 million people today. The growth rate is close to the national average. The City of Chicago's population has decreased while the growth has been in the suburbs.

The strong economic base, good transportation facilities and continued growth of the suburban population all are indications of a continuation of a strong demand for housing in the suburbs. This should have a positive effect upon house values in Typicaltown and the property being appraised.

COMMUNITY DATA

Typicaltown, Illinois, is primarily a residential suburb located 18 miles northwest of Chicago, Illinois. It is the fourth stop along the northwest finger of communities paralleling the Chicago and Northwestern Railroad's wide right of way.

The post World War II expansion of Chicago northwestwards as well as in several other directions has had a direct effect on the growth of Typicaltown. The census shows an increase at the rate of over 1,000 people per year during the past 10 years to the current estimated population of about 80,000. Housing starts have kept pace with the population growth. The vacancy rate in multiple family units is about three percent.

3

Typicaltown's economy is tied to metropolitan Chicago's economy because over 8,000 commuters work in the city. The local economic base industries consist of the national headquarters of a large insurance company and the world headquarters of an international fraternal organization. Over 4,000 people are employed at these two headquarters. Other base industries are several food processing plants, a large printing plant and a variety of other small manufacturing companies.

Chicago's major airport, O'Hare Field, has attracted many businesses, industries and service companies into the area which has affected the growth of the area favorably.

The town is divided into six neighborhoods. The downtown neighborhood, which was developed primarily between World War I and World War II, has several medium-size department stores and a variety of specialty stores and other commercial buildings. The active Chamber of Commerce has spearheaded an imaginative redevelopment program and so far retail sales have remained at a level high enough to stop any flight of merchants to the two community shopping centers. The Sears Center is located on the east side of town and the West Mall is located on the west side of town. The two major employers and most of the other commercial activity are on the east side of town.

There are three residential neighborhoods. Southville was the first developed and some of the housing stock is now substandard. Little has been done to stop this neighborhood from going into a state of decline. Wrightville is in the vicinity of the commuter railroad station. Its development started in the 1930s but primarily occurred in the 1950s. Some lots are still available and are being developed now. Most of the houses are well maintained. Hoppiville is to the north; its development started after World War II. About half its inhabitants live in single family, detached dwellings and the other half in condominiums, rental apartment units and townhouses. This neighborhood still has several large tracts of land available for future development.

Utilities in the town are provided by a municipal water company, public gas company, a Bell Telephone subsidiary and a public electric company. Their rates are typical of the region. All of the existing residences, commercial and industrial buildings are served by sanitary sewers. However, the pipes have not been extended to the undeveloped tracts. The treatment plant is now operating close to capacity.

The public school system is about average for the region. Municipal government is stable. The police department is typical for this type of community but like many others is unable to stop the steadily increasing crime rate.

4

The fire department is above average consisting of both paid firemen and volunteers.

There is a variety of local and regional recreational facilities. There are 22 houses of worship within the town's borders and many others in surrounding communities.

The population growth is expected to slow down. There is local resistance to any major residential construction that will tax the capacity of the sewer treatment plant. There is little room left for much new commercial or industrial expansion. The two major employers seem to have stopped growing, at least temporarily.

Demand for housing in Typicaltown should remain steady for the predictable future. The Chicago area continues to grow. Other new, competing suburban communities will be further out. The lack of suitable land should prevent any substantial increase in the rate of housing starts that would produce excess housing.

Typicaltown's appeal to commuters should continue.

NEIGHBORHOOD DATA

The Wrightville neighborhood is now almost 100 percent built-up with single family and multiple family residences. It is bordered on the north by Thomas Street, on the south by Mapleton Street, on the east by Harvard Avenue, and on the west by Stevenson Road.

In 1954 and 1955 a subdivision known as Stuart Acres was developed. It consisted of 254 single family residences, including the house being appraised. About 20 lots were left undeveloped and they are currently being sold individually and developed now.

All the houses in Stuart Acres are of the same basic type and style. They have five rooms and one bathroom and contain a living room, kitchen, three bedrooms and an open side carport. Through the years owners have made changes, often by building additions for a family room or extra bedroom. Many of the carports have been converted into garages. The general effect of these improvements has been a more desirable home in a higher value range than the early basic house.

The central business district has adequate public parking and is about one mile to the east. The commuter railroad station is on the east boundary of the neighborhood. Shopping is available downtown and in the two community shopping centers, which offer a wide variety of medium-priced merchandise. Many residents do a substantial portion of their major shopping in downtown Chicago.

The range of typical incomes in Wrightville is between $11,000 and $16,000. The typical resident of the neighborhood is a young family occupying their first home. It is a "stepping stone" neighborhood and many families remain only a few years and then move up to larger, more expensive homes. Most of the houses are well maintained.

There is very little adult foot traffic in the neighborhood as shopping and other services are beyond easy walking distance. Street parking is plentiful throughout the neighborhood. Except for the commuter railroad and local taxi company, there is no public transportation. Access by automobile to downtown, local services, community shopping centers and Chicago is averge. Route #14 leading to the Chicago Interstate System is crowded at rush hours.

The school system, like the rest of the community, is average. There are two elementary schools in the neighborhood and between them they are within walking distance of all the residences. The junior high school is also within walking distance of most of the residences. The high school is two miles away and the town provides school bus transportation.

Police protection is typical of the town and crime continues to increase. The volunteer and paid fire departments provide average protection.

Like the rest of Typicaltown, the neighborhood is served with public water, gas, and telephone service. All existing buildings are connected to the sanitary sewers. Septic systems are illegal. Storm water is diverted to natural waterways through an adequate storm drainage system. The utility prices are typical for the region.

There is no other neighborhood in Typicaltown that directly competes with Wrightville. The most direct competition comes from similar neighborhoods in nearby communities. Housing in new neighborhoods tends to be more expensive for similar accommodations because of rising construction and land development costs. Zoning requirements and lack of sewer capacity make unlikely the construction of competitive housing that would reduce values in Wrightville. Competing neighborhoods are having similar problems with crime prevention and their school systems are not substantially different from those of Wrightville.

6

Chicago, plus the two major local employers and the many small industries, local service and retail establishments, provide a variety of employment opportunities for the neighborhood residents. Most of the jobs pay under $20,000. Families that earn more than $20,000 tend to move out of the neighborhood. This trend is in contrast to some neighborhoods in nearby communities where the people tend to remain even when their incomes expand.

Because of the moderate prices as compared to new competing neighborhoods, the convenience to Chicago and local employers, the stable economic base of the community and the lack of any major adverse influences, values should remain stable in Wrightville in the foreseeable future, subject to adjustments caused by inflation or other major changes in the regional or national economy.

SITE DATA

The site is an inside lot, rectangular in shape and measures 66 ft. at the front and rear and 132 ft. on the sides. Its total area is 8,712 sq. ft. It is located on the east side of North Road, 303 ft. east of Stevenson Road. It is generally level but has slight slope away from the building, which appears to afford adequate drainage. The top soil is black, sandy loam and the subsoil composition is hard clay that has proven to have suitable bearing qualities for residential weight load. There are no known settlement or related structural problems resulting from failure of the subsoil.

As mentioned under Neighborhood Data, all utilities including water, sanitary sewer, gas, electricity and telephone are connected to the property being appraised.

The street is public, tar- and gravel-paved, two lanes wide without curb or gutter and has a posted 35 miles per hour speed limit.

The adequacy of the site as a residential lot in this location is normal. It is typical in size and shape and has easy access to the carport from the street through use of the driveway. There are sufficient side yards to meet the town zoning requirements; they also provide light, air and privacy. Where larger two-car garages have replaced the original carport, it has been necessary to construct them back from the house because the sites were not sized to accommodate a two-car garage attached to the side of the building.

There is a definite adverse influence to the property caused by heavy, fast traffic on Stevenson Road. Normal traffic is heavier than would be found on a purely residential street. Stevenson Road is a main artery and carries considerable traffic.

The Fast Pace Dog Track is located one-half mile northeast of the site just across the border in Tracville. In the months when it is in operation some of its customers use Stevenson Road as a short cut. The added fast through traffic produces a danger to neighborhood children and makes access from North Road into Stevenson Road difficult. This problem is serious enough to have a measurable negative impact on the value of properties affected by the traffic.

Except for the above, the site is adequate and typical of those found in the neighborhood. No other abnormal effects on the value of the site exist.

Refer to the Addenda Section for plots and maps which will illustrate some of the points made in this section of the report.

ZONING

The property is located in an area zoned R-3, single family residential. The permitted use of the site being appraised is for a single family residence.

The height of a single family dwelling according to the zoning ordinance shall not exceed 25 feet and 2-1/2 stories.

The maximum building coverage shall not exceed 35 percent, except on a lot of less than 6,000 square feet, which coverage shall not exceed 40 percent.

Each lot with a dwelling constructed on it shall have a front yard of not less than 25 feet.

On each lot with a dwelling constructed on it there shall be a side yard on each side equal to not less than 10 percent of the width; provided, however, that an attached garage may be built at a distance of not less than three feet from the side lot line.

Every lot with a building constructed on it shall have a rear yard of not less than 30 feet.

8

No building or land shall be used, erected, structurally altered, or enlarged unless otherwise provided in the ordinance except for the following uses: R-1, R-2, or R-3 single family dwellings.

Street parking is permitted except during storm emergencies.

Every one family detached dwelling shall have a lot with a minimum area of not less than 8,750 square feet and a minimum width of not less than 70 feet.

The above zoning code regulations together with the permitted uses were dated May 3, 1965. The site has a lot width of 66 feet and a total square foot area of 8,712 feet. This does not conform to the zoning, but the site was recorded on October 19, 1953, making it a legally nonconforming site. Other than this, there is no evidence of zoning violations or nonconforming uses in the neighborhood or on the site being appraised. The improvement also represents a conforming use.

The ordinance contains a special provision that permits the building of new one family houses or rebuilding existing one family houses destroyed by fire or other accidental means on pre-existing nonconforming sites. There are no time limits in this provision. Because of this provision, the fact that the improvement is now nonconforming should not significantly affect value.

ASSESSMENT AND TAXES

Real estate taxes for the past eight years are as follows:

197_	$453.18
197_	$476.24
197_	$502.16
197_	$520.41
197_	$553.17
197_	$580.49
197_	$603.55
197_	$642.21

The property is currently assessed at 19% of 197_ market value:

Land:	$ 2,146
Improvements:	4,827
Total	$6,973

The current tax rate is 92.1 mills or $9.21 per $100 of assessed value.

9

Taxes on the appraised property are very similar to other houses in Wright-ville. The tax assessor has a good record for accurate, uniform assess-ments.

Taxes have been going up at a steady rate. This increase has been caused primarily by inflation.

There does not appear to be any reason for taxes to escalate rapidly in the future. The present school system is adequate for the current com-munity needs and could even be expanded at low cost. The municipal serv-ices are average. The political climate is such that the voters do not want any major improvements in the school system or of municipal services. The state has been increasing revenue sharing and the school enrollment has remained steady.

The ratio of taxes to value of this property is similar to that of the neighbor-hood, the balance of Typicaltown and surrounding competitive com-munities. Taxes on the property being appraised do not appear to have any measurable effect upon the overall value of the property nor should they have in the predictable future.

HISTORY OF PROPERTY

The improvements on this property were built together with 254 other houses in 1954 and 1955 as part of a subdivision known as Stuart Acres.

The original owner paid $14,500 and obtained a $12,000 conventional first mortgage. A variety of models was offered in the subdivision ranging in sale price from $14,500 to $15,300. The difference in price was for varying amounts of masonry trim. The size, design and quality of construction were the same for all 254 houses in the subdivision.

In 1958 the property was sold to its second owner. It had been well main-tained. There had been no significant improvement. The property sold for $18,300 and was financed with a new $15,000 conventional first mortgage.

The property was purchased by its present owner in 1967 for $22,500. It was financed with an FHA $20,500 mortgage. The property was in good condi-tion. The exterior had recently been repainted. There had been no additions or remodeling. Since then the present owners have continued to maintain the property, having recently painted a substantial amount of the interior and exterior. A new roof was installed four years ago.

DESCRIPTION OF THE IMPROVEMENTS

General Description:
A one-family, one-story, ranch-style, frame house built above a 4-foot crawl space; containing five rooms consisting of a living room, kitchen, three bedrooms and one bathroom. There is 1,056 sq. ft. of gross living area (GLA).

Foundation:
The footings are poured concrete. The foundation walls, which extend four feet above ground level, are 10-inch thick concrete.

Exterior Construction:
The exterior walls are covered with 5/8-inch redwood siding over 1/2-inch composition fiberboard. The roof is a high pitch, hip style, covered with asphalt shingles over 1-inch by 8-inch pine boards. There are three inches of batt type insulation in all the exterior walls and six inches of batt type insulation between the roof rafters. The gutters and downspouts are galvanized sheet metal. All the windows are wood, double hung style. The exterior doors and trim are wood. There are aluminum storm doors and screens.

Interior Construction:
All the interior walls are 2-inch by 4-inch studs covered with 1/2-inch gypsum board. They are all painted except the kitchen, which is wallpapered, and the bathroom walls and tub enclosure, which are covered with 4-foot high plastic tile wainscot. The ceilings are 1/2-inch painted gypsum board. The floors are oak strip except for the kitchen and bathroom, which are asphalt tile. The kitchen cabinets are colored steel. All the interior doors are hollow core wood and the molding is standard grade mill stock.

Mechanical Systems:
There is a 60-ampere electric service from the overhead wires in the street. The distribution box is 10 circuits, protected with circuit breakers. The wiring is all BX type cable. There are adequate duplex outlets throughout the house.

The plumbing system consists of a lead water main connected to the municipal service in the street. All the water pipes are copper. The waste pipes are cast iron and connected to the municipal sanitary sewer in the street. The kitchen has a colored porcelain-over-iron double sink. There is no garbage disposal or dishwasher. The bathroom fixtures consist of a syphon jet water closet, sink built into a vanity and 5-foot tub. They are all

11

standard grade, colored porcelain-over-iron. There is a shower over the tub and a shower curtain rod.

There is a 40-gallon, glass-lined, gas-fired hot water heater.

Heat is produced in a gas-fired, 105,000 BTU gas furnace equipped with a power humidifier. It is distributed through sheet metal perimeter heating ducts and wall registers.

Interior Layout:
There are five rooms consisting of a living room, kitchen, three bedrooms and a bathroom. The master bedroom and one bedroom have double closets. The other bedroom has a single closet. There are also a linen closet and a coat closet in the living room.

The floor plan is not conventional. The front entry leads directly into the kitchen. The side entry coming from the carport leads directly into the living room. Many of the houses in this subdivision have this floor plan and there is no evidence that it is unacceptable to the market or that any penalty is taken for it.

The house also lacks a utility room. The laundry facilities are in the kitchen. The furnace and hot water tank are in a closet off the bathroom. Inside storage space is very limited.

Carport:
A frame 10-1/2-foot by 20-1/2-foot carport is attached to the south side of the house; inside the carport there is a 3-1/2-foot by 9-foot storage shed.

Site Improvements and Landscaping:
The driveway is paved with asphalt paving. The landscaping is average and typical for this neighborhood. There are no sidewalks.

Overall Condition and Effective Age:
The overall condition of the house is average for houses in this neighborhood. The roof covering appears to have a short remaining life.

The hot water tank and furnace are seven years old.

The interior was recently repainted throughout and is in good condition.

The asphalt tile in the kitchen and bathroom show substantial signs of wear and will need replacing soon.

The driveway has several large ruts and needs repairing.

The house appears to be similar to other houses in the neighborhood. It is estimated to have an effective age of 20 years.

12

HIGHEST AND BEST USE ANALYSIS

Highest and best use is defined as:

That reasonable and probable use that will support the highest present value, as defined, as of the effective date of the appraisal.

Alternatively, that use, from among reasonably probable and legal alternative uses, found to be physically possible, appropriately supported, financially feasible, and which results in highest land value.

The definition immediately above applies specifically to the highest and best use of land. It is to be recognized that in cases where a site has existing improvements on it, the highest and best use may very well be determined to be different from the existing use. The existing use will continue, however, unless and until land value in its highest and best use exceeds the total value of the property in its existing use. See Interim Use.

Implied within these definitions is recognition of the contribution of that specific use to community environment or to community development goals in addition to wealth maximization of individual property owners. Also implied is that the determination of highest and best use results from the appraiser's judgment and analytical skill, i.e., that the use determined from analysis represents an opinion, not a fact to be found. In appraisal practice, the concept of highest and best use represents the premise upon which value is based. In the context of most probable selling price (market value) another appropriate term to reflect highest and best use would be most probable use. In the context of investment value an alternative term would be most profitable use. See Most Probable Use, Most Profitable Use.[2]

The analysis is divided into two parts: The first assumes the site is vacant and ready to be improved. A wide variety of improvements might be physically possible on this site. Current zoning regulations, however, make single-family residences the only legal use. Because the site is in the midst of a stable residential neighborhood, there is little likelihood of a zoning change or a variance for a non-conforming use. Because there appears to be a good demand for single family houses in this market, it appears likely a new single family house could be constructed that would sell for more than the combined cost of the site and the new construction and the builder would make a profit.

Selecting the type, style, size, layout, materials, mechanical systems and

---

[2]*Real Estate Appraisal Terminology,* op. cit., p. 107.

quality of construction requires an analysis of the market. It is the combination of these choices that produces the maximum profit for the developer that is the highest and best use of the site if vacant.

The one-story ranch-style house still remains popular in this market. It should be possible to correct some of the layout deficiencies and still stay within the 1,056 sq. ft. size. Anything larger probably would result in a house too expensive for this neighborhood. Since the cost of this new house is going to make it more expensive than its neighbors, quality of construction and materials should be kept at an absolute minimum acceptable in the market. Few extras, if any, should be provided.

Electric heat will reduce the construction cost and save space. It is now more acceptable in this area because of the natural gas shortage. The insulation should be increased to meet electric heating requirements. The domestic hot water system and cooking appliances should also be electric to make the house eligible for the lower all-electric utility rates and to eliminate the need of gas service into the house. The electric service must be large enough to meet the needs of an all-electric house. This market is accepting the use of plastic-coated wire and plastic pipes, both of which are permitted by the local building code. They should be used to reduce costs. Wall-to-wall carpeting is now the most popular floor covering in this market. It should be laid over plywood floor covering, again, to save costs.

Many new houses in Typicaltown and surrounding communities are now being built on a slab rather than over a 4-foot crawl space. As this also is cheaper it should be utilized here.

The functional inutility in the layout should be eliminated. There are many available plans for houses of this size which have more acceptable layouts.

Even though the market is paying for the cost of an additional room in existing houses, nothing is gained by adding one to this design as it would not produce any additional profit. The same is true for a detached garage. Again, the market is not paying a premium that would result in additional profit; it is just paying the extra cost so a carport should be used.

A house built based on these recommendations similar to the kind of existing house found throughout the subdivision is estimated to be the highest and best use of the site, if vacant.

The second part of the highest and best use analysis considers what changes and improvements, if any, are needed to put the property in the condition that would produce the maximum profit utilizing the existing improvements. In this market, as in many markets, the cost of most minor repairs will produce value greater than the cost. Therefore the driveway should be repaired and the asphalt tile in the kitchen and bathroom repaired or replaced. Since the roof still has some useful life, it should just be repaired. It does not appear that if any of the functional inutility is corrected, it will produce value in excess of the cost; therefore, nothing should be done about it. For the same reason the mechanical systems should be left as is. When the recommended work is completed, the existing improvements will be the highest and best use.

COST APPROACH TO VALUE

The cost approach is based on the assumption that the value of a property tends to reflect the value of the site, plus the current cost to produce the improvements, less any existing depreciation. The steps followed are:

1. Estimate the value of the site (land) as if vacant.

2. Estimate the reproduction cost or replacement cost new of all the improvements (excluding any that were included as part of the site value).

3. Estimate accrued depreciation from all causes (physical deterioration, functional obsolescence and economic obsolescence).

4. Deduct accrued depreciation from the cost new of the improvements to arrive at a depreciated value of the improvements.

5. Add the site (land) value (Step 1) to the depreciated value of the improvements (Step 4) to arrive at a value indicated by the cost approach.

To estimate the value of the site, comparable site sales were found in the neighborhood. They are described on the following pages. Sites in this neighborhood and most other residential neighborhoods in Typicaltown are bought and sold based on their total area. The sale price per square foot was selected as the unit of comparison that is most sensitive to the market. The differences between the comparable sites and the site being appraised are adjusted for, using adjustments that are taken from the market by comparing different sales with each other. The adjustments are explained following the descriptions of the comparable sales and they are then displayed on an adjustment grid. Finally, they are reconciled into an indicated market value of the site.

Site Sale No. 1

Address:	24 Cottken Street
	Typicaltown, Illinois
Location:	One block north in Stuart Acres
Grantor:	Stuart Development Corporation
Grantee:	John Rightman and Helen Rightman
Date of sale:	November 16, 197_
Sale price:	$9,400
Data source:	John Rightman
Confirmed by:	John Rightman
Assessment:	$2,463
Topography:	Level and cleared
Special conditions:	None reported
Frontage:	75 ft.
Average depth:	135 ft.
Square feet:	10,125
Available utilities:	Gas, water, electricity, sewers, telephone
Easements or restrictions:	None
Additional information:	Subject to heavy traffic on Stevenson Road
Sale price per square foot:	$ .93

16

Site Sale No. 2

Address:	205 Landside Street
	Typicaltown, Illinois
Location:	Three blocks east in Stuart Acres
Grantor:	Stuart Development Corporation
Grantee:	Alfred Harrog and Eileen Harrog
Date of Sale:	May 18, 197_
Sale price:	$10,100
Data source:	Typicaltown Realtors Multiple
	Listing Service
Confirmed by:	Eileen Harrog
Assessment:	$2,310
Topography:	Level and cleared
Special conditions:	None
Frontage:	70 ft.
Average depth:	131 ft.
Square feet:	9,170
Available utilities:	Gas, water, electricity, sewers,
	telephone
Easements or restrictions:	None
Additional information:	Not subject to traffic problem on
	Stevenson Road
Sale price per square foot:	$1.10

17

Site Sale No. 3

Address:	83 Hoover Road
	Typicaltown, Illinois
Location:	Four blocks east in Stuart Acres
Grantor:	Stuart Development Corporation
Grantee:	Adam Rosenfeld and Janet Rosenfeld
Date of sale:	May 25, 197_
Sale price:	$10,300
Data source:	East Side Realtors (selling brokers)
Confirmed by:	Ronald Stuart, president, Stuart Development Corporation
Assessment:	$2,375
Topography:	Level and cleared
Special conditions:	None
Frontage:	72 ft.
Average depth:	130 ft.
Square feet:	9,360
Available utilities:	Gas, water, electricity, sewers, telephone
Easements or restrictions:	Telephone line easement at rear of lot
Additional information:	Not subject to traffic problem on Stevenson Road
Sale price per square foot:	$1.10

18

Site Sale No. 4

Address:	34 Cottken Street
	Typicaltown, Illinois
Location:	One block north in Stuart Acres
Grantor:	Stuart Development Corporation
Grantee:	Randolf Johnson and Mabel Johnson
Date of sale:	May 10, 197_
Sale price:	$9,800
Data source:	Stuart Development Corporation
Confirmed by:	Randolf Johnson
Assessment:	$2,310
Topography:	Level and cleared
Special conditions:	None reported
Frontage:	70 ft.
Average depth:	135 ft.
Square feet:	9,450
Available utilities:	Gas, water, electricity, sewers,
	telephone
Easements and restrictions:	None
Additional information:	Subject to heavy traffic on
	Stevenson Road
Sale price per square foot	$1.04

19

The four vacant site sales were all in the same neighborhood. They appear to be similar except for size, date of sale, and their location with reference to the heavy traffic on Stevenson Road. By comparing these sales with each other it was possible to derive the required adjustments directly from the market. The size difference was accounted for by using the unit price per square foot.

Time Adjustment

Sale No. 1 and Sale No. 4 appeared to be similar except for date of sale. Sale No. 1 sold for $.93 per sq. ft. and Sale No. 4 for $1.04 per sq. ft. Therefore there appears to be a $.11 per sq. ft. time adjustment required for six months.

Sale No. 4 (5/10/7__):	$1.04 per sq. ft.
Sale No. 1 (11/16/7__):	.93 per sq. ft.
Time adjustment:	$ .11 per sq. ft.

Location Adjustment

Sale No. 2 and Sale No. 4 appear to be similar except for location. Sale No. 2, with no traffic problem, sold for $1.10 and Sale No. 4, with a traffic problem, sold for $1.04 per sq. ft. Therefore there appears to be a $.06 per sq. ft. adjustment required for the traffic problem.

Sale No. 2 (no traffic problem):	$1.10 per sq. ft.
Sale No. 4 (traffic problem):	1.04 per sq. ft.
Location adjustment:	$ .06 per sq. ft.

The location adjustment can also be estimated by comparing Sale No. 3 and Sale No. 4.

Sale No. 3 (no traffic problem):	$1.10 per sq. ft.
Sale No. 4 (traffic problem):	1.04 per sq. ft.
Location adjustment:	$ .06 per sq. ft.

20

The location adjustment can also be estimated by comparing Sale No. 1
with Sale No. 2.

Sale No. 1 (base sale) — 11/16/7_ with traffic problem	$ .93 per sq. ft.
Sale No. 2—5/18/7— and with a traffic problem	1.10 per sq. ft.
Time adjustment based on Sale No. 2 and Sale No. 4	−.11 per sq. ft.
Adjusted sale price of Sale No. 2	$ .99 per sq. ft.
Sale No. 1 (base sale)	−.93 per sq. ft.
Difference attributed to traffic problem	$ .06 per sq. ft.

Summary:

The accompanying grid displays how the adjustments were applied to each
sale and how the adjusted sale prices and final indications of market value
of the site were derived.

Sale No. 4 required no adjustments and was very similar to the lot being
appraised except for its size. Besides size, the other three sales required
adjustments for time and location. As all four sales produced an adjusted
sale price of $1.04 per sq. ft., this value was selected as an indicated value
for 33 North Road. Indicated market value of the site at 33 North Road is
(8,712 sq. ft. x $1.04) = $9,000 (rounded).

21

SITE SALE ADJUSTMENT GRID

	Appraised Property	Site Sale No. 1	Site Sale No. 2	Site Sale No. 3	Site Sale No. 4
Address	33 North Road	24 Cottken St.	205 Landside St.	83 Hoover Rd.	34 Cotken St.
Sale Price		$9,400	$10,100	$10,300	$9,800
Size		10,125 sq. ft	9,170 sq. ft.	9,360 sq. ft.	9,450 sq. ft.
Sale Price per Sq. Ft.		$.93	$1.10	$1.10	$1.04
Date of Sale		11/16/7— + $.11	5/18/7— —0—	5/25/7— —0—	5/10/7— —0—
Location	Affected by traffic on Stevenson Rd. —0—	Affected by traffic on Stevenson Rd. —0—	Not affected by traffic on Stevenson Rd. —$.06	Not affected by traffic on Stenveson Rd. —$.06	Affected by traffic on Stevenson Rd. —0—
Physical Characteristics	Level and cleared	Similar —0—	Similar —0—	Similar —0—	Similar —0—
Special Conditions	None reported	Similar —0—	Similar —0—	Similar —0—	Similar —0—
Total Adjustments		+ $.11	— $.06	— $.06	—0—
Adjusted Sale Price per Square Foot		$1.04	$1.04	$1.04	$1.04

Estimation of Reproduction Cost

The next step of the cost approach is to estimate the cost to build the improvements new on the date of the appraisal. Since the same type of improvements are still being built, it is possible to estimate their reproduction cost rather than replacement cost. The estimate was made by considering the reported costs of two recently built houses in the neighborhood and a summary of a cost breakdown prepared by a professional cost estimator.

Ronald Stuart, president of Stuart Development Corporation, was interviewed and he provided the following information about two houses he recently built in Stuart Acres:

House No. 1 at 81 Truman Street contains 1,056 square feet and is similar to the subject except it has electric heat. He said the direct costs are $42,500. The estimated indirect costs are $8,000. The costs include an attached carport. The total cost of $50,500 is $47.82 per square foot of gross living area, not including site.

House No. 2 at 85 Truman Street contains 1,175 square feet. It is similar to the subject except for its larger size (it included a family room) and it has electric heat. The reported cost is $62,000, which includes a two-car detached garage at an estimated cost of $3,000. The total cost of the house alone is $50.21 per square foot of gross living area, not including the site.

John Halsey, the cost estimator for the Stuart Development Corporation, helped prepare the accompanying cost breakdown summary for 33 North Road based on current costs (see next page).

Summary:
Based on the cost estimate, the reproduction cost of 33 North Road is $54,000. This is $51.17 per square foot of gross living area and includes the cost of the carport. This is higher than the cost of $47.82 reported for 81 Truman Street and $50.21 reported cost of 85 Truman Street, which did not include the garage. These lower costs may have been attributed to materials purchased earlier and the lower cost of the electric heat. The $51.17 per square foot cost is estimated to be the reproduction cost of 33 North Road.

Summary of Cost Breakdown		
Item	**% of Total**	**Cost**
Survey & Engineering	½	$ 270
Plans & Plan Checking	½	270
Site Preparation	½	270
Excavation	1	540
Footings & Foundation	4½	2,430
Basement	—	—
Framing	7½	4,050
Interior Walls & Ceilings	4	2,160
Exterior Siding	3½	1,890
Roof Covering & Flashing	4½	2,430
Insulation	2	1,080
Fireplaces & Chimneys	2	1,080
Leaders & Gutters	1	540
Exterior & Interior Stairs	1	540
Doors, Windows & Shutters	2	1,080
Storm Windows, Doors & Screens	1	540
Main Floor Covering (Carpeting)	3	1,620
Kitchen Flooring	½	270
Bathroom & Lavatory Floors	½	270
Hardware	½	270
Water Supply	1	540
Waste Disposal	1½	810
Heating	4	2,160
Cooling (no air conditioning)	—	—
Domestic Hot Water	1½	810
Piping	4	2,160
Plumbing Fixtures	4	2,160
Kitchen Cabinets & Counters	3	1,620
Built-In Appliances	1½	810
Shower Doors	½	270
Bathroom Accessories	½	270
Vanities, Medicine Cabinets & Counters	½	270
Electric Service	2½	1,350
Electric Wires & Outlets	2½	1,350
Lighting Fixtures	1½	810
Painting & Decorating	4	2,160
Porches (none)	—	—
Patios	½	270
Finish Grading	½	270
Landscaping	1	540
Garages & Carports	5	2,700
Clean Up	½	270
Sidewalks & Driveways	1½	810
Interest, Taxes & Insurance	1	540
Contractor's Overhead & Temporary Facilities	4	2,160
Professional Services, Permits & Licenses	1	540
Selling Expenses & Carrying Costs	5	2,700
Contractor's Profit	7½	4,050
Total Cost	100%	$54,000

Depreciation

Depreciation includes those things on and off the site that reduce the market value of the improvements below the current reproduction cost.

Abstraction Method

One way to estimate depreciation is to abstract it from the market based on actual sales. The following is a summary of four sales in the neighborhood from which an overall depreciation rate is abstracted. The sales at 93 and 109 North Road are affected by the traffic on Stevenson Road. The other two sales are at 17 Hoover Road and 115 Landside Street and are not affected by the traffic on Stevenson Road.

The site value was estimated based on the sales used in this cost approach. The reproduction cost was based on the data previously developed and modified with the help of a national cost service publication.

17 Hoover Road is a one-story, ranch-style house with 1,175 sq. ft. of gross living area. It is on a lot 70 ft. x 128 ft. (average depth). It sold in November 197– for $50,000. At the time of sale its effective age was estimated to be 18 years.

Sale price	$50,000
Site value (70 ft. × 128 ft. × $.99)	8,870
Depreciated value of improvements	$41,130
Reproduction cost of improvements (1,175 × $51)	59,925
Total depreciation	$18,795
Estimated effective age — 18 years	÷18
Annual amount of depreciation	$ 1,044
Annual rate of depreciation ($1,044 ÷ $59,925) .0174 or 1.75%	

115 Landside Street is a one-story, ranch-style house with 1,130 sq. ft. of gross living area. It is on a lot 75 ft. x 135 ft. (average depth). It sold in September 197– for $52,000. At the time of sale its effective age was estimated to be 16 years.

Sale price	$52,000
Site value (75 ft. × 135 ft. × $.99)	10,024
Depreciated value of improvements	$41,976
Reproduction cost of improvements (1,130 × $51.50)	58,195
Total depreciation	$16,219
Estimated effective age — 16 years	÷ 16
Annual amount of depreciation	$ 1,014
Annual rate of depreciation ($1,014 ÷ $58,195) .0174 or 1.75%	

25

93 North Road is a one-story, ranch-style house with 1,240 sq. ft. of gross living area. It is on a lot 82 ft. × 133 ft. (average depth). It sold in May 197_ for $52,500. At the time of the sale its effective age was estimated to be 17 years.

Sale price	$52,500
Site value (82 ft. × 133 ft. × $1.04)	11,342
Depreciated value of improvements	$41,158
Reproduction cost of improvements (1,240 × $50.50)	62,620
Total depreciation	$21,462
Estimated effective age — 17 years	÷ 17
Annual amount of depreciation	$ 1,262
Annual rate of depreciation ($1,262 ÷ $62,620)	.0202 or 2%

109 North Road is a one-story, ranch-style house with 1,025 sq. ft. of gross living area. It is on a lot 78 ft. × 135 ft. (average depth). It sold for $39,500 in October 197_. At the time of the sale its effective age was estimated to be 22 years.

Sale price	$39,500
Site value (78 ft. × 135 ft. × $.93)	9,792
Depreciated value of improvements	$29,708
Reproduction cost of improvements (1,025 × $52)	53,300
Total depreciation	$23,592
Estimated effective age — 22 years	÷ 22
Annual amount of depreciation	$1,072
Annual rate of depreciation ($1,072 ÷ $53,300)	.0201 or 2%

Summary:

Based on these four sales it is estimated that improvements similar to 33 North Road have depreciated at a rate of 1.75% per year when not affected by the traffic on Stevenson Road and 2% per year when affected by the traffic on Stevenson Road.

The total accumulated depreciation for 33 North Road based on the market is estimated to be [40% (2% × 20 years effective age) × $54,000] $21,600.

26

Breakdown Method

The depreciation can also be estimated by the breakdown method. In this method depreciation is divided into five classifications:

1. Physical deterioration—curable
2. Physical deterioration—incurable
3. Functional obsolescence—curable
4. Functional obsolescence—incurable
5. Economic obsolescence

Each classification of depreciation is estimated separately and then combined to give an indicated total amount of depreciation.

Physical deterioration—curable includes all the items of maintenance that should be accomplished on the date of appraisal to maximize the profit (or minimize the loss) that would result if the property were sold. The measure of physical deterioration—curable is the cost to perform the maintenance. 33 North Road: these items consist of repairing the driveway and repairing the asphalt tile in the kitchen and bathroom. The cost to repair the tile is estimated to be $275 and the driveway, $300.

Total physical deterioration—curable: $575

Physical deterioration—incurable includes all the natural aging and wear and tear of the components of the improvements which, if repaired or replaced on the date of the appraisal, would not add value greater than the cost to repair or replace them. The engineering method is used here to measure the deterioration. The improvements are divided into their components based on the cost breakdown. A percentage of depreciation is estimated for each component based on observation. A total weighted percentage of depreciation is calculated and applied to the indirect costs. The total of these two items is the total amount of physical deterioration—incurable (see next page).

Functional obsolescence—curable is usually caused by a deficiency. The measure of functional obsolescence—curable is the difference between the cost of the item if it were installed on the date of appraisal by itself and if it were installed as part of a whole house being built on the date of the appraisal.

There was no functional obsolescence—curable observed in 33 North Road.

27

Physical Incurable Deterioration — Engineering Method

Component	Cost New	Esti-mated % Deterior-ation	Accrued Deterior-ation**
Survey & engineering	$ 270	20	$ 54
Plans & plan checking	270	20	54
Site preparation	270	20	54
Excavation	540	20	108
Footings & foundation	2,430	20	486
Basement	—	—	—
Framing	4,050	20	810
Interior walls & ceilings	2,160	25	567
Exterior siding	1,890	30	540
Roof covering & flashing	2,430	75	1,823
Insulation	1,080	30	324
Fireplaces & chimneys	1,080	20	216
Leaders & gutters	540	75	405
Exterior & interior stairs	540	30	162
Doors, windows & shutters	1,080	30	324
Storm windows, doors & screens	540	35	189
Main floor covering (carpeting)	1,620	30	486
Kitchen flooring	270	40*	108
Bathroom & lavatory floors	270	40*	108
Hardware	270	35	95
Water supply	540	35	189
Waste disposal	810	30	243
Heating	2,160	35	756
Cooling	—	—	—
Domestic hot water	810	40	324
Piping	2,160	30	648
Plumbing fixtures	2,160	30	648
Kitchen cabinets & counters	1,620	35	567
Built-in appliances	810	60	486
Shower doors	270	35	95
Bathroom accessories	270	30	81
Vanities, medicine cabinets & counters	270	30	81
Electric service	1,350	30	405
Electric wires & outlets	1,350	30	405
Lighting fixtures	810	30	243
Painting & decorating	2,160	50	1,080
Porches	—	—	—
Patios	270	20	54
Finish grading	270	20	54
Landscaping	540	20	108
Garages & carports	2,700	30	810
Clean-up	270	20	54
Sidewalks & driveways	810	40*	324
SUBTOTAL	$44,010		$14,568
Weighted average ($14,568 ÷ $44,010) = 33%			
Interest, taxes & insurance	540	33	178
Contractor's overhead & temporary facilities	2,160	33	713
Professional services, permits & licenses	540	33	178
Selling expenses	2,700	33	891
Contractor's profit	4,050	33	1,336
TOTAL	$54,000		$17,864

**Rounded
*Estimate is made assuming physical curable deterioration items will be repaired.

Functional obsolescence—incurable may be caused by a deficiency or a superadequacy. It can be measured by capitalizing the rent loss caused by the deficiency or the value contributed by the superadequacy less other forms of depreciation subtracted from its cost.

There was no functional obsolescence—incurable observed in 33 North Road.

Economic obsolescence is caused by factors that affect value located off the site. The traffic problem on Stevenson Road affects the value of 33 North Road.

Economic obsolescence can be measured by capitalizing the rent loss attributable to the negative influence causing the obsolescence and apportioning the loss between the land and the improvements.

The estimated rent loss caused by the traffic on Stevenson Road is $15 per month. A gross monthly rent multiplier of 130 was developed for this neighborhood. The total loss of value is $15 × 130, or $1,950. Improvements contribute approximately 75% of the value in this neighborhood so $1.462 of the loss is allocated to the improvements ($1,950 × .75). $488 is allocated to a decrease in site value. The total economic obsolescence based on the rent loss is $1,462.

Economic obsolescence was also previously measured by comparing sites that sold that were affected by the traffic on Stevenson Road with sites that were not so affected. Based on these sales the effect of the traffic problem was estimated to be $.06 per square foot or $522 (8,712 × .06) for the site being appraised. This estimate supported the above estimate made using the rent loss and GMRM.

Summary:

The depreciation estimated by the breakdown method is:

Physical deterioration—curable	$ 575
Physical deterioration—incurable	17,864
Functional obsolescence—curable	—
Functional obsolescence—incurable	—
Economic obsolescence	$1,462
Total depreciation	$19,901

Age Life Method

A direct way to measure the total depreciation in a property is the age life or economic life method. The basis of this technique is that percentage of depreciation is the effective age of the improvement divided by its estimated typical economic life.

Based on an overall observation of the improvements as compared with other houses in the neighborhood, it is estimated that 33 North Road has an effective age of 20 years.

29

The estimated typical economic life of the improvements of houses on North Road affected by the traffic conditions on Stevenson Road is 50 years.

$$\frac{\text{Effective Age}}{\text{Typical Economic Life}} = \text{Total percentage of depreciation}$$

$$\frac{20 \text{ years}}{50 \text{ years}} = 40\% \text{ total depreciation}$$

Summary:

The depreciation estimated by the age life method is:

Reproduction cost	$54,000
Total % of depreciation	.40
Total depreciation	$21,600

Summary of the Cost Approach:

Three different methods of estimating depreciation were used. The abstraction method indicated that properties not affected by the traffic on Stevenson Road have depreciated at an annual rate of 1.75% and houses affected by the traffic on Stevenson Road depreciated at the annual rate of 2%. This indicated a total depreciation on North Road of $21,600 (.40 × $54,000).

The breakdown method, which broke the depreciation into its component parts, produced a total estimated depreciation of $19,901, which is 36% of the estimated reproduction cost.

The age life method based on observation indicated a total depreciation of $21,600 (.40 × $54,000).

Most weight was given to the depreciation estimate taken from the market by the abstraction method, which was well-supported by the breakdown method and age life method.

The total depreciation is estimated to be $21,600.

Estimated market value of the site		$ 9,000
Estimated reproduction cost of the improvements	$54,000	
Estimated depreciation ($54,000 × .40)	−21,600	
Depreciated value of the improvements		32,400
Total indicated market value via the cost approach		$41,400

30

INCOME APPROACH

The income approach for single family residences is based on the relationship between the monthly rent of a residence and its market value. This relationship produces a figure known as the gross monthly rent multiplier (GMRM). The steps of the income approach are as follows:

1. Find houses that have recently sold in the neighborhood that are comparable and were rented at the time of sale.

2. Divide the sale price of each comparable by the monthly rental to derive a gross monthly rent multiplier (GMRM).

3. Reconcile the multipliers developed in Step 2 to obtain a single multiplier or range of multipliers applicable to the appraised property. This is *not* an average, but rather a judgment of comparability and applicability.

4. Find comparable rentals in the neighborhood.

5. Analyze each comparable rental and compare its features with those of the appraised property.

6. Estimate the adjustments required to obtain an indicated rental for the property being appraised.

7. Consider each comparable carefully, with emphasis on the need for adjustments, and formulate an opinion of the market (economic) rent of the appraised house based upon the actual rents of the comparables.

8. Multiply the estimated market rent by the estimated monthly multiplier (or range of multipliers) to obtain the indicated market value of the property being appraised via the income approach.

To estimate the gross monthly rent multiplier, data was obtained on four properties in Stuart Acres that were sold within the past two years and were rented at the time they were sold. These properties were similar to the appraised property except that some had garages instead of carports and some had rooms added since their initial construction.

Comparable Sale/Rental No. 1 was located at 96 Hoover Road. It was similar to 33 North Road except it had a two-car garage. It sold for $43,000 in October, 197__. It was rented at the time of sale for $330 per month.

31

Comparable Sale/Rental No. 2 was located at 26 Hoover Road. It was similar to 33 North Road except it had an addition that was an extra bedroom. It was in poor condition. It sold for $40,500 in January, 197__. It was rented at the time of the sale for $325 per month. It was reported that the tenants had caused most of the damage.

Comparable Sale/Rental No. 3 was located at 27 North Road. It was similar to 33 North Road except it had an addition that was a family room. It was in good condition. It sold for $39,000 in September, 197__. It was rented at the time of the sale for $300 per month.

Comparable Sale/Rental No. 4 was located at 210 Daley Road. It was similar to the subject except that it was not affected by the traffic condition on Stevenson Road. It was in good condition. It sold for $40,000 in May, 197__, for $295 per month. It had been rented on a two-year lease two years ago.

Comparable Sale/Rental	Address	Monthly Rent	Sale Price	GMRM
No. 1	96 Hoover Road	$330	$43,000	130.3
No. 2	26 Hoover Road	$325	$40,500	124.6
No. 3	27 North Road	$300	$39,000	130.0
No. 4	210 Daley Road	$295	$40,000	135.6

The indicated gross monthly rent multipliers range from 124.6 to 135.6. The multiplier developed by Comparable Sale/Rental No. 2 was given little weight because the property had been damaged by the tenants during the rental period. Comparable Sale/Rental No. 4 was given little weight because the property had been leased two years prior to the sale and the rental probably was not the current market rent of the property. Comparable Sale/Rental No. 1 and Comparable Sale/Rental No. 3 were good indicators of a gross monthly rent multiplier. The differences between these two comparables and 33 North Road should have been reflected in both the sale price and the monthly rent. Both these comparables indicated a gross monthly rent multiplier of 130, which was selected as the indicated GMRM for 33 North Road.

To estimate the market rent of 33 North Road, five houses were found in Stuart Acres that had been rented within the past year. None of these houses had been sold since they had been rented. No special conditions were discovered.

32

Comparable Rental No. 1 was located at 63 North Road. It was similar to 33 North Road except for a two-car detached garage. It was rented in May, 197__, for $330.

Comparable Rental No. 2 was located at 75 Cottken Street. It was similar to the appraised property except for an addition consisting of an extra bedroom and a two-car garage. It rented in September, 197__, for $335.

Comparable Rental No. 3 was located at 71 McKinley Street. It was similar to 33 North Road except for an addition consisting of an extra bedroom. It rented in November, 197__, for $320.

Comparable Rental No. 4 was located at 16 Jefferson Street. It was similar to 33 North Road except that it had a garage. It was not affected by the traffic on Stevenson Road. It was rented two weeks ago for $340.

Comparable Rental No. 5 was located at 53 North Road. It was similar to the 33 North Road except for a two-car detached garage. It was rented in October, 197__, for $315.

By comparing these rentals with each other, the adjustments for their differences were extracted from the market data. The following shows how these rentals were compared with each other and how the adjustments were estimated:

Time Adjustment

Comparable Rental No. 1 and Comparable Rental No. 5 are similar except for the time they were rented. Comparable Rental No. 1 rented for $330 and Comparable Rental No. 5 rented for $315. Based on these rentals, a $15 time adjustment is indicated for a half year.

Comparable Rental No. 1 (May 197__)	$330
Comparable Rental No. 5 (Oct. 197__)	315
Time adjustment	$ 15

Garage Adjustment

Comparable Rental No. 2 and Comparable Rental No. 3 are similar except for the two-car garage. Comparable No. 2 rented for $335 and Comparable No. 3 rented for $320. Based on these rentals, a $15 adjustment is indicated for a two-car garage.

Comparable Rental No. 2 (2-car garage)	$335
Comparable Rental No. 3 (carport)	320
Two-car garage adjustment	$ 15

33

Adjustment For Bedroom Addition

Comparable Rental No. 2 and Comparable Rental No. 5 are similar except for addition containing an extra bedroom. Comparable Rental No. 2 rented for $335 and Comparable Rental No. 5 rented for $315. The difference is $20, indicating a $20 adjustment for the addition.

Comparable Rental No. 2 (addition for bedroom)	$335
Comparable Rental No. 5 (no addition)	315
Adjustment for bedroom addition	$ 20

The adjustment for an addition containing an extra bedroom can also be extracted from the market as follows:

Comparable Rental No. 1 (base rental May 197__, 2-car garage, no addition)	$330
Comparable Rental No. 3 (November, 197__ carport, bedroom addition)	320
Adjustment for carport vs. 2-car garage	+ 15
Adjustment for time	+ 15
Adjusted Comparable Rental No. 3	$350
Comparable Rental No. 1	− 330
Indicated adjustment for bedroom addition	$ 20

and

Comparable Rental No. 1 (base rental May, 197__, 2-car garage, no addition)	$330
Comparable Rental No. 2 (September, 197__ 2-car garage, addition for bedroom)	335
Adjustment for time	+ 15
Adjusted Comparable Rental No. 2	$350
Comparable Rental No. 1	− 330
Indicated adjustment for bedroom addition	$ 20

34

Location Adjustment

Comparable Rental No. 1 and Comparable Rental No. 4 are similar except for their location to the traffic problem on Stevenson Road. Comparable Rental No. 1 rented for $330 per month and Comparable Rental No. 4 rented for $340. Based on these rentals, a $10 location adjustment is indicated for the traffic problem.

Comparable Rental No. 1 (affected by traffic)	$330
Comparable Rental No. 4 (not affected by traffic)	340
Location Adjustment:	$ 10

The location adjustment for the traffic problem can also be extracted from the market as follows:

Comparable Rental No. 2 (base rental — affected by traffic, rented 6 months ago, bedroom addition)	$335
Comparable Rental No. 4 (not affected by traffic, rented 2 weeks ago, no bedroom addition).	340
Adjustment for time	− 15
Adjustment for bedroom addition	+ 20
Adjusted Comparable Rental No. 4	$345
Comparable Rental No. 2	335
Indicated adjustment for location	$ 10
Comparable Rental No. 3 (base rental — affected by traffic, rented 6 months ago, carport, bedroom addition)	$320
Comparable Rental No. 4 (not affected by traffic, rented 2 weeks ago, 2-car garage, no bedroom addition)	$340
Adjustment for time	− 15
Adjustment for bedroom addition	+ 20
Adjustment for 2-car garage vs. carport	− 15
Adjusted Comparable Rental No. 4	$330
Comparable Rental No. 3	$320
Indicated adjustment for location	$ 10

35

Comparable Rental No. 5 (base rental — affected
   by traffic, rented 6 months ago) $315

Comparable Rental No. 4 (not affected by traffic,
   rented 2 weeks ago)   340

Adjustment for time   −   15

Adjusted Comparable Rental No. 4 $325

Comparable Rental No. 5   315

Indicated adjustment for location $ 10

On the following page is a grid chart showing the adjustments to comparable rentals.

Summary of the Income Approach:

The final step of the income approach is to multiply the gross monthly rent multiplier of 130 developed from the market for this property by the estimated market rent of $315 to give an indicated value via the income approach of $40,950 ($315 market rent × 130 GMRM = $40,950).

Indicated market value of property being appraised based on the income approach: $41,000.

COMPARABLE RENTALS — ADJUSTMENT GRID

	Appraised Property	Comparable Rental No. 1	Comparable Rental No. 2	Comparable Rental No. 3	Comparable Rental No. 4	Comparable Rental No. 5
Address	33 North Rd.	63 North Rd.	75 Cottken	71 McKinley	16 Jefferson	53 North Rd.
Monthly rent		$330	$335	$320	$340	$315
Date rented		May, 197— —0—	Sept, 197— +$15	Nov., 197— +$15	2 weeks ago —0—	Oct., 197— +$15
Location	Affected by traffic on Stevenson Rd.	Same	Same	Same	Not affected by traffic on Stevenson Rd. -$10	Same
Addition for a bedroom	None	None	Addition for bedroom -$20	Addition for bedroom -$20	None	None
Car storage	Carport	2-car garage -$15	2-car garage -$15	Carport —0—	2-car garage -$15	2-car garage -$15
Special conditions	None	None	None	None	None	None
Total adjustments		-$15	-$20	-$5	-$25	—0—
Adjusted rental		$315	$315	$315	$315	$315

Comparable Rental No. 1 was most like 33 North Road. The only difference was the 2-car garage. Its adjusted rental was $315, which was supported by the other comparable rentals that required additional adjustments. $315 was the indicated market rent of 33 North Road.

MARKET DATA APPROACH

The market data approach utilizes the sales of similar properties as the basis for an indication of market value for the appraised property. Direct comparisons are made between them on an item-by-item basis as to location, time of sale, conditions of sale, and physical characteristics. Adjustments are made to the sale price of the comparative property to arrive at an indication of what the property would have sold for had it been essentially similar to the appraised property. These adjusted sale prices are reconciled into an indication of value by this approach.

Following are five sales which are pictured and described. They are all in Stuart Acres. They were selected because they were the most similar to the property being appraised of all the sales about which information was available.

They were all inspected and were found to be similar except for their size (some had an extra room), lot size, location with reference to the Stevenson Road traffic condition, their car storage and effective age. Their other minor differences did not appear to cause any measurable difference in sale price.

Each sale is described on a separate page that includes a photograph. The sales are compared with each other to obtain adjustments for date of sale, car storage, location and effective age from this market data. The site size difference was accounted for by using the information developed in the cost approach to value. The difference in house size was accounted for by converting all the information to price per square foot of gross living area. There is an adjustment page for each sale that explains how the adjustments were applied. The information is summarized and displayed on the comparable sale adjustment grid. Finally all the data is reconciled to give an indicated value via the market data approach.

Comparable Sale No. 1

Address: 65 North Road, Typicaltown, Illinois
No. of Families: one *Type:* one story *Style:* ranch
Date of Sale: 5/18/7__ *Grantor:* Anthony and Jane Atwood
Sale Price: $46,000 *Grantee:* John and Mary Ackerman
Financing: conv. mtg. *Data Source:* MLS *Verification:* J. Atwood
Lot Dimensions: 68' x 134' (avg. depth) *Lot Size:* 9,112 sq. ft.
Site Improvements/Landscaping/Topography: average/average/level
Zoning: residential *Conforming:* yes *View:* average
Neighborhood Life Cycle: stable *Improvement Conformity:* conforms
No. of Rooms: 6 *No. of Baths:* 1 *No. of Bedrooms:* 3
Other Rooms: living room, dining room, family room
Car Storage: 1-car carport *Functional Utility:* average

Assessment	**Services and Mechanical Equipment**	
Site: $ 2,369	*Water:* municipal	*Type of Heat:* hot air
House: 5,324	*Sewage:* municipal	*Fuel:* gas
Other: –	*Electricity:* public	*Hot Water:* gas 40-gal.
Total: $ 7,693	*Gas:* public	*Plumbing:* copper water/ cast iron waste

Construction	**Extra Features**	
Type: frame	*Air Conditioning:* none	
Quality: average	*Storm Windows/Doors/Screens:* aluminum comb.	
Kitchen Style: average	*Pool:* none	*Other:* none
Bath Style: modern		
Condition: average	*Appeal:* average	*Date Inspected:* 6/21/7_
Effective Age: 20 years	*Rent and GMRM:* Not rented	
Basement % of 1st flr: crawl space	*Sq. ft. of Finished Space:* n/a	

Special Considerations: No special conditions. Affected by heavy traffic on Stevenson Road
Sq. Ft. of GLA: 1,165 *Sale Price/Sq. Ft. of GLA:* $39.48

Comparable Sale No. 2

Address: 38 Cottken Street, Typicaltown, Illinois
No. of Families: one   *Type:* one story   *Style:* ranch
Date of Sale: 11/14/7_   *Grantor:* Leonard and Lois Ultamine
Sale Price: $42,300   *Grantee:* Arthur and Diane Croteau
Financing: conv. mtg.   *Data Source:* MLS   *Verification:* D. Croteau
Lot Dimensions: 75' × 135' (avg. depth)   *Lot Size:* 10,125 sq. ft.
Site Improvements/Landscaping/Topography: average/average/level
Zoning: residential   *Conforming:* yes   *View:* average
Neighborhood Life Cycle: stable   *Improvement Conformity:* contorms
No. of Rooms: 6   *No. of Baths:* 1   *No. of Bedrooms:* 3
Other Rooms: living room, dining room, family room
Car Storage: 1-car carport   *Functional Utility:* average

Assessment	**Services and Mechanical Equipment**	
Site: $ 2,632	*Water:* municipal	*Type of Heat:* hot air
House: 5,301	*Sewage:* municipal	*Fuel:* gas
Other: –	*Electricity:* public	*Hot Water:* gas 40-gal.
Total: $ 7,933	*Gas:* public	*Plumbing:* copper
		water/cast iron waste

Construction	**Extra Features**	
Type: frame	*Air Conditioning:* one window unit	
Quality: average	*Storm Windows/Doors/Screens:* aluminum comb.	
Kitchen Style: average	*Pool:* none	*Other:* none
Bath Style: modern		
Condition: average	*Appeal:* average	*Date Inspected:* 6/21/7_
Effective Age: 20 years		*Rent and GMRM:* not rented
Basement % of 1st Flr: crawl space	*Sq. Ft. of Finished Space:* n/a	

Special Considerations: No special conditions. Affected by heavy traffic
on Stevenson Road.
Sq. Ft. of GLA: 1,160   *Sale·Price/Sq. Ft. of GLA:* $36.47

40

Comparable Sale No. 3

Address: 23 McKinley Street, Typicaltown, Illinois

No. of Families: one   Type: one story   Style: ranch

Date of Sale: 10/28/7_   Grantor: Mary Downs

Sale Price: $44,700   Grantee: Harold Goldfine

Financing: conv. mtg.   Data Source: MLS   Verification:M. Downs

Lot Dimensions: 72' x 135' (avg. depth)   Lot Size: 9,720 sq. ft.

Site Improvements/Landscaping/Topography: average/average/level

Zoning: residential   Conforming: yes   View: average

Neighborhood Life Cycle: stable   Improvement Conformity: conforms

No. of Rooms: 6   No. of Bedrooms: 3   No. of Baths: 1

Other Rooms: living room, kitchen and family room

Car Storage: 2-car detached garage   Functional Utility: average

Assessment		Services and Mechanical Equipment	
Site:	$ 2,527	Water: municipal	Type of Heat: hot air
House:	5,346	Sewage: municipal	Fuel: gas
Other	800	Electricity: public	Hot Water: gas 40 gal.
Total:	$ 8,673	Gas: public	Plumbing:copper wa-ter/cast iron waste

Construction

Type: frame

Quality: average

Kitchen Style: average

Bath Style: modern

Condition: average   Appeal: average

Effective Age: 20 years

Basement % of 1st Flr: crawl space

Extra Features

Air Conditioning: one window unit

Storm Windows/Doors/Screens: aluminum comb.

Pool: none   Other: none

Date Inspected: 6/21/7_

Rent and GMRM: not rented

Sq. Ft. of Finished Space: n/a

Special Considerations: No special conditions. Affected by heavy traffic on Stevenson Road

Sq. Ft. of GLA: 1,170   Sale Price/Sq. Ft. of GLA: $38.21

41

Comparable Sale No. 4

Address: 42 Jefferson Street, Typicaltown, Illinois

No. of Families: one   *Type:* one story   *Style:* ranch

Date of Sale: 5/25/7_   *Grantor:* Mary and James Parson

Sale Price: $46,000   *Grantee:* Edward and Joanne Driggs

Financing: conv. mtg.   *Data Source:* assessor   *Verification:* E. Driggs

Lot Dimensions: 65′ x 37′ (avg. depth)   *Lot Size:* 8,905 sq. ft.

Site Improvements/Landscaping/Topography: average/average/level

Zoning: residential   *Conforming:* yes   *View:* average

Neighborhood Life Cycle: stable   *Improvement Conformity:* conforms

No. of Rooms: 5   *No. of Bedrooms:* 3   *No. of Baths:* 1

Other Rooms: living room, kitchen

Car Storage: 2-car detached garage   *Functional Utility:* average

Assessment	**Services and Mechanical Equipment**	
Site: $ 2,315	*Water:* municipal	*Type of Heat:* hot air
House: 4,934	*Sewage:* municipal	*Fuel:* gas
Other: 810	*Electricity:* public	*Hot Water:* gas 40 gal.
Total: 8,059	*Gas:* public	*Plumbing:* copper
		water/cast iron waste

Construction	**Extra Features**	
Type: frame	*Air Conditioning:* one window unit	
Quality: average	*Storm Windows/Doors/Screens:* aluminum comb.	
Kitchen Style: average	*Pool:* none	*Other:* none
Bath Style: modern		
Condition: average	*Appeal:* average	*Date Inspected:* 6/21/7_
Effective Age: 20 yrs		*Rent and GMRM:* not rented
Basement % of 1st Flr: crawl space	*Sq. Ft. of Finished Space:* n/a.	

Special Considerations: No special conditions. Not affected by traffic on Stevenson Road.

Sq. ft. of GLA: 1,080   *Sale Price/Sq. Ft. of GLA:* $42.59

42

Comparable Sale No. 5

Address: 12 Truman Street, Typicaltown, Illinois

No. of Families: one *Type:* one story *Style:* ranch

Date of Sale: 6/10/7_ *Grantor:* Jeffrey and Rita Burke

Sale Price: $46,500 *Grantee:* Sidney and Julie Chow

Financing: conv. mtg. *Data Source:* broker *Verification:* Julie Chow

Lot Dimensions: 65' x 140' (avg. depth) *Lot Size:* 9,100 sq. ft.

Site Improvements/Landscaping/Topography: average/average/level

Zoning: residential *Conforming:* yes *View:* average

Neighborhood Life Cycle: stable *Improvement Conformity:* conforms

No. of Rooms: 5 *No. of Bedrooms:* 3 *No. of Baths:* 1

Other Rooms: living room, kitchen

Car Storage: 1 car carport *Functional Utility:* average

Assessment	**Services and Mechanical Equipment**	
Site: $ 2,380	*Water:* municipal	*Type of Heat:* hot air
House: 4,827	*Sewage:* municipal	*Fuel:* gas
Other: –	*Electricity:* public	*Hot Water:* gas 40-gal.
Total: 7,207	*Gas:* public	*Plumbing:* copper
		water/cast iron waste

Construction	**Extra Features**	
Type: frame	*Air Conditioning:* none	
Quality: average	*Storm Windows/Doors/Screens:* aluminum comb.	
Kitchen Style: average	*Pool:* none	*Other:* none
Bath Style: modern		
Condition: average	*Appeal:* average	*Date Inspected:* 6/20/7_
Effective Age: 16 yrs.		*Rent and GMRM:* not rented
Basement % of 1st Flr.: crawl space	*Sq. Ft. of Finished Space:* n/a	

Special Considerations: No special conditions. Not affected by traffic on Stevenson Road

Sq. Ft. of GLA: 1,060 *Sale Price/Sq. Ft. of GLA:* $43.87

43

Time Adjustment

Comparable Sale No. 1 and Comparable Sale No. 2 appear to be similar except for their lot size, house size and time of sale. Sale No. 1 sold for $39.48 per sq. ft. of GLA. Sale No. 2 sold for $36.47 per sq. ft. of GLA.

Comparable Sale No. 1 (base sale)
(5/18/7—, lot size 9,112 sq. ft.) $39.48 per sq. ft. of GLA

Comparable Sale No. 2 (11/14/7—,
lot size 10,125 sq. ft.) $36.47 per sq. ft. of GLA

Adjustment for difference
attributable to lot size:

Sale No. 1, 9,112 sq. ft.
@ $1.04 per sq. ft. $ 9,476

Sale No. 2, 10,125 sq. ft.
ft. @$1.04 per sq. ft.   10,530
                                 $ 1,054

Difference per sq. ft. of
GLA attributable to lot
size ($1,054 ÷ 1,160 sq. ft.)   −.91

Adjusted Comparable Sale No. 2 $35.56

Comparable Sale No. 1   39.48

Difference in sale price per
sq. ft. of GLA attributable to
difference in time of sale $ 3.92

Location Adjustment

Comparable Sale No. 3 and Comparable Sale No. 4 appear to be similar except for their lot size, house size and location. Sale No. 3 is affected by the traffic problem on Stevenson Road. Sale No. 4 is not affected by the traffic problem on Stevenson Road. Sale No. 3 sold for $38.21 per sq. ft. of GLA. Sale No. 4 sold for $42.59 per sq. ft. of GLA.

Comparable Sale No. 3 (base sale— affected by traffic on Stevenson Road, lot size 9,720 sq. ft., sold 10/28/7_)	$38.21 per sq. ft. of GLA
Comparable Sale No. 4 (not affected by traffic on Stevenson Road, lot size 8,905 sq. ft., sold 5/28/7_)	$42.59 per sq. ft. of GLA

Adjustment for difference attributable to lot size:

Sale No. 3, 9,720 sq. ft. @$1.04 per sq. ft.	$10,109	
Sale No. 4, 8,905 sq. ft. @$1.04 per sq. ft.	9,261	
	$ 848	
Difference per sq. ft. of GLA attributable to lot size ($848 ÷ 1,080 sq. ft.)		+ .79
Adjustment for difference in date of sale		− 3.92
Adjusted Comparable Sale No. 4		$39.46
Comparable Sale No. 3		38.21
Difference in sale price per sq. ft. of GLA attributable to difference in location		$ 1.25

45

Car Storage Adjustment

Comparable Sale No. 2 and Comparable Sale No. 3 appear to be similar except for their lot size, house size and car storage. Sale No. 2 sold for $36.47 per sq. ft. of GLA. Sale No. 3 sold for $38.21 per sq. ft. of GLA.

Comparable Sale No. 2 (base sale— 1-car carport, lot size 10,125 sq. ft.)	$36.47 per sq. ft. of GLA
Comparable Sale No. 3 (2-car de- tached garage, lot size 9,720 sq. ft.)	$38.21 per sq. ft. of GLA

Adjustment for difference
attributable to lot size:

Sale No. 2, 10,125 sq. ft. @$1.04 per sq. ft.	$10,530
Sale No. 3, 9,720 sq. ft. @$1.04 per sq. ft.	10,109
	$ 421

Difference per sq. ft. of GLA attributable to lot size ($421 ÷ 1,170 sq. ft.)	+ .36
Adjusted Comparable Sale No. 3	$38.57
Comparable Sale No. 2	36.47
Difference in sale price per sq. ft. of GLA attributable to dif- ference in car storage	$ 2.10

Effective Age Adjustment

Comparable Sale No. 5 and Comparable Sale No. 4 appear to be similar except for their lot size, car storage and effective age. Sale No. 4 has an effective age of 20 years and Sale No. 5 has an effective age of 16 years. Sale No. 4 sold for $42.59 per sq. ft. of GLA. Sale No. 5 sold for $43.87 per sq. ft. of GLA.

Comparable Sale No. 4 (base sale— effective age 20 years, lot size 8,905 sq. ft., 2-car detached garage)	$42.59 per sq. ft. of GLA
Comparable Sale No. 5 (effective age 16 years, lot size 9,100 sq. ft., 1-car carport)	$43.87 per sq. ft. of GLA

Adjustment for difference attributable to lot size:

Sale No. 4, 8,905 sq. ft. @$1.04 per sq. ft.	$9,261
Sale No. 5, 9,100 sq. ft. @$1.04 per sq. ft.	9,464
	$ 203

Difference per sq. ft. of GLA attributable to lot size ($203 ÷ 1,060 sq. ft.)	− .19
Difference in sale price attributable to difference in car storage	+ 2.10
Adjusted Comparable Sale No. 5	$45.78
Comparable Sale No. 4	42.59
Difference in sale price per sq. ft. of GLA attributable to difference in effective age	$ 3.19

47

Comparable Sale No. 1
65 North Road, Typicaltown, Illinois

	Adjustments (per sq. ft. GLA)	Explanation
Sale price	$46,000	
Gross living area	1,165 sq. ft.	
Sale price per sq. ft. of gross living area	$39.48	
Date of sale	—0—	Sold within one month of date of appraisal.
Location	—0—	On North Road which is affected by traffic on Stevenson Road.
Lot size	−$.36	400 sq. ft. larger than 33 North Road (400 sq. ft. × $1.04 ÷ 1,165 sq. ft.).
Car storage	—0—	1-car attached carport; same as 33 North Road.
Effective age	—0—	20 years; same as 33 North Road.
Special conditions	—0—	None
Total adjustments	−$.36	
Adjusted sale price per sq. ft. of gross living area	$39.12	
Adjusted sale price	$41,300 (rounded)	Sale price per sq. ft. of GLA × GLA of house being appraised ($39.12 × 1,056).

48

Comparable Sale No. 2
38 Cottken Street, Typicaltown, Illinois

	Adjustments (per sq. ft. GLA)	Explanation
Sale price	$42,300	
Gross living area	1,160 sq. ft.	
Sale price per sq. ft. of gross living area	$36.47	
Date of sale	+$3.92	11/14/7_
Location	—0—	Cottken Street is also affected by the traffic on Stevenson Road.
Lot size	−$1.27	1,413 sq. ft. larger than 33 North Road (1,413 sq. ft. × $1.04 ÷ 1,160 sq. ft.).
Car storage	—0—	1-car attached carport; same as 33 North Road.
Effective age	—0—	20 years; same as 33 North Road.
Special conditions	—0—	None
Total adjustments	+$2.65	
Adjusted sale price per sq. ft. of gross living area	$39.12	
Adjusted sale price	$41,300 (rounded)	Sale price per sq. ft. of GLA × GLA of house being appraised ($39.12 × 1,056).

49

Comparable Sale No. 3
23 McKinley Street, Typicaltown, Illinois

	Adjustments (per sq. ft. GLA)	Explanation
Sale price	$44,700	
Gross living area	1,170 sq. ft.	
Sale price per sq. ft. of gross living area	$38.21	
Date of sale	+$3.92	10/28/7—
Location	—0—	McKinley Street is also affected by the traffic on Stevenson Road.
Lot size	−$.90	1,008 sq. ft. larger than 33 North Road (1,008 sq. ft. × $1.04 ÷ 1,170 sq. ft.).
Car storage	−$2.10	2-car detached garage; 33 North Road has a 1-car carport.
Effective age	—0—	20 years; same as 33 North Road.
Special conditions	—0—	None
Total adjustments	+$.92	
Adjusted sale price per sq. ft. of gross living area	$39.13	
Adjusted sale price	$41,300	Sale price per sq. ft. of GLA × GLA of house being appraised ($39.13 × 1,056).

50

Comparable Sale No. 4
42 Jefferson Street, Typicaltown, Illinois

	Adjustments (per sq. ft. GLA)	Explanation
Sale price	$46,000	
Gross living area	1,080 sq. ft.	
Sale price per sq. ft. of gross living area	$42.59	
Date of sale	—0—	Sold within one month of date of appraisal.
Location	−$1.25	Jefferson Street is not affected by the traffic on Stevenson Road.
Lot size	−$ .19	193 sq. ft. larger than 33 North Road (193 sq. ft. × $1.04 ÷ 1,080 sq. ft.).
Car storage	−$2.10	2-car detached garage; 33 North Road has a 1-car carport.
Effective age	—0—	20 years; same as 33 North Road.
Special conditions	—0—	None
Total adjustment	−$3.54	
Adjusted sale price per sq. ft. of gross living area	$39.05	
Adjusted sale price	$41,200 (rounded)	Sale price per sq. ft. of GLA × GLA of house being appraised ($39.05 × 1,056).

51

Comparable Sale No. 5
12 Truman Street, Typicaltown, Illinois

	Adjustments (per sq. ft. GLA)	Explanation
Sale price	$46,500	
Gross living area	1,060 sq. ft.	
Sale price per sq. ft. of gross living area	$43.87	
Date of sale	—0—	Sold within one month of date of appraisal.
Location	—$1.25	Truman Street is not affected by the traffic on Stevenson Road.
Lot size	—$.38	388 sq. ft. larger than 33 North Road (388 sq. ft. × $1.04 ÷ 1,060 sq. ft.).
Car storage	—0—	1-car attached carport; same as 33 North Road.
Effective age	—$3.19	16 years as compared to to the 20 year effective age of 33 North Road.
Special conditions	—0—	None
Total adjustment	—$4.82	
Adjusted sale price per sq. ft. of gross living area	$39.05	
Adjusted sale price	$41,200 (rounded)	Sale price per sq. ft. of GLA × GLA of house being appraised ($39.04 × 1,056).

52

COMPARABLE SALES — ADJUSTMENT GRID
(All adjustments made on basis of sq. ft. price of GLA)

	Appraised Property	Sale No. 1	Sale No. 2	Sale No. 3	Sale No. 4	Sale No. 5
Address	33 North Rd.	65 North Rd.	38 Cottken St.	23 McKinley St.	42 Jefferson St.	12 Truman St.
Sale price	—	$46,000	$42,300	$44,700	$46,000	$46,500
GLA	1,056 sq. ft.	1,165 sq. ft.	1,160 sq. ft.	1,170 sq. ft.	1,080 sq. ft.	1,060 sq. ft.
Sale price/GLA	—	$39.48	$36.47	$38.21	$42.59	$43.87
Date of sale	6/19/7_	5/8/7_	11/14/7_ +$3.92	10/28/7_ +$3.92	5/25/7_	6/10/7_
Location	Subject to traffic problem	Subject to traffic problem	Subject to traffic problem	Subject to traffic problem	Not subject to traffic problem -$1.25	Not subject to traffic problem -$1.25
Lot size	66' × 132' (8,712 sq. ft.)	68' × 134' (9,112 sq. ft.) -$.36	75' × 135' (10,125 sq. ft.) -$1.27	72' × 135' (9,720 sq. ft.) -$.90	65' × 137' (8,905 sq. ft.) -$.19	65' × 140' (9,100 sq. ft.) -$.38
Car storage	1-car carport	1-car carport	1-car carport	2-car detached garage -$2.10	2-car detached garage -$2.10	1-car carport
Effective age	20 years	20 years	20 years	20 years	20 years	16 years -$3.19
Special conditions	None	None	None	None	None	None
Total adjustments		-$.36	+$2.65	+$.92	-$3.54	-$4.82
Adjusted sale price per sq. ft. GLA		$39.12	$39.12	$39.13	$39.05	$39.05
Adjusted sale price		$41,300 (rounded)	$41,300 (rounded)	$41,300 (rounded)	$41,200 (rounded)	$41,200 (rounded)

Summary of the Market Data Approach

The five sales produced a range of adjusted sale prices from $41,200 to $41,300—a very close range. All five sales were in the same neighborhood and very similar to 33 North Road. Most weight was given to Sale No. 1 at 65 North Road. This recent sale was very similar to 33 North Road except for having a larger lot and house. Adjustments for these two differences were taken from the market.

Based on these five sales and considering all other available sales and listing data in this market, the indicated market value of 33 North Road based on the market data approach is $41,300.

54

RECONCILIATION AND FINAL ESTIMATE OF VALUE

Thirty-three North Road. Typicaltown, Illinois, is a single family, one-story, ranch-style, five-room house with a one-car carport. Typicaltown is a residential suburb in the third largest metropolitan area in the country. A solid economic base and good transportation are strong indications of a continued demand for houses in this region and community. The neighborhood is stable. House prices are lower than newer competing communities and the supply of suitable land for direct competition is limited. These factors, together with a lack of major adverse influences, should stabilize house prices in the Wrightville neighborhood.

The site is typical for the neighborhood and is served by all the needed utilities. The zoning is residential and no change is anticipated. The improvements conform with those in the neighborhood. The selling market has been active but supply and demand have been in balance.

The improvements are acceptable to this market. The market indicates no penalty for the lack of a dining room or basement.

Taxes have been rising for the past 10 years primarily because of inflation. Adequate schools and lack of need for major budget changes and the conservative political climate indicate no unusual future tax increases. The taxes are similar to those in competitive neighborhoods and communities and do not affect the value of 33 North Road.

The highest and best use analysis indicates that the present improvement, with minor repairs, represents the highest and best use of the site as improved.

All three approaches to value were utilized to make the final value estimate.

For the cost approach there were good land sales requiring few adjustments from which to arrive at the site value estimate of $9,000. Adjustments were taken from the market using matched pairs of sales, one with and one without the differences being adjusted. Reproduction cost new was based on information from a local builder and cost estimator, plus the reported costs of some similar houses. The cost of $51.14 per square foot of gross living area provided by the cost estimator, supported by the known costs of the other houses, was selected as the indicated cost per square foot.

Depreciation was estimated by abstraction from the market based on actual sale of similar houses in the neighborhood. The breakdown method and age life method were also used. These different techniques each pro-

55

duced similar results. Because of the good quantity and high quality of the data available for the cost approach, $41,400 is a reliable indication of value for the property being appraised.

Four similar properties were located in the neighborhood that were sold within the year and were rented at the time of sale. They produced a gross monthly rent multiplier range of 124.6 to 135.6. It appeared from this data that the impact of the high traffic on Stevenson Road may affect sale prices more than it affects rentals. Five good comparable rentals were located to estimate the market rent at 33 North Road. Adjustments for the differences between these rentals and 33 North Road were made based on adjustments taken from the market. All the rentals adjusted to $315 per month. The final value estimated by the income approach of $41,000 was considered but given the least weight of the three approaches because of the doubtful accuracy of the rentals reflecting the economic obsolescence caused by the traffic on Stevenson Road.

There have been many sales of similar residences in this neighborhood as many residents remain for only short periods of time, after which they are either transferred to different locations or their income increases and they move up to a more expensive house. Despite the large number of houses for sale, the values have been maintained because of an equally high number of potential buyers attracted by the moderate prices as compared to newer neighborhoods and communities, many of which are further away from center city employment.

Five sales were selected that best reflected the value of the property being appraised. Adjustments for all significant differences were obtained by comparing the sales with each other. These adjusted sale prices fell into a narrow range. The $41,300 indicated value selected had good support from the other sales and most weight was given to this indicated value.

The $41,300 value indicated by the market data approach was selected as the final market value estimate because of the large amount of data, confidence in the adjustments made based on the market data, and the support of the value by the $41,400 and $41,000 value indications of the cost approach and income approach.

Because the data was plentiful and adjustments and depreciation estimates were also based on this data, the final value estimate has a high probability of accuracy.

The indicated market value of 33 North Road as of June 19, 197__, is Forty One Thousand Three Hundred Dollars ($41,300).

UNDERLYING ASSUMPTIONS AND LIMITING CONDITIONS SUBJECT TO THIS APPRAISAL

1. I assume no responsibility for matters legal in nature, nor do I render any opinion as to the title, which is assumed to be marketable. The property is appraised as though under responsible ownership.

2. The legal description used herein is correct.

3. I have made no survey of the property and the boundaries are taken from records believed to be reliable. The sketches in this report are included to assist the reader in visualizing the property, and I assume no responsibility for their accuracy.

4. I am not required to testify or appear in court on matters contained herein, unless previous arrangements have been made.

5. The distribution of the total valuation in this report between land and improvements applies only under the existing program of utilization. The separate valuations for land and building must not be used in conjunction with any other appraisal and are invalid if so used.

6. I assume that there are no hidden or unapparent conditions of the property, subsoil or structures which would render the property more or less valuable. I assume no responsibility for such conditions or for engineering which might be required to discover such factors.

7. The information, estimates and opinions furnished to me and contained in this report were obtained from sources considered reliable and believed to be true and accurate. However, no responsibility for accuracy can be assumed by me.

8. This report is to be used in its entirety and only for the purpose for which it was rendered.

9. Neither all nor any part of the contents of this report (especially any conclusions as to value, the identity of the appraiser or the firm with which he is connected, or any reference to the American Institute of Real Estate Appraisers and the Society of Real Estate Appraisers or to the MAI or SREA designation) shall be reproduced, published or disseminated to the public through advertising media, public relations media, news media, sales media or any other public means of communication without the prior written consent and approval of the author.

57

CERTIFICATE OF APPRAISAL

The undersigned appraiser certifies that a personal inspection of the property described herein, located at 33 North Road, Typicaltown, Illinois, was made; that the undersigned has no past, present or prospective direct or indirect interest in the said property or the use of this appraisal; that the undersigned's employment in this appraisal is not in any manner contingent upon anything else other than the delivery of this report; that, to the best of the undersigned's knowledge and belief, all of the statements and opinions contained in this report are correct; and, that this appraisal has been made in conformity with the Professional Standards of the American Institute of Real Estate Appraisers.

Respectfully submitted,

Leslie E. Clinton

Leslie E. Clinton   June 25, 197__

QUALIFICATIONS OF THE APPRAISER

Leslie E. Clinton

Education:
Wharton School of Finance and Commerce of the University of Pennsylvania, B.S., Economics, 1952
Indiana University, M.B.A., Real Estate, 1954
American Institute of Real Estate Appraisers Courses:
I-A — Basic Principles, Methods and Techniques
I-B — Capitalization Theory and Techniques
II — Urban Properties
VI — Investment Analysis
VIII — Single Family Residential Appraisal

Employment:
1954-56 United States Air Force
1956 to present: Cosgrove and Clinton, Inc.

Professional Designations:
MAI — American Institute of Real Estate Appraisers
SREA — Society of Real Estate Appraisers

Organizations:
Secretary, Chicago Chapter #6, AIREA
Vice Chairman, National AIREA Course VIII Subcommittee

Partial List of Major Clients and Types of Assignments
Employee Relocation House Appraisals: HomEquity, Inc., Western Electric, General Motors.

Mortgage Appraisals: Gong Federal Savings and Loan Association, Money National Bank of Chicago, United States Veterans' Administration

Urban Renewal Assignments: Chicago Redevelopment Authority, Oak Park Historical Development Corporation, Elmhurst Redevelopment Authority.

Commercial and Industrial Appraisals: Rock Island Railway, Sears, U.S. Synthetics Corporation, TransAmerica Corporation, General Motors, Illinois Power Authority

59

PART THREE — ADDENDA

REGIONAL MAP

CHICAGO & MAJOR PORTIONS OF THE METROPOLITAN AREA

60

COMMUNITY MAP

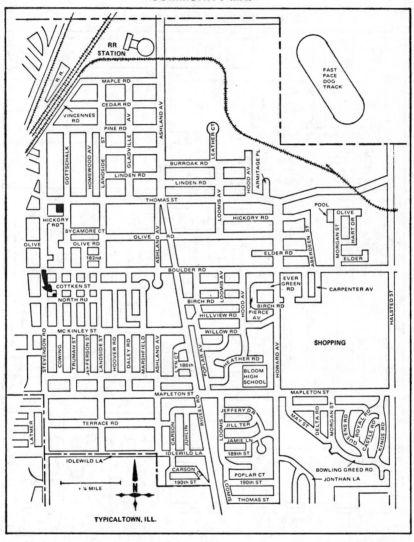

TYPICALTOWN, ILL.

NEIGHBORHOOD MAP

SHOWING COMPARABLE SALES

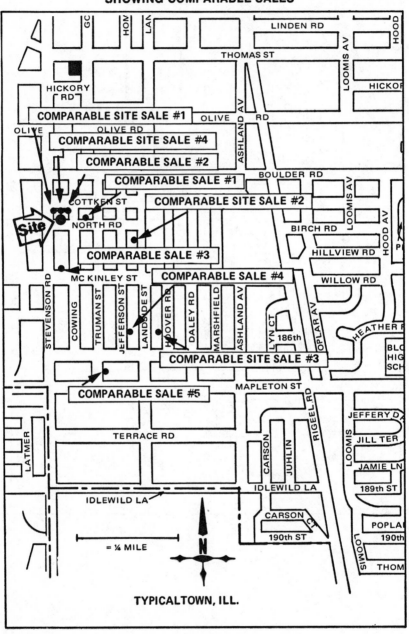

TYPICALTOWN, ILL.

ZONING MAP

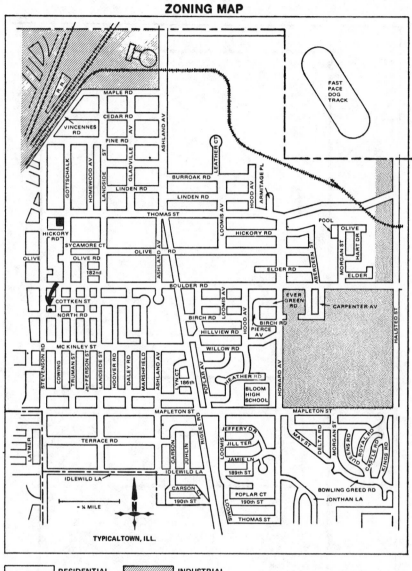

TYPICALTOWN, ILL.

= ¼ MILE

RESIDENTIAL   INDUSTRIAL

COMMERCIAL

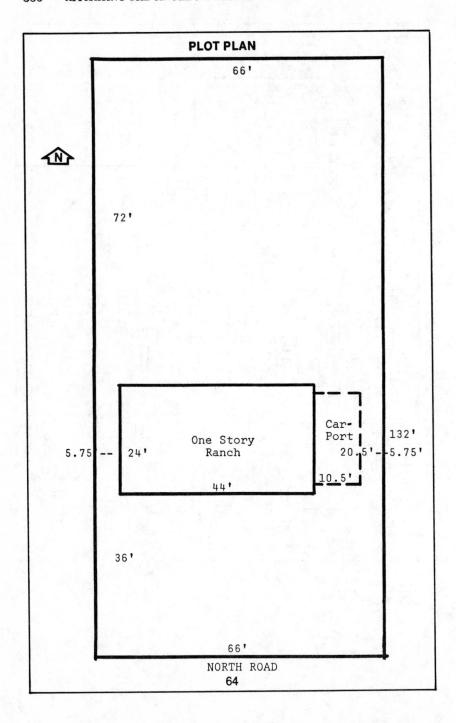

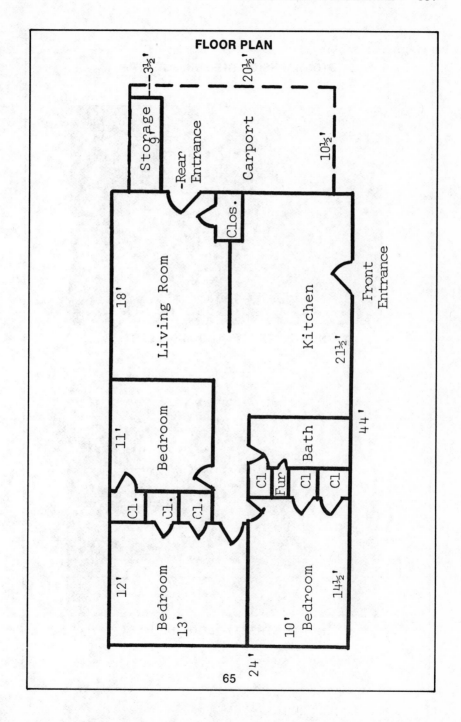

PHOTOGRAPHS OF THE SUBJECT STREET

NORTH STREET — LOOKING EAST

NORTH STREET — LOOKING WEST

66

Appendix B: Model Form Appraisal

On the following pages is a model form appraisal of a single family residence, using the form that has been developed by the Federal National Mortgage Association and the Federal Home Loan Mortgage Corporation. Requirements of this form include attachment of a sketch of the improvements, neighborhood map, photographs of the property and a form containing a definition of market value, certification and statement of limiting conditions, all of which appear here. This form appraisal is based on the same property used in the preceding model narrative appraisal. It illustrates what a typical form appraisal might look like when prepared using the techniques described in this text and when following FNMA/FHLMC guidelines.

This report is not intended to be an example of a demonstration appraisal used for credit towards a designation of the American Institute of Real Estate Appraisers.

RESIDENTIAL APPRAISAL REPORT

File No. _____

Borrower/Client **John M. Freeman & Rose B. Freeman**   Census Tract **84-9**   Map Reference **15747614**

Property Address **33 North Road**

City **Typicaltown**   County **Cook**   State **IL**   Zip Code **60119**

Legal Description **SW Qu. Sec. 19 Township 41 N, Range 11 - 66' on North Rd & 132' deep**

Sale Price $ **41,500**   Date of Sale **6/9/7-**   Property Rights Appraised ☒ Fee ☐ Leasehold ☐ DeMinimis PUD(FNMA only ☐ Condo ☐ PUD)

Actual Real Estate Taxes $ **642.21**   (yr) Loan charges to be paid by seller $ **—**   Other sales concessions $ **—**

Lender **Typa-Savings & Loan Assn**   Lender's Address **1241 Harvard Ave, Typicaltown, IL**

Occupant **Owner**   Appraiser **Leslie E. Clinton**   Instructions to Appraiser **Call for appointment**

To be completed by Lender

NEIGHBORHOOD

Location	☐ Urban	☒ Suburban	☐ Rural
Built Up	☒ Over 75%	☐ 25% to 75%	☐ Under 25%
Growth Rate ☐ Fully Dev.	☐ Rapid	☐ Steady	☒ Slow
Property Values	☐ Increasing	☒ Stable	☐ Declining
Demand/Supply	☐ Shortage	☒ In Balance	☐ Over Supply
Marketing Time	☒ Under 3 Mos.	☐ 4-6 Mos.	☐ Over 6 Mos.

Present Land Use **75** % 1 Family **5** % 2-4 Family **5** % Apts. ___ % Condo **5** % Commercial
5 % Industrial **5** % Vacant ___ %

Change in Present Land Use ☒ Not Likely ☐ Likely (*) ☐ Taking Place (*)
(*) From ___ To ___

Predominant Occupancy ☒ Owner ☐ Tenant ___ % Vacant

Single Family Price Range $ **35,000** to $ **50,000** Predominant Value $ **40,000**

Single Family Age **25** yrs to **50** yrs Predominant Age **25** yrs

	Good	Avg.	Fair	Poor
Employment Stability	☐	☒	☐	☐
Convenience to Employment	☐	☒	☐	☐
Convenience to Shopping	☐	☒	☐	☐
Convenience to Schools	☐	☒	☐	☐
Adequacy of Public Transportation	☐	☒	☐	☐
Recreational Facilities	☐	☒	☐	☐
Adequacy of Utilities	☐	☒	☐	☐
Property Compatibility	☒	☐	☐	☐
Protection from Detrimental Conditions	☐	☒	☐	☐
Police and Fire Protection	☐	☒	☐	☐
General Appearance of Properties	☐	☒	☐	☐
Appeal to Market	☐	☒	☐	☐

Note: FHLMC/FNMA do not consider the racial composition of the neighborhood to be a relevant factor and it must not be considered in the appraisal.
Comments including those factors, favorable or unfavorable, affecting marketability (e.g. public parks, schools, view, noise) **Part of a subdivision of 254 houses built in 1954-55. All houses are same basic type. Income range: $14,000-$16,000. Typical resident is young family in first home. Typical sale is financed with 75% conventional mortgage. Quality of the schools is average.**

SITE

Dimensions **66' on North Rd. x 132' deep**   • **8,712** Sq. Ft. or Acres   ☐ Corner Lot

Zoning classification **Residential**   Present improvements ☒ do ☐ do not conform to zoning regulations

Highest and best use: ☒ Present use ☐ Other (specify) ___

	Public	Other (Describe)	OFF SITE IMPROVEMENTS		Topo **Level**
Elec.	☒	___	Street Access: ☒ Public ☐ Private		Size **Typical of neighborhood**
Gas	☒	___	Surface **Bituminous paving**		Shape **Rectangular**
Water	☒	___	Maintenance: ☒ Public ☐ Private		View **Typical**
San.Sewer	☒	___	☒ Storm Sewer ☐ Curb/Gutter		Drainage **Typical - Good**

☐ Underground Elect. & Tel. ☒ Sidewalk ☒ Street Lights   Is the property located in a HUD Identified Special Flood Hazard Area? ☒ No ☐ Yes

Comments (favorable or unfavorable including any apparent adverse easements, encroachments or other adverse conditions) ___
* See notes on physical deterioration

IMPROVEMENTS

☒ Existing (approx. yr. blt.) 19 **53**   No. Units **1**   Type (det, duplex, semi/det, etc.) **detached**   Design (rambler, split level, etc.) **ranch**   Exterior Walls **⅝" redwood**
☐ Proposed ☐ Under Construction   No. Stories **1**

Roof Material **asphalt shingles**   Gutters & Downspouts ☐ None **galvanized sheet metal**   Window (Type): **double hung**   Insulation ☐ None ☒ Floor
☐ Storm Sash ☐ Screens ☒ Combination   ☒ Ceiling ☐ Roof ☒ Walls

Foundation Walls **concrete**

BSMT.
O % Basement ☐ Floor Drain   Finished Ceiling ___
☐ Outside Entrance ☐ Sump Pump   Finished Walls ___
☐ Concrete Floor ___ % Finished   Finished Floor ___
Evidence of: ☐ Dampness ☐ Termites ☐ Settlement

☐ Crawl Space
☒ Slab on Grade

Comments ___

ROOM LIST

Room List	Foyer	Living	Dining	Kitchen	Den	Family Rm.	Rec. Rm.	Bedrooms	No. Baths	Laundry	Other
Basement											
1st Level		1		1				3	1		
2nd Level											

Finished area above grade contains a total of **5** rooms, **3** bedrooms, **1** baths.

Kitchen Equipment: ☐ Refrigerator ☐ Range/Oven ☐ Disposal ☐ Dishwasher ☐ Fan/Hood ☐ Compactor ☐ Washer ☐ Dryer ☐

HEAT: Type **hot air** Fuel **gas** Cond. **good**   AIR COND: ☐ Central ☐ Other ___ ☐ Adequate ☐ Inadequate

INTERIOR FINISH & EQUIPMENT

Floors	☒ Hardwood	☐ Carpet Over ___	
Walls	☒ Drywall	☐ Plaster ___	
Trim/Finish	☐ Good	☒ Average ☐ Fair ☐ Poor	
Bath Floor	☐ Ceramic	☒ **asphalt tile**	
Bath Wainscot	☐ Ceramic	☒ **4" plastic tile**	

Special Features (including fireplaces): ___

ATTIC: ☐ Yes ☒ No ☐ Stairway ☐ Drop-stair ☐ Scuttle ☐ Floored
Finished (Describe) ___ ☐ Heated

CAR STORAGE: ☐ Garage ☐ Built-in ☒ Attached ☐ Detached ☒ Car Port
No. Cars **1** ☒ Adequate ☐ Inadequate Condition **Average**

PROPERTY RATING

	Good	Avg.	Fair	Poor
Quality of Construction (Materials & Finish)	☐	☒	☐	☐
Condition of Improvements	☐	☒	☐	☐
Rooms size and layout	☐	☒	☐	☐
Closets and Storage	☐	☐	☒	☐
Plumbing—adequacy and condition	☐	☒	☐	☐
Electrical—adequacy and condition	☐	☒	☐	☐
Kitchen Cabinets—adequacy and condition	☐	☒	☐	☐
Compatibility to Neighborhood	☒	☐	☐	☐
Overall Livability	☐	☒	☐	☐
Appeal and Marketability	☐	☒	☐	☐

Effective Age **20** Yrs. Est. Remaining Economic Life **40** Yrs.

PORCHES, PATIOS, POOL, FENCES, etc. (describe) **3.5' x 9' storage area in rear of carport**

COMMENTS (including functional or physical inadequacies, repairs needed, modernization, etc.)
Kitchen & bathroom tiles need repair
Driveway has ruts & needs repair
Entrance into kitchen and kitchen in front of house accepted in this market

FHLMC Form 70 Rev. 7/77   ATTACH DESCRIPTIVE PHOTOGRAPHS OF SUBJECT PROPERTY AND STREET SCENE   FNMA Form 1004 Rev. 7/77

VALUATION SECTION

Purpose of Appraisal is to estimate Market Value as defined in Certification & Statement of Limiting Conditions (FHLMC Form 439/FNMA Form 1004B). If submitted for FNMA, the appraiser must attach (1) sketch or map showing location of subject, street names, distance from nearest intersection, and any detrimental conditions and (2) exterior building sketch of improvements showing dimensions.

COST APPROACH

Measurements		No. Stories		Sq. Ft.
24 × 44	×	1	=	1,056
	×	×	=	
	×	×	=	
	×	×	=	
	×	×	=	
	×	×	=	

Total Gross Living Area (List in Market Data Analysis below) 1,056

Comment on functional and economic obsolescence:
Traffic on Stevenson Rd. causes economic obsolescence estimated to be $975.

Estimated physical incurable deterioration is $20,100.

ESTIMATED REPRODUCTION COST – NEW – OF IMPROVEMENTS:

Dwelling 1,056 Sq. Ft. @ $ 47.64	= $ 50,300
Sq. Ft. @ $	=
Extras	=
	=
	=
Porches, Patios, etc.	=
Garage/Car Port Sq. Ft. @ $	= 2,700
Site Improvements (driveway, landscaping, etc.)	= 1,000
Total Estimated Cost New	= $ 54,000

Less | Physical | Functional | Economic |
Depreciation $ 20,675 | $ — | $ 975 | = $ 21,650
Depreciated value of improvements . . . . = $ 32,350
ESTIMATED LAND VALUE . . . . = $ 9,000
(If leasehold, show only leasehold value)

INDICATED VALUE BY COST APPROACH . . . $ 41,400 (Rd.)

The undersigned has recited three recent sales of properties most similar and proximate to subject and has considered these in the market analysis. The description includes a dollar adjustment, reflecting market reaction to those items of significant variation between the subject and comparable properties. If a significant item in the comparable property is superior to, or more favorable than, the subject property, a minus (-) adjustment is made, thus reducing the indicated value of subject; if a significant item in the comparable is inferior to, or less favorable than, the subject property, a plus (+) adjustment is made, thus increasing the indicated value of the subject.

MARKET DATA ANALYSIS

ITEM	Subject Property	COMPARABLE NO. 1		COMPARABLE NO. 2		COMPARABLE NO. 3	
Address	33 North Road Typicaltown	65 North Road Typicaltown		38 Cottken Street Typicaltown		23 McKinley Street Typicaltown	
Proximity to Subj.		Same street		1 Block north		1 Block south	
Sales Price	$ 41,500		$ 46,000		$ 42,300		$ 44,700
Price/Living area	$ 39.30		$ 39.48		$ 36.47		$ 38.21
Data Source	Lender	Grantee-Atwood		MLS		MLS	
Date of Sale and Time Adjustment	DESCRIPTION 6-8-7-	DESCRIPTION 5-18-7-	+/-$ Adjustment -	DESCRIPTION 11-14-7-	+/-$ Adjustment +4,500	DESCRIPTION 10-28-7-	+/-$ Adjustment +4,150
Location	Average	Equal	-	Equal		Equal	
Site/View	Good/Good	Larger/Equal	-400	Larger/Equal	-1,500	Larger/Equal	-950
Design and Appeal	Average	Equal	-	Equal	-	Equal	-
Quality of Const.	Average	Equal	-	Equal	-	Equal	-
Age	20 yrs.	Equal	-	Equal	-	Equal	-
Condition	Average	Equal	-	Equal	-	Equal	-
Living Area Room Count and Total	Total 5 B-rms 3 Baths 1	Total 6 B-rms 3 Baths 1	-4,300	Total 6 B-rms 3 Baths 1	-4,000	Total 5 B-rms 3 Baths 1	-4,150
Gross Living Area	1,056 Sq.Ft.	1,165 Sq.Ft.		1,160 Sq.Ft.		1,170 Sq.Ft.	
Basement & Bsmt. Finished Rooms	Slab	Equal	-	Equal		Equal	-
Functional Utility	Average	Equal	-	Equal	-	Equal	-
Air Conditioning	None	Equal	-	Equal	-	Equal	-
Garage/Car Port	car port (1)	Equal	-	Equal	-	2-car det.	-2,450
Porches, Patio, Pools, etc.	None	Equal	-	Equal	-	Equal	-
Other (e.g. fireplaces, kitchen equip., heating, remodeling)	No kitchen or laundry equipment	Equal	-	Equal	-	Equal	-
Sales or Financing Concessions	75% conv. No concessions	Equal	-	Equal	-	Equal	-
Net Adj. (Total)		☐ Plus; ☒ Minus $ 4,700		☐ Plus; ☒ Minus $ 1,000		☐ Plus; ☒ Minus $ 3,400	
Indicated Value of Subject		$ 41,300		$ 41,300		$ 41,300	

Comments on Market Data Equal weight given to each sale. Excellent market data

INDICATED VALUE BY MARKET DATA APPROACH . . . . $ 41,300

INDICATED VALUE BY INCOME APPROACH (If applicable) Economic Market Rent $ 315 /Mo. x Gross Rent Multiplier 130 = $ 40,950

This appraisal is made ☒ "as is" ☐ subject to the repairs, alterations, or conditions listed below ☐ completion per plans and specifications.

Comments and Conditions of Appraisal: Estimated cost of kitchen and bathroom tile repair is $275. Estimated cost of driveway repair is $300.

Final Reconciliation: $41,300 indicated by market data approach is the best indication of the final value. It is well supported by the $41,400 indicated by the cost approach and the $40,950 indicated by the income approach.

This appraisal is based upon the above requirements, the certification, contingent and limiting conditions, and Market Value definition that are stated in

☐ FHLMC Form 439 (Rev. 9/75)/FNMA Form 1004B filed with client _____ 19 ___ ☒ attached.

If submitted for FNMA, the report has been prepared in compliance with FNMA form instructions.

I ESTIMATE THE MARKET VALUE, AS DEFINED, OF SUBJECT PROPERTY AS OF June 19 197- to be $ 41,300

Appraiser(s) Leslie E. Clinton _____ Review Appraiser (If applicable) _____

☐ Did ☐ Did Not Physically Inspect Property

FHLMC Form 70 Rev. 7/77 | REVERSE | SAF (American Savings and Accounting Supply Inc.) (2502-3)

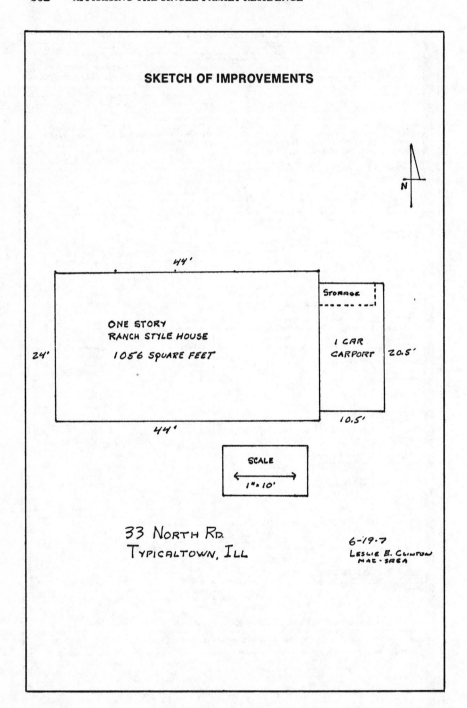

SKETCH OF IMPROVEMENTS

N

44'

ONE STORY
RANCH STYLE HOUSE

1056 SQUARE FEET

24'

STORAGE

1 CAR
CARPORT

20.5'

44'

10.5'

SCALE

1" = 10'

33 NORTH RD.
TYPICALTOWN, ILL

6-19-7

LESLIE E. CLINTON
MAE - SREA

NEIGHBORHOOD MAP

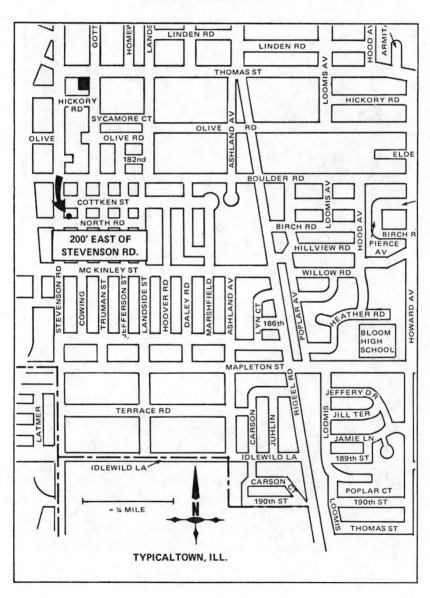

TYPICALTOWN, ILL.

PHOTOGRAPHS OF 33 NORTH ROAD

PHOTOGRAPHS OF THE SUBJECT STREET

NORTH STREET — LOOKING EAST

NORTH STREET — LOOKING WEST

DEFINITION OF MARKET VALUE: The highest price in terms of money which a property will bring in a competitive and open market under all conditions requisite to a fair sale, the buyer and seller, each acting prudently, knowledgeably and assuming the price is not affected by undue stimulus. Implicit in this definition is the consummation of a sale as of a specified date and the passing of title from seller to buyer under conditions whereby: (1) buyer and seller are typically motivated; (2) both parties are well informed or well advised, and each acting in what he considers his own best interest; (3) a reasonable time is allowed for exposure in the open market; (4) payment is made in cash or its equivalent; (5) financing, if any, is on terms generally available in the community at the specified date and typical for the property type in its locale; (6) the price represents a normal consideration for the property sold unaffected by special financing amounts and/or terms, services, fees, costs, or credits incurred in the transaction. ("Real Estate Appraisal Terminology," published 1975.)

CERTIFICATION AND STATEMENT OF LIMITING CONDITIONS

CERTIFICATION: The Appraiser certifies and agrees that:

1. The Appraiser has no present or contemplated future interest in the property appraised; and neither the employment to make the appraisal, nor the compensation for it, is contingent upon the appraised value of the property.

2. The Appraiser has no personal interest in or bias with respect to the subject matter of the appraisal report or the participants to the sale. The "Estimate of Market Value" in the appraisal report is not based in whole or in part upon the race, color, or national origin of the prospective owners or occupants of the property appraised, or upon the race, color or national origin of the present owners or occupants of the properties in the vicinity of the property appraised.

3. The Appraiser has personally inspected the property, both inside and out, and has made an exterior inspection of all comparable sales listed in the report. To the best of the Appraiser's knowledge and belief, all statements and information in this report are true and correct, and the Appraiser has not knowingly withheld any significant information.

4. All contingent and limiting conditions are contained herein (imposed by the terms of the assignment or by the undersigned affecting the analyses, opinions, and conclusions contained in the report).

5. This appraisal report has been made in conformity with and is subject to the requirements of the Code of Professional Ethics and Standards of Professional Conduct of the appraisal organizations with which the Appraiser is affiliated.

6. All conclusions and opinions concerning the real estate that are set forth in the appraisal report were prepared by the Appraiser whose signature appears on the appraisal report, unless indicated as "Review Appraiser." No change of any item in the appraisal report shall be made by anyone other than the Appraiser, and the Appraiser shall have no responsibility for any such unauthorized change.

CONTINGENT AND LIMITING CONDITIONS: The certification of the Appraiser appearing in the appraisal report is subject to the following conditions and to such other specific and limiting conditions as are set forth by the Appraiser in the report.

1. The Appraiser assumes no responsibility for matters of a legal nature affecting the property appraised or the title thereto, nor does the Appraiser render any opinion as to the title, which is assumed to be good and marketable. The property is appraised as though under responsible ownership.

2. Any sketch in the report may show approximate dimensions and is included to assist the reader in visualizing the property. The Appraiser has made no survey of the property.

3. The Appraiser is not required to give testimony or appear in court because of having made the appraisal with reference to the property in question, unless arrangements have been previously made therefor.

4. Any distribution of the valuation in the report between land and improvements applies only under the existing program of utilization. The separate valuations for land and building must not be used in conjunction with any other appraisal and are invalid if so used.

5. The Appraiser assumes that there are no hidden or unapparent conditions of the property, subsoil, or structures, which would render it more or less valuable. The Appraiser assumes no responsibility for such conditions, or for engineering which might be required to discover such factors.

6. Information, estimates, and opinions furnished to the Appraiser, and contained in the report, were obtained from sources considered reliable and believed to be true and correct. However, no responsibility for accuracy of such items furnished the Appraiser can be assumed by the Appraiser.

7. Disclosure of the contents of the appraisal report is governed by the Bylaws and Regulations of the professional appraisal organizations with which the Appraiser is affiliated.

8. Neither all, nor any part of the content of the report, or copy thereof (including conclusions as to the property value, the identity of the Appraiser, professional designations, reference to any professional appraisal organizations, or the firm with which the Appraiser is connected), shall be used for any purposes by anyone but the client specified in the report, the mortgagee or its successors and assigns, mortgage insurers, consultants, professional appraisal organizations, any state or federally approved financial institution, any department, agency, or instrumentality of the United States or any state or the District of Columbia, without the previous written consent of the Appraiser; nor shall it be conveyed by anyone to the public through advertising, public relations, news, sales, or other media, without the written consent and approval of the Appraiser.

9. On all appraisals, subject to satisfactory completion, repairs, or alterations, the appraisal report and value conclusion are contingent upon completion of the improvements in a workmanlike manner.

Date:. 6/19/7-   Appraiser(s) . Leslie E Clinton

PHLMC FORM 439 REV. 9/75   FNMA FORM 1004B

Appendix C:
Metric Conversion Tables

Linear Measurements

1 inch	=	2.54 centimeters
1 foot	=	30.48 centimeters or .3048 meters
1 yard	=	.9144 meters or 91.44 centimeters
1 mile	=	1.609347 kilometers or 1609.347 meters
1 centimeter	=	0.3937 inches
1 meter	=	3.2808 feet
1 kilometer	=	.62135 miles

Square Measurements

1 square inch	=	6.4516 square centimeters
1 square foot	=	.0929 square meters
1 square yard	=	.83613 square meters
1 acre	=	40.467 square meters
1 square mile	=	2.59 square kilometers
1 square centimeter	=	.1550 square inches
1 square meter	=	1550 square inches or 10.764 square feet
1 square kilometer	=	.3861 square miles

Land Measurements

Linear Measurements

12 inches	=	1 foot
3 feet	=	1 yard
5½ yards (16½ ft.)	=	1 rod
40 rods	=	1 furlong
8 furlongs (320 rods or 5,280 feet)	=	1 mile
7.92 inches	=	1 link
25 links	=	1 rod
4 rods (66 feet)	=	1 chain
80 chains	=	1 mile

Square Measurements

43,560 square feet	=	1 acre
144 square inches	=	1 square foot
9 square feet	=	1 square yard
30¼ square yards	=	1 square rod
40 square rods	=	1 rood
4 roods (43,560 sq. ft.)	=	1 acre
640 acres	=	1 square mile
625 square links	=	1 pole
16 poles	=	1 square chain
10 square chains	=	1 acre
640 acres	=	1 square mile
36 square miles	=	1 township

Appendix D: Mortgage Tables

The mortgage tables on the following pages are included to provide the reader with a broad range of information about the mortgages commonly written to secure loans on single family residences. The tables cover annual interest rates ranging from 6% to 12% in quarter percent intervals and terms from 5 to 30 years in 5-year intervals.

The tables give the monthly payment for each of these mortgages and the balance of the loan remaining at the end of each year throughout the life of the loan. Payments for loans of other terms and balances for periods during the year can be calculated approximately by simple interpolation.

All the figures shown are for $1,000 initial loans. The figures can be directly converted for other loan amounts by multiplying them by the amount of the loan to be calculated. For example, the monthly payment for a 9.25%, 20-year mortgage is shown as $9.16. This is the payment for a $1,000 loan. To find the payment for a $17,250 loan at the same interest and for the same term, multiply $9.16 by $17,250 which gives $158,010. Since the table is per thousand dollars move the decimal point three places to the left, giving $158.01.

The balance at the end of 18 years for the same loan is shown as $199.97. Again, multiply by $17,250 and move the decimal point three places to the left. ($199.97 x $17,250 = 3449482.5 converted to $3,449.48). When using these tables, multiply the shown figure by the amount of the loan and move the decimal point three places to the left.

6% MONTHLY MORTGAGE PAYMENTS

Monthly Payments (Debt Service Requirements) and Projected Loan Balances
Per $1,000 of Loan

Mortgage Term	5 YR.	10 YR.	15 YR.	20 YR.	25 YR.	30 YR.
Monthly Payments	$19.33	$11.10	$ 8.44	$ 7.16	$ 6.44	$ 6.00

Year-end Mortgage Balances

Year						
1	823.20	924.73	957.58	973.30	982.20	987.72
2	635.49	844.81	912.55	944.96	963.30	974.68
3	436.20	759.97	864.74	914.86	943.24	960.84
4	224.63	669.89	813.98	882.92	921.94	946.15
5	000.00	574.26	760.09	849.00	899.32	930.54
6		472.73	702.88	812.98	875.31	913.98
7		364.94	642.13	774.75	849.82	896.39
8		250.49	577.65	734.16	822.76	877.72
9		128.99	509.18	691.07	794.02	857.90
10		000.00	436.49	645.31	763.52	836.86
11			359.32	596.74	731.13	814.51
12			277.38	545.17	696.75	790.79
13			190.40	490.42	660.25	765.61
14			098.05	432.29	621.49	738.87
15			000.00	370.58	580.34	710.49
16				305.06	536.66	680.35
17				235.50	490.28	648.36
18				161.65	441.04	614.39
19				083.24	388.77	578.32
20				000.00	333.27	540.04
21					274.35	499.39
22					211.79	456.23
23					145.37	410.41
24					074.86	361.77
25					000.00	310.12
26						255.29
27						197.08
28						135.28
29						069.66
30						000.00

6¼% MONTHLY MORTGAGE PAYMENTS

Monthly Payments (Debt Service Requirements) and Projected Loan Balances
Per $1,000 of Loan

Mortgage Term	5 YR.	10 YR.	15 YR.	20 YR.	25 YR.	30 YR.
Monthly Payments	$19.45	$11.23	$ 8.57	$ 7.31	$ 6.60	$ 6.16

Year-end Mortgage Balances

Year						
1	824.13	925.66	958.43	974.05	982.85	988.28
2	636.94	846.53	914.19	946.44	964.61	975.81
3	437.72	762.32	867.10	917.05	945.18	962.54
4	225.68	672.69	816.99	885.77	924.51	948.41
5	000.00	577.30	763.65	852.47	902.51	933.37
6		475.77	706.88	817.04	879.09	917.37
7		367.71	646.45	779.32	854.17	900.34
8		252.69	582.14	739.18	827.64	882.21
9		130.28	513.70	696.46	799.41	862.91
10		000.00	440.85	650.99	769.36	842.38
11			363.32	602.59	737.38	820.52
12			280.80	551.08	703.34	797.26
13			192.97	496.26	667.12	772.50
14			099.49	437.91	628.56	746.15
15			000.00	375.81	587.52	718.10
16				309.72	543.84	688.25
17				239.37	497.36	656.48
18				164.50	447.88	622.67
19				084.81	395.22	586.68
20				000.00	339.17	548.38
21					279.52	507.61
22					216.03	464.22
23					148.46	418.04
24					076.54	368.89
25					000.00	316.58
26						260.90
27						201.64
28						138.57
29						071.44
30						000.00

6½% MONTHLY MORTGAGE PAYMENTS

Monthly Payments (Debt Service Requirements) and Projected Loan Balances
Per $1,000 of Loan

Mortgage Term	5 YR.	10 YR.	15 YR.	20 YR.	25 YR.	30 YR.
Monthly Payments	$19.57	$11.35	$ 8.71	$ 7.46	$ 6.75	$ 6.32

Year-end Mortgage Balances

Year						
1	825.06	926.58	959.27	974.79	983.49	988.82
2	638.39	848.24	915.81	947.89	965.87	976.90
3	439.23	764.66	869.44	919.19	947.08	964.17
4	226.73	675.48	819.96	888.57	927.02	950.60
5	000.00	580.33	767.17	855.89	905.62	936.11
6		478.80	710.85	821.03	882.79	920.65
7		370.48	650.75	783.83	858.43	904.16
8		254.90	586.63	744.14	832.44	886.57
9		131.58	518.21	701.80	804.70	867.79
10		000.00	445.21	656.62	775.11	847.76
11			367.32	608.41	743.54	826.39
12			284.22	556.97	709.86	803.58
13			195.55	502.09	673.91	779.25
14			100.94	443.53	635.56	753.29
15			000.00	381.05	594.64	725.59
16				314.39	550.99	696.04
17				243.26	504.40	664.50
18				167.37	454.70	630.86
19				086.40	401.67	594.96
20				000.00	345.09	556.65
21					284.72	515.78
22					220.30	472.18
23					151.57	425.65
24					078.24	376.01
25					000.00	323.04
26						266.53
27						206.23
28						141.89
29						073.24
30						000.00

6¾% MONTHLY MORTGAGE PAYMENTS

Monthly Payments (Debt Service Requirements) and Projected Loan Balances
Per $1,000 of Loan

Mortgage Term	5 YR.	10 YR.	15 YR.	20 YR.	25 YR.	30 YR.
Monthly Payments	$19.68	$11.48	$ 8.85	$ 7.60	$ 6.91	$ 6.49

Year-end Mortgage Balances

Year	5 YR.	10 YR.	15 YR.	20 YR.	25 YR.	30 YR.
1	825.98	927.50	960.09	975.51	984.10	989.34
2	639.84	849.94	917.40	949.31	967.10	977.94
3	440.75	766.99	871.74	921.29	948.92	965.75
4	227.79	678.26	822.90	891.32	929.47	952.71
5	000.00	583.35	770.67	859.26	908.66	938.76
6		481.84	714.79	824.96	886.40	923.84
7		373.25	655.02	788.28	862.60	907.87
8		257.11	591.09	749.05	837.14	890.80
9		132.88	522.71	707.09	809.90	872.54
10		000.00	449.57	662.20	780.77	853.01
11			371.34	614.19	749.61	832.12
12			287.65	562.83	716.28	809.77
13			198.15	507.90	680.63	785.87
14			102.41	449.14	642.50	760.30
15			000.00	386.30	601.71	732.95
16				319.07	558.09	703.70
17				247.17	511.42	672.41
18				170.26	461.51	638.95
19				087.99	408.12	603.15
20				000.00	351.01	564.86
21					289.93	523.91
22					224.59	480.10
23					154.71	433.24
24					079.96	383.12
25					000.00	329.51
26						272.17
27						210.84
28						145.23
29						075.06
30						000.00

7% MONTHLY MORTGAGE PAYMENTS

Monthly Payments (Debt Service Requirements) and Projected Loan Balances
Per $1,000 of Loan

Mortgage Term	5 YR.	10 YR.	15 YR.	20 YR.	25 YR.	30 YR.
Monthly Payments	$19.80	$11.61	$ 8.99	$ 7.75	$ 7.07	$ 6.65

Year-end Mortgage Balances

Year						
1	826.90	928.40	960.90	976.21	984.70	989.84
2	641.29	851.63	918.98	950.70	968.30	978.95
3	442.26	769.30	874.02	923.35	950.71	967.27
4	228.84	681.03	825.82	894.02	931.85	954.75
5	000.00	586.37	774.13	862.57	911.62	941.32
6		484.87	718.70	828.84	889.93	926.92
7		376.03	659.27	792.68	866.68	911.47
8		259.33	595.54	753.90	841.74	894.92
9		134.19	527.20	712.32	815.01	877.16
10		000.00	453.93	667.74	786.33	858.12
11			375.35	619.93	755.59	837.71
12			291.10	568.66	722.62	815.82
13			200.75	513.69	687.27	792.35
14			103.88	454.75	649.37	767.18
15			000.00	391.54	608.72	740.19
16				323.77	565.14	711.25
17				251.09	518.41	680.22
18				173.16	468.29	646.94
19				089.60	414.56	611.26
20				000.00	356.94	573.00
21					295.15	531.97
22					228.90	487.98
23					157.86	440.81
24					081.68	390.23
25					000.00	335.99
26						277.83
27						215.47
28						148.60
29						076.89
30						000.00

7¼% MONTHLY MORTGAGE PAYMENTS

Monthly Payments (Debt Service Requirements) and Projected Loan Balances
Per $1,000 of Loan

Mortgage Term	5 YR.	10 YR.	15 YR.	20 YR.	25 YR.	30 YR.
Monthly Payments	$19.92	$11.74	$ 9.13	$ 7.90	$ 7.23	$ 6.82

Year-end Mortgage Balances

Year						
1	827.82	929.30	961.70	976.90	985.28	990.32
2	642.74	853.30	920.53	952.06	969.46	979.92
3	443.78	771.60	876.27	925.37	952.45	968.73
4	229.90	683.78	828.70	896.67	934.16	956.71
5	000.00	589.38	777.56	865.82	914.51	943.79
6		487.90	722.59	832.66	893.38	929.90
7		378.82	663.49	797.01	870.67	914.96
8		261.55	599.97	758.70	846.26	898.91
9		135.50	531.68	717.51	820.01	881.65
10		000.00	458.28	673.23	791.80	863.10
11			379.37	625.63	761.48	843.16
12			294.55	574.47	728.88	821.73
13			203.37	519.47	693.84	798.69
14			105.36	460.34	656.17	773.92
15			000.00	396.79	615.67	747.29
16				328.47	572.15	718.67
17				255.03	525.35	687.91
18				176.09	475.06	654.83
19				091.22	420.99	619.28
20				000.00	362.87	581.06
21					300.39	539.98
22					233.23	495.82
23					161.03	448.35
24					083.42	397.32
25					000.00	342.47
26						283.50
27						220.12
28						151.98
29						078.74
30						000.00

7½% MONTHLY MORTGAGE PAYMENTS

Monthly Payments (Debt Service Requirements) and Projected Loan Balances
Per $1,000 of Loan

Mortgage Term	5 YR.	10 YR.	15 YR.	20 YR.	25 YR.	30 YR.
Monthly Payments	$20.04	$11.87	$ 9.27	$ 8.06	$ 7.39	$ 6.99

Year-end Mortgage Balances

Year						
1	828.74	930.19	962.49	977.57	985.84	990.78
2	644.18	854.96	922.06	953.39	970.58	980.85
3	445.29	773.89	878.50	927.34	954.14	970.14
4	230.97	686.53	831.55	899.27	936.42	958.61
5	000.00	592.38	780.96	869.02	917.33	946.17
6		490.93	726.44	836.42	896.75	932.78
7		381.60	667.69	801.29	874.57	918.34
8		263.78	604.38	763.43	850.68	902.78
9		136.82	536.15	722.63	824.93	886.02
10		000.00	462.63	678.67	797.18	867.95
11			383.40	631.29	767.27	848.48
12			298.02	580.24	735.04	827.50
13			206.00	525.22	700.32	804.89
14			106.85	465.93	662.89	780.52
15			000.00	402.03	622.56	754.27
16				333.18	579.10	725.97
17				258.98	532.27	695.48
18				179.02	481.80	662.62
19				092.86	427.41	627.21
20				000.00	368.80	589.05
21					305.63	547.93
22					237.57	503.62
23					164.22	455.86
24					085.18	404.40
25					000.00	348.95
26						289.18
27						224.78
28						155.38
29						080.59
30						000.00

7¾% MONTHLY MORTGAGE PAYMENTS

Monthly Payments (Debt Service Requirements) and Projected Loan Balances
Per $1,000 of Loan

Mortgage Term	5 YR.	10 YR.	15 YR.	20 YR.	25 YR.	30 YR.
Monthly Payments	$20.16	$12.00	$ 9.41	$ 8.21	$ 7.55	$ 7.16

Year-end Mortgage Balances

Year						
1	829.65	931.07	963.26	978.22	986.38	991.22
2	645.62	856.61	923.57	954.70	971.67	981.74
3	446.81	776.17	880.69	929.28	955.78	971.50
4	232.03	689.26	834.37	901.83	938.61	960.43
5	000.00	595.38	784.33	872.17	920.07	948.48
6		493.96	730.27	840.12	900.03	935.56
7		384.39	671.86	805.51	878.39	921.61
8		266.02	608.77	768.11	855.00	906.54
9		138.15	540.61	727.71	829.74	890.25
10		000.00	466.97	684.06	802.45	872.66
11			387.42	636.91	772.97	853.66
12			301.49	585.98	741.12	833.13
13			208.65	530.95	706.71	810.95
14			108.35	471.50	669.54	786.99
15			000.00	407.28	629.38	761.11
16				337.90	586.00	733.14
17				262.95	539.14	702.94
18				181.97	488.51	670.30
19				094.50	433.81	635.04
20				000.00	374.72	596.96
21					310.89	555.81
22					241.93	511.36
23					167.43	463.34
24					086.95	411.46
25					000.00	355.42
26						294.87
27						229.46
28						158.80
29						082.47
30						000.00

8% MONTHLY MORTGAGE PAYMENTS

Monthly Payments (Debt Service Requirements) and Projected Loan Balances
Per $1,000 of Loan

Mortgage Term	5 YR.	10 YR.	15 YR.	20 YR.	25 YR.	30 YR.
Monthly Payments	$20.28	$12.13	$ 9.56	$ 8.36	$ 7.72	$ 7.34

Year-end Mortgage Balances

Year						
1	830.56	931.95	964.02	978.86	986.91	991.65
2	647.06	858.25	925.06	955.97	972.73	982.60
3	448.32	778.43	882.86	931.18	957.38	972.80
4	233.09	691.99	837.16	904.33	940.75	962.19
5	000.00	598.37	787.66	875.26	922.74	950.70
6		496.98	734.06	843.77	903.24	938.25
7		387.18	676.01	809.66	882.11	924.77
8		268.26	613.14	772.73	859.24	910.18
9		139.48	545.05	732.73	834.46	894.37
10		000.00	471.31	689.41	807.63	877.25
11			391.45	642.49	778.58	858.70
12			304.97	591.68	747.11	838.62
13			211.30	536.65	713.03	816.88
14			109.86	477.06	676.12	793.32
15			000.00	412.52	636.14	767.82
16				342.62	592.85	740.19
17				266.92	545.97	710.27
18				184.94	495.19	677.87
19				096.16	440.20	642.78
20				000.00	380.65	604.78
21					316.15	563.62
22					246.30	519.05
23					170.65	470.78
24					088.73	418.50
25					000.00	361.88
26						300.56
27						234.16
28						162.24
29						084.35
30						000.00

8¼% MONTHLY MORTGAGE PAYMENTS

Monthly Payments (Debt Service Requirements) and Projected Loan Balances
Per $1,000 of Loan

Mortgage Term	5 YR.	10 YR.	15 YR.	20 YR.	25 YR.	30 YR.
Monthly Payments	$20.40	$12.27	$ 9.70	$ 8.52	$ 7.88	$ 7.51

Year-end Mortgage Balances

Year						
1	831.47	932.81	964.77	979.49	987.42	992.05
2	648.49	859.87	926.52	957.22	973.76	983.42
3	449.84	780.68	885.00	933.04	958.92	974.05
4	234.16	694.70	839.91	906.79	942.82	963.88
5	000.00	601.35	790.97	878.29	925.34	952.84
6		500.00	737.82	847.35	906.36	940.85
7		389.97	680.13	813.76	885.75	927.83
8		270.51	617.49	777.29	863.38	913.70
9		140.81	549.48	737.69	839.09	898.36
10		000.00	475.65	694.70	812.72	881.70
11			395.48	648.02	784.09	863.61
12			308.45	597.35	753.00	843.98
13			213.96	542.33	719.25	822.66
14			111.38	482.60	682.61	799.52
15			000.00	417.76	642.83	774.39
16				347.35	599.64	747.11
17				270.91	552.75	717.49
18				187.92	501.84	685.33
19				097.82	446.57	650.42
20				000.00	386.57	612.52
21					321.42	571.36
22					250.69	526.68
23					173.89	478.18
24					090.52	425.51
25					000.00	368.34
26						306.26
27						238.86
28						165.69
29						086.25
30						000.00

8½% MONTHLY MORTGAGE PAYMENTS

Monthly Payments (Debt Service Requirements) and Projected Loan Balances
Per $1,000 of Loan

Mortgage Term	5 YR.	10 YR.	15 YR.	20 YR.	25 YR.	30 YR.
Monthly Payments	$20.52	$12.40	$ 9.85	$ 8.68	$ 8.05	$ 7.69

Year-end Mortgage Balances

Year	5 YR.	10 YR.	15 YR.	20 YR.	25 YR.	30 YR.
1	832.37	933.67	965.51	980.10	987.91	992.44
2	649.92	861.48	927.97	958.44	974.75	984.21
3	451.35	782.91	887.11	934.86	960.43	975.26
4	235.23	697.40	842.64	909.20	944.84	965.51
5	000.00	604.32	794.24	881.27	927.87	954.90
6		503.02	741.56	850.88	909.40	943.36
7		392.76	684.22	817.79	889.30	930.79
8		272.76	621.82	781.78	867.43	917.11
9		142.15	553.90	742.59	843.62	902.23
10		000.00	479.97	699.94	817.71	886.03
11			399.52	653.51	789.50	868.39
12			311.95	602.98	758.80	849.20
13			216.64	547.99	725.39	828.31
14			112.90	488.13	689.03	805.57
15			000.00	422.99	649.45	780.83
16				352.08	606.38	753.90
17				274.91	559.49	724.58
18				190.92	508.46	692.68
19				099.50	452.92	657.96
20				000.00	392.48	620.16
21					326.69	579.03
22					255.08	534.26
23					177.15	485.53
24					092.32	432.50
25					000.00	374.78
26						311.95
27						243.58
28						169.16
29						088.16
30						000.00

8¾% MONTHLY MORTGAGE PAYMENTS

Monthly Payments (Debt Service Requirements) and Projected Loan Balances
Per $1,000 of Loan

Mortgage Term	5 YR.	10 YR.	15 YR.	20 YR.	25 YR.	30 YR.
Monthly Payments	$20.64	$12.53	$ 9.99	$ 8.84	$ 8.22	$ 7.87

Year-end Mortgage Balances

Year						
1	833.27	934.52	966.23	980.69	988.38	992.81
2	651.36	863.08	929.39	959.63	975.71	984.97
3	452.87	785.13	889.19	936.64	961.88	976.41
4	236.30	700.08	845.33	911.56	946.79	967.08
5	000.00	607.28	797.47	884.20	930.33	956.89
6		506.03	745.26	854.34	912.37	945.77
7		395.56	688.29	821.77	892.77	933.65
8		275.02	626.12	786.22	871.39	920.41
9		143.50	558.30	747.44	848.05	905.98
10		000.00	484.29	705.13	822.60	890.22
11			403.55	658.96	794.82	873.04
12			315.45	608.58	764.51	854.28
13			219.32	553.62	731.45	833.82
14			114.44	493.65	695.37	811.49
15			000.00	428.21	656.00	787.13
16				356.82	613.05	760.56
17				278.92	566.18	731.56
18				193.92	515.05	699.91
19				101.19	459.25	665.39
20				000.00	398.38	627.72
21					331.96	586.62
22					259.49	541.77
23					180.41	492.84
24					094.14	439.46
25					000.00	381.20
26						317.65
27						248.30
28						172.64
29						090.08
30						000.00

9% MONTHLY MORTGAGE PAYMENTS

Monthly Payments (Debt Service Requirements) and Projected Loan Balances
Per $1,000 of Loan

Mortgage Term	5 YR.	10 YR.	15 YR.	20 YR.	25 YR.	30 YR.
Monthly Payments	$20.76	$12.67	$10.14	$ 9.00	$ 8.39	$ 8.05

Year-end Mortgage Balances

Year						
1	834.17	935.37	966.95	981.27	988.84	993.17
2	652.78	864.67	930.79	960.79	976.64	985.70
3	454.38	787.34	891.25	938.38	963.29	977.52
4	237.37	702.76	847.99	913.88	948.69	968.58
5	000.00	610.24	800.68	887.07	932.72	958.80
6		509.04	748.93	857.75	915.26	948.10
7		398.35	692.32	825.68	896.15	936.40
8		277.28	630.41	790.60	875.25	923.61
9		144.85	562.68	752.23	852.39	909.61
10		000.00	488.61	710.26	827.39	894.30
11			407.58	664.35	800.04	877.55
12			318.95	614.14	770.13	859.23
13			222.01	559.22	737.41	839.19
14			115.98	499.14	701.62	817.28
15			000.00	433.43	662.48	793.30
16				361.55	619.66	767.08
17				282.94	572.82	738.40
18				196.94	521.59	707.03
19				102.88	465.56	672.72
20				000.00	404.27	635.18
21					337.23	594.13
22					263.90	549.22
23					183.69	500.10
24					095.96	446.38
25					000.00	387.61
26						323.34
27						253.03
28						176.13
29						092.01
30						000.00

9¼% MONTHLY MORTGAGE PAYMENTS

Monthly Payments (Debt Service Requirements) and Projected Loan Balances
Per $1,000 of Loan

Mortgage Term	5 YR.	10 YR.	15 YR.	20 YR.	25 YR.	30 YR.
Monthly Payments	$20.88	$12.80	$10.29	$ 9.16	$ 8.56	$ 8.23

Year-end Mortgage Balances

Year						
1	835.06	936.20	967.65	981.84	989.29	993.51
2	654.21	866.24	932.17	961.92	977.54	986.39
3	455.90	789.53	893.27	940.09	964.66	978.58
4	238.44	705.42	850.62	916.14	950.54	970.03
5	000.00	613.19	803.85	889.89	935.05	960.64
6		512.05	752.57	861.10	918.07	950.35
7		401.15	696.33	829.53	899.45	939.07
8		279.55	634.67	794.92	879.03	926.69
9		146.21	567.05	756.96	856.64	913.13
10		000.00	492.91	715.34	832.09	898.25
11			411.61	669.70	805.17	881.93
12			322.47	619.66	775.65	864.05
13			224.72	564.78	743.29	844.43
14			117.53	504.61	707.79	822.92
15			000.00	438.64	668.88	799.34
16				366.29	626.20	773.48
17				286.96	579.41	745.12
18				199.97	528.10	714.03
19				104.59	471.84	679.94
20				000.00	410.15	642.55
21					342.50	601.56
22					268.32	556.61
23					186.98	507.32
24					097.80	453.27
25					000.00	394.00
26						329.02
27						257.76
28						179.63
29						093.95
30						000.00

9½% MONTHLY MORTGAGE PAYMENTS

Monthly Payments (Debt Service Requirements) and Projected Loan Balances
Per $1,000 of Loan

Mortgage Term	5 YR.	10 YR.	15 YR.	20 YR.	25 YR.	30 YR.
Monthly Payments	$21.00	$12.94	$10.44	$ 9.32	$ 8.74	$ 8.41

Year-end Mortgage Balances

Year						
1	835.96	937.03	968.34	982.39	989.72	993.83
2	655.63	867.81	933.53	963.03	978.41	987.06
3	457.41	791.71	895.27	941.76	965.99	979.60
4	239.52	708.07	853.22	918.37	952.33	971.41
5	000.00	616.12	806.99	892.65	937.31	962.41
6		515.05	756.17	864.39	920.81	952.51
7		403.95	700.31	833.32	902.66	941.63
8		281.82	638.90	799.17	882.72	929.67
9		147.57	571.40	761.63	860.79	916.53
10		000.00	497.21	720.36	836.69	902.08
11			415.64	675.00	810.20	886.19
12			325.98	625.13	781.08	868.73
13			227.43	570.32	749.07	849.54
14			119.09	510.07	713.88	828.44
15			000.00	443.83	675.20	805.24
16				371.03	632.68	779.75
17				290.99	585.95	751.72
18				203.01	534.57	720.91
19				106.31	478.09	687.05
20				000.00	416.01	649.82
21					347.77	608.90
22					272.75	563.92
23					190.29	514.47
24					099.64	460.12
25					000.00	400.37
26						334.69
27						262.50
28						183.13
29						095.90
30						000.00

9¾% MONTHLY MORTGAGE PAYMENTS

Monthly Payments (Debt Service Requirements) and Projected Loan Balances
Per $1,000 of Loan

Mortgage Term	5 YR.	10 YR.	15 YR.	20 YR.	25 YR.	30 YR.
Monthly Payments	$21.12	$13.08	$10.59	$ 9.49	$ 8.91	$ 8.59

Year-end Mortgage Balances

Year						
1	836.85	937.85	969.02	982.93	990.13	994.14
2	657.05	869.36	934.87	964.12	979.25	987.69
3	458.93	793.88	897.25	943.39	967.27	980.58
4	240.60	710.71	855.79	920.54	954.06	972.74
5	000.00	619.05	810.09	895.37	939.51	964.11
6		518.05	759.74	867.62	923.47	954.59
7		406.75	704.26	837.05	905.79	944.11
8		284.10	643.12	803.36	886.32	932.55
9		148.94	575.74	766.24	864.85	919.82
10		000.00	501.49	725.33	841.20	905.79
11			419.67	680.25	815.14	890.32
12			329.51	630.57	786.42	873.28
13			230.15	575.83	754.77	854.51
14			120.66	515.50	719.89	833.81
15			000.00	449.02	681.45	811.01
16				375.76	639.10	785.88
17				295.03	592.42	758.19
18				206.07	540.99	727.68
19				108.03	484.31	694.05
20				000.00	421.86	657.00
21					353.03	616.16
22					277.18	571.16
23					193.60	521.58
24					101.50	466.93
25					000.00	406.71
26						340.36
27						267.23
28						186.65
29						097.85
30						000.00

10% MONTHLY MORTGAGE PAYMENTS

Monthly Payments (Debt Service Requirements) and Projected Loan Balances
Per $1,000 of Loan

Mortgage Term	5 YR.	10 YR.	15 YR.	20 YR.	25 YR.	30 YR.
Monthly Payments	$21.25	$13.22	$10.75	$ 9.65	$ 9.09	$ 8.78

Year-end Mortgage Balances

Year						
1	837.73	938.66	969.68	983.45	990.53	994.44
2	658.47	870.89	936.19	965.17	980.07	988.30
3	460.44	796.03	899.19	944.98	968.51	981.52
4	241.67	713.33	858.32	922.67	955.74	974.02
5	000.00	621.97	813.17	898.02	941.64	965.74
6		521.05	763.29	870.80	926.06	956.60
7		409.55	708.18	840.72	908.84	946.49
8		286.38	647.31	807.50	889.83	935.33
9		150.31	580.06	770.79	868.82	923.00
10		000.00	505.77	730.24	845.61	909.38
11			423.70	685.45	819.98	894.33
12			333.03	635.96	791.66	877.71
13			232.88	581.30	760.37	859.34
14			122.23	520.91	725.81	839.06
15			000.00	454.19	687.62	816.65
16				380.49	645.44	791.89
17				299.07	598.85	764.54
18				209.13	547.37	734.32
19				109.77	490.50	700.94
20				000.00	427.68	664.07
21					358.28	623.33
22					281.62	578.33
23					196.92	528.62
24					103.36	473.70
25					000.00	413.03
26						346.01
27						271.97
28						190.18
29						099.82
30						000.00

10¼% MONTHLY MORTGAGE PAYMENTS

Monthly Payments (Debt Service Requirements) and Projected Loan Balances
Per $1,000 of Loan

Mortgage Term	5 YR.	10 YR.	15 YR.	20 YR.	25 YR.	30 YR.
Monthly Payments	$21.37	$13.35	$10.90	$ 9.82	$ 9.26	$ 8.96

Year-end Mortgage Balances

Year						
1	838.61	939.46	970.34	983.96	990.92	994.72
2	659.89	872.42	937.49	966.20	980.85	988.88
3	461.96	798.17	901.11	946.53	969.71	982.41
4	242.76	715.94	860.82	924.75	957.37	975.25
5	000.00	624.88	816.20	900.63	943.71	967.31
6		524.04	766.79	873.92	928.57	958.52
7		412.35	712.07	844.33	911.81	948.79
8		288.67	651.47	811.57	893.25	938.01
9		151.69	584.36	775.28	872.70	926.08
10		000.00	510.03	735.10	849.93	912.86
11			427.72	690.60	824.72	898.22
12			336.56	641.31	796.80	882.01
13			235.61	586.73	765.88	864.05
14			123.81	526.29	731.64	844.17
15			000.00	459.35	693.72	822.15
16				385.22	651.72	797.76
17				303.12	605.21	770.75
18				212.20	553.70	740.85
19				111.51	496.66	707.72
20				000.00	433.49	671.04
21					363.53	630.42
22					286.06	585.43
23					200.25	535.60
24					105.23	480.43
25					000.00	419.32
26						351.65
27						276.71
28						193.71
29						101.79
30						000.00

10½% MONTHLY MORTGAGE PAYMENTS

Monthly Payments (Debt Service Requirements) and Projected Loan Balances
Per $1,000 of Loan

Mortgage Term	5 YR.	10 YR.	15 YR.	20 YR.	25 YR.	30 YR.
Monthly Payments	$21.49	$13.49	$11.05	$ 9.98	$ 9.44	$ 9.15

Year-end Mortgage Balances

Year						
1	839.49	940.26	970.98	984.46	991.29	994.99
2	661.30	873.93	938.77	967.21	981.61	989.44
3	463.47	800.29	903.00	948.06	970.87	983.27
4	243.84	718.54	863.29	926.79	958.95	976.42
5	000.00	627.78	819.21	903.19	945.71	968.82
6		527.02	770.27	876.98	931.02	960.38
7		415.15	715.93	847.88	914.70	951.00
8		290.96	655.61	815.58	896.59	940.60
9		153.08	588.64	779.71	876.48	929.05
10		000.00	514.28	739.90	854.15	916.22
11			431.74	695.69	829.37	901.99
12			340.10	646.62	801.85	886.18
13			238.36	592.14	771.30	868.63
14			125.40	531.65	737.39	849.15
15			000.00	464.49	699.73	827.52
16				389.94	657.93	803.51
17				307.17	611.52	776.85
18				215.28	559.99	747.25
19				113.26	502.79	714.39
20				000.00	439.28	677.91
21					368.77	637.41
22					290.50	592.45
23					203.59	542.53
24					107.11	487.11
25					000.00	425.58
26						357.27
27						281.44
28						197.24
29						103.77
30						000.00

10¾% MONTHLY MORTGAGE PAYMENTS

Monthly Payments (Debt Service Requirements) and Projected Loan Balances
Per $1,000 of Loan

Mortgage Term	5 YR.	10 YR.	15 YR.	20 YR.	25 YR.	30 YR.
Monthly Payments	$21.62	$13.63	$11.21	$10.15	$ 9.62	$ 9.33

Year-end Mortgage Balances

Year						
1	840.37	941.04	971.61	984.95	991.65	995.25
2	662.71	875.43	940.02	968.19	982.35	989.97
3	464.98	802.40	904.86	949.54	972.00	984.09
4	244.92	721.13	865.73	928.79	960.48	977.54
5	000.00	630.67	822.18	905.69	947.66	970.26
6		530.00	773.71	879.98	933.39	962.15
7		417.95	719.76	851.37	917.52	953.13
8		293.25	659.72	819.52	899.84	943.09
9		154.47	592.90	784.08	880.17	931.92
10		000.00	518.53	744.64	858.28	919.48
11			435.75	700.74	833.92	905.64
12			343.63	651.88	806.81	890.23
13			241.11	597.50	776.63	873.08
14			127.00	536.98	743.04	854.00
15			000.00	469.62	705.66	832.76
16				394.66	664.06	809.12
17				311.22	617.76	782.81
18				218.37	566.23	753.53
19				115.02	508.87	720.95
20				000.00	445.04	684.68
21					374.00	644.31
22					294.94	599.39
23					206.94	549.39
24					109.00	493.74
25					000.00	431.81
26						362.88
27						286.16
28						200.78
29						105.76
30						000.00

11% MONTHLY MORTGAGE PAYMENTS

Monthly Payments (Debt Service Requirements) and Projected Loan Balances
Per $1,000 of Loan

Mortgage Term	5 YR.	10 YR.	15 YR.	20 YR.	25 YR.	30 YR.
Monthly Payments	$21.74	$13.78	$11.37	$10.32	$ 9.80	$ 9.52

Year-end Mortgage Balances

Year						
1	841.25	941.82	972.24	985.42	991.99	995.50
2	664.12	876.92	941.26	969.15	983.05	990.48
3	466.50	804.50	906.70	950.99	973.08	984.87
4	246.01	723.70	868.14	930.74	961.96	978.62
5	000.00	633.55	825.12	908.14	949.55	971.65
6		532.97	777.11	882.93	935.70	963.86
7		420.76	723.56	854.80	920.25	955.18
8		295.55	663.81	823.41	903.01	945.49
9		155.86	597.14	788.39	883.78	934.68
10		000.00	522.76	749.32	862.32	922.63
11			439.77	705.73	838.38	909.17
12			347.17	657.09	811.67	894.16
13			243.86	602.83	781.87	877.41
14			128.60	542.28	748.62	858.72
15			000.00	474.73	711.52	837.87
16				399.37	670.12	814.61
17				315.28	623.94	788.66
18				221.46	572.41	759.70
19				116.79	514.93	727.39
20				000.00	450.78	691.34
21					379.22	651.12
22					299.37	606.25
23					210.29	556.18
24					110.90	500.33
25					000.00	438.00
26						368.47
27						290.89
28						204.33
29						107.75
30						000.00

11¼% MONTHLY MORTGAGE PAYMENTS

Monthly Payments (Debt Service Requirements) and Projected Loan Balances
Per $1,000 of Loan

Mortgage Term	5 YR.	10 YR.	15 YR.	20 YR.	25 YR.	30 YR.
Monthly Payments	$21.87	$13.92	$11.52	$10.49	$ 9.98	$ 9.71

Year-end Mortgage Balances

Year						
1	842.12	942.60	972.85	985.88	992.32	995.73
2	665.52	878.39	942.48	970.08	983.74	990.96
3	468.01	806.58	908.51	952.41	974.13	985.62
4	247.09	726.26	870.51	932.65	963.39	979.65
5	000.00	636.42	828.02	910.54	951.38	972.97
6		535.94	780.49	885.82	937.94	965.51
7		423.56	727.33	858.16	922.91	957.15
8		297.85	667.86	827.23	906.10	947.81
9		157.26	601.36	792.64	887.30	937.36
10		000.00	526.97	753.94	866.27	925.67
11			443.77	710.67	842.75	912.59
12			350.71	662.26	816.44	897.97
13			246.63	608.12	787.01	881.61
14			130.21	547.56	754.10	863.32
15			000.00	479.83	717.29	842.86
16				404.07	676.11	819.97
17				319.34	630.06	794.37
18				224.56	578.55	765.74
19				118.56	520.94	733.72
20				000.00	456.50	697.90
21					384.42	657.84
22					303.81	613.03
23					213.65	562.91
24					112.80	506.86
25					000.00	444.16
26						374.04
27						295.60
28						207.87
29						109.75
30						000.00

11½% MONTHLY MORTGAGE PAYMENTS

Monthly Payments (Debt Service Requirements) and Projected Loan Balances
Per $1,000 of Loan

Mortgage Term	5 YR.	10 YR.	15 YR.	20 YR.	25 YR.	30 YR.
Monthly Payments	$21.99	$14.06	$11.68	$10.66	$10.16	$ 9.90

Year-end Mortgage Balances

Year						
1	842.98	943.36	973.45	986.32	992.64	995.96
2	666.93	879.86	943.67	970.99	984.40	991.42
3	469.52	808.65	910.29	953.79	975.15	986.34
4	248.18	728.81	872.86	934.51	964.78	980.64
5	000.00	639.29	830.89	912.89	953.15	974.25
6		538.91	783.83	888.65	940.11	967.08
7		426.36	731.06	861.47	925.50	959.04
8		300.16	671.90	830.99	909.11	950.03
9		158.66	605.56	796.82	890.73	939.93
10		000.00	531.17	758.51	870.12	928.60
11			447.77	715.55	847.02	915.90
12			354.25	667.38	821.11	901.66
13			249.40	613.37	792.06	885.69
14			131.83	552.81	759.49	867.79
15			000.00	484.90	722.97	847.71
16				408.77	682.03	825.20
17				323.40	636.11	799.97
18				227.67	584.63	771.67
19				120.34	526.91	739.93
20				000.00	462.19	704.36
21					389.62	664.46
22					308.25	619.73
23					217.01	569.58
24					114.71	513.34
25					000.00	450.28
26						379.58
27						300.31
28						211.42
29						111.75
30						000.00

11¾% MONTHLY MORTGAGE PAYMENTS

Monthly Payments (Debt Service Requirements) and Projected Loan Balances
Per $1,000 of Loan

Mortgage Term	5 YR.	10 YR.	15 YR.	20 YR.	25 YR.	30 YR.
Monthly Payments	$22.12	$14.20	$11.84	$10.84	$10.35	$10.09

Year-end Mortgage Balances

Year						
1	843.85	944.12	974.04	986.76	992.95	996.17
2	668.33	881.31	944.85	971.87	985.03	991.86
3	471.04	810.70	912.05	955.14	976.13	987.02
4	249.27	731.34	875.17	936.33	966.12	981.58
5	000.00	642.13	833.72	915.19	954.87	975.47
6		541.86	787.13	891.43	942.22	968.59
7		429.16	734.76	864.72	928.01	960.86
8		302.47	675.90	834.70	912.03	952.18
9		160.07	609.73	800.95	894.07	942.42
10		000.00	535.36	763.02	873.89	931.44
11			451.76	720.38	851.20	919.11
12			357.80	672.45	825.69	905.24
13			252.17	618.58	797.03	889.66
14			133.45	558.02	764.80	872.14
15			000.00	489.96	728.58	852.45
16				413.45	687.87	830.31
17				327.45	642.10	805.44
18				230.79	590.66	777.47
19				122.13	532.84	746.04
20				000.00	467.85	710.70
21					394.79	670.99
22					312.67	626.35
23					220.37	576.17
24					116.62	519.77
25					000.00	456.37
26						385.11
27						305.00
28						214.97
29						113.76
30						000.00

12% MONTHLY MORTGAGE PAYMENTS

Monthly Payments (Debt Service Requirements) and Projected Loan Balances
Per $1,000 of Loan

Mortgage Term	5 YR.	10 YR.	15 YR.	20 YR.	25 YR.	30 YR.
Monthly Payments	$22.24	$14.35	$12.00	$11.01	$10.53	$10.29

Year-end Mortgage Balances

Year						
1	844.71	944.87	974.61	987.18	993.25	996.37
2	669.72	882.74	946.01	972.73	985.64	992.28
3	472.55	812.74	913.77	956.46	977.07	987.67
4	250.36	733.86	877.45	938.11	967.41	982.48
5	000.00	644.97	836.52	917.44	956.53	976.63
6		544.82	790.40	894.15	944.27	970.04
7		431.96	738.44	867.91	930.45	962.61
8		304.78	679.88	838.34	914.88	954.24
9		161.48	613.89	805.01	897.33	944.81
10		000.00	539.54	767.46	877.56	934.18
11			455.75	725.15	855.29	922.20
12			361.34	677.47	830.18	908.71
13			254.96	623.75	801.89	893.50
14			135.08	563.21	770.02	876.37
15			000.00	494.99	734.10	857.06
16				418.13	693.63	835.30
17				331.51	648.02	810.78
18				233.91	596.64	783.16
19				123.93	538.73	752.03
20				000.00	473.48	716.95
21					399.95	677.42
22					317.10	632.88
23					223.74	582.69
24					118.54	526.14
25					000.00	462.41
26						390.60
27						309.69
28						218.51
29						115.77
30						000.00

Appendix E: Mathematics of Appraising

Today appraising a single family residence requires the use of a wide variety of mathematical techniques ranging from simple arithmetic through the use of algebraic formulas to the statistical techniques of stepwise multiple regression analyses. Often simple adding, subtracting, multiplying and dividing can be done with only the aid of pencil and paper or a simple calculator. More sophisticated calculators are helpful for solving algebraic formulas and some linear regression analysis. Computers are required for almost all stepwise multiple regression analysis. The trend towards use of the more sophisticated techniques is increasing in the appraisal of single family residences.

This section provides a review of the mathematical techniques and language used by appraisers of single family residences. It begins with a review of basic arithmetic. Familiar processes are shown with the rules that apply to each calculation. They are presented primarily as a basis for the subsequent material on algebra, statistics and regression analysis that follows.

Basic Arithmetic

Data is the information that is collected in the market and analyzed in the appraisal process to produce an estimate of value. Types of data include building dimensions, population figures, reproduction costs, rentals and sales among many others. The numbers that represent this data can be processed to produce other numbers or *results*. There are four basic arithmetic operations known as addition, subtraction, multiplication and division.

Addition is the process of adding two or more numbers together to produce the *sum* of the numbers. The symbol for addition is a plus sign (+).

426

Example: $120 + $135 + $130 = $385.

Subtraction is the process of deducting one number from another to produce the *difference* between the numbers. The symbol for subtraction is a minus sign (−).

Example: 93 inches − 10 inches = 83 inches

Multiplication is the process of multiplying one number, the *multiplicand*, by another number, the *multiplier*, to produce a result which is called the *product*. The multiplier is also sometimes known as a *coefficient*. The symbols for multiplication are a times sign (×) or a period (·). In algebra it is also a sign to multiply when one number is inside a bracket and the other is outside the bracket.

Example: $4 \times 5 = 20$
$6 \cdot 7 = 42$
$8(9) = 72$

In the above examples 4 could be called the coefficient of 5; 6 the coefficient of 7; and 8 the coefficient of 9.

When a series of different multiplicands are multiplied by the same multiplier, that multiplier is also known as a *constant*.

Example: $6 \times 7 = 42$
$6 \times 8 = 48$
$6 \times 14 = 84$

In this example, 6 can be called a multiplier, coefficient or constant. In algebra the symbol for a constant is "k".

When a series of numbers is multiplied by each other, the results are the same no matter in what sequence the numbers are multiplied.

Example: $6 \cdot 4 \cdot 8 = 192$
$8 \times 6 \times 4 = 192$
$6(8) \times 4 = 192$

Division is the process of dividing one number, the *dividend*, by another number, the *divisor,* to produce a result which is called a *quotient.* The symbol for division is (÷) or a line placed under the dividend and over the divisor.

Example: $18 \div 9 = 2$

$$\frac{20}{5} = 4$$

In the above examples 18 and 20 are the dividends and 9 and 5 are the divisors and 2 and 4 are the quotients. The number 20 is also known as the *numerator* and 5 the *denominator* when the numbers are shown as a fraction. Therefore, the value of a fraction is found by dividing the numerator by the denominator.

Rules for Processing Numbers
- In addition and multiplication the order of the numbers does not affect the results.
- In subtraction the order of the numbers does make a difference in the results.
- In division the sequence of the numbers may affect the results.
- When a series of operations is performed, the ones within brackets (grouping symbols) are done first.

Example: $2 (4 + 6) \times (6 - 2) =$
$2 (10) \times (4) =$
$20 \times 4 = 80$

- When there are brackets within brackets, the innermost operations are done first.

Example: $2 [(8 + 2) + (6 - 3)] =$
$2 [(10) + (3)] =$
$2 [13] = 26$

- When there are no grouping symbols, all the multiplication and division operations are performed before the addition and subtraction operations.

Example: $4 \times 5 \div 2 \times 10 + 12 =$
$20 \div 2 \times 10 + 12 =$
$10 \times 10 + 12 =$
$100 + 12 = 112$
or
$3 \times 6 + 9 \div 3 - 10 =$
$18 + 3 - 10 = 11$

There are many more rules that apply to the addition, subtraction, multiplication and division operations that cover what to do when the signs are different, how to use absolute numbers, fractions, etc. These are beyond the scope of this introductory material.

Ratios

Ratios are the result of dividing one number by another number. The three different ways to express a ratio are as a whole number (integer), decimal figure or fraction.

Example: In a community school there is a ratio of 58 students to 2 teachers.

The ratio of 58 to 2 is $58 \div 2 = 29$

The ratio of 2 to 58 is $2 \div 58 = .0345$ (rounded)

The ratio of 2 to 58 is $\dfrac{2}{58} = \dfrac{1}{29}$

Percentages

Percentages are ratios multiplied by 100 (or expressed on a base of 100).

Continuing the above example:

$\dfrac{2}{58} = .0345 \times 100 = 3.45\%$ of a teacher for each student.

Rates

Rates are percentages expressed in terms of a time period. $8.00 interest per year on $100 principal = 8% interest per year; $.50 interest per month on $100 = .005 or 1/2% interest per month.

Decimals

Decimals are added, subtracted, multiplied and divided similar to the way whole numbers (integers) are with some additional rules being applied. When decimals are added and subtracted, the number of places to the right of the decimal point is equal to the largest number of places in any of the numbers being added or subtracted.

Example: 242.071
          + 63.12
          + 4.2
          + 2.7983
          _____
            312.1893

            621.0037
          − 11.02
          _____
            609.9837

When decimals are multiplied, the number of places to the right of the decimal point is the total number of places to the right of the decimal point in the numbers being multiplied.

Example: $3.23 \times 7.459 = 24.09257$
           $17.31 \times 6.9 \times 41.27 = 4929.24753$

This does not mean the number cannot be rounded in the appraisal process.

When decimals are divided, the decimal points in the dividend (numerator) and divisor (denominator) are moved to the right to make the divisor a whole number (integer); the decimal point is moved the same number of places and in the same direction in both numbers.

Example: $896.487 \div 57.31 =$

$$57.31\,\overline{\smash{)}\,896.487}$$

$$5731\,\overline{\smash{)}\,89648.7}^{\;15.64\;(rd.)}$$

Algebra

The same rules that apply to basic arithmetic apply to algebra. The main difference is that in algebra letters and symbols are used together with numbers.

Algebra makes use of equations to solve problems. An equation is a

MATHEMATICS OF APPRAISING **431**

statement of fact that a number or group of quantities on one side of an equal sign is equal to another quantity or group of quantities on the opposite side of the equal sign.

Example: $6 + 10 = 16$

$12 - 8 = 3 + 1$

$44 + (5 + 4) = 53$

$15 + (6 \times 5) = 25 + (5 \times 4)$

$$\frac{200}{20} = 10$$

$\sqrt{36} = 3 \times 2$

$(\frac{12}{3} + 1)(11 - 1) = (7 \times 8) - 6$

The most important rule in solving equations is that with every change in the statement of the equation the integrity or accuracy of the equation must always be maintained. One side of the equation must always equal the other side.

There are three laws or rules that illustrate the application of symbols.

1. The commutative laws state that as with regular addition the sum of two or more symbols is the same no matter in what order they are added together.

Example: $2 + 4 + 10 = 10 + 4 + 2$

$16 = 16$

or

$X + Y + Z = Y + Z + X$

The commutative laws state that as with regular multiplication the product of two or more symbols is the same no matter in what order they are multiplied by each other.

Example: $8 \times 12 \times 5 = 12 \times 5 \times 8$

$480 = 480$

or

$X \cdot Y \cdot Z = Z \cdot X \cdot Y$

2. The associative laws state that as with regular addition and multiplication when brackets are used the operations within the brackets are always performed first. When two or more brackets are used, the operation within the innermost bracket is performed first and then each outer one is performed successively.

Example: $5 \cdot (6 + 3) + 12 - 10 =$
$5 \cdot (9) + 12 - 10 \quad =$
$45 + 12 - 10 \quad\quad = 47$
or
$18 + \left[(5 \bullet 9) - (18 - 3) + (4 \times 5) \right] =$
$18 + \left[(45) - (15) + (20) \right] \quad\quad =$
$18 + \left[50 \right] \quad\quad =$
$18 + 50 \quad\quad\quad = 68$
or
$X + (Y + Z) = (X + Y) + Z$
or
$X \cdot (Y \cdot Z) = (X \cdot Y) \cdot Z$

3. The distributive law states that the number or symbol outside the bracket is actually multiplied by each number or symbol within the bracket.

Example: $8 (4 + 12) =$
Can be solved:
$= 8(16)$
$= 8 \cdot 16$
$= 128$

but according to the distributive law may also be solved:

$8 (4 + 12) = 32 + 96 = 128$

or using symbols:

$X (Y + Z) = X Y + X Z$

(each symbol within the bracket is multiplied by the symbol outside the bracket).

In algebra in order to solve equations it is necessary to simplify them. The commutative, associative and distributive laws are used for this process.

Example of simplification using the commutative law:

$10 + (2 Y + 3 Y + 6 Y) = 10 + 11 Y$

Example of simplification using the associative law:

$$(7 + 8 \text{ X}) + 3 \text{ X} = 7 + (3 \text{ X} + 8 \text{ X})$$

This same equation can be simplified using the distributive law:

$$(7 + 8 \text{ X}) + 3 \text{ X} = 7 + (8 + 3)\text{X}$$
$$= 7 + 11 \text{ X}$$

Equations are mathematical expressions which relate one group of numbers and symbols to another group of numbers and symbols.

$$3 \text{ X} = 4 \text{ Y}$$

If we know that X equals 4, we can solve the equation to find that Y equals 3:

$$3 \text{ X} = 4 \text{ Y}$$
$$3 \cdot 4 = 4 \text{ Y}$$
$$12 = 4 \text{ Y}$$
$$3 = \text{Y}$$

The key to solving algebraic equations is the assertion that two different combinations of numbers and symbols called *groups* or *quantities* are equal to each other. This fact is usually shown in the equation by the use of an equal sign. Groups or quantities are made up of constants, coefficients and variables.

The following are examples of some different types of algebraic equations. In them the variables are unknowns and are represented by letters of the alphabet.

Reflective equation: X = Y
Symmetric equation: if X = Y then Y = X
Transitive equation: if X = Y and Y = b then X = b

Another key to solving algebraic equations is the axiom that both sides of an equation will remain equal after equal amounts are added, subtracted, multiplied by or divided into both sides of the equation.

Example of adding equal amounts to both sides of an equation:

$$X + 15 = 21$$

Add 8 to both sides

$$X + 23 = 29$$

Example of subtracting equal amounts to both sides of an equation:

$$X + 15 = 21$$

Subtract 10 from both sides

$$X + 5 = 11$$

Example of multiplying both sides of an equation by equal amounts:

$$X + 15 = 21$$

Multiply both sides by 7

$$7(X + 15) = 147$$

Example of dividing both sides of an equation by equal amounts:

$$X + 15 = 21$$

Divide both sides by 7

$$\frac{X + 15}{7} = \frac{21}{7}$$

Another key to solving algebraic equations is that any term may be transposed from one side of an equation to the other side and the sides will remain equal provided that the sign of the transposed term is changed (+ to −, or − to +, or × to ÷, or ÷ to ×).

Example of moving a plus term in an equation to the other side of the equation:

$$9X + 2 = 29$$

Move the + 2 to the other side: $9X + \cancel{2} + (-\cancel{2}) = 29 + (-2)$

$$9X = 29 - 2$$

(the effect is the same as subtracting − 2 from both sides)

Example of moving a minus term in an equation to the other side of the equation:

$$9 X - 2 = 25$$

Move the $- 2$ to the other side: $9 X - \cancel{2} + (+ \cancel{2}) = 25 + (+2)$

$$9 X = 25 + 2$$

(the effect is the same as adding $+ 2$ to both sides)

Example of moving a multiplier in an equation to the other side of the equation:

$$3 (9 X) = 81$$

Move the multiplier 3 to the other side: $\dfrac{\cancel{3}(9 X)}{\cancel{3}} = \dfrac{81}{3}$

$$9 X = \frac{81}{3}$$

(the effect is the same as dividing both sides by 3)

Example of moving a divisor in an equation to the other side of the equation:

$$\frac{9 X}{3} = 9$$

Move the divisor 3 to the other side: $\cancel{3} \cdot \dfrac{9 X}{\cancel{3}} = 9 \cdot 3$

$$9 X = 3 (9)$$

(the effect is the same as multiplying both sides by 3)

NOTE: In all of the above transposition examples the value of X is 3.

The purpose of this algebra review is to demonstrate the skills needed to solve simple equations of the type encountered by appraisers. Here is an example of how to use the previously explained techniques to solve an equation.

Example: Find the value of X when

$$13 X - 6 X + 12 = - 6 X + 3 X + 32$$

Step 1: Collect like terms

$$7 X + 12 = - 3 X + 32$$

Step 2: Clear the negative terms by adding equal amounts to both sides.

$$
\begin{array}{rl}
7X + 12 = & -3X + 32 \\
+3X & \quad +3X \\
\hline
10X + 12 = & \quad\quad 32
\end{array}
$$

Step 3: Clear the equation by adding or substituting equal numbers to both sides.

$$
\begin{array}{rl}
10\,X + & 12 = \quad 32 \\
- & 12 \quad -12 \\
\hline
10\,X & \quad\quad = \quad 20
\end{array}
$$

Step 4: Divide each side of the equation by equal numbers to find the value of the unknown letter (X)

$$
\begin{array}{c}
10X = 20 \\
\dfrac{10X}{10} = \dfrac{20}{10} \\
X = 2
\end{array}
$$

This algebra review provides a basis upon which to proceed to statistics, which is a quantitative tool used to analyze data.

Basic Statistics

An appraisal by one popular definition is a supportable estimate of a defined value. Statistics is rapidly becoming an effective tool with which to make and support the value of a single family residence and to better understand available data.

In the language of statistics a *population* is a complete data set or all the data in a certain group. Conclusions must often be reached with incomplete data but if, for example, the group to be studied were houses in Chicago, then the population would be all the houses in Chicago.

Statistics is a field of knowledge that enables an appraiser (or any investigator) to derive and evaluate conclusions about a population from sample data. A sample is only part of the population and conclusions about a population based on a sample may be erroneous.

Observations about a population when they can be measured are called *quantitative*. The numerical value of a quantitative observation is a *variate*.

Observation about a population that cannot be measured is called *qualitative*. They are *attributes*.

For appraisal purposes one of the most useful functions of statistics is to forecast what some variate in a population will be or do. A variate is one item in a population. It is called *discrete* when it can assume only a limited number of values on a measuring scale and *continuous* when it can assume an infinite number of values on a measuring scale.

A continuous variate can become an unlimited number of values.

A typical population of attributes would be house types, i.e., one-story houses, one and one-half story houses, two-story houses, split levels, etc. It is usually easy to display or tell about a population of attributes.

It is much harder to display or tell about a population of variates because there are many different ones.

One of the problems in statistics is to describe a population in universally understandable terms. This is a very difficult thing to do. How does one describe all the houses in a community that have sold in the past year without an individual description of each sale?

One way is to use a single number to describe the whole population. This is called a *parameter*.

One parameter that is used to describe a population is an *aggregate*. It is a sum of all the variates. It is possible to describe all the house sales in a community in any given year by the total dollar amount of all the sales. This is written in statistical language as:

$A = \Sigma X$
where
A = aggregate
Σ = sigma = sum of
X = variate

Three other commonly used parameters are the mean, median or mode.

The *mean*, which is denoted by the symbol μ, is commonly called the average. It is obtained by dividing the sum of all the variates in the population by the number of variates.

The mean is by far the most commonly used parameter. In real estate appraising some common uses of the mean are average sale price, average number of days for sale, average apartment rent and average cost per square foot. What is usually meant by each of the statements (unless specifically stated otherwise) is the mean sale price, days for sale, apartment rent, or cost per square foot.

The problem with the use of the mean to describe these and other populations is that it can be distorted by extreme variates. For example, on the following page is a grouping of 36 house sales in a neighborhood. The "average" (or mean) price in this example — $43,494 — does not give a fully accurate picture of the population of houses that have been sold.

The *median* is also used to describe a population or at least the average variate in the population. The median divides the variates of a population into equal halves. To compute the median of a population the variates are arranged in numerical order (as are the 36 sale prices in the example). If the total number of variates is odd, the median is the middle variate. If the total number of variates is even (as it is in this example), the median is the arithmetic mean of the two middle variates.

In the example of 36 house sales the middle two variates are $43,900 and $43,900. The mean of these two variates is $43,900, which is the median of the 36 sales in the example ($43,900 + $43,900 = $87,800 ÷ 2 = $43,900).

$ 36,000
37,300
38,000
38,600
39,000
39,500
39,900
39,900
41,000
41,000
42,000
42,800
42,900
43,000
43,500
43,600
43,700
43,900
43,900 ←median = Md. = $43,900
43,900
44,000
44,900
45,000 ⎫
45,000 ⎬ mode = Mo = $45,000
45,000
45,000 ⎭
45,300
45,500
45,500
46,900
46,900
48,300
48,500
48,600
48,600
49,400
―――――
$1,565,800

A = Sum of the variates
N = Number of variates = 36

$$\text{Mean} = \overline{X} = \frac{A}{N} = \frac{\$1,565,800}{36} = \$43,494$$

Here is another example of an odd number of variates:

Monthly Rent

    $180
    $180
    $190
    $200 ◄——— Middle variate (the median)
    $210
    $215
    $220

Like the median and mean, the *mode* is another parameter that describes the typical variate of a population. The mode is the most frequently appearing variate or attribute in a population. The following is an example of a population of monthly rentals showing the mode:

    $170
    $175
    $180
    $180
    $185
    $190 ⎫
    $190 ⎬ The most frequent variate is the mode
    $190 ⎭
    $195
    $200

Below is another example showing a population of types of condominium apartments available in a 9-unit complex:

    efficiency
    efficiency
    efficiency
    town house ⎫
    town house ⎪
    town house ⎬ The most frequent attribute is the mode
    town house ⎪
    town house ⎭
    multi-bedroom

In the example of 36 houses, four of them sold for $45,000. This is the most frequent sale price and therefore is the mode. Sometimes two houses of different price may be of the same frequency in the sample or population. Both prices would be modes and the sample would be said to be bi-modal.

One of the problems that must be solved by the appraiser using statistics is to select the appropriate average to describe the population being used. In the previous example the following single numbers can be used to describe the 36 variates in the group of house sales:

$$\Sigma\, X = \$1,565,800 = \text{sum of all the sales}$$
$$\overline{X} = \$\quad 43,494 = \text{the mean of all the sales}$$
$$Md = \$\quad 43,900 = \text{the median of the sales}$$
$$Mo = \$\quad 45,000 = \text{the mode of the sales}$$

The mean is often selected to describe the sample or population because it is the most commonly used and most people are familiar with it.

Measures of Variation

The parameters mean, median and mode all are used to describe central tendencies of the population. Other sets of parameters are used to provide more information about the population being described. They measure the disparity among values of the various variates comprising the population. These parameters, called *measures of variation* or *dispersion*, are designed to indicate the degree of uniformity among the variates.

One way to measure the disparity between the variates is known as the *range* (denoted by R). It is the difference between the highest and lowest variate.

R = Maximum variate − minimum variate

Using the figures in the example of 36 house sales:

R = $49,400 to $36,000

R = $13,400

The range as a measure of variation is of limited usefulness since it considers only the highest and lowest values and neglects the variation in the remaining values. It also does not lend itself to further statistical treatment.

Average Deviation

Another parameter used to measure deviations between the variates is the *average deviation* which is also known as the average absolute deviation because plus or minus signs are ignored. It is a measure of how much the actual values of the population or sample deviate from the mean or the average. It is the mean of the sum of the absolute (no plus or minus signs) differences of each of the variates from the mean of the variates.

The calculations of the average deviation of the 36 sales, summarized again on page 443, using traditional statistical formula and symbols, follows:

$$\text{A.D. (ungrouped data)} = \frac{\Sigma |X - \overline{X}|}{n}$$

$$\text{A.D. (grouped data)} = \frac{\Sigma f |X - \overline{X}|}{n}$$

where

A.D. = average deviation
Σ = sum of
f = frequency
X = observed value
| | = ignore the + or − signs
n = number of observations in sample (N = population)
$\overline{X}$ = means of sample (σ = population)

$$\text{Mean} = \frac{\$1,565,800}{36} = \$43,494$$

$$\text{Average deviation from the mean} = \frac{\$96,048}{36} = \$2,668$$

Sale price	Absolute deviation between each variate and the mean sale price
$ 36,000	$ 7,494
37,300	6,194
38,000	5,494
38,600	4,894
39,000	4,494
39,500	3,994
39,900	3,594
39,900	3,594
41,000	2,494
41,000	2,494
42,000	1,494
42,800	694
42,900	594
43,000	494
43,500	6
43,600	106
43,700	206
43,900	406
43,900	406
43,900	406
44,000	506
44,900	1,406
45,000	1,506
45,000	1,506
45,000	1,506
45,000	1,506
45,300	1,806
45,500	2,006
45,500	2,006
46,900	3,406
46,900	3,406
48,300	4,806
48,500	5,006
48,600	5,106
48,600	5,106
49,000	5,906
$1,565,800 Total of the sale prices	$96,048 Total deviation from the mean

X	$\lvert X-\overline{X}\rvert$	f	$f\lvert X-\overline{X}\rvert$
$36,000	$7,494	1	$ 7,494
37,300	6,194	1	6,194
38,000	5,494	1	5,494
38,600	4,894	1	4,894
39,000	4,494	1	4,494
39,500	3,994	1	3,994
39,900	3,594	2	7,188
41,000	2,494	2	4,988
42,000	1,494	1	1,494
42,800	694	1	694
42,900	594	1	594
43,000	494	1	494
43,500	6	1	6
43,600	106	1	106
43,700	206	1	206
43,900	406	3	1,218
44,000	506	1	506
44,900	1,406	1	1,406
45,000	1,506	4	6,024
45,300	1,806	1	1,806
45,500	2,006	2	4,012
46,900	3,406	2	6,812
48,300	4,806	1	4,806
48,500	5,006	1	5,006
48,600	5,106	2	10,212
49,400	5,906	1	5,906
		36	$96,048

Mean = $43,494

$$\text{A.D.} = \frac{\Sigma f\lvert X-\overline{X}\rvert}{n} = \frac{\$96,048}{36} = \$2,668$$

This indicates that on the average the individual values in the sample population deviate from the mean $2,668 or about 6%. This is a fairly tight fit and suggests that the mean is an acceptable descriptive representation of this sample.

Like the range, the average deviation does not lend itself to further statistical calculations.

Standard Deviation

The *standard deviation* provides a way of describing a sample or a population that lends itself to further mathematical treatment. In particular it permits application of rules of probability to draw inferences of populations from samples.

In this method the square of the difference between each observation and the mean of the observations is used as a calculation step. This serves to magnify the effects of extreme variance from the mean.

In the illustration, for instance, the mean sale price is $43,494. Therefore, the measure of deviation for a $41,000 sale would be $2,494 squared or $6,220,036.

When standard deviation of a *whole* population is being calculated, it is symbolized by a sigma (σ). Expressed verbally the formula is "standard deviation of a population is the square root of the sum of the squared differences between each observation's value and the mean of all of the observations in the population divided by the number of observations in the population."

When the standard deviation of a *sample* of a population is being calculated, it is symbolized by the letter "s". Expressed verbally the formula is "standard deviation of a sample is the square root of the sum of the squared differences between each observation's value and the mean of all the observations in the sample divided by the number of observations in the sample minus 1."

The reason 1 is subtracted from the number of observations in a sample is to adjust for one degree of freedom that is lost when the mean is calculated. A set of data originally has as many "degrees of freedom" as there are observations. Every time a statistic is calculated directly from the data a degree of freedom is lost.

Formulas for calculating the standard deviation are as follows:

For a population:

$$\sigma = \sqrt{\frac{\Sigma(X-\bar{X})^2}{N}}$$

For a sample:

$$s = \sqrt{\frac{\Sigma (X-\bar{X})^2}{n-1}} \quad \text{or} \quad \sqrt{\frac{\Sigma f(X-\bar{X})^2}{n-1}}$$

In real estate appraising samples are usually used so the second formula is generally applied, as in the example of 36 house sales (see next page).

The standard deviation is an important way to describe the variance of a population or sample. It tells how representative of the whole sample or population the mean is by explaining a standard variance. It is a number that is used and understood by many disciplines. With the availability of electronic calculators it now can be calculated easily. It undoubtedly will become more widely used by appraisers in the future.

When used for this purpose the standard deviation can indicate what percent of the sample of the population may be expected to fall within selected ranges or *confidence intervals* (see page 452).

Approximately 68.2% of the sample or population will generally fall within plus or minus one standard deviation from the mean, if the data meets certain tests of "distribution normalcy" (as discussed later). Many types of real estate data, including residential sales, are commonly found to be approximately normally distributed, or normal distributions can be approximated by appropriate sampling techniques.

In this example, 68.2% of the house sales in the population are expected to be between $40,080 and $46,908 ($43,494 − $3,414 and $43,494 + $3,414), if the data is normally distributed. Also approximately 95% of the sales should fall within two standard deviations from the mean and approximately 99.74% should fall within three standard deviations from the mean.

Because the standard deviation lends itself to further mathematical treatment, it can be used for analytical purposes other than to describe a population.

Statistical Inference

This technique (useful to forecast actions) is based on the assumption that past actions in the market are a valid basis for forecasting present or future actions in the market. In the example past sale prices are used to estimate current sale prices. This technique

Standard Deviation for 36 House Sales

X	f	$(X-\overline{X})$	$(X-\overline{X})^2$	$f(X-\overline{X})^2$
$36,000	1	$7,494	$56,160,036	$ 56,160,036
37,300	1	6,194	38,365,636	38,365,636
38,000	1	5,494	30,184,036	30,184,036
38,600	1	4,894	23,951,236	23,951,236
39,000	1	4,494	20,196,036	20,196,036
39,500	1	3,994	15,952,036	15,952,036
39,900	2	3,594	12,916,836	25,833,672
41,000	2	2,494	6,220,036	12,440,072
42,000	1	1,494	2,232,036	2,232,036
42,800	1	694	481,636	481,636
42,900	1	594	352,836	352,836
43,000	1	494	244,036	244,036
43,500	1	6	36	36
43,600	1	106	11,236	11,236
43,700	1	206	42,436	42,436
43,900	3	406	164,836	494,508
44,000	1	506	256,036	256,036
44,900	1	1,406	1,976,836	1,976,836
45,000	4	1,506	2,268,036	9,072,144
45,300	1	1,806	3,261,636	3,261,636
45,500	2	2,006	4,024,036	8,048,072
46,900	2	3,406	11,600,836	23,201,672
48,300	1	4,806	23,097,636	23,097,636
48,500	1	5,006	25,060,036	25,060,036
48,600	2	5,106	26,071,236	52,142,472
49,400	1	5,906	34,880,836	34,880,836
				$407,938,896

$$s = \sqrt{\frac{\sum f(X-\overline{X})^2}{n-1}}$$

$$s = \sqrt{\frac{\$407,938,896}{36-1}}$$

Mean: $43,494

$$s = \sqrt{\$11,655,397}$$

$$s = \quad \$3,414$$

can also be used to forecast rentals, costs, depreciation, etc., using rules of probability.

The *normal-curve* plots a normal distribution and is a technique to illustrate a distribution of data. Where original data may not be normally distributed, repeated random samples may be drawn with results which approximate a normal distribution. Sales are often treated as though they were normally distributed in competitive, open market situations. The normal curve is often graphed in a form known as a bell curve.

A major characteristic of a bell curve is that it is symmetrical. Both halves have exactly the same shape and contain the same number of observations. The mean, median and mode are the same value and this value is the midpoint (apex) of the curve.

Fig. A illustrates a bell curve and shows that 68.26% of the observations will fall within the range of the mean plus or minus one standard deviation, 95.44% within plus or minus two standard deviations and 99.74% plus or minus three standard deviations. It depicts an analysis of the probable population distribution for the 36 sales, assuming a normal distribution.

In this example the ranges for one, two and three standard deviations are shown. It is also possible to calculate the percentage of the population that will fall within any given distance from the mean.

Continuing the example it is possible to calculate the percentage of sales that will fall within any specified ranges. For example, $2,500 plus or minus the mean of $43,494 (between $40,994 and $45,994) may be estimated by calculating the Z value using the following formula:

Z = the deviation of X from the mean measured in standard deviations

$$Z = \frac{X - \text{mean}}{\text{Standard deviation}}$$

$$Z = \frac{\$45,994 - \$43,494}{\$3,414} = \frac{\$2,500}{\$3,414} = .7323$$

This shows that $45,994 deviates from the mean $43,494 (or $40,994 deviates from the mean $43,494) by .7323 standard deviations.

FIG. A: Area under the Normal Curve

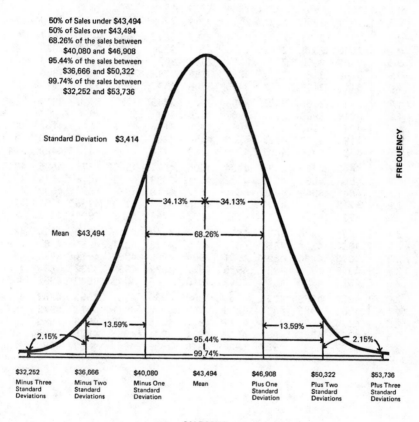

50% of Sales under $43,494
50% of Sales over $43,494
68.26% of the sales between
$40,080 and $46,908
95.44% of the sales between
$36,666 and $50,322
99.74% of the sales between
$32,252 and $53,736

Standard Deviation $3,414

FREQUENCY

34.13% — 34.13%

Mean $43,494

68.26%

13.59% — 13.59%

2.15%   95.44%   2.15%

99.74%

$32,252	$36,666	$40,080	$43,494	$46,908	$50,322	$53,736
Minus Three Standard Deviations	Minus Two Standard Deviations	Minus One Standard Deviation	Mean	Plus One Standard Deviation	Plus Two Standard Deviations	Plus Three Standard Deviations

SALE PRICE

Areas under the normal curve

z	.00	.01	.02	.03	.04	.05	.06	.07	.08	.09
0.0	.0000	.0040	.0080	.0120	.0160	.0199	.0239	.0279	.0319	.0359
0.1	.0398	.0438	.0478	.0517	.0557	.0596	.0636	.0675	.0714	.0753
0.2	.0793	.0832	.0871	.0910	.0948	.0987	.1026	.1064	.1103	.1141
0.3	.1179	.1217	.1255	.1293	.1331	.1368	.1406	.1443	.1480	.1517
0.4	.1554	.1591	.1628	.1664	.1700	.1736	.1772	.1808	.1844	.1879
0.5	.1915	.1950	.1985	.2019	.2054	.2088	.2123	.2157	.2190	.2224
0.6	.2257	.2291	.2324	.2357	.2389	.2422	.2454	.2486	.2517	.2549
0.7	.2580	.2611	.2642	.2673	.2704	.2734	.2764	.2794	.2823	.2852
0.8	.2881	.2910	.2939	.2967	.2995	.3023	.3051	.3078	.3106	.3133
0.9	.3159	.3186	.3212	.3238	.3264	.3289	.3315	.3340	.3365	.3389
1.0	.3413	.3438	.3461	.3485	.3508	.3531	.3554	.3577	.3599	.3621
1.1	.3643	.3665	.3686	.3708	.3729	.3749	.3770	.3790	.3810	.3830
1.2	.3849	.3869	.3888	.3907	.3925	.3944	.3962	.3980	.3997	.4015
1.3	.4032	.4049	.4066	.4082	.4099	.4115	.4131	.4147	.4162	.4177
1.4	.4192	.4207	.4222	.4236	.4251	.4265	.4279	.4292	.4306	.4319
1.5	.4332	.4345	.4357	.4370	.4382	.4394	.4406	.4418	.4429	.4441
1.6	.4452	.4463	.4474	.4484	.4495	.4505	.4515	.4525	.4535	.4545
1.7	.4554	.4564	.4573	.4582	.4591	.4599	.4608	.4616	.4625	.4633
1.8	.4641	.4649	.4656	.4664	.4671	.4678	.4686	.4693	.4699	.4706
1.9	.4713	.4719	.4726	.4732	.4738	.4744	.4750	.4756	.4761	.4767
2.0	.4772	.4778	.4783	.4788	.4793	.4798	.4803	.4808	.4812	.4817
2.1	.4821	.4826	.4830	.4834	.4838	.4842	.4846	.4850	.4854	.4857
2.2	.4861	.4864	.4868	.4871	.4875	.4878	.4881	.4884	.4887	.4890
2.3	.4893	.4896	.4898	.4901	.4904	.4906	.4909	.4911	.4913	.4916
2.4	.4918	.4920	.4922	.4925	.4927	.4929	.4931	.4932	.4934	.4936
2.5	.4938	.4940	.4941	.4943	.4945	.4946	.4948	.4949	.4951	.4952
2.6	.4953	.4955	.4956	.4957	.4959	.4960	.4961	.4962	.4963	.4964
2.7	.4965	.4966	.4967	.4968	.4969	.4970	.4971	.4972	.4973	.4974
2.8	.4974	.4975	.4976	.4977	.4977	.4978	.4979	.4979	.4980	.4981
2.9	.4981	.4982	.4982	.4983	.4984	.4984	.4985	.4985	.4986	.4986
3.0	.4987	.4987	.4987	.4988	.4988	.4989	.4989	.4989	.4990	.4990

The .7323 can be interpreted from the above table by first finding .7 under the Z column and then looking across the top of the page for the next digits. Accordingly, 26.73% of the sales are shown to fall between $43,494 and $45,994 or between $43,494 and $40,994 and 53.46% of the sales will be between $45,994 and $40,994.

Another question that can be answered using the Z value is the probability of a randomly selected sale falling inside a given range.

Continuing to use the population based on the sample of 36 sales, which has a mean of $43,494 and a standard deviation of $3,414, it is possible to calculate the probability of a randomly selected sale falling in any selected range of values.

For example, the probability of a randomly selected sale falling between $43,494 and $44,494 ($1,000 over the mean) is calculated as follows:

$$Z = \frac{X - \text{mean}}{\text{standard deviation}} = \frac{\$44,494 - \$43,494}{\$3,414} = \frac{\$1,000}{\$3,414} = .29$$

Looking at the table of areas under the normal curve, a Z of .29 = .1141. This indicates an 11.41% chance the sale will fall within $1,000 above the mean. The same process is repeated to find the probability of the sale falling within $1,000 below the mean.

$$Z = \frac{X - \text{mean}}{\text{standard deviation}} = \frac{\$42,494 - \$43,494}{\$3,414} = \frac{\$1,000}{\$3,414} = .29$$

Again, .29 on the table shows .1141, or a 11.41% chance the sale will fall within $1,000 below the mean.

Probability a sale will fall between $44,494 and $43,494 is:	11.41%
Probability a sale will fall between $42,494 and $43,494 is:	11.41%
Probability a sale will fall between $42,494 and $44,494 is:	22.82%

If the range is expanded in the same example to $2,000 plus or minus to the mean of $43,494, to $41,494 and $45,494 respectively, the probability of a randomly selected sale falling within this range woud be increased.

$$Z = \frac{X - \text{mean}}{\text{standard deviation}} = \frac{\$45,494 - \$43,494}{\$3,414} = \frac{\$2,000}{\$3,414} = .59$$

Looking at the areas under the normal curve table .59 = .2224.

Probability a sale will fall between $45,494 and $43,494 is:	22.24%
Probability a sale will fall between $41,494 and $43,494 is:	22.24%
Probability a sale will fall between $41,494 and $45,494 is:	44.48%

In the above two examples, the range being tested is equally above and below the mean sale. However it is also possible to test the probability of a randomly selected sale falling between any selected range in the population. Continuing the example, the probability of a randomly selected sale falling between $40,000 and $50,000 can be calculated as follows:

$$Z\ area_1 = \frac{X_1 - mean}{standard\ deviation} = \frac{\$40,000 - \$43,494}{\$3,414} = \frac{\$3,494}{\$3,414} = 1.02$$

$$Z\ area_2 = \frac{X_2 - mean}{standard\ deviation} = \frac{\$50,000 - \$43,494}{\$3,414} = \frac{\$6,506}{\$3,414} = 1.91$$

Looking at 1.02 on the areas under the normal curve table gives:	.3461
Looking at 1.91 on the areas under the normal curve table gives:	.4719
Probability:	.8180

This indicates the chance a randomly selected sale in this sample will fall between $40,000 and $50,000 is 81.80%.

Confidence Level

Using statistical inference and the laws of probability for a normal distribution, the previous examples have shown how *confidence intervals* may be constructed for a sample where there is a presumption (or approximation) of normally distributed data. These calculations may be valuable in a number of real estate decision-making situations, including loan administration, housing development, and appraising.

As seen in the previous examples, with 36 sales as a sample, an appraiser may say *with a 95% degree of confidence* that any sale randomly selected from the population will fall between $36,664 and $50,332. Similarly, there is a 68% confidence of the sample falling between $40,080 and $46,908. Such measures may be meaningful in connection with other statistical measures.

Since such measures are dependent upon the accuracy of the estimated mean (as a representative of the true population mean), it is also important to establish some degree of confidence about the mean itself. Regardless of population size there is a given sample size which will permit a given level of confidence in the estimated mean.

In the continuing example of 36 sales the standard deviation for price has been calculated as $3,414. The arithmetic mean is $43,494, or about $43,500. If an appraiser wants to be 95% certain that the true mean is within $500 of the estimated mean ($43,494) or between about $43,000 and $44,000, calculations of the necessary sample size are as follows:

n = Sample size required
z = Z statistic at 95% confidence level
s = Standard deviation of the sample
e = Required maximum difference in the mean

And: $n = \dfrac{z^2 s^2}{e^2}$

$$n = \frac{(1.96)^2 (3,414)^2}{(500)^2} = 179 \text{ sales}$$

Thus, with 179 sales in a sample the required standard of confidence could be met. Likewise, for a confidence interval of not more than $750, calculations would be as follows:

$$n = \frac{(1.96)^2 (3,414)^2}{(750)^2} = 80 \text{ sales}$$

In the original sample of 36 sales, an appraiser may ask, "At a 95% confidence, what are the limits between which the true population mean may fall?" By substitution:

$$e^2 = \frac{z^2 s^2}{n}$$

And: $e^2 = \dfrac{(1.96)^2 (3,414)^2}{36} = \$1,115$

Thus, the appraiser in this case may be statistically 95% certain that the true population mean falls between \$42,399 and \$44,609.

While such calculations may seem to have obscure reasoning for single family appraising, professional appraisers must have adequate data, knowledge and understanding of the markets in which they appraise. Calculations such as these assist in quantifying change and in performing the neighborhood analyses essential to value estimation. They are also important for appraisal review, loan underwriting and other analyses.

Regression Analysis

Simple Linear Regression Analysis

Trying to estimate the most probable sale price of a residence in the market is the goal of many appraisers. It is seldom sufficient to take a sample of sales and then calculate the standard deviation and base the estimate upon these results. The range of values is usually too great at the confidence level required to be directly useful.

Appraisers long ago discovered that the accuracy of the estimate could be substantially increased by considering in addition to the sale prices of individual properties one or more characteristics of each sale property.

Looking again at the 36 sales in the original example it has been shown there appears to be a relationship between sale price and the number of square feet of living area. The 36 sales with their square feet of gross living area in are exhibited in Table A. In traditional appraisals it is likely that an appraiser would use only those sales

Table A

Comparable Sales Data Set for Simple Regression Analysis

Sale No.	GLA/Sq. Ft.	Sale Price	Price per Sq. Ft. of GLA
1	1,321	$38,000	$28.77
2	1,372	$44,000	$32.07
3	1,394	$39,000	$27.98
4	1,403	$37,300	$26.59
5	1,457	$42,900	$29.44
6	1,472	$43,700	$29.69
7	1,475	$42,000	$28.47
8	1,479	$42,800	$28.94
9	1,503	$36,000	$23.95
10	1,512	$38,600	$25.53
11	1,515	$41,000	$27.06
12	1,535	$39,500	$25.73
13	1,535	$43,900	$28.60
14	1,577	$45,500	$28.85
15	1,613	$45,000	$27.90
16	1,640	$39,900	$24.33
17	1,666	$45,500	$27.31
18	1,681	$39,900	$23.74
19	1,697	$43,600	$25.69
20	1,703	$43,500	$25.54
21	1,706	$44,900	$26.32
22	1,709	$45,300	$26.51
23	1,709	$46,900	$27.44
24	1,720	$46,900	$27.27
25	1,732	$41,000	$23.67
26	1,749	$48,600	$27.79
27	1,771	$48,600	$27.44
28	1,777	$43,000	$24.20
29	1,939	$43,900	$22.64
30	1,939	$45,000	$23.21
31	1,939	$45,000	$23.21
32	1,939	$45,000	$23.21
33	1,939	$48,300	$24.91
34	1,940	$43,900	$22.63
35	2,014	$49,400	$24.53
36	2,065	$48,500	$23.49

which have approximately the same square footage as the appraised property in direct comparison and essentially ignore the others.

Note the appraiser's dilemma in appraising a 1,375 square foot dwelling. Sales 1, 2 and 3 are reported as $28.77, $32.07 and $27.98 per square foot respectively. Other sales may give a clue to the "right answer," but Sales 5 and 6 do little to resolve the conflict. Adjustments will likely be made for other differences, but the complication of multiple hand adjustments has already been noted in Chapter 13.

Sales 1 through 3 indicate a range of $27.98 to $32.07 per square foot, or when applied to the appraised property's 1,375 square feet, an indicated value range of $38,473 to $44,096. (These would be rounded in practice.) However, the remaining market information cannot effectively be applied to the analysis in traditional appraising except to generally reinforce the "appraiser's judgment."

Simple linear regression provides a technique in which more market data may be applied to this analysis — and avoids the zero intercept fallacy illustrated in Chapter 13. For application in the simple linear regression formula, $Y_c = a + bX$, the 36 sales were analyzed by calculator and produced the following:

a = $24,630
b = $11.29
r = .6598 (simple correlation coefficient) ·

Thus, for the 1,375 square foot property appraised:

Y_c = $24,630 + $11.29 (1,375)
Y_c = $40,154
        (or $29.20 per square foot)

The calculated regression line and a plot of the 36 sales is shown in Figure B. Also shown is another statistical measure called the *standard error of the estimate* which allows construction of confidence intervals about the regression line. Calculations in this example produce a standard error estimate of $2,603. When applied to property appraised, the appraiser may now state that the 36 sales in this market support an estimate of about $40,150 for the appraised property (based only upon comparison of square footage). Further, at a

FIG. B: Plot of Sales. Regression Line and Standard Error — 36 Sales

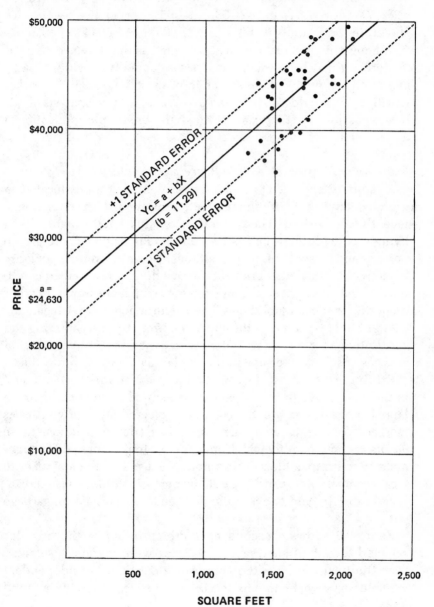

68% confidence level, the market price should lie between $40,150 ± $2,603 (or $37,547 to $42,753). At a 95% confidence level, price should lie between $40,150 ± (2) ($2,603) or $34,944 to $45,356.

Although other statistical measures such as the *standard error of the forecast* may be used, this analysis is generally considered sufficient and reasonably representative of most single family market situations. It should also be noted that a more refined analysis of this data is possible, but this example illustrates the simple application of a regression technique.

Example of Stepwise Multiple Regression Analysis*

An appraiser is asked to appraise a residential property located on a lot containing 7,575 square feet, improved with a residence recently constructed. The residence contains 1,720 square feet of living area with three bedrooms and two full baths. There are no porches and no swimming pool, although some swimming pools are found within the neighborhood. The dwelling has central air conditioning and other physical characteristics which are similar to other properties in the neighborhood. There is an attached two-car garage.

After field inspection of the appraised property and gathering and verification of comparable sales, a stepwise multiple regression analysis is selected for use in the market data approach to value.

Exhibit 1 summarizes the comparable sales information contained in the computer file of comparable sales by the appraiser. From a large list of sales on file, the computer selected these properties as most comparable, based upon the appraiser's determination of those factors of comparability which appear most important to this assignment. The comparable sales printout was used by the appraiser to locate comparables in making field inspections, to allow visual scanning of the file and to avoid the problems of "garbage in, garbage out".

Exhibit 2 shows a second computer printout of the 36 sales selected for initial analysis. These sales were randomly selected from the total file once the appraiser identified the independent variables of porch, bedrooms, lot size, garage area and living area and

---

*(The model illustrated in the exhibits shown on pp. 460-475 was developed by Valuation Systems Company, 1722 South Carson, Tulsa, Oklahoma 74119, and is used with permission.)

any time parameters as the essential elements of the search. As shown in the last column, sale price was selected as the dependent variable for multiple regression analysis.

Exhibit 3 summarizes arithmetic means of each of the variables and their standard deviations. Also shown is a simple correlation matrix of the calculated interaction among each of the variables selected. Next, Exhibit 4 summarizes each of the steps of multiple regression analysis applied to the comparable sales data set.

Once the initial regression equation has been computer-calculated (as shown in Step 5 of Exhibit 4), the computer then uses the regression equation to calculate the expected prices of each of the 36 comparable sales considered. By comparing actual sales prices with estimated sales prices for each, differences are shown in Exhibit 5 as the "residuals," along with calculated percentages of error in estimate. In this projection of actual comparable sales information, only two sales were found to have more than a 10% error and the bulk had approximately 5% or lower error.

The percent of error on residuals is also printed in Exhibit 6, which is a dynamic plot of residual error showing the lowest amount of error to the left-hand side of the plot and the highest error to the right.

Next, a second run of the regression equation was made, deleting those variables which produced the highest amount of error and/or which were indicated by visual analysis to have the lowest degree of comparability with the property appraised. The results of the second run are shown in Exhibits 7 through 11. With the deletion of the least comparable variables, the second run produces a highest amount of residual error equal to 3.44% of the actual price.

Once the appraiser accepts the reasonableness of the regression projections and their statistical reliability, the computer is instructed to produce a final indication of value using the stepwise multiple regression analysis method. Final results of the projection for the property appraised are shown in Exhibit 12. The final projection indicates an estimated price almost equal to the actual price of the property in a recent sale and establishes for a 95% confidence interval a range of approximately ± $2,000 as the reasonable selling price of the property appraised.

EXHIBIT 1: Summary of Comparable Sales

COMPARABLE SALES
RESIDENTIAL PROPERTIES

SECTION - TOWNSHIP - RANGE :

PROP I.D.	ADDRESS	L AREA	BDRMS	BATHS	HT'NG	CL'NG	PARK'NG	L SIZE	C DATE	D SLD	PRICE	APPR I.D.
6358500000230	13129 93 AVE NO	1,666	THREE	TWO	CNTRL	CNTRL	2 GR'GE	8,100	1975	07 76	$45,500	421X
6358500000290	13152 93 AVE NO	1,457	THREE	TWO	CNTRL	CNTRL	2 GR'GE	8,100	1975	11 76	$42,900	422X
6358500000110	9290 132 ST NO	1,720	THREE	TWO	CNTRL	CNTRL	2 GR'GE	7,575	1976	10 76	$46,900	732Z
6358500000270	13196 93 AVE NO	1,749	THREE	TWO	CNTRL	CNTRL	2 GR'GE	9,936	1976	08 76	$48,600	987Y
6358500000120	9322 132 ST NO	1,709	THREE	TWO	CNTRL	CNTRL	2 GR'GE	7,568	1976	04 76	$46,900	7Z
6358500000150	13198 94 AVE NO	2,014	FOUR	TWO	CNTRL	CNTRL	2 GR'GE	10,002	1976	07 76	$47,400	325Z
6358500000100	9250 132 ST NO	1,709	THREE	TWO	CNTRL	CNTRL	2 GR'GE	7,560	1976	02 76	$45,300	681Y
6358500000070	13198 92 AVE NO	1,771	THREE	TWO	CNTRL	CNTRL	2 GR'GE	10,781	1976	01 76	$48,600	561Y
6358500000140	9376 132 ST N	1,479	TWO	TWO	CNTRL	CNTRL	2 GR'GE	9,033	1976	01 76	$42,800	552Y
6594300000220	12735 90 AVE NO	1,939	THREE	TWO	CNTRL	CNTRL	2 GR'GE	7,861	1976	03 76	$43,900	886Y
6594300000150	9153 127 ST NO	1,939	THREE	TWO	CNTRL	CNTRL	2 GR'GE	13,040	1976	08 76	$45,000	454Z
6594300000300	12744 91 AVE NO	1,940	THREE	TWO	CNTRL	CNTRL	2 GR'GE	7,700	1976	04 76	$43,900	941Y
6594300000250	9035 127LANE NO	1,939	THREE	TWO	CNTRL	CNTRL	2 GR'GE	9,800	1976	01 76	$45,000	630Y
6594300000010	9002 127LANE NO	1,706	THREE	TWO	CNTRL	CNTRL	2 GR'GE	8,400	1976	09 76	$44,900	666Z
6594300000100	12267 91 AVE NO	1,939	THREE	TWO	CNTRL	CNTRL	2 GR'GE	11,085	1976	08 76	$45,000	468Z
6594300000110	12745 91 AVE NO	1,939	THREE	TWO	CNTRL	CNTRL	2 GR'GE	11,022	1976	08 76	$48,300	486Z
6594300000080	12795 91 AVE NO	1,681	THREE	TWO	CNTRL	CNTRL	2 GR'GE	19,300	1976	01 76	$39,900	560Y
6268800040010	13625 CLARDON RD	1,475	THREE	TWO	CNTRL	CNTRL	2 GR'GE	9,191	1976	05 76	$42,000	305Y
6268800010070	13422 90 TERR N	1,515	THREE	TWO	CNTRL	CNTRL	2 GR'GE	8,500	1975	03 76	$41,000	874Y
6268800010120	13520 90 TERR N	1,697	THREE	TWO	CNTRL	CNTRL	2 GR'GE	8,800	1975	07 76	$43,600	28Y
6268800030090	9256 134 WAY N	1,732	THREE	TWO	CNTRL	CNTRL	2 GR'GE	7,700	1976	01 76	$41,000	477Y
6268800030060	13485 91 AVE N	1,613	THREE	TWO	CNTRL	CNTRL	2 GR'GE	8,580	1973	07 76	$45,000	320V

(Continued)

SECTION - TOWNSHIP - RANGE :

PROP I.D.	ADDRESS	L AREA	BDRMS	BATHS	HT'NG	CL'NG	PARK'NG	L SIZE	C DATE	D SLD	PRICE	APPR I.D.
6473900110150	11455 131 AVE N	1,777	THREE	TWO	CNTRL	CNTRL	2 GR'GE	11,000	1972	11 76	$43,000	16108
6473900110100	11450 132 AVE N	1,640	THREE	TWO	CNTRL	CNTRL	2 GR'GE	11,000	1972	10 76	$39,900	16105

SECTION - TOWNSHIP - RANGE :

PROP I.D.	ADDRESS	L AREA	BDRMS	BATHS	HT'NG	CL'NG	PARK'NG	L SIZE	C DATE	D SLD	PRICE	APPR I.D.
6473900600020	11027 129 AVE NO	1,512	THREE	TWO	CNTRL	CNTRL	2 GR'GE	7,125	1972	02 76	$38,600	360Y
6473900300060	12740 110 ST NO	1,403	THREE	TWO	CNTRL	CNTRL	2 GR'GE	7,500	1975	07 76	$37,300	366Y
6473900700120	12853 112 ST NO	1,703	THREE	TWO	CNTRL	CNTRL	2 GR'GE	8,040	1974	06 76	$43,500	958Y
6473900300160	10907 126 TER NO	1,503	THREE	TWO	CNTRL	CNTRL	2 GR'GE	7,763	1975	04 76	$36,000	250X
6473900500140	11026 129 AVE NO	1,577	THREE	TWO	CNTRL	CNTRL	2 GR'GE	7,125	1974	09 76	$45,500	852X
6473900500080	10911 128 AVE NO	1,394	THREE	TWO	CNTRL	CNTRL	2 GR'GE	7,600	1976	10 76	$39,000	180Z
6473900050060	10919 128 AVE NO	1,372	TWO	TWO	CNTRL	CNTRL	2 GR'GE	7,410	1973	10 76	$44,000	750Z
6473900010570	11243 130 AVE NO	1,472	THREE	TWO	CNTRL	CNTRL	2 GR'GE	8,036	1972	04 76	$43,700	24W
6473900010020	10923 130 AVE NO	1,321	TWO	TWO	CNTRL	CNTRL	2 GR'GE	7,500	1973	03 76	$38,000	17493
6473900012250	11051 130 AVE NO	2,065	THREE	TWO	CNTRL	CNTRL	2 GR'GE	7,995	1976	09 76	$48,500	573Z
6473900010290	13119 11 LANE NO	1,535	THREE	TWO	CNTRL	CNTRL	2 GR'GE	7,500	1975	03 76	$43,900	747X
6473900020060	10914 126 TER NO	1,535	THREE	TWO	CNTRL	CNTRL	2 GR'GE	8,000	1974	02 76	$39,500	55X

EXHIBIT 2: Selected Sales — First Analysis

```
STEPWISE MULTIPLE REGRESSION ANALYSIS


OBSERVATIONS
```

OBS NUM ***	PROPERTY I.D. # *************	INDEPENDENT VARIABLE					DEP VAR.
		1 PORCH *****	2 BDRMS *****	3 LT SZ *****	4 GAR A *****	5 LIV A *****	PRICE *****
1	6358500000230	1	3	8100	468	1666	45500
2	6358500000290	1	3	8100	484	1457	42900
3	6358500000110	1	3	7575	520	1720	46900
4	6358500000270	3	3	9936	448	1749	48600
5	6358500000120	1	3	7568	459	1709	46900
6	6358500000150	3	4	10002	501	2014	49400
7	6358500000100	1	3	7560	459	1709	45300
8	6358500000070	1	3	10781	449	1771	48600
9	6358500000140	4	2	9033	421	1479	42800
10	6594300000220	1	3	7861	444	1939	43900
11	6594300000150	1	3	13040	444	1939	45000
12	6594300000300	1	3	7700	444	1940	43900
13	6594300000250	3	3	9800	444	1939	45000
14	6594300000010	1	3	8400	459	1706	44900
15	6594300000100	1	3	11085	444	1939	45000
16	6594300000110	3	3	11022	444	1939	48300
17	6594300000080	1	3	19300	479	1681	39900
18	6268800040010	1	3	9191	441	1475	42000
19	6268800010070	1	3	8500	430	1515	41000
20	6268800010120	3	3	8800	441	1697	43600
21	6268800030090	1	3	7700	451	1732	41000
22	6268800030060	3	3	8580	524	1613	45000
23	6473900110150	0	3	11000	419	1777	43000
24	6473900600020	3	3	7125	422	1512	38600
25	6473900300060	3	3	7500	421	1403	37300
26	6473900700120	1	3	8040	454	1703	43500
27	6473900300160	1	3	7763	469	1503	36000
28	6473900500140	3	3	7125	458	1577	45500
29	6473900500080	3	3	7600	430	1394	39000
30	6473900050060	2	2	7410	455	1372	44000
31	6473900010570	3	3	8036	477	1472	43700
32	6473900010020	1	2	7500	460	1321	38000
33	6473900010250	1	3	7995	466	2065	48500
34	6473900010290	3	3	7500	471	1535	43900
35	6473900020060	3	3	8000	471	1535	39500
36	6473900110100	1	3	11000	427	1640	39900

EXHIBIT 3: Means, Standard Deviations and Simple Correlation Coefficients of Variables — First Analysis

```
MEANS

VARIABLE NO.  1 - PORCH =      1.8055
VARIABLE NO.  2 - BDRMS =      2.9444
VARIABLE NO.  3 - LT SZ =  8,978.5555
VARIABLE NO.  4 - GAR A =      455.5000
VARIABLE NO.  5 - LIV A =  1,670.4722
VARIABLE NO.  6 - PRICE = 43,494.4444


STANDARD DEVIATIONS

VARIABLE NO.  1 - PORCH =      1.0642
VARIABLE NO.  2 - BDRMS =      0.3333
VARIABLE NO.  3 - LT SZ =  2,277.2125
VARIABLE NO.  4 - GAR A =     25.0855
VARIABLE NO.  5 - LIV A =    199.4894
VARIABLE NO.  6 - PRICE =  3,414.0001


SIMPLE CORRELATION COEFFICIENTS

    1       2       3       4       5    DEP VAR
  PORCH   BDRMS   LT SZ   GAR A   LIV A   PRICE

1.0000 -0.0313 -0.1746 -0.0069 -0.2225  0.0224
        0.9999  0.1511  0.2596  0.5082  0.2909
                1.0000 -0.0168  0.3232  0.0686
                        0.9999  0.0720  0.3210
                                1.0000  0.6598
                                        0.9999
```

EXHIBIT 4: Summary of Comparable Sales — First Analysis

```
                        STEPS

************ STEP NUMBER  1 ENTER VARIABLE  5 LIV A ***********

MEAN OF THE DEPENDENT VARIABLE . . . . . . . . . .    43,494.44
STANDARD ERROR OF THE ESTIMATE  . . . . . . . . . .     2,602.72
MULTIPLE CORRELATION COEFFICIENT   . . . . . . . . .    0.659848
CONTRIBUTION TO MULTIPLE CORRELATION COEFFICIENT . . .  .659848
NUMBER OF VARIABLES IN REGRESSION EQUATION  . . . . . . .      1
DEGREES OF FREEDOM  . . . . . . . . . . . . . . . . . .       34
F RATIO  . . . . . . . . . . . . . . . . . . .          26.2195
CONSTANT TERM OF REGRESSION EQUATION  . . . . . .     24630.7425

VAR      BETA COEFF      S D COEFF       T VALUE       C COEFF

 5        11.2924         2.2053         5.1205         0.6598


************ STEP NUMBER  2 ENTER VARIABLE  4 GAR A ***********

MEAN OF THE DEPENDENT VARIABLE . . . . . . . . . .    43,494.44
STANDARD ERROR OF THE ESTIMATE  . . . . . . . . . .     2,459.75
MULTIPLE CORRELATION COEFFICIENT   . . . . . . . . .    0.714532
CONTRIBUTION TO MULTIPLE CORRELATION COEFFICIENT . . .  .054684
NUMBER OF VARIABLES IN REGRESSION EQUATION  . . . . . . .      2
DEGREES OF FREEDOM  . . . . . . . . . . . . . . . . . .       33
F RATIO  . . . . . . . . . . . . . . . . . . .          17.2118
CONSTANT TERM OF REGRESSION EQUATION  . . . . . .      8158.1402

VAR      BETA COEFF      S D COEFF       T VALUE       C COEFF

 4        37.4073        16.6174         2.2510         0.2748
 5        10.9533         2.0896         5.2417         0.6400


************ STEP NUMBER  3 ENTER VARIABLE  1 PORCH ***********

MEAN OF THE DEPENDENT VARIABLE . . . . . . . . . .    43,494.44
STANDARD ERROR OF THE ESTIMATE  . . . . . . . . . .     2,421.98
MULTIPLE CORRELATION COEFFICIENT   . . . . . . . . .    0.734745
CONTRIBUTION TO MULTIPLE CORRELATION COEFFICIENT . . .  .020212
NUMBER OF VARIABLES IN REGRESSION EQUATION  . . . . . . .      3
DEGREES OF FREEDOM  . . . . . . . . . . . . . . . . . .       32
F RATIO  . . . . . . . . . . . . . . . . . . .          12.5142
CONSTANT TERM OF REGRESSION EQUATION  . . . . . .      6120.3021

VAR      BETA COEFF      S D COEFF       T VALUE       C COEFF

 1       563.2193       394.6035         1.4273         0.1755
 4        37.1891        16.3630         2.2727         0.2732
 5        11.6240         2.1105         5.5076         0.6792
```

(Continued)

```
************ STEP NUMBER  4 ENTER VARIABLE  2 BDRMS ***********

MEAN OF THE DEPENDENT VARIABLE . . . . . . . . . .    43,494.44
STANDARD ERROR OF THE ESTIMATE  . . . . . . . . . .    2,404.12
MULTIPLE CORRELATION COEFFICIENT  . . . . . . . . .    0.748853
CONTRIBUTION TO MULTIPLE CORRELATION COEFFICIENT . . .  .014107
NUMBER OF VARIABLES IN REGRESSION EQUATION  . . . . . .    4
DEGREES OF FREEDOM  . . . . . . . . . . . . . . . . . .   31
F RATIO  . . . . . . . . . . . . . . . . . . . . .     9.8949
CONSTANT TERM OF REGRESSION EQUATION  . . . . . .    6332.8066

VAR      BETA COEFF      S D COEFF      T VALUE      C COEFF

  1       610.2820       393.6028       1.5505       0.1902
  2     -1790.3544      1473.0339      -1.2154      -0.1748
  4        42.5047        16.8208       2.5269       0.3123
  5        13.1522         2.4433       5.3829       0.7685


************ STEP NUMBER  5 ENTER VARIABLE  3 LT SZ ***********

MEAN OF THE DEPENDENT VARIABLE . . . . . . . . . .    43,494.44
STANDARD ERROR OF THE ESTIMATE  . . . . . . . . . .    2,401.97
MULTIPLE CORRELATION COEFFICIENT  . . . . . . . . .    0.758756
CONTRIBUTION TO MULTIPLE CORRELATION COEFFICIENT . . .  .009902
NUMBER OF VARIABLES IN REGRESSION EQUATION  . . . . . .    5
DEGREES OF FREEDOM  . . . . . . . . . . . . . . . . . .   30
F RATIO  . . . . . . . . . . . . . . . . . . . . .     8.1413
CONSTANT TERM OF REGRESSION EQUATION  . . . . . .    7357.4683

VAR      BETA COEFF      S D COEFF      T VALUE      C COEFF

  1       565.1095       395.7003       1.4281       0.1761
  2     -1781.6589      1471.7387      -1.2105      -0.1739
  3        -0.1949         0.1897      -1.0274      -0.1300
  4        41.7828        16.8204       2.4840       0.3070
  5        13.8170         2.5254       5.4711       0.8073
```

EXHIBIT 5: Comparison of Actual and Estimated Sale Prices of Comparables, Showing Residuals and Percentages of Error — First Analysis

RESIDUALS LISTING

OBS	I.D. #	ACTUAL	ESTIMATE	RESIDUAL	% ERROR
1	6358500000230	45,500.00	43,572.00	1,927	4.23
2	6358500000290	42,900.00	41,352.77	1,547	3.60
3	6358500000110	46,900.00	46,593.18	306	0.65
4	6358500000270	48,600.00	44,655.44	3,944	8.11
5	6358500000120	46,900.00	43,893.81	3,006	6.40
6	6358500000150	49,400.00	48,736.92	663	1.34
7	6358500000100	45,300.00	43,895.37	1,404	3.10
8	6358500000070	48,600.00	43,706.24	4,893	10.06
9	6358500000140	42,800.00	42,319.52	480	1.12
10	6594300000220	43,900.00	46,387.87	-2,487	-5.66
11	6594300000150	45,000.00	45,378.19	-378	-0.84
12	6594300000300	43,900.00	46,433.07	-2,533	-5.77
13	6594300000250	45,000.00	47,140.06	-2,140	-4.75
14	6594300000010	44,900.00	43,690.15	1,209	2.69
15	6594300000100	45,000.00	45,759.33	-759	-1.68
16	6594300000110	48,300.00	46,901.83	1,398	2.89
17	6594300000080	39,900.00	42,055.36	-2,155	-5.40
18	6268800040010	42,000.00	39,592.11	2,407	5.73
19	6268800010070	41,000.00	39,819.90	1,180	2.87
20	6268800010120	43,600.00	43,865.95	-265	-0.60
21	6268800030090	41,000.00	43,851.60	-2,851	-6.95
22	6268800030060	45,000.00	46,216.18	-1,216	-2.70
23	6473900110150	43,000.00	41,927.86	1,072	2.49
24	6473900600020	38,600.00	40,842.47	-2,242	-5.80
25	6473900300060	37,300.00	39,221.52	-1,921	-5.15
26	6473900700120	43,500.00	43,509.97	-9	-0.02
27	6473900300160	36,000.00	41,427.31	-5,427	-15.07
28	6473900500140	45,500.00	43,244.76	2,255	4.95
29	6473900500080	39,000.00	39,453.72	-453	-1.16
30	6473900050060	44,000.00	41,447.90	2,552	5.80
31	6473900010570	43,700.00	42,410.24	1,289	2.95
32	6473900010020	38,000.00	40,369.49	-2,369	-6.23
33	6473900010250	48,500.00	49,021.91	-521	-1.07
34	6473900010290	43,900.00	43,134.51	765	1.74
35	6473900020060	39,500.00	43,037.03	-3,537	-8.95
36	6473900110100	39,900.00	40,934.29	-1,034	-2.59

EXHIBIT 6: Residuals Percentage of Error — First Analysis

```
                    RESIDUALS  AS  A  PERCENT  OF  ACTUAL
6358500000230 *               4.23                                        * 1
6358500000290 *             3.60                                          * 2
6358500000110 *    0.65                                                   * 3
6358500000270 *                                    8.11                   * 4
6358500000120 *                         6.40                              * 5
6358500000150 *      1.34                                                 * 6
6358500000100 *          3.10                                             * 7
6358500000070 *                                          10.06            * 8
6358500000140 *      1.12                                                 * 9
6594300000220 *                    -5.66                                  * 10
6594300000150 *   -0.84                                                   * 11
6594300000300 *                     -5.77                                 * 12
6594300000250 *                  -4.75                                    * 13
6594300000010 *           2.69                                           * 14
6594300000100 *     -1.68                                                 * 15
6594300000110 *            2.89                                           * 16
659430000080 *                    -5.40                                   * 17
6268800040010 *               5.73                                        * 18
6268800010070 *           2.87                                            * 19
6268800010120 *   -0.60                                                  * 20
6268800030090 *                         -6.95                             * 21
6268800030060 *       -2.70                                              * 22
6473900110150 *          2.49                                            * 23
6473900600020 *                    -5.80                                  * 24
6473900300060 *                 -5.15                                    * 25
6473900700120 * -0.02                                                    * 26
6473900300160 *                                              -15.07 * 27
6473900500140 *                4.95                                       * 28
647390050008O *    -1.16                                                  * 29
6473900050060 *                     5.80                                  * 30
6473900010570 *        2.95                                              * 31
6473900010020 *                      -6.23                                * 32
6473900010250 *    -1.07                                                  * 33
6473900010290 *      1.74                                                 * 34
6473900020060 *                                 -8.95                      * 35
6473900110100 *        -2.59                                              * 36
```

EXHIBIT 7: Selected Sales — Second Analysis

```
STEPWISE MULTIPLE REGRESSION
ANALYSIS

OBSERVATIONS
```

OBS NUM	PROPERTY I.D. #	INDEPENDENT VARIABLE					DEP VAR.
		1 PORCH	2 BDRMS	3 LT SZ	4 GAR A	5 LIV A	PRICE
2	6358500000290	1	3	8100	484	1457	42900
3	6358500000110	1	3	7575	520	1720	46900
6	6358500000150	3	4	10002	501	2014	49400
7	6358500000100	1	3	7560	459	1709	45300
9	6358500000140	4	2	9033	421	1479	42800
11	6594300000150	1	3	13040	444	1939	45000
14	6594300000010	1	3	8400	459	1706	44900
15	6594300000100	1	3	11085	444	1939	45000
16	6594300000110	3	3	11022	444	1939	48300
19	6268800010070	1	3	8500	430	1515	41000
20	6268800010120	3	3	8800	441	1697	43600
22	6268800030060	3	3	8580	524	1613	45000
23	6473900110150	0	3	11000	419	1777	43000
26	6473900700120	1	3	8040	454	1703	43500
29	6473900500080	3	3	7600	430	1394	39000
31	6473900010570	3	3	8036	477	1472	43700
33	6473900010250	1	3	7995	466	2065	48500
34	6473900010290	3	3	7500	471	1535	43900
36	6473900110100	1	3	11000	427	1640	39900

**EXHIBIT 8: Means, Standard Deviations and Simple Correlation
Coefficients of Variables — Second Analysis**

```
MEANS

VARIABLE NO.  1 - PORCH =      1.8421
VARIABLE NO.  2 - BDRMS =      3.0000
VARIABLE NO.  3 - LT SZ =  9,098.3157
VARIABLE NO.  4 - GAR A =    458.6842
VARIABLE NO.  5 - LIV A =  1,700.6842
VARIABLE NO.  6 - PRICE = 44,294.7368


STANDARD DEVIATIONS

VARIABLE NO.  1 - PORCH =      1.1672
VARIABLE NO.  2 - BDRMS =      0.3333
VARIABLE NO.  3 - LT SZ =  1,605.3780
VARIABLE NO.  4 - GAR A =     31.2908
VARIABLE NO.  5 - LIV A =    202.1781
VARIABLE NO.  6 - PRICE =  2,739.9257


SIMPLE CORRELATION COEFFICIENTS

    1       2       3       4       5    DEP VAR
  PORCH   BDRMS   LT SZ   GAR A   LIV A   PRICE

 1.0000 -0.1427 -0.1895  0.1232 -0.2878  0.0431
         0.9999  0.1005  0.4261  0.4410  0.4014
                 0.9999 -0.3764  0.5334  0.1066
                         0.9999  0.0870  0.5390
                                 1.0000  0.7721
                                         1.0000
```

EXHIBIT 9: Summary of Comparable Sales — Second Analysis

```
                              STEPS

************ STEP NUMBER  1 ENTER VARIABLE  5 LIV A ***********

MEAN OF THE DEPENDENT VARIABLE . . . . . . . . . .    44,294.73
STANDARD ERROR OF THE ESTIMATE  . . . . . . . . . .    1,791.55
MULTIPLE CORRELATION COEFFICIENT  . . . . . . . .     0.772143
CONTRIBUTION TO MULTIPLE CORRELATION COEFFICIENT . . . .772143
NUMBER OF VARIABLES IN REGRESSION EQUATION  . . . . . .        1
DEGREES OF FREEDOM  . . . . . . . . . . . . . . . . . .       17
F RATIO  . . . . . . . . . . . . . . . . . . .         25.1007
CONSTANT TERM OF REGRESSION EQUATION  . . . . . .   26498.5669

VAR     BETA COEFF      S D COEFF      T VALUE      C COEFF

 5       10.4641         2.0886        5.0100        0.7721


************ STEP NUMBER  2 ENTER VARIABLE  4 GAR A ***********

MEAN OF THE DEPENDENT VARIABLE . . . . . . . . . .    44,294.73
STANDARD ERROR OF THE ESTIMATE  . . . . . . . . . .    1,231.17
MULTIPLE CORRELATION COEFFICIENT  . . . . . . . . .    0.905826
CONTRIBUTION TO MULTIPLE CORRELATION COEFFICIENT . . . .133682
NUMBER OF VARIABLES IN REGRESSION EQUATION  . . . . . . .       2
DEGREES OF FREEDOM  . . . . . . . . . . . . . . . . . .       16
F RATIO  . . . . . . . . . . . . . . . . . . . .       36.5738
CONSTANT TERM OF REGRESSION EQUATION  . . . . . .    8357.6367

VAR     BETA COEFF      S D COEFF      T VALUE      C COEFF

 4       41.6297         9.3093        4.4718        0.4754
 5        9.9031         1.4407        6.8734        0.7307


************ STEP NUMBER  3 ENTER VARIABLE  1 PORCH ***********

MEAN OF THE DEPENDENT VARIABLE . . . . . . . . . .    44,294.73
STANDARD ERROR OF THE ESTIMATE  . . . . . . . . . .    1,111.04
MULTIPLE CORRELATION COEFFICIENT  . . . . . . . . .    0.928963
CONTRIBUTION TO MULTIPLE CORRELATION COEFFICIENT . . . .023136
NUMBER OF VARIABLES IN REGRESSION EQUATION  . . . . . . .       3
DEGREES OF FREEDOM  . . . . . . . . . . . . . . . . . .       15
F RATIO  . . . . . . . . . . . . . . . . . . . .       31.4893
CONSTANT TERM OF REGRESSION EQUATION  . . . . . .    7213.0588

VAR     BETA COEFF      S D COEFF      T VALUE      C COEFF

 1      511.2167       237.1465        2.1556        0.2177
 4       38.7790         8.5044        4.5598        0.4428
 5       10.7913         1.3639        7.9119        0.7962
```

(Continued)

```
*********** STEP NUMBER  4 ENTER VARIABLE  3 LT SZ ***********

MEAN OF THE DEPENDENT VARIABLE . . . . . . . . . .    44,294.73
STANDARD ERROR OF THE ESTIMATE  . . . . . . . . . .     1,050.50
MULTIPLE CORRELATION COEFFICIENT  . . . . . . . . .     0.941098
CONTRIBUTION TO MULTIPLE CORRELATION COEFFICIENT . . .  .012135
NUMBER OF VARIABLES IN REGRESSION EQUATION  . . . . . .        4
DEGREES OF FREEDOM  . . . . . . . . . . . . . . . . . .       14
F RATIO  . . . . . . . . . . . . . . . . . .          27.1122
CONSTANT TERM OF REGRESSION EQUATION  . . . . . .    11197.1810
```

VAR	BETA COEFF	S D COEFF	T VALUE	C COEFF
1	525.9293	224.3977	2.3437	0.2240
3	-0.3516	0.2109	-1.6669	-0.2060
4	31.0079	9.2946	3.3361	0.3541
5	12.4101	1.6143	7.6873	0.9157

```
*********** STEP NUMBER  5 ENTER VARIABLE  2 BDRMS ***********

MEAN OF THE DEPENDENT VARIABLE . . . . . . . . . .    44,294.73
STANDARD ERROR OF THE ESTIMATE  . . . . . . . . . .     1,012.75
MULTIPLE CORRELATION COEFFICIENT  . . . . . . . . .     0.949381
CONTRIBUTION TO MULTIPLE CORRELATION COEFFICIENT . . .  .008282
NUMBER OF VARIABLES IN REGRESSION EQUATION  . . . . . .        5
DEGREES OF FREEDOM  . . . . . . . . . . . . . . . . . .       13
F RATIO  . . . . . . . . . . . . . . . . . .          23.7492
CONSTANT TERM OF REGRESSION EQUATION  . . . . . .    11015.6410
```

VAR	BETA COEFF	S D COEFF	T VALUE	C COEFF
1	495.1224	217.3957	2.2775	0.2109
2	-1279.8154	891.0417	-1.4363	-0.1556
3	-0.3353	0.2037	-1.6463	-0.1965
4	36.8626	9.8442	3.7445	0.4209
5	13.1415	1.6375	8.0251	0.9697

EXHIBIT 10: Comparison of Actual and Estimated Sale Prices of Comparables, Showing Residuals and Percentages of Error — Second Analysis

RESIDUALS LISTING

OBS	I.D. #	ACTUAL	ESTIMATE	RESIDUAL	% ERROR
2	6358500000290	42,900.00	41,943.43	956	2.22
3	6358500000110	46,900.00	46,902.79	-2	-0.00
6	6358500000150	49,400.00	48,962.46	437	0.88
7	6358500000100	45,300.00	44,514.64	785	1.73
9	6358500000140	42,800.00	42,362.46	437	1.02
11	6594300000150	45,000.00	45,146.33	-146	-0.32
14	6594300000010	44,900.00	44,193.49	706	1.57
15	6594300000100	45,000.00	45,802.02	-802	-1.78
16	6594300000110	48,300.00	46,813.39	1,486	3.07
19	6268800010070	41,000.00	40,580.90	419	1.02
20	6268800010120	43,600.00	44,267.78	-667	-1.53
22	6268800030060	45,000.00	46,297.27	-1,297	-2.88
23	6473900110150	43,000.00	42,284.91	715	1.66
26	6473900700120	43,500.00	44,090.49	-590	-1.35
29	6473900500080	39,000.00	40,282.86	-1,282	-3.28
31	6473900010570	43,700.00	42,894.22	805	1.84
33	6473900010250	48,500.00	49,305.18	-805	-1.66
34	6473900010290	43,900.00	43,680.73	219	0.49
36	6473900110100	39,900.00	41,274.54	-1,374	-3.44

EXHIBIT 11: Residuals Percentage of Error — Second Analysis

RESIDUALS AS A PERCENT OF ACTUAL

Property ID	Residual %	Index
6358500000290 *	2.22	2
6358500000110 *	-0.00	3
6358500000150 *	0.88	6
6358500000100 *	1.73	7
6358500000140 *	1.02	9
6594300000150 *	-0.32	11
6594300000010 *	1.57	14
6594300000100 *	-1.78	15
6594300000110 *	3.07	16
6268800010070 *	1.02	19
6268800010120 *	-1.53	20
6268800030060 *	-2.88	22
6473900110150 *	1.66	23
6473900700120 *	-1.35	26
6473900500080 *	-3.28	29
6473900010570 *	1.84	31
6473900010250 *	-1.66	33
6473900010290 *	0.49	34
6473900110100 *	-3.44	36

EXHIBIT 12: Final Summary of Data Analyzed

```
              HOME  FEDERAL  SAVINGS  AND  LOAN
                   MARKET  DATA  ANALYSIS


PROPERTY ADDRESS    9290  132 ST  NO

APPRAISER                              DATE -

PARAMETERS FOR COMPARABLES SEARCH:

PORCHES      GENERAL    BEDROOMS    GENERAL    LOT SIZE    GENERAL
GARAGE AREA GENERAL     LIVING AREA GENERAL


COMPARISON GRID:
                                     COMPARABLE PROPERTIES
                       PROPERTY  ************************************
      ITEM             APPRAISED     #1          #2          #3
***************        *********  **********  **********  **********
DATE SOLD               10 76       09 76       11 76       10 76
LOT SIZE                7,575       8,400      11,000      11,000
CONSTRUCTION DATE        1976        1976        1972        1972
PORCHES                  NONE        NONE        UNKWN       NONE
BEDROOMS                THREE       THREE       THREE       THREE
BATHS                    TWO         TWO         TWO         TWO
LIVING AREA             1,720       1,706       1,777       1,640
POOL                     NONE        NONE        NONE        NONE
PARKING                2 GR'GE     2 GR'GE     2 GR'GE     2 GR'GE
COOLING                 CNTRL       CNTRL       CNTRL       CNTRL
FINANCING               CNVTL       CNVTL       UNKWN       UNKWN
EXTRAS                   N           N           N           N
SALES PRICE            $46,900     $44,900     $43,000     $39,900

ADDRESSES              # 1   9002  127LANE NO
                       # 2  11455  131 AVE  N
                       # 3  11450  132 AVE  N
```

(Continued)

STEPWISE MULTIPLE REGRESSION VALUATION ANALYSIS

SUMMARY DATA FOR ALL COMPARABLE SALES ANALYZED:
```
    TOTAL NUMBER OF SALES ANALYZED . . . . . . . . . . . .    19
    MEAN SALES PRICE FOR ALL SALES . . . . . . . . . . .  $44,294
    STANDARD DEVIATION IN PRICE FOR ALL SALES . . . . . .  $2,739
```

SUMMARY DATA FOR THE MULTIPLE REGRESSION ANALYSIS:
```
    MULTIPLE CORRELATION COEFFICIENT . . . . . . . . . . . 0.9493
    STANDARD ERROR OF THE ESTIMATE . . . . . . . . .   1012.7576
    NUMBER OF VARIABLES IN REGRESSION EQUATION . . . . . . . .    5
    DEGREES OF FREEDOM . . . . . . . . . . . . . . . . . .    13
    F RATIO  . . . . . . . . . . . . . . . . . . . . .   23.7492
```

APPLICATION OF REGRESSION RESULTS FOR PROPERTY VALUATION:

VARIABLE NAME	SIGNIFICANCE (T VALUE)	MULTIPLIER CALCULATED	DATA FOR SUBJECT	EXTENSION FOR SUBJECT
PORCH	2.2775	495.1224	1.0000	$495
BDRMS	-1.4363	-1279.8154	3.0000	$-3,839
LT SZ	-1.6463	-0.3353	7575.0000	$-2,540
GAR A	3.7445	36.8626	520.0000	$19,168
LIV A	8.0251	13.1415	1720.0000	$22,603

```
    CONSTANT TERM OF THE REGRESSION EQUATION  . . . . . $  11,015
    INDICATED VALUE FOR THE PROPERTY APPRAISED . . . . .  $46,902
```

CONFIDENCE INTERVALS FOR THE VALUE ESTIMATE:

DEGREE OF CONFIDENCE	RANGE OF CONFIDENCE IN PERCENT	CONFIDENCE IN DOLLARS	REASONABLE VALUE INTERVAL MINIMUM	TO MAXIMUM
68.26%	+/- 0.0228	+/- $1,012	$45,890	$47,915
95.44%	+/- 0.0457	+/- $2,025	$44,877	$48,928

Appendix F: Flood Insurance

Throughout the United States hundreds of millions of dollars in property losses can be suffered annually from floods and mud slides. Until 1968, with few exceptions, such losses were borne without any insurance reimbursement to the property owners and/or lending institutions who held mortgages. In that year the National Flood Insurance Act made flood insurance available for the first time to the typical single family residence owner at an affordable premium.

One of the problems that had to be overcome to make flood insurance workable was the possibility that the program inherently would encourage the continued unwise use of flood-prone areas, which in turn would increase future losses. To prevent this from happening, Congress limited the use of the program to those communities where future development would be controlled through flood plain management designed to minimize losses.

The Flood Disaster Protection Act of 1973 required the Department of Housing and Urban Development to publish information on known flood-prone communities. Upon notification of designation as a flood-prone area, these communities were required to participate in the flood insurance control and regulation programs by July 1, 1975, or face the loss of future federally-funded projects. Nonparticipation in the program would result in denial of mortgages from federally-backed lending institutions.

Maps known as Flood Hazard Boundary Maps (FHBM) are prepared by the Federal Insurance Administration, a department of HUD. This agency also works closely with local governments, helping them adopt and enforce land use and control measures aimed at avoiding or reducing future flood damage.

The insurance aspects of the program are operated by the property and casualty insurance industry which formed the National Flood Insurers Association (NFIA). The NFIA has in turn contracted with different insurance companies throughout the country which act as servicing organizations for designated territories (often whole states). The insurance industry thereby provided a percentage of the risk capital, bears a portion of the

476

losses, and through licensed property and casualty insurance agents (who work through the servicing organizations in their territory) sells and services flood insurance policies.

There are two insurance programs: the Emergency Program and the Regular Program. The Emergency Program is intended as an interim device to provide coverage until Flood Insurance Rate Maps are prepared. These maps, prepared by the Federal Insurance Administrator, show the precise location of flood areas and establish minimum first-floor elevations for land use within the designated areas. Flood areas generally have a one percent chance of being flooded each year.

Within the flood area actuarial rate zones are designated. The degree of potential flooding and mud-slide hazard is indicated by these zones. Special actuarial rates are set for each zone. The annual rates range from $.01 to $50 per $100 of coverage. The current FIA subsidized first layer rates are $.25 per $100 of coverage for single family dwellings and $.35 per $100 of coverage for contents within single family dwellings.

After the flood maps of the community are complete and appropriate hearings are held and notice given, the community is converted to the Regular Insurance Program and actuarial rates are established for the flood areas.

Two layers of insurance are offered to the property owner. The first layer (up to $35,000 on all single family dwellings except those in Alaska, Hawaii, Guam and the Virgin Islands where the limit is $50,000)[1] is available at the actuarial rate or subsidized rate, whichever is less ($10,000 on the contents is also available on the same basis). The second layer of insurance is available in an equal amount only at the actuarial rates. Once the regular first layer program has started, subsidized rates are not available on buildings newly constructed or substantially improved after December 31, 1974, or the effective date of the Flood Insurance Rate Map.

The appraiser must first determine if the community in which the property being appraised has been identified by the FIA as containing one or more areas of special flood hazards. This information can be obtained from the chief executive officer of the

---

[1]As of June 1, 1977.

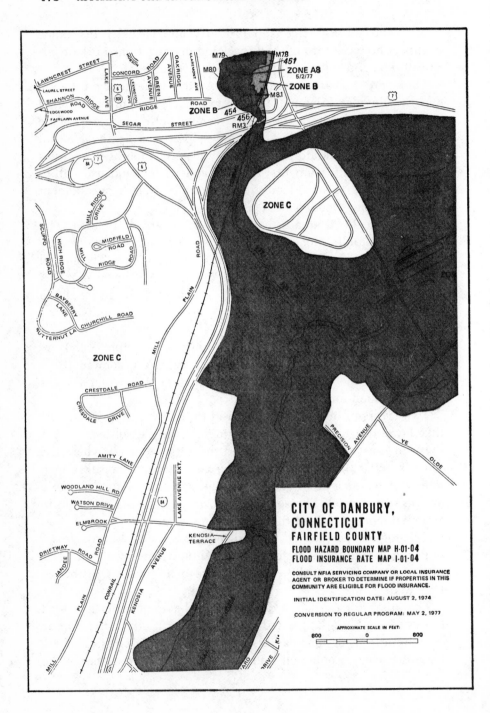

KEY TO SYMBOLS

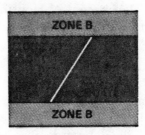

ZONE DESIGNATIONS* WITH
DATE OF IDENTIFICATION
ie., 12/2/74

Base Flood Elevation Line
with elevation in feet

~~~~~*513*~~~~~

Base Flood Elevation
where uniform within zone

(EL. 987' MSL)

Elevation Reference Mark

RM7 ×

River Mile

· M1.5

*EXPLANATION OF ZONE DESIGNATIONS

A flood insurance map displays the zone designations for a community
according to areas of designated flood hazards. The zone designations
used by FIA are:

Zone	Explanation
A	Areas of 100-year flood; base flood elevations and flood hazard factors not determined.
AO	Areas of 100-year shallow flooding; flood depth 1 to 3 feet; product of flood depth (feet) and velocity (feet per second) less than 15.
A1-A30	Areas of 100-year flood; base flood elevations and flood hazard factors determined.
A99	Areas of 100-year flood to be protected by a flood protection system under construction; base flood elevations and flood hazard factors not determined.
B	Area between limits of 100-year flood and 500-year flood; areas of 100-year shallow flooding where depths less than 1 foot.
C	Areas outside 500-year flood.
D	Areas of undetermined, but possible, flood hazards.
V	Areas of 100-year coastal flood with velocity (wave action); base flood elevations and flood hazard factors not determined.
VO	Areas of 100-year shallow flooding with velocity; flood depth 1 to 3 feet; product of depth (feet) and velocity (feet per second) more than 15.
V1-V30	Areas of 100-year coastal flood with velocity (wave action); base flood elevations and flood hazard factors determined.

community (mayor, city manager, county commissioner, etc.), or the National Flood Insurance Program, Federal Insurance Administration, U.S. Department of Housing and Urban Development, Box 34294, Bethesda, Maryland 20034.

If the property is within such a community, the appraiser must next determine from the same sources whether or not the community is eligible for either the emergency program or the regular program. The appropriate FHBM or FIRM map should be located to determine if the property being appraised is within a designated flood hazard area, and if so, more specifically what zone (see illustration, pages 478-479).

Maps are usually available in the administrative offices of the community. Appraisers may obtain their own copies through the offices of the servicing insurance company for the area. The name and address of the servicing insurance company can be obtained from the National Foood Insurers Association.

If the property is within a flood hazard zone, the appraisal report should indicate this fact. The rates for coverage should be determined by contacting a local insurance agent familiar with the program or the servicing insurance company for the area. Consideration should be given to how this additional expense affects the value of the property being appraised. If the comparable properties in the market are all in the same flood area, there probably will be little effect. If, on the other hand, there is a substantial premium difference, an appropriate adjustment must be made to reflect this difference. The best way to estimate this adjustment is to find and compare properties that have sold both in and out of the flood-hazard zone.

Relationships between the Department of Housing and Urban Development, the National Flood Insurers Association, insurance companies and local insurance agents involved in the program are constantly being revised. Also, the deadlines for community participation in flood prevention and hazard controls have been extended. Appraisers must keep current as to the status of the program, the amount of insurance available, how the program is being administered and the cost of the insurance in the communities involved.

Appendix G: The Appraiser's Work Tools

A professional appraiser should have a complete set of work tools to do an efficient job in the field. The following are suggested items with which the appraiser may be equipped:

- *Tool bag.* A standard attache case is commonly used. Leather briefcases that open from the top are easier to get into when standing and less likely to spill their contents if tipped over.
- *Maps.* Community and street maps will be needed to locate properties. Flood maps and topographical maps will also be helpful.
- *Measuring tools.* A 50- to 100-foot tape is standard equipment. Also useful are a six-foot folding carpenter's rule, a 12-inch ruler and a 12-inch triangular scale. A variety of rolling and optical measuring devices are also available.
- *Photographic equipment.* An instant type of camera is suitable for jobs that require only one copy of each picture. A 35mm camera is necessary for jobs that require more complex pictures, enlargements or many copies. A slightly wide angle lens is useful for many house pictures. A flash attachment is useful for interior photographs.
- *Electronic calculators.* A variety of calculators is now available which are programmed with the six functions of $1. It is possible to make many mortgage calculations with these machines. Some appraisers carry only a very simple machine for field work.
- *Dictating equipment.* Many compact portable machines are now available that are mechanically satisfactory. Care must be exercised when using them not to skip needed information. Codes are useful for negative comments in the presence of owners.

• *Folder of papers and supplies.* Include pad of lined paper, tracing paper, grid paper, plain bond paper, stationery, envelopes, business cards, and postage stamps. A box of other supplies might include pens, pencils, magic markers, grease pencils, stapler and supply of staples, pencil sharpener; marble (for testing for level floors), magnifying glass, paper clips, hole punch, masking tape, scissors, rubber bands and glue.

• *Miscellaneous equipment.* Flashlight, clipboard and scaling knife (useful for testing for wood rot, holding a measuring tape and opening locked doors).

Appendix H: Construction Cost Services

A number of services that regularly issue data on construction and building component costs are available to the appraiser. Among them are:

Boeckh Building Valuation Manual (Volume 1—Residential and Agricultural). American Appraisal Company, Inc., Milwaukee, WI. (Built up from unit-in-place costs converted to cost-per-square-foot of floor or ground area.)

Building Construction Cost Data. Robert Snow Means Co., Duxbury, MA. (Gives "average unit prices on a wide variety of building construction items for use in making up engineering estimates." Issued annually.)

Dodge Building Cost Calculator & Valuation Guide. McGraw-Hill Information Systems Co., New York, NY. (Building costs arranged by frequently occurring types and sizes of buildings; local cost modifiers and historical cost index tables included. Looseleaf service; quarterly supplements.)

Marshall Valuation Service. Marshall and Swift Publication Co., Los Angeles, CA. (Cost data for determining replacement costs of buildings and other improvements in the U.S. and Canada; includes current cost multipliers and local modifiers. Looseleaf service; monthly supplements.)

Residential Cost Handbook. Marshall and Swift Publication Co., Los Angeles, CA. (Presents square foot method and segregated cost method; local modifiers and cost trend modifiers included. Looseleaf service; quarterly supplements.)

Appendix I: Suggested Reading

The following books and articles will further provide the appraiser with information and insights into valuing residential property.

American Institute of Real Estate Appraisers. *The Appraisal of Real Estate*. 7th ed. Chicago, IL, 1978.

American Institute of Real Estate Appraisers and Society of Real Estate Appraisers. *Real Estate Appraisal Terminology*. Edited by Byrl N. Boyce, Cambridge, MA, Ballinger Publishing Co., 1975.

Becker, Boris W. "On the Reliability of Multiple Listing Service Data," *The Appraisal Journal*, April 1972.

Breckenfeld, Gurney. "Housing Subsidies Are a Grand Delusion," *The Real Estate Appraiser*, May-June 1972.

Browne, Dan. *The House Building Book*. New York, NY, McGraw-Hill Paperbacks, 1974.

Clifton, Russell B. "The Secondary Market Concerns with Real Estate Appraising," *The Appraisal Journal*, January 1975.

Cowley, Leonard M. "Gathering Data for an Appraisal," *Encyclopedia of Real Estate Appraising*. Revised & enlarged ed. Englewood Cliffs, NJ, Prentice-Hall, Inc., 1968.

Davidson, Harold A. *Housing Demand: Mobile, Modular or Conventional?* New York, NY, Van Nostrand Reinhold Co., 1973.

Dombal, Robert W. *Residential Condominiums: A Guide to Analysis and Appraisal*. Chicago, IL, American Institute of Real Estate Appraisers, 1976.

Downs, James C., Jr., "The Demand and Market for Housing: the Balance of the Decade," *The Appraisal Journal*, January 1972.

Grier, Eunice and George Grier. *Equality and Beyond: Housing Segregation and the Goals of the Great Society.* Chicago, Quadrangle, 1966.

Grier, George and Eunice Grier. *Privately Developed Interracial Housing: An Analysis of Experience.* Berkeley, CA, University of California Press, 1960.

Harrison, Henry S. *Harrison's Illustrated Guide How to Fill Out a Freddie Mac-Fannie Mae Residential Appraisal Report (FHLMC Form 70-FNMA Form 1004).* New Haven, CT, Collegiate Publishing Co., 1977.

Harrison, Henry S. *Houses—The Illustrated Guide to Construction, Design and Systems.* Revised ed. Chicago, IL, REALTORS National Marketing Institute®, 1976.

Harrison, Henry S. *Houses—Student Workbook.* Chicago, IL. REALTORS National Marketing Institute®, 1977.

Harrison, Henry S. "The Residential Appraiser" (a series of columns in *The Real Estate Appraiser*): "Highest and Best Use Analysis," March-April 1975. "Community Analysis," May-June 1975. "Neighborhood Analysis," September-October 1975. "Site Data Analysis," January-February 1976. "What Is an Amenity?" March-April 1976. "Inspecting a House," September-October 1976, November-December 1976, January-February 1977, and March-April 1977. "Description of the Interior," May-June 1977. "Inspecting a House," July-August 1977, September-October 1977, November-December 1977, and January-February 1978.

Joint Center for Urban Studies of Massachusetts Institute of Technology and Harvard University, *America's Housing Needs: 1975-1985.* Cambridge, MA, 1977.

Karr, James N. *The Condominium Buyers Guide.* New York, NY, Frederick Fell Publishers, Inc., 1973.

Laurenti, Luigi. *Property Values and Race: Studies in Seven Cities.* Berkeley, CA, University of California Press, 1960.

Maga, Peter J. "Cost Estimating," *Encyclopedia of Real Estate Appraising.* Revised & enlarged ed. Englewood Cliffs, NJ, Prentice-Hall, Inc., 1968.

McEntire, Davis. *Residence and Race.* Berkeley, CA, University of California Press, 1960.

O'Flaherty, John D. "An Appraiser's Dilemma: The Cost Approach to Value," *The Real Estate Appraiser*, January-February 1969.

Ratcliff, Richard U., and Dennis G. Swan. "Getting More from Comparables by Rating and Regression," *The Appraisal Journal*, January 1972.

Rule, Thomas M. "The Metropolitan Analysis in the Appraisal Report," *The Appraisal Journal*, April 1972.

Schuler, Stanley. *Home Renovation: Making Your Home More Attractive, Modern and Valuable*. Englewood Cliffs, NJ, Prentice-Hall, 1974.

Smith, Charles B. "How to Write a Poor Report," *The Appraisal Journal*, April 1973.

Taeuber, Karl and Alma Taeuber. *Negroes in Cities: Residential Segregation and Neighborhood Change*. Chicago, IL, Aldine, 1965. (Reprinted in paperback by Atheneum, 1972.)

Von Furstenburg, George M., ed. *Patterns of Racial Discrimination: Housing*. Lexington, MA, Lexington Books, 1974.

Weimer, Arthur M., Homer Hoyt and George Bloom. *Real Estate*. New York, NY, John Wiley & Sons, Inc., 1978.

Winger, Alan R. "How Important is Distance from the Center of the City as a Determinant of Urban Residential Land Values?," *The Appraisal Journal*, October 1973.

Appendix J:
Requirements for the MAI and RM Designations

Membership in the American Institute of Real Estate Appraisers is effected when an individual is awarded one of two designations of the Institute: the MAI (Member, Appraisal Institute) and RM (Residential Member). Qualifications for candidacy and membership for these designations are shown below[1].

The RM designation was established in 1968 and is awarded to persons who demonstrate ability to appraise single family houses. To be a candidate for the RM designation, an individual must:

1. Have graduated from an accredited four-year high school or have the equivalent of a four-year high school education.
2. Have good moral character, integrity and sincerity of purpose.

To be awarded the RM designation, an individual must:

1. Be an RM Candidate in good standing.
2. Have acquired credit for three years of real estate experience including at least two years of residential appraisal experience.
3. Have received a passing grade on the Institute's Required Examination No. I or I-A prior to January 1, 1973, and within the previous 10 years; or have received a passing grade on the Institute's Examination VIII after January 1, 1973.*
4. Have acquired credit for either three demonstration appraisal reports relating to single family residential property (one short narrative report and two form reports) which are acceptable to the Institute's Admissions Committee; or two demonstration reports (one a narrative report that meets the standards of a demonstration appraisal report acceptable for the MAI designation and the other a form report).*
5. Have a recommendation as to good moral character, integrity, sincerity of purpose and general fitness from the Institute's local chapter having jurisdiction over the applicant's principal place of business.
6. Hold some form of membership in the National Association of

[1] This is a summary; detailed requirements are contained in the Institute's Regulation No. 1 and in Form A2a, Criteria for the Awarding of Experience Credits. For further information, readers should contact the Institute's Admissions Department, 430 N. Michigan Ave., Chicago, IL 60611.

* As of January 1, 1980, the requirements for examinations, demonstration reports and experience were changed. Readers should contact the Admissions Department for details of these changes before applying.

REALTORS® (there are some exceptions to this requirement for individuals employed by a government agency, educational institution, insurance or financing organization and not engaged in the real estate brokerage business or other real estate fee work).

To qualify for candidacy for the MAI designation, an individual must:

1. Have graduated from an accredited four-year college or have the equivalent of a four-year college education.
2. Have good moral character, integrity and sincerity of purpose.

To be awarded the MAI designation, an individual must:

1. Be an MAI Candidate in good standing.
2. Have acquired credit for Required Examination I or I-A and I-B; Required Examination II; one elective examination; and the comprehensive examination.*
3. Have acquired credit for five years of "creditable appraisal experience" which must include three years in "specialized appraisal."
4. Have acquired credit for two acceptable demonstration appraisal reports, at least one of which is on an income-producing property.*
5. Meet the same requirements as specified in Nos. 5 and 6 for obtaining the RM designation.

"Creditable appraisal experience" is that acquired in the appraisal of real estate as a field appraiser, as a review appraiser, a real estate analyst or consultant or as a teacher of the real estate appraisal process.

"Specialized appraisal experience" is experience acquired in ONE of the following classifications (for other than one- to four-family residential real estate): 1) in the valuation of real estate as a "field appraiser"; 2) in the review of real estate appraisals as a "reviewing appraiser"; 3) in the evaluation of real estate as a "real estate analyst and consultant"; 4) as a teacher of courses relating to the appraisal of real estate. To receive credit, the appraisal work performed must either deal with more than one type of real estate or demonstrate that substantially different knowledge, skills or techniques were required to perform such appraisal work competently.

---

* As of January 1, 1980, the requirements for examinations, demonstration reports and experience were changed. Readers should contact the AIREA Admissions Department for details of these changes.

Appendix K:
AIREA Code of Professional Ethics and Standards of Professional Conduct (Regulation No. 10)

All members and candidates of the American Institute of Real Estate Appraisers sign an agreement with the Institute to be governed by its Code of Ethics, which states:

"The purpose of the Code of Professional Ethics and Standards of Professional Conduct is two-fold. Its primary purpose is to establish clear, precise, ethical and professional guidelines for the real estate appraiser who earnestly seeks to discharge all professional responsibilities in a manner consistent with duty to the public and the profession. Its secondary purpose is to provide minimum standards by which to judge Members of the Institute and Candidates for membership whose conduct is in question."

All members and candidates must determine for themselves the extent to which their actions should rise above these minimum standards. Although the threat of disciplinary action does provide an incentive towards ethical conduct, in the final analysis it is the desire for individual excellence, coupled with a desire for the respect and confidence of their profession and of the society which they serve, that provides professional people with the most effective incentive towards the highest degree of ethical conduct and the most effective deterrent to unethical conduct.

Regulation No. 10 consists of seven basic Canons, each of which is followed by disciplinary rules and explanatory comments. It is not practical to incorporate the entire Code into this text. However, each Canon is set forth together with some comments and illustrations. Hereafter, the word "Member" means both designated members

489

and candidates of the Institute. Because Regulation No. 10 changes from time to time, students and applicants for membership are advised to obtain a current copy of Regulation No. 10 for study, along with this text.

Canon 1: A Member of the Institute must refrain from conduct that is detrimental to the real estate profession.

Highlights of the Disciplinary Rules

D.R. 1-1. It is unethical to engage in conduct that is detrimental to or has an adverse effect upon the real estate profession.

D.R. 1-2. It is unethical to conduct one's self in a dishonest or fraudulent manner.

D.R. 1-3. It is unethical to be convicted of a felony involving moral turpitude.

Highlights of the Explanatory Comments

The success of the real estate appraisal profession and the American Institute of Real Estate Appraisers depends upon the confidence and trust the public has in the profession and in the Institute. Therefore, a member must refrain from all conduct that has a tendency to cast discredit upon the profession.

Canon 2: A Member of the Institute must assist the Institute in carrying out its responsibilities to the public and to the other members of the Institute.

Highlights of the Disciplinary Rules

D.R. 2-1, 2-2, 2-5. Members must cooperate with the Admissions Committee, Professional Ethics Committee, and Appraisal Review Committee by submitting only true information and not withholding any relevant information they have.

D.R. 2-3. Members must not withhold information from disciplinary proceedings of the Ethics Committee, or fail to comply with the terms of a summons from this Committee.

D.R. 2-4. Members must prepare a written appraisal report or complete memorandum before testifying in court or before a public commission or other tribunal as an appraiser. The document must be preserved for at least two years from the disposition of the proceeding, for examination by authorized committees or representatives of the Institute when necessary.

D.R. 2-6. If a member accepts an assignment on a Committee of the Institute, especially those committees that have the responsibility for admissions matters, enforcing the Code of Ethics and administering the Appraisal Review process, then the member must carry out such responsibilities with diligence and objectivity.

D.R. 2-7. A member cannot accept employment that precludes the member from complying with the By-Laws or Regulations of the Institute.

Highlights of the Explanatory Comments

The Institute depends upon its members to discharge its responsibilities to the public. Successful enforcement of the Code of Ethics and the functioning of the many committees also depends upon the help of the members. It is essential for the success of these functions that every member cooperate and assist the officers and committees as fully as possible. Not to do so is against the public interest and in itself a violation of the Code of Ethics. This is especially true of the functions that pertain to the screening of applicants for membership, the enforcement of the Code of Ethics, and the Appraisal Review Committee.

Canon 3: When performing a real estate appraisal assignment, a Member of the Institute must render professional services without advocacy for the client's interests or the accommodation of one's own personal interest.

Highlights of the Disciplinary Rules

D.R. 3-1. All opinions must be objective and unbiased.

D.R. 3-2. No assignment can be accepted which is contingent upon reporting a predetermined value or conclusion.

D.R. 3-3. No fee can be based on a percentage of the value estimated or a percentage of the difference between the value estimated and some other value.

D.R. 3-4. No fee may be accepted which is contingent upon some damages to be awarded.

D.R. 3-5. No assignment may be accepted on a property in which the appraiser has an interest, or contemplated future interest, unless the appraiser discloses this interest and concludes that this interest will not bias the value opinion, and a reasonable person would also conclude that the interest would not bias the appraiser's opinion.

D.R. 3-6. From the time of the first contact until a reasonable time after the completion of the assignment, no position in the property may be taken that will affect the appraiser's professional judgment, or violate the fiduciary relationship with the client.

D.R. 3-7. From the time of the first contact until a reasonable time after the completion of the assignment, no position in the property may be taken that could affect the appraiser's professional judgment, or violate professional duty to the client, *unless* the member concludes this will not happen, and the member obtains the consent of the client after full disclosure of all the facts, and the client is given the opportunity to terminate the appraisal assignment without payment of any fee or charge.

D.R. 3-8. No false or misleading statements about professional qualifications may be made.

D.R. 3-9. Professional help received in making the analysis or value conclusion must be acknowledged unless the persons rendering the assistance specifically request that their names not be used.

D.R. 3-10. A member who signs a report assumes full responsibility for the entire report.

Highlights of the Explanatory Comments

An appraisal prepared by a member must be factual and objective, and made without advocacy for the client's or member's own interest. This does not prohibit explaining, defending, or advocating the correctness of one's appraisal.

An appraisal based on hypothetical conditions may be made when the member concludes there is a reasonable possibility that the hypothetical conditions may in fact come into being, and that a reasonable person would conclude the same thing.

When appraising a property in which one has an interest, full disclosure of this interest must be made. In addition, the appraiser must conclude that this interest is such as not to make the appraiser biased, and that a reasonable person would also conclude the same.

When receiving professional help in rendering an appraisal opinion, the help must be acknowledged. Any member who signs a report assumes full responsibility for the entire report.

Canon 4: In rendering professional real estate appraisal services, a Member of the Institute must perform competently at all times.

Highlights of the Disciplinary Rules

D.R. 4-1. An appraisal cannot contain an error of commission or omission which substantially and materially affects the analysis, opinion or conclusion.

D.R. 4-2. A member may not repeatedly render appraisal services in a careless and negligent manner as evidenced by a series of minor errors over a period of time.

D.R. 4-3. The appraiser must have or acquire the knowledge to do the assignment.

D.R. 4-4. The appraiser must have the experience a reasonable person would expect in order to do an assignment, unless help is obtained from a qualified appraiser having the necessary experience.

D.R. 4-5. It is required that normal appraisal procedures be followed unless there is a valid reason for a departure from the normal procedures and the facts of the departure are set forth in the report.

D.R. 4-6, 4-7. Limited assignments and expanded assignments may be accepted only if the appraiser advises the client that the report will be qualified in that it is based on the limiting or expanding conditions and the scope of the assignment is not so limited or expanded that the results are meaningless or that the public or client will be misled.

Highlights of the Explanatory Comments

This Canon concerns itself with the substance of an appraisal as distinguished from the appraisal report, which is covered by Canon 5.

A member must always act with competence and proper care in rendering real estate appraisal services to clients. It is not sufficient for a member simply to maintain skills and the basic levels of proficiency. It is required that these skills continually be improved.

A simple human error is not in itself a violation of the Code of Ethics. Two types of errors are in violation of the Code:

1. An error of omission or commission which is substantial and materially affects the analysis, opinion or conclusions concerning real estate contained in an appraisal.

2. A series of errors which, considered individually, do not substantially or materially affect the results of individual appraisal assignments, but nevertheless evidence the fact that an appraiser is repeatedly rendering professional services in a careless and negligent manner.

If an appraiser lacks the knowledge to do an appraisal, the knowledge must be acquired or the assignment declined. If an appraiser lacks the experience to do an appraisal assignment (or if it would appear so to a reasonable person), then the fact must be disclosed to the client before acceptance of the assignment, or experienced help must be obtained to do the assignment.

The appraiser must use all of the recognized methods and techniques that will materially contribute to a proper evaluation. When a valuation is predicated on anticipated rentals and expenses, the probability of these anticipated items must be demonstrated by clear and competent evidence.

An appraisal of a proposed project must be based on definite plans and specifications or on another similar project that has been examined by the appraiser. When applicable the appraiser must make and rely on an independent estimate of the projected income and expenses and take into account the time reasonably required to obtain normal occupancy or usage.

All existing and proposed zoning regulations and legal restrictions must be considered. When proposed public improvements are considered, there must be a high degree of probability of their completion. The estimated time of completion must also be taken into account.

When appraising leased property, the terms of the lease must be considered along with their effect on the value of the various estates created by the lease, unless such consideration is precluded by the terms of the appraisal assignment. When making an appraisal of leasehold improvements as security for loans, the terms and conditions of the lease and their effect on the value of the leasehold estate must be considered.

The effect, if any, of assemblage on a property's value musł be considered.

When the client limits or expands the scope of an appraisal assignment, the appraiser must advise the client that the report will state this fact and will be so qualified. The limited or expanded scope of the assignment must be clearly stated in the report. The limited or expanded appraisal report must not be unmeaningful or misleading.

Canon 5: In making written and oral real estate appraisal reports, a Member of the Institute must comply with the rules relating to the contents of such reports.

Highlights of the Disciplinary Rules

D.R. 5-1. All oral appraisals must comply with the specific reporting rules of the Institute.

D.R. 5-2. All written appraisals must comply with the specific reporting rules of the Institute.

D.R. 5-3. Limited and expanded assignments can be accepted only after advising the client that the report called for will not be complete and will contain a qualifying statement to that effect. How it is limited or expanded must be clearly explained in the report and the report must not be such as to mislead the public.

Highlights of the Explanatory Comments

This Canon concerns the rules relating to the contents of an appraisal report. All the recognized appraisal methods and techniques that will materially contribute to a proper evaluation must be used.

Written reports are preferred. When oral reports are made, the notes and factual records together with a complete memorandum of each analysis, conclusion and opinion must be made and preserved.

To aid its members the Institute has adopted specific reporting rules which spell out what each written and oral report must contain. The following is a summary of these rules regarding the items that must be included in each report:

1. A clear and reasonably complete description of the property.
2. All the facts, assumptions and conditions upon which the appraisal is based.
3. Date of the valuation and reasoning of the appraiser in support of the valuation.
4. When the appraisal is of an estate less than fee simple, a clear statement that the report relates to a fractional interest only, and that the value of this fractional interest plus all the other fractional interests may or may not equal the value of the entire fee simple estate considered as a whole.
5. When the appraisal is of a geographical portion of a larger parcel or tract, a clear statement that the value reported relates only to the portion being appraised, and not the larger parcel or tract, and that the value of this portion plus all the other portions of the larger tract or parcel may or may not equal the value of the larger parcel or tract when considered as a whole.
6. A statement that the appraiser has no present or contemplated future interest in the property being appraised, or a clear and frank statement of what personal interest or bias does exist.
7. A certificate substantially in the form prescribed by the Institute.
8. A statement acknowledging the professional contributions of others or a statement that none exist.
9. A statement restricting public disclosure.

When the report is of an appraisal made under the terms of a limited or expanded assignment, statements are required that clearly set forth the conditions of the limited or expanded assignment.

Canon 6: A Member of the Institute must not violate the confidential nature of the appraiser-client relationship by improperly disclosing the confidential portions of a real estate appraisal report.

Highlights of the Disciplinary Rules

D.R. 6-1, 6-2. The report in its *entirety* or any conclusions or confidential, factual data may be disclosed only to persons specifically authorized by the client to receive such information; to third parties when and to the extent legally required to do so; and to duly consti-tuted committees of the Institute or their members when acting in their official capacity.

D.R. 6-3. If a member has confidential, factual data that cannot be used in an assignment, which will affect the result of the assignment, the assignment must be refused.

D.R. 6-4. All written contracts for appraisal services should provide that the appraisal report will be prepared in conformity with and will be subject to the requirements of the Code of Professional Ethics and Standards of Professional Conduct of the Institute.

Highlights of the Explanatory Comments

The client who employs the appraiser as a professional expects the appraiser to preserve and protect the confidential nature of the appraiser-client relationship. If the member does not preserve this confidential relationship, the public will lose confidence in the appraiser and in the Institute.

The Institute has developed guidelines to help the appraiser de-termine what may and may not be disclosed. The following is a summary of these guidelines:

1. Neither the report in its *entirety* nor any value conclusions may be disclosed except to persons specifically authorized by the client to receive such information, to third parties when and to the extent legally required to do so, and to duly constituted committees of the Institute or their members when acting in their official capacity.

2. Some *portions* of an appraisal report are not considered to be confidential and may be disclosed and used as the appraiser sees fit to do. Some of the *non-confidential parts* include fac-tual and statistical data secured by the appraiser from personal resources, general conclusions regarding the community and general charts, maps and graphs that relate to more than the subject property.

3. When a member possesses confidential information, it cannot be used in another appraisal, and if knowledge of this informa-tion would substantially affect the result of the appraisal as-signment, then the assignment must be declined.

4. All written appraisal employment contracts should contain a

provision giving the member permission to disclose the appraisal report to duly constituted committees of the Institute by stating that it is subject to the Code of Ethics of the Institute.

Canon 7: A Member of the Institute must refrain from unprofessional conduct in securing real estate assignments and in using advertising media in connection with the practice of real estate appraisal.

Highlights of the Disciplinary Rules

D.R. 7-1. Appraisal assignments may not be solicited other than through the limited and restricted use of advertising media permitted by this Regulation.

D-R. 7-2. All fees must be fair.

D.R. 7-3. No referral fees may be paid or collected.

D.R. 7-4. Resumes and statements of qualifications must be true and not misleading.

D.R. 7-5. No advertising is permitted except that specifically permitted by this Regulation.

D.R. 7-6. Members who are employees of corporations must use their best efforts to have the corporation comply with this Regulation.

D.R. 7-7. All appraisal reports must contain a statement prohibiting the dissemination of any of the report through advertising, public relations, news or sales media or any other public means of communication.

Highlights of the Explanatory Comments

A primary goal of the Institute and its members is to be accepted by the public as professionals. A traditional hallmark of a profession is that a professional does not secure assignments by unrestricted advertising but rather through individual reputation and the confidence the public places in the professional designations.

The Institute prohibits its members from soliciting real estate appraisal assignments except by the limited and restricted use of selected advertising media.

Professional fees must neither be excessive nor inadequate. Ex-

cessive fees imply advocacy and inadequate fees are unfair competition. Giving or receiving fees for referrals of assignments is prohibited. Fees may be shared if both appraisers perform services. Resumes of qualifications submitted to a client at the client's request
must be prepared carefully and accurately so as not to mislead the
client or the public.

Appraisers may conduct their business activities in corporate
form. The Institute's advertising regulations do not apply to corporations if such advertisements do not refer to the Institute's professional designations. If the advertisement does refer to the Institute
or the Institute's designations, those portions of the advertisement
that pertain to appraising must comply with this Regulation.

With respect to the distribution of books, pamphlets and
brochures by corporations, if the book, pamphlet, or brochure
mentions *only* the fact that an individual is a member of the Institute
or holds an Institute designation, then the corporation may distribute the book, pamphlet or brochure as it sees fit.

Members of the Institute who are employed by corporations must
make their best effort to have the corporation comply with this
Regulation. Continual violations by the corporation may place the
member in the position of having to resign from the corporation or
the Institute.

To prevent clients from using a member's name or the Institute's
name, logo or designations in their commercial advertising, all reports must contain a statement prohibiting such an act.

Institute regulations may be subject to change and readers are
advised to contact the American Institute of Real Estate Appraisers
for current information.

Index

Index